SOUNDING THE MODERN WOMAN

SOUNDING THE MODERN WOMAN

The Songstress in Chinese Cinema · JEAN MA

Duke University Press · Durham and London · 2015

Printed in the United States of America on acid-free paper ∞
Cover design by Amy Ruth Buchanan. Text design by Courtesy Leigh Baker.
Typeset in Whitman by Westchester Publishing Services

Library of Congress Cataloging-in-Publication Data
Ma, Jean, 1972–
Sounding the modern woman : the songstress in Chinese cinema / Jean Ma.
pages cm
Includes bibliographical references and index.
ISBN 978-0-8223-5865-7 (hardcover : alk. paper)
ISBN 978-0-8223-5876-3 (pbk. : alk. paper)
ISBN 978-0-8223-7562-3 (e-book)
1. Motion pictures—China—History. 2. Women singers in motion pictures. 3. Women
singers—China. I. Title.
PN1993.5.C6M354 2015
791.43'65220951—dc23   2014044250

Cover art: Grace Chang in *The Wild, Wild Rose* (directed by Wong Tin-lam, 1960). Permission
of Cathay-Keris Films Pte. Ltd. Background pattern from illustrart/Alamy.

CONTENTS

ACKNOWLEDGMENTS

In the summer of 2010 I visited the Hong Kong Film Archive for the first time, with a vague notion of starting a book project about the films and songs of the postwar star Grace Chang. What I found after immersing myself in the archive led me to fundamentally rethink my understanding of Chinese film history, resulting in a different book from what I had initially conceived. The following individuals helped bring this project to fruition and shaped many of its twists and turns.

It is difficult to imagine how this book would have come together without the encouragement and support of Sam Ho, who was head of programming at the Hong Kong Film Archive for the duration of my research. Sam was unfailingly generous in sharing his expertise, recommending films and readings, helping me navigate the archive, and acting as a sounding board for my ideas. Even though I am very happy to be finished, I miss the pleasure of his company and the delicious food at our lunches in Sai Wan Ho.

Andrew Jones not only inspired many of the questions asked in this book with his innovative scholarship, but he also played an instrumental role in its development. I am deeply grateful for his rigorous critical feedback, which has benefited this study from beginning to end in countless ways and helped me better articulate its main ideas. I owe a debt of gratitude to Jason McGrath for being a terrific colleague and also a staunch ally when I needed it most. Guo-Juin Hong has been a consistently enlivening presence. I treasure his friendship and wit, and I thank him for being a wonderful host when I presented my research at the Asian/Pacific Studies Institute at Duke University.

Emilie Yeh and Darrell Davis provided me with an intellectual anchor and a reason to look forward to my trips to Hong Kong. On many occasions they have been gracious hosts and invigorating interlocutors. I thank Emilie for including me in the excellent conference she organized at Hong Kong Baptist University in 2013. Sze Wei Ang was a lifesaver on multiple occasions; I thank her for amazing culinary adventures, giving me refuge, and helping me obtain images for the book. I had a great time exploring Hong Kong with Giorgio Biancorosso and thank him for making me feel at home there.

At Stanford University I have relied much on the support of my colleagues Beth Kessler, Pavle Levi, and Rick Vinograd. I could not ask for a better colleague and mentor than Scott Bukatman has been to me; his enthusiasm for this book was a sustaining force and a constant reminder of why it was worth writing. I am grateful to Pavle for his editorial input on the book proposal at a critical stage in the process, and to Scott for giving the introduction a thorough reading near the end. Charlie Kronengold offered some key musicological pointers. I thank him and Carol Vernallis for sharing in the gratifications of songstress performance. I found an extraordinarily vibrant intellectual community in the Performance Focal Group from 2011 to 2012, and I thank its members for their insightful responses when I presented a portion of chapter 3 to them. My thanks also go to the graduate students in my Chinese cinema seminar and to the faculty fellows at the Michelle R. Clayman Institute for their thoughtful engagement with my work.

I am grateful to the colleagues and friends who read portions of the manuscript, extended opportunities to present my work, and kept my spirits afloat through the ups and downs of the past few years: Weihong Bao, Rob Culp, Barbara Ess, Leah Gilliam, Chika Kinoshita, Akira Lippit, Dan Morgan, Dan O'Neill, Abé Markus Nornes, Lisa Outar, John David Rhodes, Nerina Rustomji, Karl Schoonover, and Julie Sze. The result of my editorial collaboration with Karen Beckman many years ago was not only a book but also an ongoing conversation that never ceases to teach, energize, and inspire me.

I've been lucky to find an amazing research assistant in Hsinyi Tiffany Lee. I thank Tiffany for her contributions to the research and translations in this book, and Chenshu Zhou for her help with archival research.

I thank Ken Wissoker at Duke University Press for championing this project and for his wise editorial guidance. Elizabeth Ault was wonderful to work with as an editor, and Danielle Szulczewski skillfully steered it through production. The three anonymous reviewers of the manuscript offered much helpful feedback, and I thank them for their rigorous readings and constructive criticism. The staff at the Hong Kong Film Archive accommodated all of my research requests with great patience and professionalism. I am grateful to Diana Miu for her invaluable assistance in securing permissions and reproductions, and to Cathay-Keris Films and the Shaw Organisation for allowing me to reprint their images. Thanks to the Performing Arts Collection at Arts Centre Melbourne for the beautiful photograph of Lolinda Raquel and to Lucy Spencer for her kind assistance. Thanks to Zhaohui Xue and Grace Yang at Stanford's East Asia Library for helping me to navigate the Chinese collection. A portion of chapter 4 was previously published in *Camera Obscura*.

My research was supported by a Freeman-Spogli Institute Hewlett Faculty Grant and a Michelle R. Clayman Institute for Gender Research Fellowship.

I can always count on Amber, Yvette, Ayling, and Cheng-Quinn Ma for their loving support and, whenever required, an infusion of good humor. This book is especially indebted to my mother, Ayling, who possesses a stunning memory for music and spent many hours with me listening to songs, watching film clips, and poring over old film magazines. Experiencing the material through her eyes and ears made it meaningful in ways I couldn't have anticipated.

Ed Simnett has been with me through the entire process of researching and writing this book. I share with him completely the victory of reaching the finish line, along with all of the happiest things in life. This book is dedicated to him with much love.

The disembodied voices of bygone songstresses course through the soundscapes of many recent Chinese films that evoke the cultural past. In a mode of retrospection, these films pay tribute to a figure who, although rarely encountered today, once loomed large in the visual and acoustic spaces of popular music and cinema. The audience is invited to remember the familiar voices and tunes that circulated in these erstwhile spaces. For instance, in a film by the Hong Kong director Wong Kar-wai set in the 1960s, *In the Mood for Love*, a traveling businessman dedicates a song on the radio to his wife on her birthday.[1] Along with the wife we listen to "Hua yang de nianhua" ("The Blooming Years"), crooned by Zhou Xuan, one of China's most beloved singers of pop music. The song was originally featured in a Hong Kong production of 1947, *All-Consuming Love*, which cast Zhou in the role of a self-sacrificing songstress.[2] Set in Shanghai during the years of the Japanese occupation, the story of *All-Consuming Love* centers on the plight of Zhou's character, who is forced to obtain a job as a nightclub singer to support herself and her enfeebled mother-in-law after her husband leaves home to join the resistance. "The Blooming Years" refers to these recent political events in a tone of wistful regret, expressing the homesickness of the exile who yearns for the best years of her life: "Suddenly this orphan island is overshadowed by miseries and sorrows, miseries and sorrows; ah, my lovely country, when can I run into your arms again?"[3] Wong Kar-wai picks up on these sentiments of homesickness in his use of the song as a pop cultural artifact of the Shanghainese émigré community whose members sought refuge in Hong Kong during and after the tumultuous war years, a community from which he himself hails.[4] The inclusion of "The Blooming Years" in *In the Mood for Love* concatenates the longings of this displaced community for a lost homeland, the desires of the film's characters for lost or unrealized loves, and perhaps too the director's nostalgia for the disappeared milieu of his childhood. Thus Wong evokes the past through an identification with a previous generation's wish for an unattainable lost time, a wish that is immortalized in the song of the songstress. In this regard, Zhou Xuan's voice can be described as the *punctum* of *In the Mood for Love*—the vanishing point of desire and memory, the detail that pierces the spectator-auditor and unleashes a temporal vertigo.[5]

Zhou Xuan is conjured up in yet another contemporary production in the vein of Shanghai nostalgia, *Lust, Caution*, from the Taiwan-born Chinese American director Ang Lee and based on the novella of the same title by the notable modern fiction writer Eileen Chang.[6] The film's story of espionage and political intrigue takes place during the years of the Japanese occupation and centers on Wang Jiazhi, a female college student who becomes a spy for the underground resistance. In a key scene in *Lust, Caution*, Wang sings "Tianya genü" ("The Wandering Songstress"), a tune from one of Zhou's best-known films, the 1937 leftist classic *Street Angel*.[7] Zhou's character is a songstress indentured to a teahouse owner, who forces her to display her vocal talent for a lascivious male clientele; the cause of her plight, the film suggests, is the recent Japanese invasion of Manchuria. Wang Jiazhi's performance of the song in *Lust, Caution* takes place in a Japanese restaurant where she dines with Mr. Yi, the security chief in Wang Jingwei's collaborationist wartime regime, whom Wang Jiazhi has taken as a lover as part of a plot to assassinate him. Commenting on the Japanese women who entertain patrons in the adjoining rooms, Wang tells Yi, "I know why you've brought me here. You want me to be your whore." "It is I who brought you here," Yi replies, "so I know better than you how to be a whore." Wang then offers to sing for him, placing herself in a position analogous to that of both the neighboring entertainers and Zhou's *Street Angel* character. Yi responds with an uncharacteristic display of emotion: he is moved to tears by her song. Here music comes to the foreground in a historically charged exchange, to convey a profound identification and mutual recognition between Wang and Yi as prostitutes, each deprived of autonomy by historical circumstances and the masters they respectively serve. In a film that has repeatedly been accused of treading on the wrong side of national politics, song performance marks an excess that is not only affective but also ideological. Politics and pathos converge in the suffering expressed by the tragic songstress, blurring the distinction between predator and prey, collaborator and resistance spy, man and woman (Yi is feminized by his description of himself as a whore working for the Japanese). The songstress reference paradoxically at once grounds the film's representation of events of the turbulent wartime era and carves out a channel of sentiment that transcends political lines.

To offer a third and final example, in Tsai Ming-liang's *The Hole*, the song-stress enters through a more disruptive mode of citation.[8] The film centers on a nameless man and woman who live in Taipei at the turn of the millennium and who are drawn into a series of encounters when a hole appears in the wall between their apartments. Most of the narrative transpires in near silence, with minimal dialogue spoken by the characters and no musical underscore. But the voice of Grace Chang—a singer and actress in Hong Kong in the 1950s and 1960s—periodically punctuates the soundtrack as the story is interrupted by musical inserts staged in a highly theatrical fashion, at odds with its otherwise austere realism. In these interludes Chang's songs are lip-synched by Yang Kuei-mei, the actress who plays the nameless woman, as she dances in flamboyant costumes, sometimes flanked by backup dancers or accompanied by her costar Lee Kang-sheng, the nameless man. They include Latin-style dance tunes like "Calypso," the playful pop melody "Achoo Cha Cha," and a Mandarin rendition of the American blues hit "I Want You to Be My Baby." In the film's final frame, a handwritten intertitle names the vocalist as an inspiration with the epigraph: "In the year 2000, we are grateful that we still have Grace Chang's songs with us.—Tsai Ming-liang." The unabashedly nostalgic and personal tone of the epigraph is all the more striking in light of *The Hole's* futuristic atmosphere, with its story unfolding in an anxiously surreal but recognizable setting that gestures toward the far side of the impending millennial transition. Against the bleakness and anonymity of contemporary life, the film suggests, the colorful past embodied in Chang's music promises a last refuge for feeling and intensity, the triumph of fantasy over banality, and the survival of humanity in a literally dehumanizing universe (everyone in the film is turning into cockroaches).[9]

It is striking that these three prominent works of contemporary art cinema—works that map out the globalized circuits constituting Chinese cinema in the twenty-first century, encompassing Hollywood and Europe as well as mainland China, Hong Kong, and Taiwan; and popular genre as well as the transnational commerce of auteurism—look to the songstress as an avatar of history. The far-ranging scope of their collective historical imagination, from the war years through the postwar period to the present, attests to the long shadow cast by this figure over the first century of Chinese cinema. Indeed, from the very beginnings of sound filmmaking in Shanghai in the 1930s, singing actresses like Violet Wong, Wang Renmei, and Zhou Xuan captivated the attention of filmgoers and proved the symbiotic potency of sound motion picture technology. Their rise to stardom changed the course of Chinese cinema's evolution as an expressive medium, with musical performance emerging as a powerful rival to storytelling. Following the upheavals of the Japanese occupation and the civil war, and in the wake of the dispersal of the Shanghai film industry, the songstress reemerged in Hong Kong, becoming a commonplace fixture of the vibrant entertainment industry established there in the postwar decades. These years witnessed a stunning proliferation of singing stars—Chung Ching, Linda Lin Dai, Grace Chang, Ivy Ling Po, Julie Yeh Feng, and Jenny Hu—concomitant with a pronounced musical turn in commercial filmmaking. Many of these stars were affiliated with Hong Kong's two biggest production studios, the Motion Picture and General Investment Co. Ltd. (MP&GI, sometimes referred to as Cathay) and Shaw Brothers, which were the driving forces behind the arrival of what many describe as a second golden age of Mandarin cinema. In the late 1960s, the songstress retreated to the margins of popular cinema, to be occasionally resuscitated by contemporary directors like Wong, Tsai, and Lee—as well as by performers like the late Anita Mui, both an acclaimed actress and a performer extraordinaire of Cantopop, or Cantonese soft rock music. Across this historical field, the female singer comes into relief as a thematic obsession, sensory magnet, and iconic remnant of the past. Even as an anachronistic and elusive referent—a voice ventriloquized, mimetically conjured, technologically transmitted, or unattached to a visible corporeal source—she continues to haunt the screen, the light of her fading star shimmering with new meanings across the reaches of time.

Responding to this call from the past, this book follows the trail of the songstress, a figure who has received little scrutiny despite her enduring and far-reaching presence throughout Chinese films of various periods, regions, dialects, genres, and styles. The singing woman appears in many incarnations: teahouse entertainer, opera actress, nightclub chanteuse, street singer, showgirl, ancient beauty, modern teenager, country lass, and revolutionary. These diverse types offer insights into the various cultural and historical contexts in which they are rooted, and an investigation of this trope must account for the meanings the songstress carries in these specific contexts. But she also challenges us to pay attention to those large-scale temporal connections and cross-regional transactions that transcend the boundaries of any individual milieu. The sheer variety of her guises reveals her to be a figure of remarkable endurance, capable of adapting to changing circumstances, multiple locations, and shifting ideological orientations. The songstress signals latent connections that weave throughout the polycentric topography of Chinese cinema, connections that cut across and complicate the divides of war, dislocation, and politics. In tracing her repetitions and recirculations, we begin to discern a web of interrelated motifs and discursive patterns stretching across this terrain and centering on the gendered spectacle of vocal performance. The persistence of this figure throughout the first four decades of Chinese sound cinema speaks to the thematic fascination exercised by female singers on the imagination of filmmakers and audiences, as well as the sensory attractions contained in her songs. As the songstress became a ubiquitous feature of cinema, so her performances underpinned and stabilized a musical idiom that exceeded the boundaries of any single genre.

Vocal Performers and Singing Pictures

My use of the term *songstress* contains two different yet interrelated inflections, referring both to a type of performer and to a codified diegetic construct invested with particular discursive functions. Viewed from the first of these angles, the term calls attention to a phenomenon of crossover stardom fed by the intertwined economies of the motion picture and music recording industries. In *Yellow Music*, Andrew Jones reconstructs the complex media matrix that surrounds the birth of the songstress. The rise to stardom of singing actresses like Zhou Xuan in the 1930s, he shows, hinged on a symbiosis in her time between commercial cinema and popular music as mass media industries built on new technologies for the reproduction and dissemination of sounds and images—phonography, radio, and sound motion pictures.[10] The tunes of modern popular music (*shidai gequ*), such as those crooned by Zhou, composed the soundtrack of leisure time in metropolitan Shanghai, linking the spaces of the musical stage, movie theater, record store, dance hall, and nightclub. Likewise, many of the other singing actresses discussed in this study also moved fluidly between these realms to simultaneously pursue careers as screen stars and recording artists, leveraging their success in one realm as additional publicity for the other. As much as their fortunes are framed by the conjunction of these industries, they also attest to cinema's embedded place in this larger, interconnected media matrix. The professional trajectories of these performers map out a circuit from the screen to the recording studio to the stage; their songs were detachable commodities that were transmitted as both signal and script, broadcast in public and domestic spaces and circulated in print form in song sheets and fan magazines. In the heyday of these performers, the mechanical echoes of their voices, as much as their reproduced images, sustained a lucrative, multichannel star system. Positioned at the center of this system, the songstress opens up a valuable intermedia perspective on cinema.

Furthermore, the conventions of sound filmmaking evolved in tandem with commercial imperatives, so that the presence of these singing actresses also gave rise to a distinctive set of representational tropes and formal patterns. Typically the identity of these vocal performers finds an echo in the fiction of their films. They are cast as characters who themselves are defined by a superior vocal talent, a strategy that facilitates the display of the singing voice in musical interludes that periodically interrupt the narrative. More often than not, the singing characters in these films eventually become professional entertainers, featuring in stories that transpire in the world of opera, theater, stage revues, teahouses, nightclubs, movies, and the music recording industry. The discursive construction of the songstress therefore serves to justify and naturalize the inclusion of song, granting a diegetic pretext for scenes of lyrical performance. The songstress anchors a representational system in which speech must periodically give way to song, allowing the female voice to come to the fore as a locus of dramatic and affective intensity. In these song scenes, the act of performance doubles back on itself—an audience inside the film reduplicates the position of the spectator-auditor, and the performer herself is doubly inscribed as both star and fictional character when she ceases to act and marshals the lyrical powers of her voice. Beyond its existence as a soundtrack element, the song effects a break in the flow of the story's action and prompts a shift into a different narrative register and mode of address. Sound and image concentrate around the body of the singer, in such a way that the direct physicality and identificatory pull of her performance effect a fissure in the fictive world; in short, we perceive and affectively relate to the songstress in a qualitatively different way during the song numbers. Often that difference is recuperated by the film, invested with a narrative significance. But at the same time, recuperation can go only so far, and the unsettling effects of her performance can infiltrate the entirety of the film. In the transformative interval of song, the distinction between the songstress as star and the songstress as trope, between the performer and the codified character type, becomes blurred.

Insofar as she confronts us with the operations of voice and music, the songstress offers a point of entry into the soundscape of Chinese cinema. The topic of sound has been largely overlooked in critical writings in this area, which collude with film studies' long-standing analytic bias toward the image and questions of visuality. With its focus on musical expression and audiovisual dynamics, this study joins and engages a growing body of scholarship on Chinese film history—and film scholarship as a whole—that seeks to redress the imbalance between image and sound.[11] As many have observed, this history encompasses an extraordinarily wide and varied musical field—including

Western jazz and pentatonic folk melodies, which come together in the forging of the modern idiom of Mandarin pop (*shidai qu*); Western classical music; traditional regional and operatic forms; revolutionary anthems; rock and pop genres, increasingly throughout the twentieth century; and various combinations of these categories. This breadth of musical styles is matched by the plural forms of their encounter with the cinematic medium, with song numbers appearing across a far-ranging constellation of genres, including backstage musicals and revues, romantic and family melodramas, comedies, historical costume dramas, and fantastic ghost stories. Another major strand, one unique to the Chinese context, arises at the juncture of cinema and the Chinese operatic tradition of *xiqu*. In opera films we see the musical field of Chinese filmmaking further differentiated on the basis of diverse regional styles and modes of performance rooted in the musical stage.[12] Opera films can be distinguished from singing films (*gechang pian*) for their fluid alternations between singing and speaking within an integral musical structure, as opposed to the incorporation of discrete musical numbers. At the same time, the use of songs or arias as a means of expressive punctuation is common to both of these types of films. Across this broad constellation of genres, sound and image intersect in surprising ways, and mutating modes of musical signification call into question easy distinctions between background and foreground, diegetic and nondiegetic elements. The heterogeneity of this landscape necessarily inflects the individual film, as it forms a horizon of possibilities within which particular ways of mobilizing music in a narrative context can make sense and carry meaning for an audience.

It is somewhat ironic, then, to find that the interpretive frameworks brought to bear on these works often tend to flatten out this diversity. Much writing on song performance in Chinese cinema looks to the American film musical as a point of critical reference. Because the films in which the songstress features contain musical sequences and alternate between narrative exposition and song numbers, they are seen as synonymous with—or aspiring toward—the film musical à la Hollywood. Yet, as Yeh Yueh-yu astutely notes, "Hollywood-style musicals never existed in China as a major film genre."[13] To assume that they did is to use a set of tools for analyzing the cinematic functions of music derived from a different body of work and cut to the measure of its conventions. The cultural specificity of genres is nowhere more apparent than in this instance, and the impossibility of transposing a genre category derived from one regional context into another is registered in the language of film criticism. Chinese film criticism lacks an exact equivalent for the term *film musical*, instead referring to films containing discrete scenes of musical performance as either *gechang pian*, singing films in which the musical spectacle is limited to vocalization, or *gewu pian*, song-and-dance films in which dance choreography plays a greater role. Inscribed in the terminology of film criticism is a fundamental distinction between the dancing body and the singing voice, a distinction that is further entrenched by an asymmetry in which *gechang pian* vastly outnumber *gewu pian* (as chapter 4 discusses in greater detail).

The question of generic norms and their cross-cultural transposition is not reducible to a question of influence, and to be sure, the impact of the American film musical can be discerned throughout the history of both *gechang pian* and *gewu pian*. For instance, in the early sound period, we find productions like *Yinhan shuang xing* (*Two Stars in the Milky Way*, 1931), a Chinese take on the Metro-Goldwyn-Mayer (MGM) backstage musical *Show People* (1928);[14] *Yeban gesheng* (*Song at Midnight*, 1937), modeled on Universal's 1925 *Phantom of the Opera*; and numerous films inspired by the operetta-style romantic comedies of Ernst Lubitsch.[15] Not only did Shanghai filmmakers in this period often borrow from Hollywood musicals, but they also operated in a critical environment in which the impact of sound technology in the American and European film industries was intensely scrutinized and debated. But Hollywood was far from the only factor affecting the development of Chinese sound films, and in at least one notable example, it exerted a negative influence. Discussing *Genü Hong mudan* (*Songstress Red Peony*, 1931), considered to be China's first sound production, Zhou Jianyun, manager of the Mingxing Film Company, emphasizes the film's divergences from the spectacular formula of the American musical picture—which, he writes, fails to "stir the heart with pleasing sounds" despite its dazzling sets, lavish costumes, and hundreds of dancing girls.[16] In a similar vein, Hong Kong productions of the postwar period frequently "borrow and adapt important plot devices and narrative tropes from well-known Hollywood musicals, comedies, and melodramas," Gary Needham observes.[17] In the high-budget productions of MP&GI and Shaw Brothers, we see attempts to replicate Hollywood's elaborate musical spectacles; the English-language titles assigned by these studios to their productions are sometimes even lifted directly from popular American films. But as Needham goes on to note, even if many productions of this period fall within the influential orbit of American cinema and share in its surface features, deeper structural differences clearly distinguish these two bodies of work. Chief among these is the Hollywood musical's dual-focus structure and reliance on couple formation as a mechanism of narrative closure. If the musical upholds an ideology of heterosexuality by smoothing out oppositions in the "harmonious unity" of marriage, as Rick Altman has famously argued, we see in the Chinese films a consistent displacement of closure away from the heterosexual couple and toward other relational axes—familial, communal, or platonic, but hardly ever romantic.[18]

Needham's analysis participates in an ongoing endeavor by scholars of non-Western cinemas to challenge, in his words, "the normative alignment between Hollywood and genre in both film studies and the popular imagination."[19] Indeed, a comparative perspective that looks solely to Hollywood as a benchmark runs the danger of overlooking and marginalizing those elements that do not map onto this model. Moreover, the problems of such an approach are compounded by the normative alignments that emerge from within the critical construction of a genre like the musical. For example, Richard Dyer has noted that "for a long period the ideal of the musical was seen to be integration," defined as an overcoming of the disruptive effects of song and dance "by smoothing out the transition between [registers], by having the numbers do narrative work."[20] The ideal of integration is realized in the heyday of the "Metro musical," and some accounts of the Hollywood musical view the MGM works of the early 1950s as the culmination of the genre. Such accounts in turn reprise a credo that permeates histories of the Broadway stage musical, "according to which all elements of a show—plot, character, song, dance, orchestration, and setting—should blend together into a unity, a seamless whole."[21] Scott McMillin points out that this model of the organically unified work, so influential in American musical theater, finds a basis in nineteenth-century opera and the Wagnerian ideal of the *Gesamtkunstwerk*, or the synthetic total work of art.[22]

To privilege integration and unity as the telos of the American film musical is to overlook the manifold aspects of these films that do not square with these representational values, and therefore to oversimplify the genre. It is precisely such a reduced understanding of the musical genre that we see informing analyses that compare *gechang* and *gewu pian* with the Hollywood musical. For example, the film historian Stephen Teo offers an overview of the history of *gechang pian* with a focus on formal innovations driven by, as he puts it, the industry's desire "to be as Western as possible."[23] In tracing a lineage of songstresses from Zhou Xuan to her postwar descendants like Chung Ching and Grace Chang, Teo identifies a progression in their films from simple, interpolated song sequences—known as *chaqu*, or inserted film songs—to "the development of the full-fledged musical genre."[24] While the *chaqu* format allows for the inclusion of musical scenes that have no necessary connection to the story and transpire in a suspended space and time, as we see in many of Zhou's films, Teo denigrates this format as "technically awkward and underdeveloped."[25] In his reading, the achievement of postwar musical films resides in their departure from the simplicity of the interpolated song sequence, endowing film songs with a narrative function and thematic significance. Yet the progression from a primitive, interruptive form to a mature, integrated one quickly collapses. Teo laments that "the musical in its integrative form where music, songs, characters and plots were inter-related to each other, survived only for a short period in the late 50s," before reverting to its earlier interruptive tendencies.[26]

The difficulty of sustaining a developmental account of *gechang pian* that takes integration as its main criterion, and the considerable number of films that must be dismissed on such a basis, tells us that this notion cannot fully account for what these films are doing and that their musical content is not just a means to narrative ends. As Altman asks in his study of the American film music, "are there texts commonly called musicals which in fact operate according to a logic different from the vast majority of other musicals?"[27] My discussion of *gechang pian* grapples with this question, beginning from the premise that their musical attractions—inextricable from the appeal of the singing star—must be analyzed on their own terms. I treat the figure of the songstress as key to articulating the specific logic, forms, and modes of address of *gechang* and *gewu pian*. In doing so, my aim is not only to flesh out a historical understanding of Chinese cinema and its soundscape, but also to work toward a more nuanced and expansive reflection on the intersections of music and cinema on a global plane, in which Hollywood occupies a decentered position. Do the musical and vocal manifestations of Chinese cinema indeed mobilize logics of presentation, performance, and identification that confound our expectations? To borrow a phrase from Dyer, what happens in the space of a song?

Dyer's own exploration of this last question endeavors to articulate the unique ways in which songs in film make sense—a process steeped in linguistic and narrative conventions but also spilling beyond these conventions with the immediate, visceral, and sensuous impact of song performance. As Dyer argues, songs seem to hold out a direct channel to feeling and physicality and therefore to collapse the distance between singer and listener, to transcend the ordinary. They entail a transformation in the phenomenal experience of the spectator-auditor because "song, as befits an oral art, makes great use of repetition and redundancy and thus has an overall tendency towards a sense of stasis, towards not going or getting anywhere, to a sense of tableau, of suspended time. This is highly suggestive in the context of time and space in film."[28] The effects described by Dyer apply as well to *gechang pian*, in which songs also pause the flow of diegetic time, prolong a moment and mood, heighten the emotional temperature, and even create an alternative reality. In giving the "singing" of singing pictures its proper due, then, my objective consists not so much in asserting an essential difference between *gechang pian* and Hollywood musicals (or, for that matter, between *gechang pian* and musicals from any other region). Rather, it is to probe difference as internal to the individual work—where it marks a distance between its explicit and latent meanings—and consequently as inscribed in the fundamental mechanisms of Chinese song films. This approach is inspired by a strand of thinking about works of musical narration that understands heterogeneity and disjunction, rather than unity and integration, to lie at their core. Scholars like Gerald Mast, Richard Dyer, and Amy Herzog have all made compelling arguments for the importance of apprehending this difference in aesthetic and political terms, as the basis of the musical's expressive modalities as well as its ideological work.[29] In Herzog's formulation, the disruption of what she terms "the musical moment" refracts the genre's conservative tendencies to "prescribe and reinforce meanings according to the dominant rationale of a particular historical moment." Against and concurrent with these tendencies, the uneven flux of sound and image creates a space available for surplus meanings and "interventions of difference. . . . The musical moment is unusual in its capacity to make this tension palpable; it is at once one of the most conservative and most irreverent filmic phenomena."[30]

Voices, Bodies, and Gender

If a close scrutiny of the difference constituted in the musical moment—or, alternatively, in the space of a song—discloses political effects that are related to filmic codings of nation, race, gender, or sexuality, as Herzog suggests, this insight has particular relevance for the *gechang pian*. For the Chinese songstress has no male equivalent. A clear division of labor informs these films from the outset: their singing stars are invariably women, while men contribute to the musical performance chiefly as composers, instrumentalists, or occasional duet partners. The songstress phenomenon points to a distinctive gendering of lyrical expression and a persistent alignment of femininity with musical spectacle in the Chinese filmic tradition. This pattern arose in the Shanghai period as part of what Zhang Zhen terms the "acoustic dominant" of the 1930s, as the gradual adoption of synchronized sound technologies transformed the aesthetic structure and sensorial parameters of Chinese film.[31] Zhang observes that "early sound films commonly privileged singing girls and self-reflexive references to the theater world," beginning with the release of Shanghai's first sound-on-disc production in 1931, *Songstress Red Peony*, which featured the movie queen Hu Die as a Peking opera singer.[32] Solo performances by singing actresses predominated throughout the transition to sound, and many of the female stars of early sound cinema, like Zhou Xuan, came to filmmaking by way of the musical stage and recording industry. As the mainland-based filmmaking and popular music industries entered a phase of nationalism and mass mobilization starting in the late 1930s, the female singing voice was joined by male voices and eventually swallowed up in a revolutionary chorus. But this did not mark the last gasp of the solo female vocalist, for she would emerge with even greater force in the postwar period of Mandarin cinema, as the singing women of early sound cinema were borne along on the tides of the wartime exodus of cultural workers and intellectuals to Hong Kong. Stars like Zhou Xuan, after building successful careers on the mainland, resumed their work in the colony's reconstituted entertainment industry and were eventually succeeded by a new generation of performers cast in their mold. These singing actresses reigned over the Hong Kong movie world in the postwar years, overshadowing their male costars. Their voices dominated the airwaves, and their images graced the screen in picture after picture dedicated to displaying their talents to the fullest advantage. The gendering of lyrical expression grew even more pronounced during this period, as the idea of "no film without a song"— to use an oft-cited phrase from the popular music historian Wong Kee-chee— became something of an industry watchword.[33]

The songstresses of Chinese cinema call to mind counterparts from filmmaking traditions around the world: in Hollywood, stars like Jeanette Mac-Donald, Marlene Dietrich, Judy Garland, and Doris Day; *enka* singers of Japanese cinema, such as Hibari Misora;[34] and the playback singers whose voices permeate the soundtracks of Indian cinema, to name just a few examples. But in most global traditions of musical filmmaking, song performance is not the exclusive province of female vocalists. Given the tight association between song and femininity in Chinese films, the Chinese songstress is more akin to the *chanteuse réaliste* of French cinema in the 1930s and 1940s. Kelley Conway has described the ways in which the adoption of sound technology catalyzed an absorption of performers and styles from a culture of popular music rooted in the *café-concert*, cabaret, and music hall. As realist singers like Fréhel, Damia, and Edith Piaf became involved in film production, their chanteuse personas were mythologized in stories that unfolded in a working-class underworld of cafés, nightclubs, and city streets. The earthiness and bold sexuality that characterizes the personas of these singers set them apart from their Chinese counterparts, who were for the most part more idealized and held accountable to restrictive notions of feminine virtue (a point to which I will return). But the affective disposition of these *chanteuses réalistes*, with their world-weary songs of heartbreak and abuse, their lyrical expressions of "female loss and suffering," closely mirrors that of the Chinese songstress, who plays for pathos and uses her voice as a testament to suffering and pain.[35] The turn to song as a signifier of female subjectivity and desire suggests an alternative vector of musical expression in the cinema, one that can be mapped with respect to culturally specific songstress traditions and isolated moments of song performance that erupt even in films that are not musicals.[36]

Like the *chanteuse réaliste*, the Chinese songstress embodies the traces of a live entertainment culture predating and paralleling sound cinema, anchored in a milieu of teahouses, cabarets, and concert halls. The feminization of vocal performance can be explained in part by recourse to what Emilie Yeh describes as the "female-centered musical amusements" of the urban demimonde, with the songstress finding a kindred relative in the singsong girls and other "female entertainers who [sold] nocturnal delights to pleasure-seekers in colonial Shanghai."[37] According to Meng Yue, the presence of these female singers contributed greatly to the "decadent anarchism" and heady, seductive ambiance of entertainment districts like Baoshan Street.[38] We see this world recreated in numerous songstress films that nod to the singer's origins in this culture of stage performance, from the seedy teahouses where she works to attract customers (*Street Angel*) to the luxurious art deco nightclubs where she reigns over the dance floor (*Song of a Songstress*).[39] The lyrical offerings of these stage performers included regional forms like *tanci* (Suzhou-based storytelling songs) and other urban folk melodies; opera arias, sung individually without the props, costumes, gestures, and interspersed dialogue associated with stage performance, in a practice known as *qing chang* (pure singing); and the jazzy tunes of Western-influenced modern pop music (*shidai qu*). These female singers continued to maintain their central position with the advent of mass-mediated music, moving into the sphere of radio performance and phonograph recording as *shidai qu* gained a foothold in the urban soundscape. In this period there was a dearth of male vocalists in modern popular music, which was dominated instead by songstresses like Li Minghui, Zhou Xuan, Yao Lee, Bai Hong, Gong Qiuxia, and Ouyang Feiying.[40] The division of musical labor onscreen was thus consonant with the actual division of labor in the modern music industry, where the vast majority of professional singers were female and most songwriters were male. Yet this fact alone cannot account for the extreme imbalance between female and male pop stars that uniquely characterizes this context, nor does it explain how things came to be this way in the first place.

In grappling with the gendering of vocal performance, it is necessary to consider the historical moment in which this modern mass culture of sounds and images took shape, situated at the endpoint of a long-standing culture of music in which "singing in a performance context" was "culturally coded as feminine," in the words of Judith Zeitlin.[41] Music making and lyrical performance were an integral part of the courtesan culture that flourished throughout the late imperial period. The female entertainers of this milieu engaged in the practice of pure singing. Along with the operatic repertory, their performances also drew upon a long-lived tradition of popular ballads, consisting of lyric verse—usually written in the first person—set to existing melodies. Grace Fong writes: "The Chinese lyrical tradition has a history of female-voiced songs that are often anonymous [in authorship] and have folk or popular origins." On the one hand, these songs "represent some of the strongest expressions of a female lyrical subject in the Chinese tradition."[42] On the other hand, they also represent a reified expression of the social and erotic relationships that transpired in the pleasure quarters, with their status as melodies performed by courtesans for the pleasure of male literati listeners. These relationships were constituted through a highly formalized exchange of entertainment services, money, objects of literary or material value, and—in some instances—sexual favors and companionship between courtesans and male literati.[43]

As many scholars have emphasized, courtesans were not prostitutes in the Western sense of the word because they did not extract payment for sexual services in the manner of a commercial transaction. Even the less elite among them were artists and performers who, in the words of Gail Hershatter, "prided themselves on 'selling their voices rather than their bodies.'"[44] The distinction between the courtesan and the common prostitute, however, is further complicated by the strongly erotic connotations of song performance itself. Zeitlin's work is illuminating on this point. She writes: "Singing was fundamental to the courtesan's art in China not only because song was a social and sexual lubricant and the lyrics were appreciated for their literary and sentimental value, but because singing itself, when offered as entertainment at banquets or other settings, was culturally gendered as feminine. To perform a song was to submit oneself to the gaze as well as the ears of another, and there was a perpetual tendency for the audience to conflate the physical beauty of the singer with the acoustic beauty of the song."[45] These comments point to a decidedly corporeal and sensuous understanding of song in the performative context, one that metonymically relates the quality of the singing voice to the beauty and sexuality of the singer. In Zeitlin's description, the performance of song is a gateway to physical arousal as well as to more refined forms of aesthetic delectation, with the pleasures of intangible notes and fleshly substance converging in the body of the female singer.

The dawning of the republican era of modernity brought with it the end of the courtesan, and the elite entertainment culture centering on this figure gave way to a panoply of mass-accessible cultural productions catering to an urban petty bourgeoisie. Hershatter notes that by the 1920s, the courtesan performer was "completely absorbed" into the category of the common prostitute.[46] Yet the figure of the courtesan continued to adumbrate and permeate public perceptions of a new class of female entertainment professionals. As Jones argues, "the lingering taint of the popular musician's (particularly the female vocalist's) traditional association with unorthodox pleasures" persisted well into the twentieth century, enshrined in conservative prejudicial views of popular song as morally corrupting and of singers as déclassé and unwholesome. The endurance of this association is evident in the musical culture wars of the 1930s, he continues, when "the rhetorical equation of mass-mediated sing-song girls with courtesans and prostitutes" was leveraged in order to ideologically discredit their tunes as decadent, thus clearing the way for a masculine and revolutionary idiom of mass music.[47] The taint of the courtesan-cum-prostitute is also preserved in the cinematic pedigree of the songstress: time and again, she is imagined as a kind of *jiaoji hua* (social flower) who lives off the largesse of the male admirers to whom she makes her voice and body available. Alternatively, she is targeted as an object of social stigma and moral disapproval by others, deemed as unfit for respectable society on the basis of her lowly profession—most often by the parents of the well-bred young men who inevitably fall in love with her and want to marry her. The protest raised against the hapless songstress, in countless romantic melodramas whose plots turn on the collision between young love and parental prohibition, is that she exposes herself to public scrutiny, or *paotou loumian*—a phrase inscribing the transgressive physicality of female song performance. As will become evident in the following chapters, the songstress is plagued by this perceived transgression—and by a stubborn cultural logic that conflates *maige* (selling songs) and *maishen* (selling the body)—for the entirety of her existence.

The haunting of the songstress by her predecessors attests to the way in which residual codes are preserved in the very cultural discourses that have displaced them. On the one hand, the construal of the female singer according to an older set of cultural practices amounts to an anachronism, if not an outright excuse for the perpetuation of long-standing traditional social and sexual hierarchies. On the other hand, it pinpoints the historical truth of the commercial objectification of the female body in an emerging modern culture of entertainment and mass media. The birth of the filmic songstress occurred in a moment when women's images and voices were consumed by others through the media of pictorial magazines, films, phonograph records, and radio on an unprecedented scale as well as in live amusement venues, and when even the experience of tactile proximity to their bodies was available to paying male customers in Shanghai's dance halls.[48] The sensuous and erotic cultural connotations of female song performance in the late imperial period did not die out with the latter's passing but rather were reanimated by and redistributed through the circuits of "the larger sensorial and libidinal economy of a modernizing society."[49] Transposed to the screen, female-voiced songs retained the electrifying charge of seduction, intimacy, and invitation to fantasy, as the examples discussed in this book will attest.

The Songstress as Modern Woman

The central position of the commodified female body in the cultural landscape of early twentieth-century Chinese modernity has been explored from numerous angles by historians attuned to, in the words of Catherine Russell, "a wider field of global visual culture in which the commodification of the female image intersected—and often conflicted—with received norms of gendered behavior."[50] The images of women circulating throughout this culture of consumption and modern media are a reflection of changing gender roles and newly available identities, as well as an active agent in the reconfiguration of femininity. Their impact can be discerned in the iconic construction of the New Woman and/or Modern Girl (translated alternatively as *xin nüxing, xiandai nüxing, modeng nulang,* and *modeng nüxing*), who flaunted the styles of the time—short hair, cosmetics, *qipao,* and Western fashions—along with new ways of being: independent, educated, athletic, professionally active, and politically conscious.[51] Such images can be understood as a crucial element of those "simple surface manifestations of an epoch" that, in Siegfried Kracauer's view, afford a flash of insight into underlying historical processes.[52] Viewed as an amalgam of political aspiration, anxiety, and voyeuristic fascination, the discourse of modern femininity—in China as in other parts of the world—emerges as a vivid index of these processes. In the words of Weihong Bao, "as the battleground among residual, emergent, and alternative discourses of sociobiopolitical reorganization, and as the eroticized embodiment of capitalist circulation, the female body provided the experience of modernity with a tangible image in early-twentieth century China."[53]

It is only against such a historical background that the significance of the gendering of song performance can be fully grasped. This book is premised on the idea that the songstress belongs to the lineage of the modern woman, alongside those creatures of fashion and glamour, the independent new women and the fallen women who have riveted the attention of filmgoers since the silent era and whose echoes continue to permeate the transition to sound and the postwar decades. Like these antecedents, the songstress possesses an irresistible appeal to the senses as an embodied display of the new, the fashionable, and the allures of modern mass culture. Like the fallen women featured in many of the most notable works of Chinese silent cinema—such as *Tianming* (*Daybreak*, 1933) and *Shennü* (*Goddess*, 1934)—the songstress is also obliged to exploit her body, looks, and voice for a living, in the process violating traditional prescriptions related to gender, labor, and public space. Both the fallen woman and the songstress are invested with a high degree of affective and identificatory power, while simultaneously being shrouded in social opprobrium and marginalized within their fictive worlds. Even as they are aesthetically idealized, they are also rendered as passive objects to be disciplined, sacrificed, rescued, or redeemed—ultimately reined in by narrative impulses that betray the deep anxieties surrounding women, performance, and publicity in the age of mass media. And like so many fallen women of the silent screen, the songstress often meets a tragic end. As in the sad case of the great silent film actress Ruan Lingyu (who took her own life at the age of twenty-four, after starring in a film about a young mother and aspiring author who was driven to suicide by a hypocritical and corrupt society), the diegetic fate of the female singer is disconcertingly echoed in the actual fates of the stars who play these roles, many of whom have died in a tragic, untimely fashion, and frequently by their own hand.

To insert the songstress into this lineage is to engage the project of feminist film historiography, building on its investigations of the interrelations among femininity, modernity, and mediatized spectacle that have found a unique articulation in cinema—indeed, that have obsessed Chinese filmmakers from the beginnings of the industry. With this move, my objective is twofold: first, to extend the historical and regional parameters of a critical discourse that has focused on Shanghai cinema of the silent era, and second, to move beyond the primarily visual terms in which this discourse casts mass media. The historical boundaries of this discussion are largely consistent with standard accounts that equate the dawning of a revolutionary mass culture with the terminus of the cultural imagination of the modern woman. Already by the late 1930s, she has set off on a path to disappearance, subsumed by a genderless ideal of the militant and patriotic worker that would define a subsequent era of socialist cinema. From the emancipated New Woman of the May Fourth period, she morphs into the "materialistic, urban femme fatale" and finally the "socially conscious Marxist Girl, who was to become an ancestor to the desexualized female communist cadre after 1949," as Shu-mei Shih writes.[54] As a consequence of the displacement of the urban imaginary of the Shanghai era by a rural revolutionary imaginary, the modern woman fades into a collective of militant workers and national martyrs.

Yet a different perspective on the fate of the modern woman comes into focus when we turn away from a mainland-centric account of film history and consider configurations of urban modernity in other parts of the Chinese-speaking world. The events that led up to the modern woman's disappearance from mainland Chinese cinema also led to her reanimation in another context, Hong Kong in the postwar years. The massive influx of migrants into the colony in the years around the war and the Communist revolution spurred a wave of urbanization that would lay the foundations for Hong Kong's current status as a cosmopolitan megalopolis. During the 1950s and 1960s, a vibrant commercial film industry was created in Hong Kong against the backdrop of urban concentration; industrialization; the absorption of Western and other foreign influences; transformations of the traditional family; the large-scale entrance of women into the workforce; the rise of a white-collar class; and the emergence of a distinct new pop culture erected on the sectors of design, fashion, and manufacturing. The impact of these developments is vividly registered in the cinematic productions of postwar Hong Kong, concretely indexed by the images and sounds of female stars circulating in this period. Here we encounter a new generation of modern girls, attesting to the ways in which this figure is constituted across translocal circuits of capitalist and colonial exchange. Returning to Bao's formulation, in postwar Hong Kong as much as in prewar China, the female body stands out as the "eroticized embodiment of capitalist circulation." From the vantage point of a longer temporal trajectory, the modern woman stands out even more clearly as a figure who mediates the tensions between residual and emergent historical forces, tradition and modernity, and the local and the global.

Many commentators have pointed to the contradictions at play in screen portrayals of modern femininity. These are perhaps nowhere more apparent than in *Goddess*, where Ruan Lingyu memorably portrays that most archetypal fallen woman of the silent screen, the prostitute. The film's impact is inseparable from the charismatic, melancholic beauty of its star—cannily mined in shots that linger on her face and body—even as Ruan's character is subjected to a condemnatory, punitive gaze within the spaces of the fiction. This gives rise to a disparity between the film's presentation of the prostitute as physically desirable and its narrative construction of her as abject and pitiable—a disparity between its showing and its telling. Such a disparity can be construed as the outcome of a process of textual disavowal: the film fetishistically exploits the visual appeal of the very figure it narratively exiles from social and familial existence, with its story about a streetwalker and devoted single mother who ends up separated from her son and imprisoned despite her best efforts to provide for her child. In doing so, *Goddess* caters to a hypocritical morality that sees female sexuality as simultaneously alluring and deserving of punishment. This equivocation perhaps ultimately boils down to the duplicity of the cinematic medium itself, which allows a filmmaker to have it both ways.[55] Conversely, it also attests to the semiotic surplus of images, capable of undercutting and contravening narrative ascriptions of meaning.

Contradictions like these constitute a fundamental component of what Miriam Hansen describes more broadly as the fallen woman cycle of Chinese cinema. Hansen suggests that we might view these films as inscriptions of the contradictions of modernity itself, "enacted through the figure of the woman, very often, literally, across the body of the woman who tries to live them but more often than not fails."[56] *Goddess* is just one of many melodramas of the silent era that evoke a sense of the dead end of feminine subjectivity, "trapped between the rock of societal bigotry and the hard place of sexual commodification."[57] An object of media fantasy and male authorship, the modern woman is often divested of agency and autonomy and shaped by reactionary undercurrents that reaffirm traditional gender values, despite her outwardly up-to-the-minute appearance.[58] But as much as films like *Goddess* and *Daybreak* collude in these fantasies of regulation and discipline, they also clearly display the limits of their ability to determine the reception of the fallen woman figure. Hansen writes: "The meanings of a film are not only determined by directorial intention and an underlying social, masculinist discourse, but are significantly shaped by other voices, such as the mode of performance and the degree of agency, however precarious, that accrues to female actors in the star system. . . . [While] female figures may well be the privileged fetish of male/modernist projection and stereotyping, they are also the sites of greatest ambivalence and mobility, as traditional binarisms may be at once invoked and undermined through performance and masquerade."[59]

For Hansen, the fallen woman's capacity to transcend the discourses that struggle to contain her stems from a specifically cinematic mode of porosity and affect, which is traceable to the power of the medium to elicit unanticipated responses and forms of viewer identification that run obliquely to narrative currents. These instances of mobility, narrative agency, and excessive identification might be provoked by performance, the presence of the star, or other visual elements like mise-en-scène, and—as Hansen argues—Chinese silent cinema abounds with examples of the semiotic vagrancy of the fallen woman. They demand to be approached symptomatically rather than allegorically, with a view to those dissonances, inconsistencies, and tensions that are internal to the film's discursive construction.

Going beyond silent cinema, however, we are also confronted with channels of oblique meaning that extend beyond the visual to the registers of sound and music. For instance, considering a cycle of left-wing sound productions of the 1930s that feature female singers, Jones identifies a "curious doubleness" in their presentation of song. Made in a time of rising nationalist sentiment and class consciousness, these films mounted a bid to harness the songstress's popular appeal for the political edification and mobilization of the masses by rewriting her sybaritic songs as leftist political anthems. They staged her transformation from fallen woman or sentimental heroine into "an oppressed subaltern eager to add her voice to the chorus of enlightened citizens crying out for national salvation."[60] Yet these strategies of "leftist political ventriloquism" could only partially succeed because they ultimately retraced the same "circuit of pleasure" that they purported to disrupt, with their reliance on the star power and alluring presence of the singer.[61] Analyzing films like *Feng yun ernü* (*Children of Troubled Times*, 1935), *Yasuiqian* (*New Year's Coin*, 1937), and *Street Angel*, Jones shows how this doubleness manifests itself most markedly in musical moments. If song was invoked as a powerful political tool by leftist filmmakers and composers, it also proves to be a double-edged weapon, opening up a realm of indeterminacy where sound and image diverge in meaning, the performer's star identity readily erupts out of the fictional façade of the oppressed subaltern, and the lingering echoes of past performances undermine the attempt to rewrite the messages of well-known tunes. The representation of the songstress in such films enacts a repetition of the disavowal that attends the fallen woman, insofar as "the fetishized star appeal of [singers like Zhou Xuan] is exploited at the same time that it is defused and rewritten by the presence of a larger discourse."[62] But in this case the sleight of hand transpires as an act of ventriloquism, an appropriation of the *genü*'s voice.

As Jones demonstrates, the struggles for control over the meaning of the filmed female body continue from the silent to the sound era. The tensions between male authorship and female performance, commercial and pedagogical agendas, and gender and nation are crucial dimensions of the difference that unfolds in the space of a song. To further pursue the question of this difference requires both a shift beyond cinematic visuality to include the complex audio-visual interactions that constitute the female body as a fetish, and a leap across space and time—from the silent era to the age of sound, from the prewar to the postwar period, and from Shanghai to Hong Kong. In the explosion of female stars in the postwar film and music industry, we encounter an intensifying traffic of images and sounds by which the feminine is imagined, circulated, and contested throughout mass media. The entrenchment of musical performance in the films of this period carves out an important arena for an ongoing gendered reflection on modernity. It is the performative nature of this reflection that is most compelling for my analysis, for the interlude of song and dance is often a conduit for meanings that run counter to the film's more overtly didactic political messages. It marks the point at which these works, steeped as they are in formulaic production strategies and dominant ideologies, betray a textual unconscious and thereby disclose their historical significance—not merely as a transparent reflection of a sociohistorical context, but rather in their "complex, mediated, and decentered relationship with this context."[63]

Voices in Time

Inasmuch as the musical moment in film is an interval of difference, the discovery and articulation of this difference is critical to this study as a work of feminist historiography. My endeavor to construct in these pages a gendered history of Chinese cinema through the figure of the songstress is directly inspired by Hansen's work. As a historian, Hansen engaged continuously with the question of how to locate the female subject within the experience of cinema and against the backdrop of the exclusionary effects of patriarchy, the constraints of the industry, and the assertions of the female spectator's structural impossibility made by proponents of certain strands of feminist psychoanalytic film theory. From one angle, this question entails a careful reconstruction of the historical conditions of filmgoing, looking to the material evidence of how a female viewing public came into being in the early twentieth century, concomitant with the rise of a mass culture that targeted women as consumers. Such an approach to spectatorship aims to restore its culturally and historically specific features, countermanding a theoretical tendency to reduce the spectator to a structural or textual effect.[64] But at the same time, Hansen also looks to the film itself as an archive of material traces of gendered spectatorship, even if these traces exist only in the form of internal tensions, conflicting forms of address, and gaps "between patriarchal ideology on the one hand and the recognition of female experience, needs, fantasies on the other."[65] That is, in its appeal to female filmgoers, the cinema necessarily "both recognized and absorbed discourses of experience" that conflicted with "the masculinization of the spectator position endemic to classical cinema."[66] For Hansen, the task of feminist historiography therefore necessarily implicates a politics of close analysis that aims "to establish a usable past" by identifying cracks in the individual film's textual system—detours in its enunciatory mechanisms that open onto multiple, gendered pathways of reception and interpretation. The search for the female spectator must pull us into the film itself, so that we can ask: "Are processes of identification necessarily synchronous with the temporal structures of classical narrative, and to what extent is closure effective? How do films construct what we remember of them?"[67]

Hansen's writings on early American cinema explore these questions through a consideration of cases of an explicit address to the female gaze, whether in the star cult of Rudolph Valentino, patterns of address in D. W. Griffiths's *Intolerance*, or perverse restagings of the desiring female consumer in works of early cinema like *The 'Teddy' Bears*. Her late work is marked by a turn to transnational dimensions of film history—in dialogue with Chinese and Japanese film history—along with an increasing focus on what might be called the affective dimensions of performance and how these give rise to countercurrents of identification that inflect the experience and memory of watching films. In her writing on the fallen women, modern girls, *moga* (modern Japanese girls), and maternal madonnas of Chinese and Japanese cinema, Hansen emphasizes those "moments of mimetic identification that were more often than not partial and excessive in relation to narrative comprehension and closure."[68] The politics of close reading are thus oriented toward dimensions of performance that cannot be boiled down to the construction of the character as a psychologically and diegetically consistent entity. Rather, these dimensions consist of more inchoate, ephemeral, at times even incongruous elements of body language, gesture, and appearance. The persistence of such elements in the memory of the viewer demands an acknowledgment of the authorial agency of the actress: her capacity to determine identification and meaning and to elicit flash points of recognition and affect that interrupt the flow of the narrative. These moments of disjunction, no matter how fleeting, Hansen suggests, are the kernel from which new perspectives on the past can spring, ones responsive to the "junctures between, and heterogeneities within, national film histories, whether virtual or actual, politically blocked or historiographically repressed."[69] The writing of gender-specific history therefore begins by locating fault lines in the individual work and seeing them as openings through which a female subject can be read back into the discursive structures and processes of reception that comprise the experience of cinema.

The seam between sound and image presents one such opening in the case of the songstress, and throughout this book, building on Hansen's historiographic framework, I unfold the ways in which film music expands the range of possibilities by which this performative flux is manifested. The songs of the songstress present us with a veritable archive of identifications that are "partial and excessive in relation to narrative comprehension and closure." Given their autonomous existence as cultural commodities, at once imbedded in and existing outside of the film, songs carry a host of extratextual meanings not fully contained by the framework of narration. With the performance of song, other temporalities are woven into the reception of cinema—temporalities that stem from the pleasures of repeated listening, or from the resonance of songs in space and memory, even long after the film has ended. Just as the singing voice involves a mode of address that is different from the speaking voices in a film, more presentational than representational, so it also makes particular demands on the memory of the audience. Songs have a special relation to repetition, to the extent that they are made to be heard again and again. The affective charge of songs does not expire in the interval of projection but rather builds on each rehearing. This book delves into the ways that female voices inhabit films and carry across time.

Locating the Songstress

The genealogy of the songstress constructed in these pages traverses a historical terrain that is usually conceptualized in distinct and separate units. Periodization is an act of division on the basis of selection, identifying certain events, agents, and political forces as capable of conferring sense and order on the past while discarding others. Thus, this book takes the songstress as a starting point for a remapping of Chinese film history against an international horizon. Although throughout her history the songstress has been claimed as a potent symbol of national, class, and anticolonial politics, she also discloses crossings and currents that are occluded by these politics. Her circuitous trail points to the need for an internally comparative understanding of Chinese film history—a history that is geographically dispersed, polycentric, and all too readily trifurcated into more digestible components, or, conversely, anchored by recourse to totalizing national frameworks. The endpoint of the songstress's trail is not just a disclosure of cultural identity, but also a confrontation with Chinese cinema as a self-differing and heterogeneous entity.

As I have already noted, the songstress phenomenon was not confined to a single regional locus; rather, it bridged two notable epicenters of film production. The phenomenon demands to be understood as part of what Poshek Fu has termed the "Shanghai–Hong Kong nexus," referring to the "extensive movement of people, capital, and ideas across the border" from 1935 until the closing of the borders of the People's Republic of China in 1950.[70] As Fu argues in his important study on this topic, the links between the film and entertainment industries of these regions were critical to Shanghai's standing as the so-called Hollywood of the East in the 1930s, and to Hong Kong's subsequent assumption of this mantle after the decline of the Shanghai film industry. During these years, waves of migrants poured into Hong Kong, nearly quadrupling its population. Among these were a large number of literati, filmmakers, composers, writers, and performing artists, all of whom would play a crucial role in the colony's rise as a new center of cultural production for the Chinese-speaking world. The passage of the songstress across these regions attests to the tightness of these connections as well as to the continuing impact of the Shanghai–Hong Kong nexus throughout the 1950s and 1960s.

The remnants of prewar film culture circulated throughout postwar cinema, evident in the latter's forms and conventions, story lines (many of which were recycled from earlier Shanghai productions), and even musical content (a significant fraction of the songs featured in postwar *gechang pian* were Shanghai oldies, rearranged and sometimes set to new lyrics). As reminders of another place and time, these remnants and echoes point to postwar film culture's emergence at the unstable historical juncture of a great divide, when China's geopolitical map was reconfigured in the aftermath of the country's civil war. To a large extent, the era of film history over which the songstress reigned was the creation of an émigré generation, whose members were steeped in their memories of the past and deeply marked by their experiences of displacement. The affective resonance of these songs for their audience finds a basis in a long-standing popular mythology of the songstress as a figure of existential homelessness—orphan, refugee, or exile. This mythology was crafted in films from *Street Angel*—which casts the songstress as a refugee from the Northeast, one of many millions of people displaced by the Japanese invasion—to *Da lu* (*The Big Road*, 1934)—where she is embodied in the familiar cultural icon of the wandering flower drum singer from Fengyang, forced to flee her home by natural disasters and political unrest. Significantly, it is only through the performance of song that the audience learns of the background of these characters. In the volatile political atmosphere of the 1930s, songs functioned as coded references to contemporary historical events; in subsequent decades, their sentiments of pathos would reverberate against a larger background of recent traumas and dislocations.

On the other side of the fallout of the great divide, the songstress is intercepted by another set of transregional currents. Only through the lens of a double historical vision do her contours come into focus. Singing actresses were not just holdovers from the past, they were also the building blocks of a new commercial film culture. The principal driving forces in the postwar Hong Kong film industry were based in Southeast Asia: MP&GI, part of the Cathay conglomerate, and its longer-lived rival, Shaw Brothers (whose past incarnation was the Tianyi Film Company in Shanghai). The studios were founded by Loke Wan Tho and Run Run Shaw, respectively. Both men were Chinese Malayan property magnates who saw a lucrative opportunity in the export market for Chinese-language films throughout the trans-Pacific diaspora: Malaya, Singapore, Borneo, Taiwan, Thailand, Vietnam, and the Philippines. They turned to Hong Kong as a stable environment in which to pursue commercial filmmaking. In 1956 MP&GI's studios were established in Kowloon, and in the following year, Shaw Studios was founded in Clearwater Bay; competing with them were numerous smaller film studios like Xinhua and Changcheng (Great Wall). In Fu's description, the films made by the two major studios reflect the "cosmopolitan, border-crossing consciousness" of the producers and their desire to forge a polished, technically sophisticated, modern cinema with cross-regional appeal.[71] The songstresses of the postwar period display this cosmopolitan orientation and border-crossing agility. The circulation of their images and voices traced the perimeter of a cultural space known as *nanyang* (south seas), constituted by migratory flows throughout the South China Sea and overlaid with networks of colonial power.

As Jeremy Taylor points out, the large-scale population movements precipitated by the war and the communist victory also gave rise to large communities of dialect speakers dispersed throughout the Chinese diaspora.[72] The cultural space of *nanyang* was marked by linguistic heterogeneity, as the postwar period saw the flowering of dialect film industries catering to these communities (the largest of which were Cantonese and Amoy).[73] Song performance featured prominently in all of these dialect cinemas, drawing on localized musical traditions such as Cantonese opera, *nanyin*, and Hokkien opera. Although this book focuses on song performance in Mandarin films from the early sound era to postwar Hong Kong and on the performers who worked exclusively in this linguistic realm—Zhou Xuan, Chung Ching, Yao Lee, and Grace Chang—it bears noting that these figures have parallels in other dialect industries. Singing actresses and crossover stars appeared across the polylinguistic terrain of diasporic film culture. They flourished in a milieu constituted by movements across borders, hybridity, and multiple locations (and dislocations) of culture.

The Mandarin film industry of postwar Hong Kong has been largely sidelined by Chinese film historiography, even though it marks a crucial juncture— the emergence of Chinese cinema's first fully functioning vertically integrated commercial studio system.[74] The vast majority of English-language scholarship on Hong Kong cinema refers to the Cantonese-language film industry that was consolidated in the 1970s, a moment that postdates the disappearance of Mandarin and other dialect industries from the colony's filmmaking landscape. Although the kinetic action genres that are today such an object of worldwide fixation and cultish veneration have their roots in this later phase of Hong Kong filmmaking,[75] a glance at the preceding decades reveals a very different genre ecology, composed largely of romantic and family melodramas, historical costume epics, and opera films. Indeed, the rise of Hong Kong's popular genres of action—kung fu, swordplay, and crime thrillers—was coterminous with the decline of the female-centered dramas of the preceding era. The edging out of singing heroines by fighting heroes signaled a sea change in the taste and sensibilities of the moviegoing public. Viewed in the context of Hong Kong cinema as we know it today, the films of the postwar era look like stranded objects. They are further disadvantaged within a critical milieu where debates on regional identity, postcolonialism, and transnationalism lie front and center.[76]

Although a large part of this book is devoted to a detailed account of the postwar era of Hong Kong cinema, I steer clear of situating this cinema within a linear narrative of identity formation, in which a uniquely local filmmaking idiom emerges from amidst the dissipating miasma of a "Shanghai hangover."[77] By the same token, however, neither is my objective to fold this cinema into a narrative that looks to the mainland as its main reference, thereby marginalizing it with respect to a sinocentric point of origin. Rather, what interests me about postwar Hong Kong film culture is the challenge it poses to entrenched nation-based paradigms of historiography and rubrics of cultural identity, as a stranded object capable in turn of decentering these discourses. The period over which the songstress reigns marks a historical juncture in which Chinese cinema becomes irrevocably pluralized, henceforth referring to three distinct industries divided by territory, economic organization, and political orientation. The geopolitical reconfigurations and dispersions precipitated by the great divide challenge the setting up of tidy demarcations, confronting the researcher with a centrifugal field. With her multiple locations and interstitial temporal positioning, the songstress embodies the elusiveness of this period of film history.

Returning to the contemporary examples with which this introduction began, we can comprehend how this elusive quality is the basis of the continuing appeal of the songstress as an intensive locus of cultural memory. In her own time, her songs emanated from a space of loss and dispossession, poignantly evoking the sense of an elsewhere. From the perspective of the present, the tunes and voices become even more untimely and phantom-like in their reverberation, as sonic remainders of the past. They evoke a sense of historical residues yet to be fully discharged, of something yet to be fully remembered and that therefore compels repeated listening.

Chapters

The book begins by tracing the birth of the songstress during the transition from silent to sound filmmaking in Shanghai. From an early point in this process, filmmakers explored the new possibilities of synchronized sound technology in a musical register, anchoring sound to image in the body of the female vocalist and thus constructing a soundscape dominated by female singing voices. Sound film developed only a short step behind recorded music as a lucrative entertainment commodity, with the film song marking an intersection between the technologies of cinema, radio, and gramophone. Film producers were highly attuned to the cross-marketing opportunities enabled by synchronized sound technologies, as demonstrated in the strategies that an early generation of singing actresses—including Li Minghui, Yang Naimei, and Violet Wong—used to navigate the transition from silent to sound film.

All of these performers came to filmmaking by way of the musical stage, and their productions shed light on another important aspect of the film song—its emergence from exhibitor practices of matching projected images with live music. Thus, chapter 1 situates early sound films within a history of multimedia performances, combining the attractions of the musical stage with cinematic entertainment. In this context, film songs were associated with the effect of direct address and the immediacy of live performance; at the same time, this effect was produced from within an environment of mechanical reproduced sounds and repetitive listening. In *Two Stars in the Milky Way*, one of a number of partial-sound productions from the transitional period, we witness how the incorporation of film songs transforms narrative space. The chapter concludes with a discussion of Zhou Xuan, the first proper star of the era of the sound film. Zhou's films cemented the conventions of the singing film while also forging a mythology of the songstress as melodramatic victim, one that would leave an imprint on Chinese cinema for decades to come.

The following chapters build on this genealogy of the songstress by turning to postwar Hong Kong, where a new generation of performers followed in Zhou's footsteps between the music recording and film industries. As *gechang pian* evolved in the postwar period, they built on the conventions of an earlier era and further cemented the equation between femininity and lyrical expression. Chapter 2 provides the basic historical groundwork for my analysis of the postwar songstress. It describes the industry developments that led to Hong Kong's rise as an epicenter of Mandarin popular music and movies in the 1950s and 1960s, ushering in an era of modern images and sounds for Chinese audiences in the trans-Pacific diaspora. This period also saw a new phase in the evolution of *gechang pian*, within the context of a vibrant, polyglot culture of music. Film songs flourished in this period, which was bookended by the Chinese jazz age and the era of rock and roll.

Chapter 3 discusses a particular songstress type: the wildcat, or singing country lass, associated with a highly popular cycle of rustic singing films and most famously embodied by the actress Chung Ching. Chung was a somewhat idiosyncratic case—typecast as a songstress despite her lack of vocal talent. Her film songs were regularly dubbed by other singers, such as the famed pop star Yao Lee, who collaborated with Chung as a behind-the-scenes singer in a large number of productions. Precisely for this reason, these films shed light on the ambivalent location of the voice in songstress films—at once corporeally anchored and mechanically detachable, coexisting with but not necessarily belonging to the on-screen singer. The ambivalence of the voice in turn points to the specific assumptions about performance and stardom that were operative in this period.

Chapter 4 focuses on another postwar performer: Grace Chang, arguably the most emblematic of postwar songstresses as well as one of the most popular recording artists of Mandarin pop. Chang made her screen debut in the 1957 film *Mambo Girl*,[78] which introduced to Chinese cinema the figure of the carefree singing and dancing teenager. Her performances introduced new, foreign musical styles—such as American rock and roll, swing, mambo, calypso, and cha-cha—to Chinese audiences; they channeled and remediated the otherness and exoticism of these styles. Moreover, Chang's rise to stardom precipitated an important turn in the evolution of the songstress film. Until this moment, singing films had far outnumbered song-and-dance films, and musical expression had centered primarily on vocal performance. But in Chang's vehicles, we see dance promoted to an equal partner of song, incorporated into songstress routines on a regular basis, and even in some instances supplanting vocal performance as a main musical attraction. Dance is tied to another significant dimension of Chang's star persona—an adeptness at crossing cultural boundaries, whether in the acquisition of foreign languages or the mastery of international musical styles. Chang's career illustrates how in this era of Hong Kong modernity, what counted as talent was modulated by an aspiration to cosmopolitan worldliness, embodied in the performer as a kind of cultural chameleon able to absorb, adapt to, and perform difference with virtuosic grace.

The final chapter shifts to a longer historical perspective of postwar Hong Kong cinema, taking a single film as its starting point: *The Wild, Wild Rose*,[79] a singing film inspired by the music and plot of Bizet's opera *Carmen*. The film's portrayal of its songstress amalgamates two very different iconic fictional personas, the fiery temptress Carmen and the self-sacrificing courtesan Camille, from *The Lady of the Camellias* by Alexandre Dumas *fils*. The citational strategies of *The Wild, Wild Rose* demand to be situated in a history of adaptation, translation, and hybridizing exchanges that extended back to the early twentieth century and helped form a tradition of popular sentimental fiction. In its unruly intertextuality, the film serves as a case study for tracking the ways in which this tradition passed from the printed page to the screen and consequently generated a distinctive strand of Chinese film melodrama. *Gechang pian* developed in the orbit of this melodramatic mode; female singer and film songs arose from dialogic interactions between cinema, literature, theater, and opera.

A note on romanization: the names of managers, directors, writers, and performers are romanized according to the conventions of the places where they worked, following as closely as possible the form in which these names are most commonly printed in English. All titles of films and print references are romanized using the Hanyu Pinyin system. All translations are the author's unless otherwise noted.

A SONGSTRESS IS BORN

. . . .

The songstress was born with the introduction of sound to the Shanghai-based filmmaking industry, as a figure who from the outset made a special claim on the capacities of emerging audiovisual technologies. As in other parts of the world, in China the cinema's transition to sound took place in fits and starts during a prolonged period of technical experimentation. Filmmakers drew on divergent, often imperfect, approaches to the synchronization of sound with moving images, making use of preexisting phonograph records, sound-on-disc soundtrack recordings, and both imported and homegrown sound-on-film systems. But even amidst the fractured landscape of filmmaking before the standardization of the sound picture, a strand of consistency can be discerned in the tendencies to acoustically spotlight the singing voice and to visually anchor that voice in the body of the female singer. These tendencies are already apparent in the first full-sound Chinese film, *Genü Hong mudan* (*Songstress Red Peony*, 1931, directed by Zhang Shichuan and produced by Mingxing Film Studio). The film featured an opera singer as its eponymous heroine, played by the movie queen Hu Die. It included four sequences from Peking opera as musical highlights; these were dubbed by the famed male opera performer Mei Lanfang, although—as noted in the introduction—this fact was downplayed in the film's publicity.

On the one hand, *Songstress Red Peony* illustrates the influence of the Chinese operatic tradition on filmmaking practices. Opera was an important precedent for sound cinema, constituting a preexisting matrix of possibilities for the combination of songs and storytelling, for endowing music with an emphatic expressive function within a narrational context. This matrix of possibilities would find its fullest and most systematic elaboration in the opera film, a category that flourished after the introduction of synchronized sound technology. But on the other hand, *Songstress Red Peony* marks the inception of a filmmaking approach distinct from the opera film genre. In contrast to the latter, where an entire cast of singers participates in the performance of song, the film presents one singer as the lone lyrical agent. The labor of musical production is rendered as singular, not collective, within the space of the fiction, embodied within a solitary figure. The framing of the singer's voice as a solo instrument elicits a perception of that voice as an individual entity, freighted with connotations of interiority and depth. Such stories about female entertainers proliferated throughout the period of transition to sound and beyond, along with various strategies for supplementing filmic narration with scenes of musical display. The songstress exerted a magnetic pull on the powers of film sound, promising the full release of its expressive possibilities. In doing so, she would also propel the subsequent development of Chinese cinema in a musical direction.

This chapter surveys the songstress's beginnings in prewar Shanghai film culture, approaching this figure as a starting point from which to map the crossings of sound and image throughout the transitional period. Her ubiquitous presence attests to the predominance of the singing voice in the soundscape of prewar Chinese cinema. If the term *talkie* in Western film critical parlance signals a sonic regime that privileges dialogue above other kinds of sounds, the partial-sound productions that were made throughout the 1930s—like *Yinhan shuang xing* (*Two Stars in the Milky Way*, 1931), discussed in greater detail below—suggest the workings of a different sonic hierarchy and audiovisual logic. These partial-sound films endowed their singing characters with audible voices, even as those around them remained consigned to silence, their speech communicated only through intertitles. The singing voice alone penetrated the soundtrack, mingling with instrumental accompaniment and sound effects. Even after the standardization of full-sound pictures closed the audible gap between speech and song, the singing voice retained a distinctive presence and emphasis. This special status would be preserved in the formal structures of *gechang pian* (singing films) in ensuing decades. Moreover, the disproportionate number of chanteuses featured in early Chinese cinema introduces yet another facet to the distinction of singing voices: it is the female voice that commands the soundtrack, accrues dramatic force, and rises to a privileged position in the acoustic field of film. Thus the musical register in which the marriage of sound and image takes place is inseparable from the evolution of patterns of gendered display, representational tropes, and associations between femininity and song that would inflect films for years to come.

The musical styles of film songs in the prewar period ran a gamut that included traditional regional opera, regional folk ballads, revolutionary anthems, Western-influenced art songs, and *shidai qu* (jazz-influenced Mandarin pop). The soundtrack's incorporation of such tunes attests to the symbiotic connections forged between the film and music industries in the age of sound technology. As both Zhang Zhen and Andrew Jones have pointed out, film sound arrived in an era when songs were already lucrative cultural commodities. Republican-era Shanghai was a base not just for the Chinese film industry, but also for the burgeoning commercial record industry and wireless broadcasting network. To a large extent, the introduction of songs to film soundtracks reflected a nascent awareness on the part of cultural producers of the lucrative possibilities of cross-platform marketing and tie-ups—as evidenced in the collaboration that spawned *Songstress Red Peony*, between Mingxing Film Studio and Pathé Records, a major producer of gramophone records in China.[1] Jones demonstrates how new recording, play-back, and wireless transmission technologies catalyzed the emergence of a distinctive hybrid and polyglot culture of modern popular music in the contact zones of the semicolonial city. As a medium of popular songs, early sound cinema was imbricated in the crisscrossing networks of convergence and feedback that constituted the "urban media marketplace" of the Shanghai culture industry.[2] Along parallel lines, Zhang situates early film songs within a new regime of "acousticized spectatorship" that cut across disparate media and spaces of consumption—cinema, phonograph, radio, magazines, theater, shops, the home, and the street. To the extent that "the proliferation of the Chinese character for song (*ge*) is indicative of a film culture captivated by the sonic spell," as Zhang observes, this sonic spell was part and parcel of a broader restructuring of perceptual experience within a technologically mediated cultural geography.[3] Film songs developed in tandem with a sea change in the soundscape of modernity, as musical sounds previously experienced only in the context of live performance were diffused across a host of new spaces, both private and public, and transformed by processes of mechanical reproduction.

Film songs call for an extrinsic approach, one attuned to cinema's embedded place in a mass culture of urban leisure, but they also demand to be understood as the basis of an intrinsic set of representational codes taking shape around the encounter between film narrative and synchronized music. More than discrete cultural objects simply inserted into the space of the screen and the movie theater, songs also expanded cinema's expressive repertoire, thereby transforming the very process of narration and audience engagement. With the act of singing, new modes of performance were incorporated into the conventions of the sound film and multiple and disjunctive forms of address conjoined with narrative illusionism. The scene of musical performance constitutes a discursive fold, in which diegetic space and time are overlaid with other spatiotemporal configurations. As the main vocal agent of lyrical performance, the pivot on which speech turns into song and vice versa, the songstress not only absorbed the effects of this discursive flux; she also functioned as the interface through which these effects were correlated with specific thematic motifs and formal techniques. The countless tales about female singers in the first decade of sound cinema document a process through which the external, cross-media resonances of song performance congealed into distinctive generic codes, structures of identification, and ideologemes. This chapter details the ways in which this process plays out in several important works that showcase an early generation of stars who crossed the divide between silent and sound cinema—Yang Naimei, Li Minghui, Violet Wong [Zi Luolan], and Wang Renmei. The second part of the chapter focuses on Zhou Xuan, the first proper star of the age of sound technology. After rising to celebrity in the Shanghai film and recording industries, Zhou moved to Hong Kong to continue her filmmaking career during the wartime period. In tracing her footsteps, this chapter paves the way for a consideration of the *gechang pian* in its postwar phase and of a new generation of singing actresses. The continuities between these filmmaking periods disclose a hitherto imperceptible strand of Chinese film history—one rooted in a musical idiom that cuts across genres and periods, predicating modes of performance and address that defy the logic of narrative integration.

Film Songs in the Silent Era: Rethinking the Sound Transition

The transition to sound filmmaking in Shanghai spans a period of roughly six years. It begins with the introduction of sound projection to the city's top-tier movie theaters in 1929 and the first attempts by Chinese filmmakers to synchronize sound and image in 1930, and it ends around 1935, when sound films became the industry norm.[4] *Songstress Red Peony* holds a prominent place in accounts of this period as the first instance of a made-in-Shanghai full-sound production, using a sound-on-disc system. The film went into production in 1930 and, after a long and arduous journey, was released in March 1931. Heralded in numerous press accounts as China's "first all-talking and singing sound picture," it was an enormous box-office success, notwithstanding the poor technical quality of its soundtrack and its faulty synchronization. A string of releases from other studios deploying various kinds of sound technology followed in rapid succession, making 1931 a pivotal year in the Chinese film industry's move toward sound cinema. These included *Yu meiren* (*The Singing Beauty*), a sound-on-disc production from Youlian Film Company; *Yu guo tian qing* (*Peace after Storm*), China's first sound-on-film production, made by Da Zhongguo Film Company and Jinan Film Company in collaboration with Japanese technicians; *Gechang chunse* (*Pleasures of the Opera*), a sound-on-film production made by Tianyi Film Company with Movietone technology imported from America at great expense and advertised as China's first "real" sound film;[5] and *Two Stars in the Milky Way*, a sound-on-disc production from United Photoplay Service (Lianhua Film Company). Meanwhile, silent film production continued throughout the transitional period, with the 1930s witnessing the release of some of the most highly regarded works of Chinese silent cinema. As Li Suyuan and Hu Jubin point out, it was only after the advent of sound that silent cinema somewhat paradoxically reached its zenith as an art form in China.[6]

A glance at these examples of early sound films reveals that already in this initial wave of sound filmmaking, a pattern had begun to crystallize in the equation of the newfound powers of sound with the allures of song, both of which were embodied in the female singer. This figure is frequently inscribed in the titles of these productions—whether directly named, as in the case of *The Singing Beauty*, or invoked allusively, as in *Pleasures of the Opera*. In the publicity for these pictures, the attractions of sound are enumerated individually in terms of music, song, and dialogue, with musical performance receiving a special emphasis. For instance, the story line of *The Singing Beauty*—about the doomed love between two members of a theater company, a playwright and a singer-actress—incorporates numerous scenes of musical performance. A full-page ad for the film appearing in the daily newspaper *Shenbao* describes it as a "made-in-China sound-music-singing-talking-moving masterpiece" (figure 1.1).[7] One section of the ad is devoted to the film's musical highlights; among these were a duet sung by the male and female leads, Xu Qinfang

··· FIGURE 1.1 ···

Advertisement for *The Singing Beauty*, *Shenbao*, May 25, 1931.

and Shang Guanwu, and the film's theme song, "Fang cao meiren" ("Fragrant Beauty"), whose lyrics are transcribed in their entirety in the ad. The reader is informed that a recording of these songs has already been produced, reflecting a move in the early sound period toward releasing gramophone records of film songs simultaneously with—sometimes even in advance of—the film's theatrical debut. Furthermore, the ad announces a twice-daily "simultaneous radio broadcast of the film's music and songs" by the Tianling Wireless Broadcast Station. The ad registers in various ways a dawning conception of the film song as a featured soundtrack component, a special attraction for moviegoers, as well as a cultural object with a life of its own—existing apart from the film in the form of sheet music and gramophone records and functioning as the basis for a three-way tie-up between the film studio, record company, and radio station. Such a conception is evident throughout the marketing strategies of the early sound period, which frequently combine notices for gramophone record releases with film advertisements and devote as much space to detailing the musical content of new films as to describing their plots.[8]

Even more intriguing in this particular case is the special radio broadcast of *The Singing Beauty*'s musical soundtrack. The practice of simultaneously transmitting film screenings on the airwaves seems to have occurred with some regularity in this period, as suggested by its portrayal in a partial-sound film of the same year, *Two Stars in the Milky Way*. A self-reflexive "metafilm" about the movie industry, *Two Stars* depicts the rise to stardom of Yueying, a young singer and actress.[9] Yueying makes her screen debut after signing a contract with the Yinhan Film Studio, a fictional stand-in for the actual producer, United Photoplay. (The film even includes cameo appearances by notable real-life directors affiliated with United Photoplay, like Sun Yu and Cai Chusheng.) To celebrate the opening night of the new picture, "Love's Sorrow in the Eastern Chamber," Yinhan throws a lavish party in an art deco nightclub. The festivities are briefly interrupted when the host exhorts the partygoers to turn their attention to a radio broadcast of a song scene performed by Yueying: "Ladies and gentlemen! The Chui Wah Garden scene is now on the screen. To prove what I say, let us turn on the radio and listen to the song of the Empress, Mei Fee." With these words, he turns to a wireless transmission unit built into the front of the nightclub stage and switches it on. The appearance of the wireless radio as part of the stage, in lieu of a flesh-and-blood singer, stands as a stark visual illustration of the detachment of musical sounds from their material sources in an era of technological recording and recirculation. This detachment serves as the basis for the tie-up between film and radio, enabling a spatial expansion of the sound film's experiential scope via the transmission of the wireless signal—from the movie theater to the home and other public spaces where radio broadcasts could be heard, like the street, cafés, restaurants, shops, and cabarets, as we see in *Two Stars*.

At the same time, the reproduction and spatial diffusion of prerecorded sound are also contained here in the framework of a singular performance event, the opening-night show. Even as technology enabled the accelerating incursion of mediated sounds into the soundscape of mass culture, modes of display and reception more readily associated with live performance continued to assert themselves in the encounter with mediated sounds. In portraying on-screen one of the exhibition practices of its time, *Two Stars* dramatizes the early sound film's participation in a temporal horizon of simultaneous mediated listening. The translation of the movie audience's audiovisual experience into a sonic experience for a larger community of listeners rests on a prior conception of the film screening itself as a performance event, on a par with a concert or theater show, available to be transmitted simultaneously on the airwaves. During an era when radio was a medium for live programming as much as for prerecorded music, the quality of simultaneous presence in time anchored the emergence of a listening audience at the juncture of these technological systems. Film sound took shape at the juncture of two distinct medium ontologies: one of pastness, associated with film as a medium of recording and storing time, and the other of liveness, associated with broadcasting media like radio and television that are capable of transmitting events as they occur.[10] The examples of *The Singing Beauty* and *Two Stars in the Milky Way* demonstrate the ways in which the transition to sound brought a new and complex set of temporalities to bear on cinematic spectatorship. These temporalities were woven into the fabric of the film just as the songs themselves were inserted (*chuancha*) into the narrative.

Indeed, in following the cue of these early sound productions to consider the film screening as audiovisual event, we arrive at a more nuanced account of the transition from silent to sound cinema. A look back at the years immediately preceding this transition confirms that the impulse to combine images and sounds preceded the arrival of synchronized sound technology. The practice of silent films with on-site musical accompaniment existed in China as it did in other parts of the world. High-end exhibition venues in Shanghai catering to an American and European clientele, like the Capitol Carlton Theatre, arranged for live music to accompany their film programs on a regular basis, with some even retaining an in-house orchestra for this purpose. Some of the local theaters that screened Chinese films adopted the exhibition strategies of top-tier Western theaters. In doing so, they promoted themselves and laid claim to a certain degree of distinction, as demonstrated by the example of the Grand Beijing Theater (Beijing Da Xiyuan), which vaunted its investment in on-site musical entertainment in a 1929 *Shenbao* article titled "Movie Theaters and Music." "Based on today's trend," the theater's manager stated, "the sophistication of moviegoers develops day by day, and they will only visit theaters offering delightful music."[11] Zhang Yiwei contextualizes these exhibition practices in a semicolonial environment, where public tastes were influenced by Western film culture and musical accompaniment was consequently equated with aesthetic refinement and sophistication.[12] Surveying the advertising and media discourse of the day, Zhang identifies an increasing attention to music's capacity to enhance silent storytelling in the late 1920s. Paving the way for the prolonged transition to sound cinema was a turn to music as a tool for creating a mood and deepening the audience's emotional engagement with the narrative. One newspaper article from 1929 argued: "With the power to tug at human emotions, everything that happens on screen can trigger happiness or remorse in rapid alternation. When set to appropriate music, the visual and aural senses are both stimulated, and this impact is even more pronounced."[13]

In this context, the film song must be situated as a phenomenon propelled not only by developments in sound recording technology, but also by exhibitor practices of matching projected images with live music. Film songs were not an invention of the age of the soundtrack; rather, they featured among the sounds of silent cinema. In *Liangxin fuhuo* (*Resurrection of Conscience*, 1926), directed by Bu Wancang,[14] we find an example of a silent film whose script included a song scene (figure 1.2). Adapted from Tolstoy's final novel, *Resurrection*, the film centers on the travails of a servant girl impregnated by the young master of the wealthy family she serves. The song scene marks one of the film's melodramatic climaxes: while working as a wet nurse for another child, the servant comes home to find that her own newborn child has died. In response to this tragedy, the destitute heroine—played by the silent film star Yang Naimei—sings "The Ballad of the Wet Nurse," a heart-rending ballad of maternal love.[15] The debut of *Resurrection of Conscience* at Shanghai's Grand Central Theater included a special appearance by the film's star. Press accounts describe the program as a combination of a film screening with musical stage show: when it came time for the song scene, the projection paused, the screen lifted, and the lights turned on to reveal Yang Naimei in person on stage. Dressed like her character in the film, against a backdrop duplicating the mise-en-scène of the interrupted film scene, Yang sang the entirety of "The Ballad of the Wet Nurse." When she had completed her song, the lights

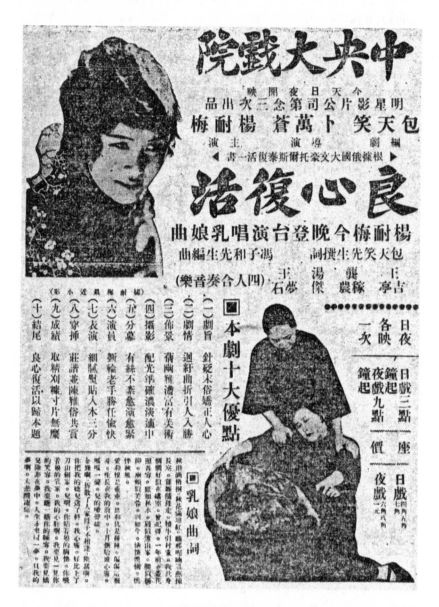

Advertisement for *Resurrection of Conscience*, *Shenbao*, December 22, 1926.

were once again dimmed, the screen lowered, and the screening of the film resumed.[16] In this instance, the live singing voice was introduced as a supplement to silent narration, transforming the screening into a multimedia audiovisual event. The song became an interface between filmic and theatrical modes of performance, its duration constituting an interval in which diegetic space and time were overlaid with the real space and time of the audience. By incorporating externally sourced music into its narrative design, *Resurrection* unlocked the expressive possibilities of the song as cinematic attraction. Song performance crossed the boundary between real exhibition space and diegetic space. At the same time, it carried a sense of liveness and copresence, distinct from the recorded images on the screen. And through the body of the singer— presented here as a flesh-and-blood counterpart to her filmic character—this sense of copresence was marshaled for narrative purposes, channeled into the emotional intensity of her performance and the ensuing identificatory rapport with her character at the point of extreme pathos (as attested to by the teary reactions reported in press accounts of the screening).[17]

"The Ballad of the Wet Nurse" is considered to be one of Chinese cinema's earliest successful film songs. The public's enthusiastic response to the show inspired subsequent attempts to promote new film releases and entice moviegoers with in-person stage appearances and musical performances by stars. (The practice would continue to prove its viability into the postwar years, when conglomerates like the Motion Picture and General Investment Co. Ltd. (MP&GI) and Shaw Brothers dispatched their stars to premiere festivities in their own movie theaters.) The strategy was repeated at the Grand Central Theater in the following year with *Kelian de Qiuxiang* (*The Miserable Life of Qiuxiang*, 1927), another example of a silent film featuring a theme song. The film, featuring the actress Li Minghui in the title role, was one of a string of productions from the Great China–Lily Film Company (Dazhonghua Baihe), which was known for its socially conscious dramas. Li had gone into filmmaking after having made a name for herself as a popular singer, spoken drama performer, and musical revue star. *The Miserable Life of Qiuxiang* made reference to Li's musical career by appropriating the title of one of her best-known songs, "Kelian de Qiuxiang," composed by her father, Li Jinhui, in 1921 and released as a recording by Great China Records in 1926. At the film's debut at the Grand Central Theater, audiences were treated to a rendition of "Kelian de Qiuxiang" by Li Minghui in person. For four nights, the evening screening of *The Miserable Life of Qiuxiang* was accompanied by a special program, a musical stage play based on the song. Advertised as a "narrational-style musical play" (*shu shi di geju*), the program was specially commissioned by the studio to mark the film's premiere. It was scripted and directed by the song's composer, Li Jinhui, and featured the film's star as a solo vocalist, together with fifteen dancers from her father's China Song and Dance Institute.

The strategy of combining silent film projection with on-site music has particular importance in light of the background of "Kelian de Qiuxiang." The song's composer, Li Jinhui, was one of the most prolific songwriters of the 1920s and 1930s and is regarded today as the father of modern Chinese music. Jones has described the indelible impact made by Li on the urban media culture of republican Shanghai—as an artist who forged an idiom of sinified jazz that would shape the development of modern pop music for decades to come, an educator, an impresario, and an entrepreneur whose work propelled the growth of a budding mass-mediated culture industry. "Li Jinhui," Jones observes, "was single-handedly responsible for launching the careers of almost every notable singer, popular musician, and movie star of the era."[18] The song-and-dance troupes he led throughout his career functioned as training institutions for an entire generation of film stars, including Wang Renmei, Li Lili, and Zhou Xuan. Li Jinhui also played an important role in the transition to sound cinema, enlisted by major studios like United Photography Service and Tianyi as a music director for their first forays into sound filmmaking. Underpinning his career was a fruitful collaboration with his daughter Minghui. Her recordings and performances of his songs contributed to their popularity, especially among young listeners, and her increasing fame as a singer and dancer went hand in hand with the success of his compositions and musical productions. "Kelian de Qiuxiang" was one of a number of children's songs written by Li Jinhui in the early 1920s; some of these tunes were so-called performance songs, which circulated as sheet music accompanied by stage instructions for acting out scenarios associated with the song. By the time of the production of the film that took its name, the song had become a standard cherished by young listeners and was frequently performed in schools as a musical play involving various combinations of singing, dancing, and stage acting. Li Minghui's commercial recording from the previous year further boosted the song's popularity, leading one reviewer of the film to note that "all of the country's students and teachers delight in singing this song[;] . . . young people from all walks of life in Shanghai love humming the tune."[19]

The naming of The Miserable Life of Qiuxiang after the children's song makes clear the studio's desire to bank on the prior success of the tune and its singer, while returning the favor by prolonging the song's shelf life as a cultural commodity. In contrast to later theme songs that were composed with specific films in mind, this film appropriated a preexisting musical hit as the basis for a narrative treatment that took the subject of the song, a pitiable orphan girl named Qiuxiang, as its main character[20]—in a movement paralleling Li Minghui's own trajectory from the stage and recording studio to the screen as Chinese cinema's first crossover star. An advertisement for the film explicitly invokes the popularity of the song along with that of its teenage singer, whose sprightly stage persona garnered an enthusiastic following and inspired imitation by so many schoolchildren: "This lively girl, previously seen on stage singing 'The Grape Fairy' and 'Kelian de Qiuxiang' to resounding applause, is now the great movie star Li Minghui."[21] "Kelian de Qiuxiang" emerges here as a complex intertextual and intermediated musical event. The film represents only one part of the longer history of the song's stage enactments. The participation of Li Jinghui—a composer as well as a scenarist who pioneered a revue format combining narrational elements (sets, characters, and dramatic scenarios) with dance and lyrical expression—further cements the film's connections to modern musical drama (gewu ju).[22] Conversely, the song functions as an open channel between cinema and theater, a unifying framework for a variety program encompassing both stage and screen, and an index of the star who stands at the center of this musical event. Through Li Minghui's body and voice, the familiar resonances of "Kelian de Qiuxiang" are reactivated in a filmic context, notwithstanding the limitations of synchronized sound technology at this point in time.

The musical play was not the only means by which The Miserable Life of Qiuxiang offered its audience the audiovisual experience of a theme song. Li's recording of the song also made an appearance in one of the film's scenes, played by one of the characters on a gramophone. Contemporary reviews suggest that this action served as a musical cue to play the record in the movie theater itself, thus dubbing the visual representation of the song with on-site audio playback. (One reviewer even complained that the scene felt like an advertisement for the record.[23]) The use of gramophone records in film screenings represents yet another facet of the kaleidoscopic character of sound-image relations in the transitional period, as a logical extension of live musical accompaniment in the age of mechanical sound reproduction. As a means of "live dubbing," or bringing sound to the projected image at the point of exhibition, the practice anticipates the sound-on-disc systems used throughout the early sound period. By many accounts, these systems were barely an improvement over the basic gramophone record player in their capacity to synchronize recorded sounds with projected images for significant periods of time.

An early pioneer of this practice was Sun Yu, who saw music as a critical part of filmmaking and experimented with the use of disc recordings in the films he directed. In two of his early silent works, Sun selected musical pieces to be played at specific moments in the narrative as nondiegetic accompaniment and worked directly with exhibitors to ensure that his instructions were correctly executed by their musicians.[24] He took this strategy a step further with *Yecao xianhua* (*Wild Flowers*, 1930), a work generally known as as China's first "dubbed sound film" or "dubbed singing film" (*peiyin yousheng/gechang pian*). *Wild Flowers* contained a musical sequence in which its two stars, Ruan Lingyu and Jin Yan, sang the theme song "Looking for My Brother" ("Xunxiong ci"). To dub this musical duet, a wax disc recording of the song (made by Great China Records and heavily advertised as a record release alongside the film) was played in the theater, carefully synched by hand with the image.[25] Later in the story, the theme song was repeated in a solo version by Ruan's character, a singer named Lilian. This performance, however, was incomplete, with Lilian collapsing after a few verses because of her emotional distress at having been forcibly separated from her lover and duet partner by his family. The film also incorporated a disc playback of Western classical music, in a scene in which Jin's character played a Dvorak humoresque to express his passionate feelings toward Lilian. In Wang Wenhe's analysis, despite being technically a silent production, *Wild Flowers* marked a breakthrough in sound filmmaking in its diegetic incorporation of songs to convey characters' emotions and narrative meanings. Beyond operating in the manner of ordinary musical accompaniment, situated at a remove from the fictional world, the songs in the film are "integrated with the drama, emphasizing its significance."[26]

The Scene of Song

As *Resurrection of Conscience* and *The Miserable Life of Qiuxiang* demonstrate, film songs predated the material convergence of sound and image recording. Furthermore, beyond the economic motives behind such tie-ups, the two productions reveal another angle of the particular allure that music held for film. What the phenomenon of the silent film song suggests is that the turn to song was motivated not just by a desire to synchronize sounds with moving pictures per se, on a par with technological developments in other parts of the world, but also by an intermedia impulse to bring the attractions of the musical stage to the cinema. The inclusion of songs offered a means of interweaving the sensation of live presentation with the experience of projected recorded images. Considered in this light, the impact of melodies like "The Ballad of the Wet Nurse" and "Kelian de Qiuxiang" derived not just from their positioning in a virtual soundtrack, for the sake of narrative enhancement, but also from their place apart from the diegetic universe, existing in the framework of the stage. Coming to the audience from within their own space, these songs carried the charge of direct address, of the vocalist's physical proximity to and copresence with her audience. They injected a sense of liveness, immediacy, and real time into the scene of exhibition. The appeal they held for filmgoers was inseparable from the metadiegetic charisma of the star and the latent theatricality of the screening as a performance event.

But at the same time, such effects of liveness were fully implicated in, and indeed the product of, a sophisticated commercial and technological apparatus built around the recording and mechanical circulation of songs for a listening public. Just as the notion of star charisma demands to be demystified from a materialist perspective—as the return of individual aura after the regime of commodification has ushered in an unprecedented fungibility between persons and things—so the felt immediacy of the star's performances must be understood as the manufactured effect of a mass-mediated system of musical production and circulation. The thrill of live performance, of shared presence in time, was the corollary of a historical moment in which reproduced sounds were becoming a ubiquitous element of the modern soundscape and canned voices, detached from the body of the performer, emerged as the baseline of everyday listening.[27]

The Miserable Life of Qiuxiang pointedly illustrates how the live musical show was itself intricately entangled in an economy of replaying, repackaging, and restaging music—bearing out James Lastra's observation that any event of performance is shaped by conventional forms and social practices and therefore is "already subject to transformations potentially identical in kind and in effect to those wrought by the recording process."[28] Even as in-person stage appearances by performers like Yang Naimei and Li Minghui introduced a degree of singularity and contingency to the screening experience, their songs rebounded across a horizon of repeated listening. Film songs, whether predating the film or newly composed for it, existed as recordings to be heard again and again both within and beyond the confines of the movie theater. As autonomous cultural objects, they could be embedded in the memory of listeners and reactivated in new contexts. And as they made their way into film, they brought this horizon of repeated listening to bear on its reception. Strategies like the adoption of preexisting songs as theme tunes evidence an incipient awareness of how the repeatable pleasures of song could be exploited to attract audiences (and anticipate the wave of already heard tunes that would engulf postwar film culture, as the next chapter discusses).[29] The doubled performance of the theme song in *Wild Flowers*—a technique lauded by Wang for effectively "expanding the song's original meaning" and opening up the narrative to the emotional reality of the characters—points to how repetition could be mobilized to deepen audience engagement.[30] The replaying of a tune could serve as a powerful evocation of the past in the manner of a flashback, and in the wake of *Wild Flowers*, filmmakers continued to explore these resonant possibilities. Songs constituted a musical memory that could reverberate both within and beyond the individual film.

From an early point in time, then, the appeal of song was bound up, on the one hand, with the pleasures of repeated listening enabled by mechanical recording and, on the other hand, with a sense of direct address and immediacy carrying over from the musical stage to the audiovisual experience of the film screening. These associations constitute a foundation for Chinese cinema's reliance on musical expression and singing actresses, thereby serving as a blueprint for decoding the expressive mechanisms of the song-and-dance films and singing films that proliferated in the years to come. The first decade of sound filmmaking witnessed the birth of the *gewu pian*—a term inscribing the early sound cinema's debts to the musical revue, or *gewu ju*—but these would soon be overtaken by *gechang pian* as dance gave way to an emphasis on song. And in due course, the standardization of synchronized sound technology rendered obsolete the live dubbing strategies of films like *Resurrection of Conscience*. Musical accompaniment as an exhibition practice was supplanted by the recorded soundtrack. But the performance of soundtrack songs in their entirety, from beginning to end, persevered as a practice of sound filmmaking. This convention preserved the traces of early exhibition practices and the song's distinctive modes of address. Even as they hastened the technological penetration of music, films continually restaged the situation of live song performance—thus reproducing liveness as a fantasy, an ideology, and an idealization of a shared time and space.

To map the process by which songs were assimilated by cinema and endowed with a set of expressive functions, I turn to the example of *Two Stars in the Milky Way*. This work is one of a number of partial-sound films from the early 1930s that bear the traces of technological disruption in their uneven textual surface and in the breaks between silence and sound. For this sound-on-disc production—billed as a "musical song-and-dance sound picture"—United Photoplay commissioned four musical advisers to create the soundtrack, including Li Jinhui (who composed two of the film's songs).[31] Li is also indirectly referred to in the film's plotline about a young woman named Li Yueying with a beautiful voice who lives in Hangzhou with her father. The story begins with her discovery by a film crew shooting near her house, depicts her transformation into a movie star, and ends with her disillusioned retreat from the glamorous world of stardom. As Kristine Harris points out, the father-daughter pair of *Two Stars* is modeled on the real-life duo of Li Jinhui and Li Minghui. The film's opening intertitle, for instance, makes reference to Li Jinhui's compositional approach by introducing the father as a composer "devoted to Occidental as well as to Chinese music."[32] Cast in the role of Yueying was Zi Luolan, also known as Violet Wong. Born and raised in Guangdong Province, Wong was widely hailed as a "queen of southern songs and dances" by the time of the film's production. She built this reputation as a stage performer working with another of the musical revue companies headed by Li Jinhui, the Bright Moon Song and Dance Troupe.[33]

Wong's identity as a "queen of southern songs and dances" is referenced in one of the film's musical centerpieces, in which she performs a scene from Cantonese opera. In her first starring role for the big screen, Yueying dons a historical costume to play the concubine Mei Fee in the opera film "Love's Sorrow in the Eastern Chamber" ("Loudong yuan").[34] The shooting of the scene in which her character performs a solo ballad is depicted at length: the actress appears on an elaborate set of an imperial garden pavilion overlooking a pond and, seated at the water's edge, staring into her reflection, sings her plaint of loneliness and disappointed love. The sorrowful mood of the song and the singer's melancholy bearing are at odds with the scenes that bracket this number, contrasting with the jubilant buzz surrounding the new production. Her solo lasts for nearly five minutes, interrupted only when Mei Fee is taken by surprise by the arrival of Emperor Tang Minghuang, who overhears her song and is drawn by the sound of her voice. It is shot in five long takes—the longest one lasting eighty seconds—that frame the singer with slight changes in angle and alternations between long and medium long shots. The only camera movement comes in the final shot, when the camera pans right to reveal the emperor listening to her song from across the garden. Zhang Zhen notes the marked shift in rhythm and framing that characterizes this extended musical interlude. She writes: "The long takes of the scene of Zi Luolan singing in her operatic role are contained in rather static framing redolent of a stage tableau as though the audience is suddenly transported to an opera theater."[35] For Zhang, the scene serves as a demonstration of the intermedia connotations of song performance in early sound films, with its incorporation of the musical stage (here an opera setting as well as a film set) and reduplication of a theatrical perspective. The terminology of the period, which refers to such numbers as "plays within the play" (*xi zhong xi*), further signals their status as autonomous attractions rather than integrated components of the narrative, as well as their relationship to theatrical performances such as Chinese opera and musical revues.[36] Thus the introduction of sound technology creates a zone of permeability between film and theater, with *xi zhong xi* operating as an interface between these media.

Zhang's observations call attention to one of the key methods by which the evolving *gewu* and *gechang pian* assimilated the theatricality of song performance into their formulas. The play within the play provided early filmmakers with a compelling diegetic pretext for the inclusion of musical attractions, and this strategy endured throughout the entire existence of this category of films. The space of the stage became a ubiquitous scenic element of musical productions—a platform for displays of song and dance, a naturalized feature of the diegetic world, and a perspectival construction directed at a diegetic audience as well as the actual audience of the film. Occupying the spotlight on this platform is the figure of the professional entertainer, who emerges as the dramatic locus of the song-and-dance film, the pivot between its onstage spectacles and offstage story. Similar conventions also appear in the early Hollywood musicals that were enthusiastically received by Shanghai audiences in this period, thus suggesting the cross-cultural influences at play in the development of early Chinese sound films. In particular, the play within the play finds an echo in a wave of American productions around 1929 that employ the backstage plot as a means of framing dramas about the lives and loves of entertainers, on the one hand, and of structuring alternation between narrative and numbers, on the other hand.[37]

Works like *Songstress Red Peony* and *The Singing Beauty* are indicative of early Chinese filmmakers' preoccupation with the stage of traditional Chinese opera—even as, somewhat ironically, their depiction of the lives of opera songstresses runs counter to the general exclusion of female performers from contemporaneous theater practices. In *Two Stars*, however, this fascination with the traditional stage coexists with a more expansive imagination of the spaces of performance, moving through different permutations as it mines a range of musical styles. The traditional opera setting of "Love's Sorrow in the Eastern Chamber" is revealed to be a film set at the end of the scene, when the camera tracks back dramatically to reveal the Yinhan studio crew at work filming the scene, and the visual interest of the elaborate historical mise-en-scène suddenly gives way to the apparatus of modern cinematic technology. Another play within the play in *Two Stars* transports the audience to the musical revue stage. While scoping out Yueying as a potential star, studio managers attend a charity show in which she is set to make an appearance. The scene motivates the insertion of a military march–style dance number, set to Li Jinhui's tune

"Work Hard" and performed by his Bright Moon Song and Dance Troupe (re-named the United Photoplay Service Follies in this context). Participating in this show were two of the troupe's most celebrated members, who would soon become film stars in their own right: Li Lili and Wang Renmei. The number is followed by an Egyptian-style dance by Yueying, presented in static long takes that are crosscut with shots of the excited response of the studio managers in the audience. In portraying and linking together multiple configurations of the stage, *Two Stars* not only self-reflexively comments on the intermedia charac-ter of its musical displays but also anticipates the future trajectory of *gechang pian*. As the spatial trope of the stage is codified as a defining feature of these films, it spins out into multiple variations: along with opera, musical theater, and film sets, this trope expands to encompass teahouses, nightclubs, schools, and eventually recording studios, radio stations, and television studios.

But what about song performances that are not framed within the space of the stage? Even as *gechang pian* tended to anchor their numbers with the play within the play, they rarely relied exclusively on this device, instead exploring other methods of weaving song performance into their stories. Another scene from *Two Stars* shows how, almost from their inception, film songs tended to migrate through narrative space, transforming it in their wake. Indeed, it is a song that sets the story in motion and precipitates the narrative's shift from the country to the city. During a location shoot in the countryside near Yueying's home in the West Lake district—a region famed for its scenic beauty—two of the actors stumble onto a scene that halts them in their tracks: a group of villagers gathered around a house, held fast as if enraptured by a spell. The ensuing shot of the house's interior reveals the object of their entrancement to be Yueying, seated next to her father, singing to him as he smokes and rocks in his chair. Absorbed by the singing and distracted from the film shoot, the two actors approach the house. After some time they are joined by the direc-tor, who comes searching for them. For the remainder of the song, the film cuts between shots of the listeners gathered outside and the father-daughter pair reposing inside, unaware of their audience. The reactions of the film crew are singled out in medium shots that capture their pleasure at Yueying's song. At its conclusion, the singer is startled by the sound of applause coming from outside; the father and daughter turn to look at the window behind them, then draw the curtains, step onto the balcony, and greet their friends (figures 1.3–1.9). Spotting Yueying, the director becomes even more excited and declares to his assistant, "How exquisitely she sings! And so pretty too! It won't be a bad idea to suggest to Mr. Wang to try her in the leading role in his play, 'Love's Sorrow in the Eastern Chamber.'"

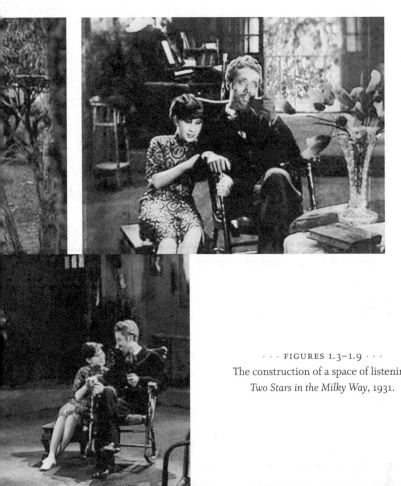

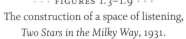
FIGURES 1.3–1.9

The construction of a space of listening,
Two Stars in the Milky Way, 1931.

Textual sources indicate that during this sequence the audience hears the well-known Cantonese ballad "Raindrops on Banana Leaves," the other of the two songs performed by Violet Wong in the film. Like the concubine Mei Fee in the scene discussed above, Yueying is not aware of her audience, and the juxtaposition of these parallel scenarios indicates how sound films drew from an operatic tradition of overheard songs. At the same time, the differences between the presentation of this song and "Love's Sorrow in the Eastern Chamber" are notable. In contrast to the fixed spatial framing and frontal perspective of the opera scene, the spatial presentation of song here is unusually dynamic, freely traversing the boundary between inside and outside as it constructs a virtual space of listening. Even though the film's original soundtrack cannot be reconstructed, its absence only casts into relief the host of ways in which this opening number strives to visualize sound and build a sonorous presence, portraying the effects of sound as it ripples throughout the fictional world and elicits responses from various characters. The beauty of Yueying's singing is indexed by the delighted expressions of her listeners, and the powers of song are conveyed as a magnetic force that irresistibly pulls them in her direction. The singer's physical separation from the scene of listening only underscores the impact of this performance, for here sound is not merely layered onto the image but also rendered tangible in the very disjunction between seeing and hearing. This sensory disjunction carves out a zone for the unhindered movement of sound and prompts one of the most film's most unusual visualizing strategies—a use of editing as a means of relating spaces that are audible yet not visible to one another. In the pattern of alternating shots between the singer and the other characters, we can recognize something akin to a standard shot–reverse shot technique that stitches these shots together according to a logic of spatial contiguity. But in this instance, the identification between the gaze of the character and that of the camera is broken insofar as Yueying remains invisible to her diegetic audience throughout the performance, enclosed within the walls of her home. Instead the shot–reverse shot alternation represents an auditory perspective, doing for the ear what the mechanisms of suture typically do for the eye and carving out a subject position of listening within the space of the fiction. With this appropriation and repurposing of an established convention, Two Stars discovers an innovative discursive strategy for the cinematic inscription of song.

The marked contrast between this and the other song numbers discussed above can be attributed to the absence of the stage and the consequent unmooring of image and sound from the spatial and temporal confines of the proscenium. Yueying's performance is naturalized as an unscripted expression of affection between father and daughter, situated in an intimate domestic setting and performed with no consciousness of an audience. At the same time, it would be inaccurate to describe the scene as fully integrated with the narrative. Even without evident visual markers, the performance retains a sense of discreteness and separation from its diegetic context. The song has the effect of seizing and pausing the story's action as it unfolds: Yueying's singing quite literally stops the two actors in their tracks and thus brings to a halt the film shoot that is in process. Not simply absorbed into a sequence of narrative events, the song intercepts this sequence and detours it into another time zone, one characterized by inaction, stillness, and intense absorption—as if the film itself has been caught in the spell that binds the characters. The spell lasts for the full duration of the song, and only after Yueying has ended her tune does the flow of story action resume. The "Raindrops on Banana Leaves" number represents an overdetermined moment: a testament to the arresting force of song, a parable of the newfound powers of film sound, and also a reprisal of an earlier scenario of interruption. When the camera in *Two Stars* stops rolling, we are reminded of another recent instance of the machinery of cinema jammed by the singing voice: the halting of the projection of *Resurrection of Conscience* to make way for Yang Naimei's performance. The sense of a collision between incompatible presentational modes, revived so pointedly in *Two Stars*, goes on to cast a shadow over the future of film songs. The film thus offers a key to comprehending the song's distinctive mode of address, how its presence in film gives rise to particular spatiotemporal configurations and perceptions— here signaled not by the differentiated space of the stage, but rather by the differentiated temporality of performance. Songs constitute an interval in which things do not move along as usual, imposing an order of time defined by suspension and repetitions of verse and rhythm. This alternative order of time is preserved in the practice of presenting songs in their entirety, which remains unchanged throughout the history of the singing picture. If songs frequently cut into the narrative, the reverse is never true: the song must be allowed to run its full course before the story can resume. This explains the convention of referring to these musical numbers as "inserted film songs" (*chaqu*), a term that emphasizes their interruptive quality.

The soundtrack of *Two Stars* is not extant, and for the present-day viewer who can experience it only as a silent film, Yueying's voice stands out as its absent center, the single element that more than anything else commands our attention and drives the story's twists and turns. The film describes a process by which the sensory fascination of the voice comes to shape the discursive strategies of *gechang pian*, and the effects of song radiate across the film's visible surfaces. Conversely, these effects also involve a centripetal movement with the fictive world contracting around the figure of the singer, as if to rekindle the promise of direct rapport and auratic copresence contained in the scene of live performance. The act of singing collapses distance and generates a zone of intimate contact, activating the illusion of proximity and direct address. This alteration of spatial perspective magnifies the presence of the singer, who looms larger in our perception as she moves to the foreground and center of the audiovisual field. Such effects of proximity and magnification are registered in the convention of depicting the singer's face in close-up during her performance, which becomes a staple device in *gechang pian* in ensuing years (its absence from *Two Stars* may be owing to the difficulties of precise synchronization when the film was made). As the camera responds to a desire to draw closer to the songstress, so her vocal expressions further absorb the audience into the temporal cohabitation of a here and now that blurs the boundary between diegetic time and the real time of the screening.

Zhou Xuan

Throughout the 1930s, as synchronized sound technology was progressively absorbed into the machinery of the movie industry, filmmakers continued to explore the expressive possibilities of sound in a musical register. The transitional period saw the release of numerous other partial-sound productions similar to *Two Stars*, combining methods of silent storytelling and dialogue intertitles with recorded instrumental accompaniment, sound effects, and interludes of synchronized song performance. Included among this group are many of the most acclaimed works of the progressive left-wing film movement that represents a signal development of the decade. They include *Yu guang qu* (*Song of the Fishermen*, 1934), starring Wang Renmei as a poor woman from a fishing family; *Da lu* (*The Big Road*, 1934), including in its star-studded cast another alumna of the Bright Moon Song and Dance Troupe, Li Lili; and *Xin nüxing* (*New Woman*, 1935), in which the great silent film actress Ruan Lingyu made her last appearance before her untimely death. In these productions, we see the coalescence of discursive conventions around the performance of song; these conventions involve specific ways of combining music, image, and text. At the level of the image, the shift into song entails a projection beyond diegetic space, calling forth scenes and pictures that have only a tenuous relation with the story and point to a larger historical reality beyond the fiction. Song numbers tend to be accompanied by subtitles that present the lyrics, inscribed directly onto the surviving prints of productions from this period. The appearance of such subtitles reinforces the sense of an abrupt shift into a direct mode of address, with the image becoming a writing surface by which nondiegetic information relating to the song is transmitted to the audience. Sometimes a bouncing ball helps the viewer to follow the lyrics, as if encouraging them to sing along during these sequences.

Song of the Fishermen, directed by Cai Chusheng, not only set box-office records with its success—remaining in theaters for nearly three months—but also became the first Chinese film to receive an international prize when it was screened at the Moscow International Film Festival in 1935. The film took its name from the theme song featured in it, a plaintive ballad inspired by the melodies of the Jiangnan region and describing the hard lot of fishing folk. The song was already on its way to becoming a popular hit by the time that the film reached theaters, having been released in advance as a recording. Song of the Fishermen incorporates the resonance of repeated listening in its recursive musical structure. The film's star, Wang Renmei, sings the theme song three times, first when her character is introduced early in the story as a little girl. She sings it again as a young woman, after having traveled to Shanghai to seek employment. In the harsh and desperate environment of the city, she resorts to working as a street singer to eke out a living, and the images of water, waves, and fishing boats that accompany her song, summoned by her lyrics, serve as visual signifiers of her homesickness. We hear a final reprisal of the ballad during the film's sad conclusion, when her ill and overworked brother lies dying in her arms. She sings to comfort him in his last moments, and as he joins in, the tune takes on overtones of fatalism and resignation. The song acquires a deep poignancy across these repetitions, which mark the turns of fortune experienced by the singer while also asserting the constancy of her identity and the natural world from which she hails.[38]

The overwhelming success of Song of the Fishermen resounded in the context of critical debates about the aesthetic implications of sound technology and the role of songs and other music in the new medium of sound cinema. In some quarters, an overreliance on music was cause for concern, seen as a hindrance to the discovery of the sound film's potential as a medium. For instance, this position was forcefully articulated by Si Bai in a 1934 article: "It is a mistake to treat music as the ideal part of the sound film, as musicians and filmmakers do not understand each other's art. . . . Music in sound films now hinders the independence of sound cinema."[39] But for other critics, Song of the Fishermen laid out a future path for sound cinema in which songs were indispensable. Tang Tangyin saw in it a demonstration of not just the profitability of film songs, but also their aesthetic contribution: "In terms of artistic effects, the addition of suitable songs can intensify spectators' understanding of the plot and the characters' experience and emotions, compensating for the artistic inadequacy of the purely visual."[40] The revolutionary composer and critic Nie Er, who also collaborated on the film's soundtrack, took a similar view, noting the effective use of the theme song to paint the reality and subject matter of the story. Encouraged by the film's runaway success, he declared that "music is the soul of the sound film."[41] In the wake of *Song of the Fishermen*, film songs became a regular feature of the cinematic soundscape, and the insertion of songs coalesced into a standard format, paving the way for a continued influx of crossover stars. Following in the steps of those who came to filmmaking by way of the musical stage and recording industry was Zhou Xuan, the most celebrated vocalist in the history of mainland Chinese popular music. Zhou's distinctively high, dulcet, and delicate voice made her a sensation with the listening public. Her position at the pinnacle of the "metal scale" of singers was indicated by the moniker given to her by her fans, the Golden Throat. Like so many of her predecessors, Zhou honed her musical skills under the tutelage of Li Jinhui, and by 1934, at the age of sixteen, she had made a name for herself as a singer of *shidai qu*. She began acting in films in the following year, and by the time of her death in 1957 had appeared in roughly forty films and recorded more than two hundred songs.[42]

Zhou's earliest film roles were minor parts, conceived without consideration of her vocal skills; her first important starring role was in *Malu tianshi* (*Street Angel*, 1937). The film is regarded as a masterpiece of the Chinese left-wing film movement, released by the Mingxing Film Company in the final year of the golden age of Shanghai cinema—and only weeks before the Japanese invasion shut down the company's operations. *Street Angel* cannily incorporated Zhou's identity as a pop star in its narrative design, naming her character Xiaohong (the singer's real name), incorporating elements of her life story into its plot, and featuring three scenes that treated audiences to her singing. The lead-up to the musical scenes deliberately plays on the audience's expectations by withholding the sound of Zhou's voice. In the first twenty-five minutes of the film, Xiaohong speaks just two words of dialogue, so that it is only when she bursts into song that her "golden throat" is exposed in its full glory. Indeed, many of *Street Angel*'s scenes are like segments of a silent film, acted out entirely without dialogue and relying on gesture, blocking, framing, and editing to convey meaning. Although technically a full-sound film, the film shares in the uneven and heterogeneous qualities of the partial-sound productions that preceded it. The songs performed by Zhou in the film, "Siji ge" ("Song of the Four Seasons" and "Tianya genü" ("The Wandering Songstress"), would endure as two of the most evocative classics in her repertoire. *Street Angel* propelled Zhou to new heights of celebrity. In doing so, it also created a benchmark for her filmmaking career, entrenched song performance as a cinematic convention, and laid the foundations for a popular mythology of the songstress that shaped film culture for years to come.

The film's story centers on a group of young people from the lowest strata of urban society: a trumpet player, newspaper hawker, prostitute, and teahouse singer.[43] Xiaohong the singer lives in bondage to the abusive and avaricious couple who own the teahouse—as does another woman, Xiaoyun, whom the couple forces to work as a streetwalker. The first song scene comes early in the film and establishes Xiaohong's downtrodden circumstances. The man who runs the teahouse calls on her to perform for some customers and she reluctantly complies, averting her gaze from the male clients who regard her with prurient interest. Her song, "Song of the Four Seasons," offers an insight into the circumstances leading to her current plight, with its lyrical description of a maiden driven away from her home accompanied by a montage of images of war that evoke Japan's recent invasion of Manchuria. Living together in a building adjacent to the teahouse are the trumpet player Xiaochen and his close friend Li. The windows of the apartments of the men and women face each other across a narrow alley and function as a portal through which the characters communicate with one another. Xiaohong finds solace in the high-spirited company of her neighbors, even crossing the eaves to sneak into their room from time to time. The film's second song scene paints this relationship in further depth by conveying the feelings of passion between her and Xiaochen. On a spring morning as she stands by her open window feeding a caged bird, Xiaochen whistles at her from his room across the street, and the two launch into a mutual serenade with Xiaohong singing as Xiaochen plays the *erhu*:

> From the end of the earth to the farthest sea
> I search and search for my soul mate.
> A young girl sings while her lover plays a tune.
> My beloved, we two are of one heart—
> Aiya, aiya, my darling,
> We two are of one heart.
>
> Gazing north from my mountain home
> My tears soak through my blouse.
> A young girl misses her lover;
> Only love that lasts through adversity is deep.

Aiya, aiya, my darling,
Only love that lasts through adversity is deep.

Who in life does not
Cherish the springtime of youth?
A young girl to her man like a thread to its needle.
My beloved, we are a threaded needle never to be separated.
Aiya, aiya, my darling,
We are a threaded needle never to be separated.

Taken together, the two song scenes mark out two possible fates lying in store for the innocent young singer, one denoted by the wealthy teahouse client who is willing to pay for the privilege of possessing her (signaled none too subtly when he tears apart a rose blossom while staring lasciviously at her), the other by the poor musician on the receiving end of her musical love letter. When Xiaohong becomes aware of the danger in store for her, the two lovers run away, get married, and set up a new home with their two friends. In the film's melodramatic final act, the teahouse owner discovers the location of their new home and breaks in; the streetwalker Xiaoyun prevents him from capturing Xiaohong but is fatally stabbed by him in the process of saving her friend.

The differences between these two scenes dramatize a dichotomy, already evident in *Two Stars*, between the framing of the song number as an independent attraction, couched as a situation of performance within the fictional world, and the representation of song as a more unpremeditated and natural vehicle of expression, taking place in ordinary and private settings rather than the public venue of the stage. Although Xiaohong's first song performance on the teahouse stage follows the format of the play within the play, her second number is presented as a counterpoint to the earlier scenario, occurring in the intimate space of her living quarters rather than the public areas downstairs, and as an impromptu form of communication with her boyfriend rather than a professional obligation to strangers. Alexander Des Forges has pointed to the theatrical construction of the film's mise-en-scène, with the windows of the lovers' apartment buildings functioning as a site of reciprocal performances, captured in shots that seem to reproduce "the view from the box seats in the theatres of previous decades."[44] The window that frames our view of Xiaohong throughout "The Wandering Songstress" lends the scene a presentational quality, setting up a visual parallel between the frame and the proscenium and also between the singer enclosed within the aperture and the caged bird she feeds. But although the visual setup evokes the play within the play, the manner in which her song is introduced suggests an attempt to erase the boundary between narrative and number. The scene begins with the chirping of the pet bird in the cage that hangs in Xiaohong's window, which we hear as Xiaochen rises from his bed, goes to the window, and whistles. When Xiaohong comes to feed the bird, his whistling takes shape as a melody, prompting her to join in with her humming. Xiaochen then reaches for an *erhu* hanging by his window without breaking the melody, chanting "aiyo, ai-aiyo," and across the way Xiaohong completes this musical phrase by singing the song's last verse. As he begins to play the *erhu*, she launches wholeheartedly into the song while continuing with her domestic chores (figures 1.10 and 1.11).

Thus the performance of "The Wandering Songstress" gradually and subtly swells forth from a mix of ambient sounds and diegetic vocalizations, naturalized as a spontaneous expression of romantic sentiment between the two lovers—on the order of words, kisses, or embraces. Not only do the lyrics describe the love between these characters, but the song functions as a medium for the materialization of these feelings: sound creates a corridor of communication between the facing windows, and melody carves out an intersubjective zone of feeling as their voices mingle in a musical pattern of call and response. A brief pause in the number—when Xiaochen is startled by a rag that Xiaohong has playfully tossed through the window and momentarily ceases his fiddling—serves to camouflage the activity of the invisible orchestra of Chinese instruments that has unobtrusively joined his accompaniment after a few stanzas. Wang Wenhe notes that the detail of this interruption strategically reinforces the "natural" and "life-like" effect of the performance.[45] A similar effect comes at the end of the number: after the last notes are sung and played, Xiaoyun storms into the room and puts an end to their interaction. With this number *Street Angel* attempts to move beyond the conventions of the play within the play, anchoring song performance in ordinary diegetic space rather than containing it in a specially demarcated zone of display like the stage. The exhibitionistic mode of address associated with the film song as autonomous musical attraction can still be glimpsed here, but it is also intercepted by a voyeuristic framing of the song as a story element that we spy on or, more pointedly, overhear. The construction of the scene as an intimate exchange between lovers deliberately dissolves the markers of performance in a sequence of fictional events, thereby denying its own status as a performance—a strategy that stands in contrast to the more self-conscious display of Xiaohong's first song scene in the film, which acknowledges the conditions of the spectator-auditor with its teahouse setting.

Moreover, the differences in the framing of the two song numbers are given an explicit thematic articulation by the film. "The Wandering Songstress"

音知覓 呀覓

琴奏郎

· · · FIGURES 1.10–1.11 · · ·
The lovers perform "The Wandering Songstress," *Street Angel*, 1937.

encodes musical performance in terms of spontaneity, authenticity, and the elective affinities of mutual love—all values embodied in Xiaohong's freely offered song. In contrast, "Song of the Four Seasons" casts a decidedly more negative light on the scene of song. In that case, the act of performance is coterminous with a tableau of sexual and economic exploitation, making Xiaohong's song into a sign of her subjection as much as an incitement to the audience's listening pleasure. When the teahouse fills with customers, the owner forces Xiaohong onto the stage and orders her to sing. Even as she obeys with a moving delivery of "Song of the Four Seasons," her body language registers a resistance to the coercive conditions of this performance: Xiaohong scowls, plays with her hair, and refuses to meet the stares of an audience composed of the teahouse's exclusively male clientele. As Ma Ning observes, the editing of the scene constructs the singer as an "object of sexual desire," using eyeline matches to frame her close-ups within the point of the view of the audience members.[46] The voice and body of the songstress are ensnared within a net of gazes and a coercive nexus of commercial exchange. The extent of the singer's reduction to an object of visual and auditory consumption for a paying public in this situation becomes apparent when the teahouse owner expresses his eagerness to sell her to the highest bidder. Xiaohong's lack of autonomy is driven home even more poignantly later in the film, when she performs "The Wandering Songstress" for a second time. After she and Xiaochen become embroiled in a fierce lover's quarrel, he drowns his sorrows in liquor at the teahouse. Spotting Xiaohong in his inebriated state, he exercises his privilege as a paying customer by demanding a song from her. With no choice but to comply, she weeps pitifully as she sings. The repetition of the tune that earlier signaled their love for one another underscores the violence of Xiaochen's gesture, and the memory of its prior performance throws into sharp relief the songstress's powerlessness and humiliation. Again the production of musical diversion amounts to a form of punishment for the singer, and the extortion of her voice consequently taints the pleasures of her song.

From the Lower Depths

In dramatizing the plight of the teahouse singer, *Street Angel* forged an archetype that would become an indelible part of Zhou Xuan's star persona as well as the broader landscape of Chinese cinema: the songstress as a tragic figure and victim of society. This archetype crystallizes tendencies and tropes already evident in the earliest examples of musical films, as we have seen, in which the performance of song punctuates scenes of suffering and singers seem fated to lose their loved ones, their voices, and even their lives. In nearly all of these films, Zhang Zhen notes, "the voice of the singing girl is the source of both attraction and eventual (self-) destruction."[47] The portrayal of the songstress as a magnet for misfortune and personification of exploitation calls to mind the melodramatic plights that showcase the talents of so many of the most renowned actresses of the silent screen, like Li Lili and Ruan Lingyu. The singing women who figure so prominently in the transition to sound are molded by the melodramatic legacy of Chinese silent cinema—where, in the words of Miriam Hansen, "female protagonists serve as the focus of social injustice and oppression; rape, thwarted romantic love, rejection, sacrifice, prostitution function as metaphors of a civilization in crisis."[48] Indeed, *Street Angel* nods to the shared lineage of the songstress and the fallen woman of the silent screen by presenting them as sisters in adversity, both ensnared in a cruel traffic in female bodies. The streetwalker Xiaoyun—a character cast in the mold of that most iconic of fallen women, the maligned prostitute—figures as a silent double to Xiaohong throughout much of the film, as well as a harbinger of the future that potentially lies in store for the younger singer. *Street Angel* also introduces a political inflection to this portrait of feminine victimhood, reflecting the left-wing sentiments of its time. As Jones argues, the montage that accompanies "Song of the Four Seasons," relating Xiaohong's personal tragedy to Japan's invasion of Manchuria, transforms the pathos of her song into "an analogue for China's national crisis."[49] Here, as in numerous other leftist films of the 1930s, the songstress is cast in the role of subaltern within a larger national narrative of resistance and salvation, instrumentalized as a political symbol of the beleaguered Chinese nation.[50]

The imagination of the songstress as a disempowered female subject, either sacrificed as a casualty of an unjust world or rescued by progressive forces, points to the affinities between musical performance and melodrama in cinema from the prewar era through to the postwar. *Gechang pian* developed within the ambit of a deeply entrenched filmic tradition of melodrama, adding songs to the latter's arsenal of techniques to appeal to the emotions and positioning the female singer in the lineage of sentimental heroines. In turn, the suffering woman acquired even more mythic proportions with the intermediation of the singing voice. At the same time, the emotional appeal of songs goes hand in hand with a recognition of the material conditions under which the vocalist labors, so that the poignancy of her song becomes inextricable from her plight as a hapless victim of forces beyond her control. The lowly status of the songstress reflects the low social position traditionally assigned to entertainers, as well as deeply entrenched prejudices against women who make a living from the public display of their bodies and voices. Such prejudices often inform the narrative traps in which the songstress is caught, given voice by other characters who declare her unfit as a wife, mother, or member of respectable society on the basis of her vocation.

The character immortalized by Zhou Xuan in *Street Angel* summons an image familiar in the public imagination: that of the teahouse singer, facing an audience of uncouth men, subject to harassment and all forms of unwanted attention as the lone woman in a rough homosocial drinking establishment. The teahouse singer quickly became a familiar incarnation of the filmic songstress, establishing her identity as a denizen of the lower depths of society. Zhou Xuan reprises the role in later productions like *Hua jie* (*Flower Street*, 1950). *Flower Street* evokes the ambiance of the famous entertainment districts of the northern port city of Tianjin. Zhou plays the daughter of a family of musicians, and the setting of the teahouse where they perform functions as a platform for the display of folk musical styles such as clapper music and drum song.[51] Many singing actresses of a later generation would also bring this figure into life and sound; an example is Linda Lin Dai in *Jin lianhua* (*Golden Lotus*, 1957). The title refers to the stage name of the main character, a feisty drum song performer, and the film re-creates in vivid detail the raucous atmosphere of the teahouse— with the air thick with smoke and flying towels, the scurrying of servers with pots of tea, and the cacophony of male voices that jeer and whistle at Golden Lotus.[52] But as Zhou's own career attests, the teahouse singer would soon be overshadowed by a type of performer more at home in a contemporary setting. If *Street Angel* represents her most memorable screen performance of the prewar period of Shanghai filmmaking, the film that stands out in a later phase of her career is *Genü zhi ge* (*Song of a Songstress*, 1948), directed by the actress's close friend Fang Peilin (figure 1.12). One of a number of Hong Kong productions in which Zhou starred after relocating to the colony in 1946, *Song of a Songstress* casts the star as a nightclub singer named Zhulan. In doing so, it fashions a prototype that comes to dominate the filmic representation of the songstress.

The nightclub chanteuse simultaneously updates the image of the teahouse singer and situates the performance of song firmly within a modern urban cult of leisure. Films like *Song of a Songstress* interweave the sensory delights of music and the glamorous and hedonistic thrills of metropolitan nightlife, drawing on a long-standing screen iconography of the nightclub as "an idyllic capitalist chronotope . . . lavish places of social leisure, romantic encounter, and public display."[53] Vivian Sobchack's description of the nightclub as a cinematic trope applies as much to Chinese filmic tradition as to classical Hollywood films, as evidenced by *Two Stars*—which depicts the nightclub as

· · · FIGURE 1.12 · · ·

Zhou Xuan as nightclub singer, publicity still for *Song of a Songstress*, 1948. Permission of Qidong Motion Picture Company. Courtesy of the Hong Kong Film Archive.

a node within the silvery world of celebrity into which the singer is drawn—and the numerous other films of its era that also make use of this setting.[54] But despite the manifest markers of difference between the teahouse and the nightclub—the one with its coarse atmosphere, largely masculine mixed-class crowd, teacups, and towels; the other with its air of elegance, tuxedoed men and gowned women, overflowing champagne glasses—both institutions are part of an economy built around the female singer as a linchpin of audiovisual spectacle. In the nightclub as in the teahouse, the songstress occupies center stage, while the musicians who accompany her fade into the background. In offering up her voice, she simultaneously makes herself available to a desiring gaze, framed in close-ups that are attributed to the point of view of male characters and thus emphasize the arousing effects of her song on them. And just as Xiaohong's teahouse performance in *Street Angel* reduces her to an object of exchange as well as an instrument for the pleasure of others, so the musical number that introduces Zhulan in *Song of a Songstress* leads directly to a transaction that puts a price on her body. A group of playboys at the nightclub react to her performance by placing bets on whether the biggest womanizer among them can seduce her. He succeeds in the course of the film, and at its conclusion we find Zhulan a fallen woman, pregnant and abandoned by the playboy.

In both the teahouse and the nightclub, the stage does not just demarcate a distinct zone of theatricality. Rather, the division between the space of the performer and that of the audience starts to break down in the portrayal of these settings as social spaces structured around relations of power and intimacy. In this regard, songstress films revive a cultural memory of the teahouse that Joshua Goldstein describes: a site of performance lacking any sense of a defined boundary "between social and representational spaces, between real and performed identities."[55] Both the layout of the teahouse and the dramatic practices it cultivated produced a continuous space crisscrossed by reciprocal interactions, where exchanges between patrons and performers constantly punctured the barrier of the fourth wall. Goldstein demonstrates that it is precisely this social aspect of performance that became a target of theater reform during the republican period. Teahouses eventually gave way to new-style theaters that were designed to foster a more passive, less distracted style of spectatorship and to reinforce the principle of the stage as a space "separate and distinct and that should command the audience's undivided attention."[56] But if the differences between these sites of cultural consumption mark a rupture in the history of modern spectatorship, then the nightclub denotes an alternative trajectory of urban entertainment, in which performing is coterminous with the functions of eating, drinking, conversation, and bodily contact. In the words of Shane Vogel, this type of establishment "describes a specific arrangement of nightlife performance as it intersects, interfaces, and interferes with a specific social arrangement." Performer and audience "occupy the same space as coequal inhabitants, each making a competing claim over the control and use of the space. . . . The cabaret performer, meanwhile, does not create and operate within a fictional world separate from that of the audience, as the performer of a dramatic performance might. Rather, the cabaret performer addresses the audience from a position continuous with the audience's time and place."[57] This sense of spatial continuity is especially pronounced in the cabaret numbers in *Song of a Songstress*, where fluid tracking shots constantly assert the contiguity of the stage with its environment. The staging of song here strikingly contrasts with the static theatricality of earlier songstress films like *Two Stars* and conspicuously breaks down the barrier between the songstress and her audience.

In restaging the conditions of musical performance, singing pictures replicate and dramatize the social arrangements that characterize the space of the show. The fact that these social arrangements are informed by hierarchies of gender also inflects the thematic and discursive contours of *gechang pian* as a set of films premised on the feminized pleasures of song. Earlier performance traditions find a new life in the modern medium of film, which absorbs the eroticized female voice into a regime of visual pleasure centering on the objectified female body.[58] In this sense, the gendering of song performance as feminine within Chinese filmic tradition bears out Kaja Silverman's thesis on the consonance between dominant cinema's sonic and scopic regimes. Analyzing a number of works from classical Hollywood, she argues that the visual construction of the woman as the object of a mastering male gaze carries over to the realm of sound, resulting in a "close identification of the female voice with spectacle and the body." Unlike male voices, which range freely over the image, female voices tend to be confined to "an inner textual space, such as a painting, a song-and-dance performance, or a film-within-a-film."[59] The dichotomy of sexual difference is reified by "a textual model which holds the female voice and body insistently to the interior of the diegesis, while relegating the male subject to a position of apparent discursive exteriority by identifying him with mastering speech, vision, or hearing."[60] There is much evidence in *gechang pian* to support Silverman's argument, given their tendency to frame the act of singing by the audiovisual perspective of male characters. As a corollary to the consistent feminization of the lyrical voice, the act of listening and watching is coded as masculine and is often laden with undercurrents of desire, possessiveness, or sadistic control. The scenario in *Street Angel* of a man who acts out his power over a woman by forcing her to sing represents both an extreme expression of this gender hierarchy and a trope to which songstress films return again and again.

Silverman's pioneering account of the female voice in cinema resonates beyond the historical specificity of American cinema, offering important insights on the gendered dynamics of songstress films and attesting to the ways that feminist film theory can illuminate the scene of song. To simply end the story here, however, would be to accept somewhat too readily the contractual terms by which the pleasures of songs are held out to the audience, colluding in the disavowal by which these films negate the agency of the female singer while simultaneously exploiting her appeal. It would also overlook those aspects of the scene of song that do not fit easily in a dichotomous schema that contrasts the mastery of a male perceiving subject with the passivity of the performing body. For instance, both *Song of a Songstress* and *Chang xiang si* (*All-Consuming Love*, 1947, another of Zhou Xuan's Hong Kong productions) begin and end with acts of listening that signify a male character's intense longing for the singer. In the opening scene of *Song of a Songstress*, an elderly man stands among a group that has gathered at the entrance of the swanky Black Cat Club. A loudspeaker blasts the music that starts to play inside the cabaret; the camera follows the gaze of the listeners to a painted poster of the singer, which dissolves into a close-up image of Zhulan as she begins her song. The film ends with another scene in which the same elderly man (whose relationship to the singer has been disclosed in the meantime) listens to Zhulan from outside the nightclub, gazing intently at the façade of the building with tears in his eyes while her performance is transmitted. *All-Consuming Love* begins with an image of a man carrying a portable gramophone and walking along a picturesque seaside; seating himself on a rock, he proceeds to play a record (visibly imprinted with the Pathé label). A dissolve moves the story into the past, depicting his relationship with the singer and the events leading up to this moment of musical reverie. *All-Consuming Love* ends with a performance by Zhou's songstress character: a close-up of her face dissolves into a shot of the gramophone record as it spins on the turntable, bringing us back into the initial scene by the shore.

In both films the act of listening functions as an epigraph and coda, thus positioning the listener as a gateway into the narrative and framing its events by his perspective. But what is also striking in these scenes is how the disjunction between the body and voice of the singer is foregrounded. While Silverman maintains that there is a fundamental congruence between sound and image, these examples play on the gap between seeing and hearing, a gap that in both instances is coded in terms of painful memories and unattainable wishes. They illustrate the powers of the singing voice to command space and time as it breaks free of the body from which it issues. Although objects—such as the spinning record, the poster, and the loudspeaker—serve as visual proxies for the voice, they do not fully anchor it, so that the listener himself becomes captive to the omnipresent voice instead of its master. The prominent role of the gramophone record and transducer speaker system in these scenes is also significant, indicating a high degree of reflexive awareness of how the experience of song is mediated by technologies of sound. Reflexive moments like these recur throughout the history of songstress films, as chapter 3 discusses in detail. They remind us that songs escape the spatiotemporal confines not only of the image, but also of the fiction. The mass accessibility of musical playback technology, in an era when the experience of film was limited to theatrical exhibition, extended the half-life of songs as cultural objects and endowed them with a temporal durability and spatial scope beyond the event of the screening. As Zhou Xuan's own body of work attests, songs persist in public memory long after the films themselves have been forgotten.

Even when films present embodied acts of musical performance, the singing voice has the power to dictate the flow of images. In some cases, the voice opens up a space in the narrative in which images that otherwise have no connection to the story can appear, as with numbers like "Song of the Four Seasons" in *Street Angel*.[61] The montage of war images that accompanies the song can be compared to the convention of song picturization found throughout the history of Indian cinema; the phrase *song picturization*, as Neepa Majumdar points out, "already shows a certain tendency toward defining the image in the terms set out by the song."[62] In other cases, the singing voice gives rise to fantastical configurations that rupture the spatiotemporal continuity of a given fictive reality, as another number from *Song of a Songstress* demonstrates. As Zhulan launches into a song titled "Springtime in the Alley" ("Lou xiang zhi chun"), the camera pans to a painting of a bustling urban alleyway, which dissolves into a photographed live-action scene identical to the image on the canvas. Thus the painting comes to life, as if animated by the song, and its virtual space unfolds before the camera in tandem with the lyrics—so that a shot of birds in trees appears with the verse "Birds in the treetops, singing their songs," and so on. Elsewhere the other space and time evoked by the song are registered on the compositional plane of the shot—for example, in *Street Angel* by means of multiple exposures. During Xiaohong's second performance of "The Wandering Songstress," an image of the two lovers from a happier earlier time is superimposed on a close-up shot of the singer's teary visage, as a contrast to her present misery.

Examples like this bear out what several critics have noted about the special discursive status of music in film, which stems from its ability to move effortlessly between the diegetic and nondiegetic realm.[63] Musical accompaniment tends to be invoked as a typically nondiegetic element of cinematic representation—perceptible to the audience alone, dissociated from diegetic reality—but music that is performed by characters constitutes a more ambiguous case. Even when situated as an event taking place within the fiction, it frequently assumes many of the narrative functions of the underscore, guiding the audience's emotional responses to the film as it blends with the instrumental sounds of an invisible orchestra. And, as in the examples above, the performance of music can even create a passage into other planes of reality. Neither exclusively diegetic or nondiegetic, performed music occupies a gray zone in between the two, what Robynn Stilwell describes as a "metadiegetic" territory that is continually traversed in its temporal unfolding. Stilwell describes this passage as a movement from background to foreground: "when the music takes the foreground, it can, literally and metaphorically, seem to spill out over/from behind the screen and envelop the audience, creating a particularly intense connection[;] . . . the metadiegetic might be conceived as a kind of musical 'direct address,' threatening to breach the fourth wall that is the screen."[64]

It is significant that the "intense connection" described by Stilwell is embodied by a single figure, the songstress, rather than distributed across a cast of characters. For insofar as only she can exercise the lyrical voice, it is the songstress alone who rises to a metadiegetic level and consequently lays claim to an expressive impact that sets her apart within the film. Songstress films set into vivid relief the core difference between voices that sing and those that speak. During the performance of song, the vocalist is not merely a character among others in the drama, but also a narrator who mediates between the audience and the fictional world, endowed with the power of direct address and summoning images into being. As Mark Booth notes, the connection that songs can build with an audience is rooted in their singular mode of address, "existing for its audience in the sense that it is going on in front of listeners as an object of their attention." Booth continues: "Because song comes to us in a voice, without dramatic context, to pass through the consciousness of the listener, it fosters some degree of identification between singer and audience . . . we are drawn into the state, the pose, the attitude, the self offered by the song."[65] Through these descriptions, we can begin to grasp the complex effects of the singing voice—how it creates a sensation of being alone with the singer, even if we listen along with others; how it rings as true, authentic, and real, even in the most theatrical of circumstances; how it ramps up our emotional involvement even as it brings into play indeterminate and nonliteral meanings.

Such accounts ultimately call attention to the identificatory command wielded by the songstress within a structure of musical narrative, contravening her characterization as a passive victim and subaltern. The paradox marked by the extremely active enunciatory role granted to the songstress, on the one hand, and the disempowered position ascribed to her within the fictional world, on the other, ultimately points to the intrinsic dissonances that haunt *gechang pian* and to the failure of its musical, diegetic, and visual codes to resolve into a fully integrated and unified system.[66] The concept of performance that emerges throughout these accounts also brings to light dynamics of identification that confound a ready equation between the female voice and embodied spectacle. As both Stilwell and Booth suggest, something in music escapes the binary structure of representation derived from the gaze. The identificatory dynamics created by musical performance have less to do with perceptual mastery than with intimacy and envelopment. Song cannot be pinned down to a visual point on the screen; rather, it surrounds and draws in the listener, collapsing the distance between subject and object. Song's effects of proximity, contact, and tactility are further reinforced by conventions like the complete elimination of dialogue and ambient noises, and the close microphoning of the singing voice, which results in a kind of sonic close-up. The contraction of space around the singer heightens our identification with her. When Zhou Xuan sings, we are submerged in an affective space—of longing, betrayal, or wounded love—that ultimately refers back to the desires and state of mind of her character. Richard Dyer writes: "Because songs are frequently in the first person, because they mobilise affects beyond discursive consciousness, because they come out of the body, it is common to consider them expressions, even emanations of someone."[67] As the formula of *gechang pian* crystallizes around the female singer as the main channel of musical expression, so the film song comes to be stamped as her direct emanation, coded in terms of femininity, interiority, and feeling.

THE MYTHOLOGY OF THE songstress constructed in Zhou Xuan's films—as a wanderer, victim, and avatar of a suffering nation—took shape at a juncture marked by national emergency, mobilization, war, and migration. The same historical forces that shaped the cultural imagination of the songstress in the first two decades of Chinese sound filmmaking also brought about a geographical repositioning of this figure. Zhou and other crossover performers of her ilk continued to play an active role in film culture during the wartime years. This period saw the rise to fame of recording artists like Bai Guang (another of the most distinctive voices of modern Chinese music) and Li Xianglan (also known as Yoshiko Yamaguchi, whose Japanese ancestry was kept a secret early in her career), both of whom forged careers in film acting under occupation cinema, working with the Sino-Japanese studio Zhonglian (China United).[68] In the aftermath of the war, the lone female singer lost her anchor in mainland cinema, dissolving into the collective chorus of a revolutionary mass subject. But she reappeared with even greater vitality in Hong Kong, energized by the colony's emergence as a new epicenter for popular film and music.

FROM SHANGHAI TO HONG KONG

Zhou Xuan's rise to stardom exemplifies the emergence of the songstress as both a narrative trope destined to become a staple of Mandarin cinema's fictive landscape and a breed of performer. Zhou's career as an entertainer took off in a moment when technologies for the recording and dissemination of sound were exerting a crucial impact on the film and music industries. Her peregrinations between live theater, film, radio, and music recording map out the strong cross-currents among media that shaped republican-era urban mass culture and persisted well into the postwar era. If Zhou represents the original prototype of the filmic songstress and Shanghai her birthplace, then Hong Kong is the ground on which this prototype would flourish and develop in subsequent decades, carried along by a younger generation of performers including Chung Ching, Grace Chang, Linda Lin Dai, Julie Yeh Feng, and Jenny Hu. Like Zhou, nearly all of these performers were part of the wartime exodus from the mainland to the colony and embarked on careers in the entertainment business after settling in Hong Kong. These stars would become the face of Mandarin cinema in a new chapter of its history, sustaining a film culture in which music featured as a principal attraction and enshrining a regional tendency toward crossover stardom that continues today. Their songs dominated the pop charts, and their images filled the screen in countless pictures as well as in the widely circulated movie magazines that further propagated the cult of stardom in this period. The popularity and predominance of these songstresses underscores the crucial role of music in postwar Hong Kong film culture, captured in the music historian Wong Kee-chee's oft-cited phrase "no film without a song."[1]

In the minds of many critics, the persistence of the songstress figure throughout the postwar years is evidence of the lingering influence of earlier filmmaking traditions. For example, in his survey of Hong Kong film history, Stephen Teo traces the singing stars of the 1950s and 1960s directly back to the sing-song girl as "a feature of Shanghai life. . . . Mandarin cinema took this particular Shanghai tradition of sing-song girls to heart and, in the great majority of its productions, regardless of genres, featured a tune or two."[2] The convention of the inserted film song associated with the songstress can also be seen as "a vertical transplant from China," in the words of Law Kar, further underscoring the continuities between these two periods.[3] But even as the songstress delineates vectors of continuity, she also bears the imprint of changing historical circumstances. The postwar generation of singing actresses brought to the screen a markedly more variegated set of character types than had been encountered in previous years. Although the familiar figures of the nightclub singer, street singer, and musical revue star remained fixtures of this new landscape, they were joined by a host of novel models of lyrical femininity—sprightly country lasses, high-spirited teenagers and college coeds, cheerily efficient air hostesses, and young working wives, all of whom were reliably inclined to burst into song. Notwithstanding their common musical proclivities, the so-called wildcats and mambo girls bursting forth on the scene of Hong Kong cinema appear to be species apart from the reluctant party girls and fallen women of the pleasure industry long associated with the Shanghai era. In departing from this earlier mold, the postwar songstress seems to announce a new sensibility and ethos in Hong Kong cinema. Her appeal anticipates the forward-looking and optimistic mind-set of a younger demographic, poised to move beyond the memories of hardship and suffering endured by the wartime generation of migrants. Thus Sam Ho argues that "the prospect of the musical woman turning away from her tragic fatalism to sunny, homespun optimism is closely related to the changing view of society in the cinema." In the changing social climate of postwar modernity the old-style songstress, "with her deprived upbringing and tragic disposition, felt absolutely out of place," while by contrast her newer counterparts appeared "decidedly urban and authentically Hong Kong."[4]

The postwar songstress found a home in a series of locales that would become imbedded in the scenic imaginary of Hong Kong cinema, spatially anchoring the particular genres and cycles of the singing pictures of this period. Some of the key topoi of this scenic imaginary include the country or seaside village, traditional street market, middle-class home, college campus, and urban nightclub, each serving as the chosen setting for stories of rural life, historical romances, youth films, family and romantic melodramas. Although Hong Kong popular cinema since the 1970s has been largely identified with kinetic genres of masculine action, the preceding decades were characterized by a strikingly different film culture. Indeed a glance at the Mandarin filmography of these years immediately reveals the predominance of female-centered narratives; a vast number of film titles contain the word *nü* (woman) or female terms of various sorts. The trail of the songstress cuts through the collective dreamscape described by these films, winding through fantasies of pastoral communality and an idealized past, of cosmopolitan glamour and upward economic mobility—all of which acquire a particular resonance at this historical juncture and find a musical and dramatic articulation through her presence. Viewed in this light, the songstress appears as a dream image of Hong Kong modernity. Her changing contours index the emergence of a postwar colonial capitalist society characterized by rapid industrialization, urban concentration, and cosmopolitan aspirations. The songstress was the commodity par excellence of a film industry in the throes of commercial acceleration, expansion, and consolidation. Her entrenchment in Hong Kong film culture coincides with the birth of Chinese cinema's first full-fledged vertically integrated studio system. She is imbricated in this system's explicit agendas of modernization and globalization, caught up in its manufactured mythologies and ideological tendencies.

For many historians, the onset of this chapter of Chinese-language film history goes hand in hand with the gradual emergence of a distinct regional film culture from the shadow of prior traditions. According to this narrative of emergence, in the years immediately following the war, Mandarin film production in the colony was dominated by filmmakers and producers from Shanghai who saw it as a temporary base of economic stability in which to conduct their business. These migrants viewed their new environment with no small degree of skepticism, many of them displaying what Poshek Fu terms a "Central Plains syndrome"—a cultural elitism rooted in a sense of sinocentric superiority and a dismissive view of Hong Kong as "backward," compromised by its colonial status, and devoid of cultural value.[5] Teo argues that the attitude of this émigré generation is clearly reflected in its films: "The Hong Kong depicted by the Mandarin directors was an abstract, cardboard city, using Hong Kong locations dressed up as the streets and quarters of Shanghai or other northern cities. Characters behaved like typical Shanghai residents, their dialogue laced with Shanghai-isms. The styles, themes and contents of Hong Kong's Mandarin films evoked the classics of Shanghai cinema of the 1930s."[6] In the latter half of the 1950s, however, there was a shift, with Hong Kong cinema shedding its "Shanghai hangover" and developing its own identity.[7] Cinema turned to the here and now, absorbed the imprint of a nascent lifestyle distinct from that of the mainland, and in doing so claimed a prominent place in what has been described as the "Hong Kong Sixties."[8] As Matthew Turner argues, this formative decade witnessed the rise of a locally rooted Hong Kong identity: "Before the sixties, Hong Kong exhibited an ambivalent identity, like many displaced *huaqiao* [diasporic Chinese] communities and overseas Chinese: conservative in cultural values but modernized in economic activity and life-style. A decade later it was evident that local life-style was displacing traditional cultural attachments as the basis of identity, to the point where, in the mid-eighties the great majority of the population identified themselves as 'Hong Kong people,' not 'Chinese people.'"[9]

Yet a closer examination of postwar Mandarin cinema discloses elements that do not square with this account. Tempting though it may be to subscribe to a narrative in which Hong Kong cinema casts off the shackles of tradition as it flowers into a newfound modernity, the historiographical conundrum posed by this filmmaking period is far more complex. It holds forth not the incipient clarity of a dissipating fog, but rather the challenges of a history glimpsed "through a dusty window pane," to quote the Hong Kong fiction writer Lau Yee Cheung.[10] Although this cinema undeniably bears the imprint of the colony's unique cultural location—steeped in the urban, consumer-oriented, cosmopolitan brand of pop modernity that would come to define Hong Kong in the twentieth century—it also evinces an undeniable disconnection from Hong Kong cinema today. A wide gulf—of language, sensibility, and ethos—separates the postwar era of filmmaking from the contemporary "cinema of speed."[11] In this respect, the postwar era appears less as a direct antecedent of contemporary film culture than as its residuum—that which is cast aside to make way for the new. Complicating this narrative, for instance, are the historical costume dramas churned out by Shaw Brothers, a cycle that reached a commercial climax in the *Huangmei diao* (yellow plum melody) opera films that were phenomenally popular in the 1960s. According to the film critic Sek Kei, the nostalgic "China dream" conjured in these films contradicts prevailing notions of a "distinct 'Hong Kong style.'"[12] At the same time, the highly artificial, fantastical, even kitschy lens through which the films envision the ancient past reveals how history and tradition become unstable referents at this point in time.

In a similar vein, Chiao Hsiung-ping turns on its head the familiar narrative of emergence that defines the period. Despite its modern surface, she argues, postwar Mandarin cinema remains steeped in the atavistic mentality of the mainland exiles, profoundly shaped by their sense of homelessness and loss. The hardships and emotionally wrenching plights endured by so many filmic heroines in the dramas that dominate this filmmaking era ultimately refer to the inability of the migrant generation to directly confront a new reality and changing times.[13] As these accounts suggest, the story of postwar Hong Kong cinema consists of throwbacks, regressions, and lingering hangovers as much as forward steps. Its peculiar temporality finds an incarnation in the songstress and is marked by a skepticism that is repeatedly voiced about her historical meaning. Although she makes tangible new forms of feminine identity in the aftermath of the great divide, a sense of anachronism and regression clings to her throughout her heyday. Even as she stands out as the face of postwar modernity, the songstress also appears as a throwback to another time, an ever-receding past.

The view of postwar cinema advanced by Chiao also calls attention to the changing and unstable valences that the Shanghai school of filmmaking accrues over time, thereby cautioning us against the easy recourse to reified and homogenized notions of tradition in the mapping of history. The legacy of Shanghai cinema is typically framed in terms of its commitment to progressive and left-wing politics, but in the exilic setting of postwar Hong Kong, it assumes a more reactionary hue, coming to denote a nostalgic stance and reverence for the past. The backward-forward slippage implied in this tradition is further elaborated by Teo:

> Even in their heyday in the 30s, the Shanghai directors were just as prone to delve into Western (meaning Hollywood) styles in efforts to "modernise" Chinese cinema. Hong Kong cinema naturally benefited from the expertise and sophistication of the Shanghai film-makers in integrating Chinese tradition with the urge for modernisation: cultural nationalism on the one hand and, on the other, a kind of aestheticised materialism. The two-faced nature of Chinese film-making became much more marked in Hong Kong and it may be argued that as the Shanghai émigrés settled down to life in the territory, they became adept in juggling

these two aspects of cinema which gradually grew to complement each other.[14]

In the context of the postwar period, the Shanghai tradition represents at once a modernizing influence necessary to the formation of a new film culture and a set of antecedents to be overcome in that very process.

The ambiguities entailed in the recirculation and displacement of older filmmaking traditions might ultimately open up an oblique perspective on their original context. The slippery historical location of postwar Mandarin cinema not only reveals the limits of entrenched ways of conceiving Chinese film history, but it also shines a different light on that history, bringing out the internal dissonances and alternative pathways embedded in it. Assertions of the modernity of postwar cinema must account for its participation in an ongoing process of vernacular appropriation, cultural translation, and hybridization dating from the prewar era. The overdetermined meanings of modernity in this context bring us face to face with the complex positioning of Hong Kong itself—a zone of contact between East and Southeast and West, a cosmopolitan hub buffered from the fray of Cold War nationalist politics, and a society of migrants whose memories and allegiances mingled with local and foreign cultural values in a new environment. From the vantage point of the twenty-first century, we might interpret the twilight quality that clings to postwar cinema as a prediction of a Hong Kong to come, what Ackbar Abbas describes as a world situated at the intersection of different places as well as different times.[15] Untimely in more than one sense, then, Hong Kong postwar cinema exists in a mode of displacement, an afterimage of something already vanished and a proleptic picture of a time yet to come.

Hong Kong's Studio Era

The beginning of the rebirth of the Mandarin film industry in Hong Kong can be traced to the arrival of two major players in the latter half of the 1950s, who would carve out a new direction for filmmaking in the colony. The first of these was the Motion Picture and General Investment Co. Ltd. (MP&GI, sometimes referred to as Cathay). MP&GI was founded by Loke Wan Tho (Lu Yuntao), a Chinese Malayan property magnate based in Singapore.[16] Shortly after taking the helm of a prosperous family business with holdings in real estate, restaurants, theaters, hotels, rubber plantations, mines, and banking, Loke set about building a movie empire, beginning with exhibition venues and distribution networks. By the early 1950s he had built one of the three largest movie theater chains in Southeast Asia, along with a thriving film distribution business. As Cathay continued to expand its network of theaters in response to growing viewer demand, Loke decided to turn his formidable family resources toward the production of films.[17] The result was the establishment of MP&GI in Kowloon in 1956. MP&GI quickly established itself as a key producer of Mandarin-language films in Hong Kong and over the next decade turned out around two hundred pictures, which included many of the notable films of the postwar period.

The second major player was Shaw Studios in Hong Kong, which was established by the youngest of the four Shaw brothers, Run Run, in 1957. The Shaw movie empire dates back to the founding of Tianyi (Unique) Film Studio in Shanghai in 1925; in 1934 the Shaws established production facilities in Kowloon and became a major producer of Cantonese dialect films. Early on the Shaws also extended their business into the distribution and exhibition of films, and by 1956 they owned more than a hundred theaters in Singapore, Malaya, Indonesia, Borneo, Vietnam, and Thailand.[18] The reorganization of their filmmaking facilities under the name of Shaw Studios was announced in 1958 and signaled their intention to move more aggressively into Mandarin film production. Unlike MP&GI, which quickly began to turn out high-quality pictures after its founding, Shaw Brothers' entry into filmmaking was slower and more labored, but conducted on a far grander scale. Run Run Shaw broadcast his ambitions for the enterprise by acquiring forty-six acres of land in Clearwater Bay, on which Shaw Brothers would build its legendary Movie Town.[19] With the completion of the last phase of construction in 1964, Movie Town became one of the largest privately held studios in the world. It included twelve sound stages and sixteen permanent sets, a color processing lab, a dubbing studio, and dormitories for Shaw Brothers' 1,200 employees.[20] The centralization of the studio's filmmaking resources eventually enabled Shaw Brothers to make substantial gains over time in the efficiency of its production process. At its peak, the studio turned out forty films per year.

These forays into film production were intended to capitalize on the decline of mainland film exports as a source of entertainment for Chinese audiences in the postwar years, responding to the changing market conditions of the Cold War era. As the political situation in the People's Republic of China (PRC) led to the erosion of the mainland film industry's ties to export markets, lucrative markets for Mandarin film exhibition were emerging elsewhere—namely, in Taiwan and Southeast Asia. As recalled by Raymond Chow, the publicity manager for Shaw Brothers and second-in-command to Run Run, the studio's strategy was motivated by the perception that production was the key to securing the profitable Mandarin film market, in an environment where a steady supply of films to show in the Shaws' theaters posed the biggest barrier to their business's success.[21] The canniness of this perception was corroborated by MP&GI's own move in that direction. In short order, MP&GI and Shaw Brothers established themselves as major producers of Mandarin cinema, catering to audiences in Hong Kong, Taiwan, Southeast Asia, and North America. The years 1956 to 1964 were a period of stabilization and consolidation for the Hong Kong–based film industry, with the two studios "becoming virtually synonymous with Mandarin cinema" for the Chinese-speaking world, as Teo puts it.[22] Consequently Hong Kong's film output increased in both quantity—more than doubling in annual production between 1955 and 1964—and quality.[23] The fierce rivalry between the two studios raised the bar for production values and laid the ground for what has been described as a second golden age of Mandarin cinema. These years witnessed the emergence of a vibrant commercial film culture with a trans-Pacific scope, and the Hong Kong film industry had no equivalent in either Taiwan or the PRC. The period saw the development of a diversified genre landscape, with MP&GI best known for its modern dramas and comedies, and Shaw Brothers building its reputation primarily on historical costume dramas. Musical performance was a central attraction across this range of genres, in MP&GI's song-and-dance films with modern settings, Shaw Brothers' *Huangmei diao* opera films with historical settings, and the Hollywood-style musicals made by both studios. Throughout the period, smaller independent studios like Changcheng (Great Wall), Fenghuang (Phoenix), and Xinhua (New China) also continued to operate. Xinhua also made important contributions to the developing musical idiom of Mandarin films, as discussed in the next chapter.

Both MP&GI and Shaw Brothers consciously modeled their movie empires on the Hollywood system of Fordist mass production and vertical integration, with their production enterprises feeding directly into the distribution and exhibition networks that they managed simultaneously. Their endeavors led to the establishment of Chinese cinema's first fully functioning commercial centralized studio system. Shaw Brothers tightly coordinated its production facilities under the control of Run Run, who reportedly exercised a high degree of personal control and input at every stage of the filmmaking process, notwithstanding the ambitious scale of the company's activities.[24] The studio also established training institutes for its employees, honing the skills of its actors and actively cultivating the expertise of its technicians. The emphasis on cutting-edge technical proficiency was one of its key signatures, with Shaw Brothers taking the lead in Hong Kong cinema's adoption of new technologies such as color cinematography and anamorphic widescreen. MP&GI was easily outdone by its rival, lacking Shaw Brothers' technical resources, finesse, and cutting-edge innovation. But what MP&GI lacked in material facilities, it made up for with the quality of its personnel. It employed scriptwriters with formidable literary pedigrees; for instance, the acclaimed modern fiction author Eileen Chang was employed a scriptwriter in the 1950s and early 1960s, authoring the screenplays for eight of the company's films. Also critical to the studio's success was its ability to spot and cultivate talent. MP&GI launched a compelling new generation of actresses and actors.

The two studios also published their own monthly movie magazines, dedicated to the promotion of their image in the print media sphere. MP&GI's *International Screen* (*Guoji dianying*) began its run in 1955, with Shaw Brothers' *Southern Screen* (*Nanguo dianying huabao*) following in 1958.[25] By contemporary standards, both publications were lavishly produced, and they numbered among Hong Kong's most widely circulated, longest running illustrated movie journals. The pages of *International Screen* were dedicated to promoting a consistent, integral image of MP&GI and its star performers. Along with news of the studio's current and forthcoming productions, the magazine included numerous in-depth features on individual performers and personnel, reporting on their biographies and professional backgrounds as well as social and charity activities in which they participated. In the category of industry and entertainment-related news, there were reports on the state of the market and technical advances and announcements of regional festival awards; visits to Hong Kong by foreign celebrities, including Alfred Hitchcock, William Holden, and Otto Preminger; openings of Cathay theaters; and new releases from Southeast Asia, Hollywood, and Europe. *Southern Screen* covered a similar territory, combining an emphasis on the latest activities and productions of Shaw Brothers with general movie news from home and abroad, celebrity gossip and interviews, and film-related features. Although more scattershot in its coverage and falling short of *International Screen*'s strong and unified editorial vision, *Southern Screen* presented a greater variety and quantity of features, including serialized fiction and comics, reproductions of storyboards, song sheets for tunes featured in Shaw Brothers productions, and more short news items for the reader to skim. Both periodicals also regularly included a letters section and games designed to solicit reader participation—for instance, by guessing the identities of stars based on isolated body parts such as eyes and legs.

The two studio publications anchored the upmarket end of a print sphere that included numerous illustrated monthly film magazines that were published in

Hong Kong and throughout Southeast Asia. Such periodicals can be situated within the print culture that developed around Chinese cinema beginning in the 1920s, when specialized film publications began to appear in Shanghai. As Zhang Zhen notes, film magazines provided mass audiences with a textual space that extended the filmgoing experience, in which they could "learn about plots, institutional organization of the industry, film technologies, biographies of Chinese or foreign stars, directors, and even cinematographers, as well as forecasts of what films were in production."[26] The circulation of these publications during the postwar era retraces the circuits of Mandarin film exhibition in this period, as suggested by the Chinese title of *Southern Screen*, which literally means "southern lands film illustrated journal." *International Screen* and *Southern Screen* further signaled their ambitions for a broader regional presence at multiple levels. Both magazines adopted a bilingual mode of textual production, with many of their main features and photo captions appearing in both Mandarin and English. This dual-language format was not employed consistently throughout the periodicals, to be sure: most of their content appeared only in Chinese or with accompanying synopses in English. But the selective criteria applied by the two periodicals to the inclusion of English text—regularly used to emphasize and expand major features on the studios' own activities, productions, and personnel, and always displayed prominently on the magazines' covers—indicates their intended address to, and desire for, a worldwide readership. *International Screen* further conveyed its cosmopolitan aspirations through a number of visual winks. For instance, in one photograph published in its "Pictures in the News" section, the American actor William Holden can be clearly seen reading an issue of *International Screen*. Similar images of foreign and Chinese stars with the magazine prominently in hand appeared in *International Screen* throughout its run. These reflexive insertions of the magazine into the film world constructed within its pages and on the screen reveal the degree of self-consciousness and assurance with which MP&GI broadcast its cosmopolitan vision and interpellated its audience.

Flipping through the pages of *Southern Screen* and *International Screen*, one is immediately struck by the magazines' zealous fashioning of a star-driven, star-centric film culture (figures 2.1 and 2.2). Both publications are dominated by colorful, glamorous, and visually appealing images of the studios' biggest stars—whether posed in glamorous portraits, captured in "candid" shots of their everyday lives, or presented in costume and character in production stills from their newest films. Alongside these images are features that entice the reader with glimpses into the stars' offscreen existence, offering details about their personal histories, domestic lives, romantic relationships, professional

··· FIGURE 2.1 ···
Jeanette Lin Tsui, cover
of *International Screen*,
March 1962.

··· FIGURE 2.2 ···
Jenny Hu, cover of
Southern Screen, May 1966.

development, training and rehearsals, leisure activities, travels, and consumption habits. The guessing games (*caimi youxi*) that appear regularly in the back pages of the magazines further foster a sense of intimacy, involvement, and possession on the part of the reader. They draw the reader into the attitude of the fan, encouraging her to "interact" with the star through the exercise of fetishistic knowledge. Moreover, fetishism bears a feminine inflection in these pictorials, given their predominant emphasis on actresses. Presenting female performers adorned in the latest fashions, on vacation, and at play—as experts in a conspicuous modern lifestyle—they embed the discourse of stardom in a broader matrix of consumer desire. In their promulgation of a cult of celebrity and personality, *Southern Screen* and *International Screen* participate in what Michael Chang describes as a progressive routinization of stardom that started in the 1930s.[27]

Just as the burgeoning film press was instrumental to the institutional coalescence of stardom in the prewar era, so postwar print media contributed to the continuing evolution of the star—and the female body—as a cultural commodity. But these two journals also signal a new stage in this evolution, one whose impact comes to light in the final instance of the studio itself as author in the discourse of stardom. With the rise of MP&GI and Shaw Brothers, the business of moviemaking absorbed the construction of stars. The influence of these studios on the collective fantasies of postwar moviegoers finds a tangible image in the faces and bodies of the studios' stars.[28] The performers featured in the pages of these journals were the human capital of the two big studios and, in some instances, their inventions—trained in their facilities and drilled in acting, dancing, elocution, and etiquette before being launched in their productions. A star-focused commercial film industry had already emerged in the republican era, writ large in the hyperbolic onscreen presence of its early luminaries, but it is the offscreen, miniaturized, print-mediated representation of the star that most clearly displays the calculus of postwar celebrity. In the pages of *Southern Screen* and *International Screen*, we see the sophisticated publicity machine of the studios at work, pulling the disparate strands of a performer's existence together into a consistent, transfilmic persona. Also clearly discernible are the disciplinary manifestations of this intensified systematization of stardom. For instance, articles in *International Screen* construct the studio's relationship to its stars—in particular, its young female stars—in paternalistic terms, repeatedly invoking the notion of the "big MP&GI family" ("Dianmao da jiating"), by way of emphasizing the studio's regard for the education and welfare of its performers and the communal bonds among all of its artists. Underlying this harmonious public image of the film studio as family was the disciplinary reality of the studio's investment in the tight management of its human assets. As Stephanie Chung notes, MP&GI's general manager Robert Chung heavily supervised the stars' media liaisons, "while controlling their private lives" as well.[29] MP&GI's paternalistic stance was replicated by Shaw Brothers, notorious for sequestering its actors (many bound to the studio by exclusive contracts) in Movie Town's dormitories. Cheng Pei-pei, one of Shaw Brothers' most vaunted starlets and an acclaimed performer in the martial arts genre, recalls: "We were almost entirely ignorant of what went on outside of the Shaw studio."[30] The scrupulous control exerted over the media images of their actresses and actors points to both studios' devising of a methodical machine for the manufacture of stardom.

Myths of Modernity

Unlike Shaw Brothers, which has been the subject of much critical attention and scholarly study in recent years, MP&GI has been overlooked in English-language film scholarship despite its paramount place in Hong Kong film culture—a lack of attention that this book seeks to redress. This asymmetry has partly to do with historical circumstance: Loke Wan Tho was killed in an airplane crash in June 1964, a blow from which MP&GI never fully recovered. In contrast, Shaw Brothers remained an active force in the film industry into the 1970s under Run Run Shaw's long-lived leadership, and it is still involved in the entertainment business today. The asymmetry also stems to some degree from the divergent specializations of the two studios. Shaw Brothers was most renowned for its historical epics and, beginning around 1965, martial arts swordplay films (*wuxia pian*), a genre that has emerged as an object of cult fascination and popular revival in contemporary film culture.[31] MP&GI's output was dominated instead by dramas of contemporary life, showcasing the glamorous and—for most viewers—unattainable lifestyles of the urban bourgeoisie. These differences, exemplified the most memorable productions of each studio, have been not only noted by many historians of the period but also repeated and elevated to a mantra on the divergent sensibilities of the two rivals. As Fu writes, Shaw Brothers catered to the longing of diasporic audiences for "an imagined homeland expressed by principally an invented tradition, a shared past, and a common language," tendering idealized images of the past and of an immemorial China.[32] Conversely, MP&GI saw its project as the projection of an idealized modern world. The sensibility of the Shaw movie enterprise was at heart nostalgic and traditional, in contrast to the forward-looking, modern, and westernized attitude of MP&GI.

Although such characterizations identify the specific strengths and the imprint of each company, they also invite an oversimplified view of the two studios and, simultaneously, of the larger film culture to which they made a vital contribution. To approach Shaw Brothers solely on the evidence provided by its historical costume dramas is to overlook the modern narratives—no less lavishly produced, star studded, heavily promoted, and commercially and critically successful—that make up a significant portion of its output.[33] And MP&GI produced its fair share of historical costume epics.[34] Indeed, the keen competition between the two studios encouraged no small amount of copying, poaching (of ideas, scripts, and creative personnel), and various other trespasses on the artistic capital of each by the other.[35]

Moreover, to portray the two studios' identities solely in terms of a bifurcation between tradition and modernity, based on only their iconographic output, obscures their deeper commonalities and the appositional influences they exerted on postwar film culture. In fact, the idealized visions of past and present crafted by both studios converged in a shared agenda of modernization and creating a world-class cinema with transnational appeal. Their agenda reflected the rising cultural visibility of Hong Kong as the hub of a new geopolitical formation. The contours of this formation can be mapped according to, on the one hand, circuits of colonial capitalist exchange between East and West that met in the open port city of Hong Kong and, on the other hand, mercantile capitalist networks linking the colony to Southeast Asia (*nanyang*)—networks typified by the holdings of the Loke and Shaw family empires. Both of these empires were based in Singapore and run by charismatic moguls who regularly mingled with the glamorous stars of moviedom that were their creation.[36] Both Loke Wan Tho and Run Run Shaw displayed, in Fu's words, "a cosmopolitan, border-crossing consciousness" as prominent members of "the global network of diasporic Chinese business and culture that played a significant role in Asia's transition to modernity."[37] Although Fu's description refers directly to Shaw, Loke embodies even more colorfully the cosmopolitan elite that Fu describes. Loke was born in Kuala Lumpur, educated at Swiss boarding schools before studying at Cambridge and the London School of Economics; he was an avid ornithologist and globe-trotting photographer and reportedly more at ease expressing himself in English than in Mandarin.

The intertwined aspirations of modernization and globalization account for the chief distinguishing characteristic of postwar Mandarin cinema history— its undeniably escapist and mythic orientation. In this regard, the two studios consciously absorbed not only the infrastructural blueprint and professional standards of American cinema but also its representational values. The modernity to which MP&GI and Shaw Brothers aspired was one incarnated by Hollywood. Kenny Ng observes that "for a film industry that mostly consisted of Chinese émigrés and a cultural elite supported by overseas Chinese capital, the Hollywood mode of filmmaking promised up-to-date systems of industrial production, mass reproduction, and consumption for a modernizing city. This aesthetic appropriation of Hollywood styles could aptly express and foresee the modern lifestyle and culture of an emerging middle class."[38] Like many others, Ng invokes the biographical profiles of the key personnel at the two studios to account for this openness to Western influences. Loke's international background finds an echo, for instance, in the résumés of many of MP&GI's most influential personnel, such as Robert Chung, a graduate of the University of Hong Kong who worked in Hollywood prior to his seven-year tenure as the studio's general manager. Shaw Brothers owed a great deal of its success to Raymond Chow, who received his education at St. John's University in Shanghai and, with his fluency in English, worked as a journalist at the Hong Kong branch of the U.S. Information Service before joining the studio as its publicity manager. The artistic departments of both studios were filled with Shanghai intellectuals and writers who were conversant with Western culture. The author and screenwriter Eileen Chang and the directors Doe Ching (Tao Qin), Evan Yang (Yi Wen), and Griffin Yueh Feng (Yue Feng)—who were responsible for many of the most important films of the era—all translated and reviewed American films in Shanghai before the war.

The sway held by an idealized Hollywood-style, bourgeois vision of modernity for audiences in Hong Kong and across the South Seas diaspora is further corroborated by their viewing habits. American movies dominated local box offices in terms of gross receipts and, with few exceptions, outsold Mandarin films until the late 1960s. Taking their cues accordingly, MP&GI and Shaw Brothers made films in this era that had little to do with everyday life in the colony—instead offering up dreams of prosperity in an urbanized present or visions of an immemorial past. The modern dramas in which MP&GI excelled consistently took place in elegant homes with staircases, Western furniture, and grand pianos that made no acknowledgment of the poverty affecting the vast majority of Hong Kong's population in the postwar years and that appear all the more fanciful when considered in the context of the severe housing crisis that gripped the colony as a result of the postwar population boom.[39] The period dramas made by Shaw Brothers were set in a historical elsewhere of "exquisite bridges, rivers, city walls, palaces and pavilions, and shops gracing the landscape of ancient China."[40] In both instances, the world projected on-screen was a studio fabrication, an index not of tangible reality but rather of fantasies of origin (depicting a traditional China that never existed) or anticipations of the future ("a picture of a society which does not yet exist").[41]

The escapist and imitative tendencies of Mandarin cinema in the postwar years have been noted by many critics. In the work of I. C. Jarvie, a sociologist and the author of one of the earliest English-language studies dedicated to Hong Kong cinema, they receive a decidedly negative review and serve to illustrate the differences between Mandarin cinema and the Cantonese films that were also produced in abundance in the colony. Although the two coexisted alongside one another as parallel industries in the postwar period, they remained separated by a massive gulf. In Jarvie's assessment, Hong Kong–made Cantonese films were charmingly naïve and unpretentious, for the most part cheaply made, but enriched by folk cultural traditions and a local southern sensibility. At the opposite end of the spectrum were Mandarin pictures, more lavishly budgeted, calculatedly arty, removed from local culture, and marked by a northern and cosmopolitan sensibility. In Jarvie's words, these productions amounted to

> pale, Chinesified copies of western movies. Leaving aside costume pictures, Mandarin movies of the 1950s and 1960s were about night clubs and pop singers, about air hostesses and travel agents, about cops and robbers, all subjects remotely if at all connected with the real lives of the mass of Chinese people living in Hong Kong. Never were the films about shopkeepers and their assistants, about colonial life and tourism, about factory work and farming, about split families and immigration, about refugees, about hard times, about the strain on the individual, about the clash between old and new values and mores, about settling down in a new life in a strange place, about disease, gambling, drugs, politics, corruption.[42]

Teo adopts a similar view. "Cantonese cinema tended towards social issues," he argues, and "by focusing on pressing social problems, it evolved a realist tradition." In contrast, Mandarin cinema was "more sophisticated than its Cantonese counterparts, with more luxurious sets and more glamorous stars, reveling in fantasy, myths, historical legends and musicals."[43]

These descriptions emphasize the ideological bent of the commercial mainstream works of postwar Mandarin cinema, which abandoned the political impulses that had been so central to the leftist filmmaking tradition of the prewar years. The revolutionary and nationalist desires animating that tradition came to be displaced by a new constellation of desires, channeled across capitalist metanarratives of modernity and upward mobility. Concomitantly the social-realist sensibility long associated with Shanghai leftist cinema gave way to an escapist and aspirational disposition. Moreover, the avoidance of issues of colonial power, nationalist politics, and the traumatic impact of the recent wars can be attributed to the political climate of the Cold War era. The British government—intent on keeping its crown colony apart from the hostilities between the PRC and the Republic of China—discouraged demonstrations of partisanship and overt provocation in either direction of nationalist politics.[44] Early in 1952 colonial authorities deported ten filmmakers with close ties to the Chinese Communist Party, an event that sent ripples throughout the film industry.[45] Censorship also exerted an impact on the places where the films were exhibited. For instance, in Malaya, whose large Chinese population represented a significant market for Hong Kong filmmakers, state censors vigilantly monitored "anything that could be interpreted, even allegorically, to represent a statement of either pro-Communist or pro-Nationalist sentiment."[46] Such pressures encouraged the Hong Kong industry to adopt a politically neutral, commercially oriented approach to filmmaking. In 1952 the PRC announced that the mainland market would be closed to Hong Kong films, except for those productions deemed to be ideologically suitable for its audiences. Among the allowable films were those made by Changcheng, Fenghuang, and Zhonglian (Union), left-wing studios based in Hong Kong which also received financial support from the PRC. These left-wing studios remained committed to the patriotism, progressive values, and social-realist ethos of prewar leftist cinema, albeit by necessity without its overt revolutionary messages.[47] Meanwhile, the two major studios set their sights elsewhere—in particular, on Taiwan, which was the home base of the Kuomintang regime under Chiang Kai-shek after its defeat and expulsion from the mainland.[48]

The desire to target Taiwan audiences can partly account for the decision of Shaw Brothers and MP&GI to concentrate their resources on film production in Mandarin, given the Kuomintang's endorsement of Mandarin as the national language (*guoyu*). Yet economic imperatives alone cannot explain this decision, in view of the vast number of dialect speakers who populated the regions served by these studios. Indeed, the period from the late 1950s to the early 1960s witnessed not only a so-called rebirth of Mandarin cinema but also a flowering of multiple dialect film industries, catering to communities of speakers of Cantonese, Amoy, Teochew (Chaozhou), and other Chinese dialects that had formed along the routes of the postwar diaspora. The number of films produced in Cantonese and Amoy, the two largest of these dialect groups, vastly exceeded the number of Mandarin films in these years.[49] Hong Kong also served as a production base for these dialect industries, and both Shaw Brothers and MP&GI dedicated departments of their studios to the making of Cantonese and Amoy films.[50] In his important study of the Amoy-dialect film industry, Jeremy Taylor locates these films in a historically specific cultural space, a "transboundary" zone that "belonged to no single city, nation or, indeed, 'place.' "[51] Taylor's research brings into view the consonances between Mandarin and Amoy cinema in this period and implicitly calls into question the tendency to conceive of individual Chinese dialect film industries as being parallel to one another, on separate tracks that do not intersect. The cultural geography of Amoy cinema was shared by Mandarin films in the postwar period, retraced in the latter's overlapping distributive routes. And although Mandarin, with its status as a standardized national language, must be distinguished from Amoy, its address was also to a Chinese subject belonging to no single nation or place.[52] Only against the background of a linguistically heterogeneous diasporic film culture can the significance of Mandarin be fully grasped—as a lingua franca, capable of transcending the particularities of origin and regional identity and of forging a common cultural identity across local and national boundaries.

The idea of a cultural space belonging to no particular single place was visually produced on screen by means of the erasure of local everyday reality. As Wendy Gan observes, the films made by MP&GI and Shaw Brothers, even those set in contemporary Hong Kong, portrayed their settings in the most generic terms and avoided concrete signifiers of locality. She writes: "What is seen of Hong Kong is partial and surprisingly nonspecific. Much of Hong Kong's diversity has been omitted from representation. There is little notion of Hong Kong's agricultural or fishing and seafaring cultures, no hint of Hong Kong's colonial status nor visual evidence of its colonial masters, no sense of Hong Kong as a thriving city of big business."[53] What is offered instead is a view from the top—of enclosed interiors and public spaces inaccessible to the masses—from which such details fade into the distant background. Somewhat paradoxically, a filmgoer eager for glimpses of everyday life in this time would do better with a film like *The World of Suzie Wong* (1960), whose portrait of Hong Kong life, "from the British bankers in Central to the fishing folk in Aberdeen and the prostitutes in Wanchai, though undoubtedly orientalist, is far more comprehensive and diverse than most local films."[54]

The World of Suzie Wong was one of a slew of Cold War–era Hollywood productions set in Hong Kong, along with *Macao* (1952), *Soldier of Fortune* (1955), *Love Is a Many-Splendored Thing* (1955), and *Flight to Hong Kong* (1956). Steeped in the Cold War geopolitical imaginary, these films tap into long-standing orientalist and paternalistic representations of the Far East—as mysterious, feminized, treacherous, and primitive—along with paranoid visions of Red China and the communist menace, on the one hand, and lurid port-city nightmares of smugglers, spies, and international crime syndicates, on the other hand. Needless to say, these films are hardly accurate portrayals of Hong Kong, given their tendency to overwrite the specificity of place with stereotypical preconceptions of the exotic East. But they frequently, if inadvertently, present a startling documentary perspective on the colony in their use of location shots to visually establish their setting.[55] Such location shots, even if limited to brief moments and the sidelines of the plot, exert a fascination in their own right, offering intriguing glimpses of public life in 1950s Hong Kong—showing the Star Ferry, colonial architecture, teeming street markets, temples, tenements, squatter settlements, floating communities of boat dwellers, and so on.[56] Ironically, in their very insistence on the otherness of their setting, these American films give flashes of actuality that break the frame of the fiction, revealing the unadorned, working-class mien of Hong Kong that is typically excluded from Mandarin films of the same period. Indeed, American portrayals of Hong Kong as a site of sojourn and business for Westerners put in stark relief the complete elision of British colonial presence in locally produced films.

The Musical Field of Postwar Cinema

Perhaps the single most conspicuous feature of Hong Kong–made films of the postwar period is their predilection for musical performance, exhibited across the divisions of genre and language. The convention of the inserted film song used by Shanghai filmmakers in the early sound period became an essential narrative component of Mandarin and dialect cinemas throughout the 1950s and 1960s. The frequency of freestanding scenes of song performance increased as *gechang pian* and *gewu pian* evolved, and it was not uncommon for films from this period to contain from six to upwards of a dozen *chaqu*. As in the earliest years of sound filmmaking, song inserts were frequently presented as diegetic scenes of performance and couched within stories about the lives of natural-born singers and professional entertainers. From the plays within the play of the early Chinese sound era, we arrive at the embedded song spectacles threaded throughout the mise-en-scène of postwar cinema, on its streets and stages and in spaces of domesticity as well as public display. If the persistence of these formulas across this historical span is indicative of the long shadow cast by the backstage musical—and its availability for local appropriation and reterritorialization—the influence of Hollywood's musical codes becomes even more pronounced in postwar Hong Kong cinema. The push toward higher production values and improved filmmaking technologies by the two major studios also opened up a pathway for new forms of musical spectacle, so that coexisting alongside traditional-style *gechang pian* with their solitary singers were large-scale, elaborate song-and-dance extravaganzas, modeled after the Hollywood musicals produced after the advent of widescreen Technicolor.[57] Moreover, filmic stagings of song were not limited to any single genre but spanned a wide range of categories, including historical costume dramas, opera films, comedies, romances, tragedies, family dramas, and melodramas along with musicals in the strict sense.

To a large degree, then, the profusion of musical modes on screen was fueled by the demands of an expanding, diversifying commercial film industry. However, this phenomenon must also be situated along the historical trajectory of twentieth-century Chinese music. The development of sound cinema occurred simultaneously with a transformation in the mass culture of listening by the introduction of technologies of recording and transmission like the gramophone record and radio, which led to the rise of popular music as a modern industry. The tie-ups and collaborative opportunities discovered by filmmakers and music producers in the Shanghai period, described in the previous chapter, continued to shape the sounds of Hong Kong cinema. The postwar years constitute another phase in the emergence of a symbiotically interwoven audiovisual and musical mass culture—situated at the crossroads of film, stage, and the recording industry, and extending across disparate regional traditions of music. For instance, looking at Amoy cinema, Taylor observes that "the inclusion of songs [was] one of the few common features of virtually all Amoy-dialect films." As Amoy filmmaking found a foothold in Hong Kong, there also arose "an entire industry of recording and printing 'modern Hokkien songs' . . . also known as 'contemporary Amoy songs.'"[58] Film songs were released as commercial records, recorded by the same stars who performed them in the films, and were even sold at screenings. The on-screen performances of these tunes were often staged in the setting of the cabaret, nodding to the origins of both these singing stars and the songs in the nightclub (*getai*) culture of Singapore and Malay.[59] Similar crossover connections are found in the Taiwanese-dialect films (*taiyu pian*) made in this same period.[60]

Cantonese cinema likewise incorporated the musical idioms of the Guangdong region. In particular, the Cantonese film industry flourished because of its close ties to Cantonese opera (*Yueju*), the dominant form of popular music for Cantonese listeners in the first half of the twentieth century. Yung Saishing describes the ongoing process by which technological mediation opened up new channels of circulation for Cantonese opera throughout the twentieth century, beginning with the gramophone records that in the 1920s first made it possible to listen to opera in private, domestic space. Recording outfits like the New Moon Gramophone Record Company built a lucrative business on sales of "Cantonese operas on disc."[61] In 1933 Cantonese opera made the leap to the big screen with the release of *Bai jin long* (*White Golden Dragon*). The film's enormous commercial success alerted theater professionals, filmmakers, and record producers alike to the possibilities for cross-marketing in the dawn of sound cinema.[62] Opera stars were approached to perform in films, their songs were sold as recordings, and some stars—like the famed Sit Kok-sin— even founded studios to produce their own films. The popularity of Cantonese opera films peaked in the 1950s, and there may be no more incontrovertible evidence for the musical bent of postwar cinema than the staggering number of opera films made in this decade: more than 500, or fully a third of the Cantonese-dialect films made in Hong Kong.[63]

The prominent position of opera films in the genre system of postwar cinema points to the deep-rooted influence of *xiqu* (Chinese opera) and traditional theater arts in Chinese filmmaking throughout its history. Cinema emerged in a cultural environment that was dominated by opera as a medium of storytelling, staged visual spectacle, and musical entertainment. The subsequent development of cinema was shaped by an ongoing dialogue and tension with the conventions of *xiqu* and long-standing traditions of lyrical storytelling. The significance of opera for Chinese cinema's archaeology and history, protocols of acting and mimesis, and conceptions of cinematic aesthetics and medium specificity has been a subject of investigation in recent scholarship.[64] In light of the tightly woven bonds between the two media, the ubiquity of performed songs in Chinese films can be seen as an effect of the gravitational pull exerted by opera on the evolution of cinema's representational strategies. These strategies reflect and respond to the habits of reception and the expectations of a viewing public accustomed to the alternation of speech and song within a musical structure of narration. "Before the introduction of Western theater," Bell Yung writes, "purely spoken drama was not known in China; all stage performances involved some form of singing and instrumental music."[65]

During the 1930s, opera served as a key point of reference for filmmakers as they explored the expressive possibilities of new synchronized sound technologies. Alongside filmed versions of stage operas like *White Golden Dragon* were many early sound productions that were not classifiable as opera films but that nonetheless featured scenes of opera performance, such as *Songstress Red Peony*, *The Singing Beauty*, and *Two Stars in the Milky Way*. The 1950s marked another phase of intense exchange between these media, as opera films experienced a revival on multiple fronts. Along with the peak in Cantonese opera film production, the decade saw an upsurge in opera films in the PRC, many of which were enthusiastically received by audiences when screened outside the mainland.[66] The opera film phenomenon eventually penetrated the sphere of Hong Kong's Mandarin film industry as well. In 1958 the Shaw Brothers Film Studio released *Diao Chan* (*Diau Charn*), an opera film loosely based on the regional style of Huangmei opera, which presented the legend of a famed beauty from the period of the Three Kingdoms; cast in the title role was Linda Lin Dai. *Diau Charn* broke box office records for Mandarin releases in Hong Kong and received five awards at the Asian Film Festival that year. Its critical and commercial success inspired a cycle of what were known as *Huangmei diao pian* that lasted into the late 1960s. The craze for *Huangmei diao pian* reached its pinnacle with *Liang Shanbo yu Zhu Yingtai* (*The Love Eterne*, 1963), a film regarded as one of the biggest popular hits in the history of Chinese-language cinema. *The Love Eterne* broke box-office records in Taiwan, where it played for sixty-two days; spawned an unprecedented phenomenon of repeat viewing, with some filmgoers claiming to have seen the film twenty to thirty times; and stoked a frenzied fan cult around the actress Ivy Ling Po, who played one of the film's two star-crossed lovers.[67]

A comparison of opera films with the *gechang* and *gewu pian* that are the subject of this book reveals notable differences between these types of musical productions. The former constitute what Emilie Yeh calls a "closed generic system," one rooted in the representational codes, expressive aesthetics, and stylized performances of the stage.[68] In contrast, song-and-dance films largely conform to the codes of narrative realism, framing their musical numbers as realistically motivated spectacles that are clearly marked off from the verisimilar performance of the story. For instance, in *Bu liao qing* (*Love without End*, 1961) Linda Lin Dai's character sings and dances when she steps onto the stage of the nightclub where she works as a lounge singer. Once off the stage, she plays her part no differently than she would in a nonmusical drama. But in the title role of *Diau Charn*, her acting bears the inflection of the stylized theatricality of opera, where "movements and speech . . . have been abstracted and refined into song and dance."[69] Lin's words and gestures are rhythmically matched to the music that runs continuously throughout the film. Her performance shifts fluidly and constantly between speaking and singing, between the formalized body language of theater and the naturalistic acting of cinema. Rather than a drama punctuated by moments of singing, *Diau Charn* can be described as a string of episodes linked together in and engulfed by a musical matrix. Bridging the episodes is an invisible chorus of female singers who describe the action in the manner of a third-person omniscient narrator and frame the story with a unified voice. The distinctive strategies of opera films, with their negotiation of conflicting codes of expressivity and realism, render them a species apart in the realm of musical filmmaking.

But before we move away from *Huangmei diao pian* to focus on songstress films of the postwar period, the flash points of porosity in these closed generic systems merit consideration. The borders dividing opera films from song-and-dance films appear less clear-cut in view of the ways that opera is interwoven throughout *gechang pian* with contemporary settings and performed by well-known singers more commonly associated with *shidai qu*. For example, in one of her films, *Qingchung ernü* (*Spring Song*, 1959), Grace Chang dons a traditional costume to perform a scene from *Kunqu* opera, as part of a talent show at her school. *Qian mian nülang* (*Girl of a Thousand Guises*, 1959) contains several Peking opera numbers performed by Chang (figure 2.3).[70] Conversely, the opera films of this period also display the influence of modern musical styles, rather than strictly adhering to theatrical traditions. Li Han-hsiang, the director of *Diau Charn* and numerous other *Huangmei diao* productions from Shaw Brothers, described the film as a "hybrid," and "a bastard not resembling opera or film."[71] *Huangmei diao pian* cast movie stars rather than trained opera performers and recruited singers from the world of modern music rather than *xiqu*. For instance, the Mandarin pop singer Tsin Ting provided the vocals for Lin's song scenes in *Diau Charn*. Lyrics were thus sung in Mandarin rather than in the regional dialect, and the tunes themselves were modernized with the addition of Western instrumentation and modern rhythms.[72]

The two genres also converged in their shared emphasis on the female lyrical voice. As Xiangyang Chen points out, a "female structuring voiceover" is a consistent feature in *Huangmei diao pian*. In *Diau Charn*, the most dominant and consistent musical element is the invisible chorus of women that functions to "propel the narrative, relate the back-story, link scenes, comment on a character's state of mind, externalize Diau Charn's interior monologues by relaying her asides, and provide a concluding coda."[73] Chen traces this emphasis on female voices to Huangmei opera as a regional form that evolved from an oral repertory of women's folk songs, sung by tea-leaf pickers in Hubei Province and expressing their hardships. In the filmic remediation of Huangmei opera, we can thus discern a tradition of female lament linking stage and screen. This tradition undergirds the expanded field of songstress performance in Chinese cinema. The gendering of the lyrical voice beyond the category of the opera film, across a spectrum of films featuring musical performance, reinforces a coding of song in terms of feminine subjectivity and interiority.

··· FIGURE 2.3 ···
Grace Chang performs
Peking opera, publicity
still for *Girl of a Thousand
Guises*, 1959. Permission of
Tao Yuen Motion Picture
Development Company.
Courtesy of the Hong
Kong Film Archive.

The musical productions of postwar Mandarin cinema were built on its close ties to the music recording industry, and its songstresses rode the wave of the relocation of modern Mandarin pop music from Shanghai to Hong Kong. Paralleling the exodus of workers in the film industry, many of Shanghai's most talented songwriters, singers, and musicians migrated to the colony and continued their careers. Among them were composers like Li Houxiang, vocalists like Chang Loo, instrumentalists from many of Shanghai's most celebrated nightclubs and ballrooms, and the brother-sister duo Yao Min and Yao Lee—one a prolific composer, the other known as the queen of Mandarin pop. Hong Kong emerged as the new epicenter of *shidai qu* in the postwar years. Although "yellow music" became the target of increasingly strident denunciations in the PRC—it was banned outright in the early 1950s, as Andrew Jones points out—it thrived in this new milieu.[74] Hong Kong's standing as the new capital of the Mandarin music industry was announced in no uncertain terms by the relocation of Pathé-EMI, one of the major producers of *shidai qu* recordings in republican Shanghai, to the colony in 1949.[75] Pathé-EMI quickly established itself as Hong Kong's biggest record company and the only producer with its own recording studio, located in Causeway Bay. (As I discuss in the next chapter, a glimpse of these facilities is offered by the 1959 film *Gemi xiaojie* [*Miss Songbird*], which contains several scenes shot on location at the studio.) The company further cemented its dominant position by fostering its connections to the film industry, hiring Yao Min to head its film music division (after his death in 1967, Yao Lee took over this role). Competing with Pathé-EMI for the Mandarin music market were local producers like Great Wall and Diamond and other transnational outfits such as Philips.[76]

In this period film songs, packaged and sold as singles, accounted for a major segment of the popular music market. Compilation albums consisting of songs associated with individual film stars were popular in the late 1950s—a phenomenon also witnessed in India, where the cultures of music and cinema were similarly intertwined. And beginning in 1963, spurred by the Huangmei opera film craze, individual film soundtrack LPs became a common feature of the record market.[77] Conversely, the most talented and sought-after vocalists of *shidai qu*—like Yao Lee—were approached by film studios to record songs for movies, a practice referred to as *muhou daichang* (behind-the-scenes substitute singing). Given the ubiquity of song scenes in postwar cinema and the limited musical talent of some stars, the demand for behind-the-scenes singers was high. A 1959 article in the movie magazine *Southern Screen* observes that by this time, not a single major recording artist had not sung for films.[78] Some vocalists went a step beyond the role of the behind-the-scenes singer to claim a greater visibility. For example, Xia Dan made a guest appearance in the 1956 hit film *Taohua jiang* (*Songs of the Peach Blossom River*), and Carrie Gu Mei played the lead role in *Xiao yunque* (*The Lark*, 1965), which used as its title the nickname by which Gu's fans referred to her. Sometimes, the star appeal of these vocalists exceeded that of the actors themselves. For instance, the program brochure for *Songs of the Peach Blossom River* featured not the visage of the film's main star, Chung Ching, but that of Yao Lee, who dubbed all of Chung's song scenes in the picture, as I discuss in greater detail in the next chapter.

In his survey of Mandarin pop from 1930 to 1970, Wong Kee Chee points to the similarities between the film and music culture of the Shanghai era and that of postwar Hong Kong. Besides creating a demand for the services of professional vocalists in the film industry, "the popularity of singing films in the 1950s . . . stimulated also a demand for recordings by film stars themselves, which is not unlike the 1930s," Wong argues.[79] But a close comparison between the two periods also discloses notable, if subtle, differences in the intermedia currents of pre- and postwar mass culture. A 1958 article from *International Screen* on the subject of the connections between the film and music industries is instructive in this regard. Titled "Pathé Records Nets MP&GI's Flock of Stars," it highlights the large number of the film studio's actresses who had signed record contracts with Pathé-EMI: Jeanette Lin Tsui, Linda Lin Dai, Grace Chang, Helen Li Mei and, most recently, Julie Yeh Feng and Kitty Ting Hao. The article pays credit for this development to Miriam Wang (Wang Shu-wei), who began working for the record company in 1938, while it was based in Shanghai, and eventually rose to the position of general manager and producer for its Hong Kong division. Wang, the article states, "early on recognized that the record industry must rely on the market forged by film" and took steps to establish the company's monopoly on Mandarin film music. As well as pursuing recording contracts with individual movie stars, Wang also secured exclusive rights to the songs of Yao Min—who by this time had become one of Hong Kong's most respected and prolific songwriters and was responsible for a vast number of the most popular film songs of the period—further ensuring that film stars would "line up under Pathé's banner."[80] The article's text is accompanied by individual photos of these stars taken during recording sessions and group shots in which they posed with Wang. Such images of Wang alongside the recording artists with whom she worked abound in the illustrated magazines of the period, testifying to her power and public visibility as a paramount player in the postwar mass culture industry—a status particularly impressive in view of the general paucity of women occupying prominent industry positions in this period.[81] Foreign managers still constituted the record company's top leadership, as had been the case in Shanghai, with Chinese compradors "relegated to providing musical expertise and negotiating with performers and local distributors."[82] But Wang's distinct media presence suggests a more substantial role as the public face of Pathé for the Chinese market. Her leadership was essential to the fortunes of the company in Hong Kong. Wong credits her with discovering a new path for the popular music industry in the postwar decades as well "recapturing Pathé's former glory in the space of two to three years" following its move to the colony.[83]

The *International Screen* article sheds light on the complex and interarticulated mass cultural ecosystem of the postwar years, bound together by currents of symbiosis and feedback. The announcement of Pathé-EMI's contracts with MP&GI's stars in the film studio's house publication is a calculated publicity maneuver, harnessing the prestige of the record company to bolster the standing of the studio's star assets. Conversely, Pathé-EMI's targeting of these artists indicates its own calculations regarding the recognition and cultural capital already accrued by these figures in the domain of film. Publicity begets more publicity; music helps sell the films that create a viable market for music. To be sure, such strategies were already established in the early years of sound cinema, as scholars like Jones, Sue Touhy, and Zhang Zhen have demonstrated. The introduction of sound technology, Zhang points out, quickly gave rise to the theme song as an audiovisual commodity that extended the filmic experience beyond the confines of the theater, rode on the success of the picture, and even promoted films in advance by luring new viewers into the theater.[84] But Miriam Wang's strategy of signing film stars as recording artists also reveals an important directional shift in the expansion of postwar mass media. During the Shanghai era, the music profession supplied early sound cinema with its first generation of performers—with singers like Zhou Xuan, Wang Renmei, Li Lili, and Li Minghui moving into film acting only after having already established careers as musical stage performers and recording artists. Musical revue troupes like the Bright Moon Song and Dance Troupe supplied cinema with a stream of skilled professionals in music and theater arts, functioned as training institutes for a film industry that had none of its own, and laid the foundations for the star system of prewar mass media.[85] In 1950s Hong Kong, however, we see a reversal of this movement, with the region's largest record company capitalizing on the talent incubated by the movie industry. Although Grace Chang and Julie Yeh Feng were accomplished singers in their own right, their status as stars of the screen nonetheless preceded, and enabled, their musical careers.[86] In contrast to the Shanghai era, in this period none of Hong Kong's major film actors came from the music industry. In this reversal we can discern the ascendance of cinema as the main driving force in the star culture of the 1950s and 1960s, as well as the far-reaching impact of the powerful publicity machines created by the big film studios (Shaw Brothers as much as MP&GI) on the broader mass media landscape.

The popular music landscape of the postwar period was remarkably variegated and polyglot, in continuity with the "colonial bricolage" that Jones identifies as the prevalent mode of *shidai qu* in the Republican era. In the 1920s and 1930s, modern Mandarin pop music combined Eastern and Western instrumentation and scales and melded Chinese urban folk melodies (*xiaodiao*) with American jazz, Hollywood film music, Broadway show tunes, and dance rhythms such as those of the tango, rumba, and foxtrot.[87] In the 1950s and 1960s, a period bookended by the jazz age and the rock and roll era, *shidai qu* entered a phase of even greater hybridity and promiscuity. One of the signal trends of these years was the popularity of Latin Caribbean music and dance styles, discussed in chapter 4. On the heels of a global mambo craze, the rhythms of mambo, cha-cha, and calypso were absorbed into the soundscape of *shidai qu*, percolating from the big band and nightclub scene into film soundtracks and the sphere of pop music. Blues, swing, and rock and roll music from the United States also had a significant impact on the development of postwar Mandarin pop. These idioms affected Hong Kong's music culture not only by way of stylistic influence but also through the invention of new strategies by which to assimilate foreign music, beyond the modes of bricolage encountered in the prewar colonial era. As Wong Kee-chee observes, "Hong Kong was responsible for a new type of Mandarin pop—plugging Chinese lyrics into western or Japanese tunes."[88] Although some Chinese-language versions of foreign songs were recorded in the 1930s, the practice was far from common. In postwar Hong Kong, however, Mandarin covers of foreign songs took off and gave rise to the category of *yiqu* (translated songs). Among them were remakes of American hit songs like "Achoo Cha Cha," a 1958 release by the McGuire Sisters that was covered by Grace Chang.[89] Another of Chang's hit songs, the 1957 "I Want Your Love" ("Wo yao ni di ai")—a cover of the American jump blues song "I Want You to Be My Baby"—represents a variation on *yiqu*, mixing together Mandarin verses and the song's original English lyrics.[90] Another set of *yiqu* consisted of Mandarin versions of Japanese songs, like Chang Loo's "Hong shuilian" ("Red Lotus"), a song originally recorded in Japanese by Li Xianglan (Shirley Yamaguchi) as "Akai Suiren."[91]

The practice of covering songs did more than serve as a mechanism through which Mandarin music absorbed an international corpus of contemporary pop hits. It also extended along a historical axis, reaching back in time to draw on an archive of golden oldies, which were newly arranged and sometimes set to rewritten lyrics. A 1960 article on film and popular music in *International Screen* points out that "one of the hottest tunes in Hong Kong nightclubs today" is "Cheek to Cheek," a song that came from an American film released in 1935, *Top Hat*.[92] The song came into vogue after a translated version of it appeared in a more recent film. The article goes on to mention several Mandarin pop oldies from the 1920s and 1930s that had been similarly resuscitated in recent productions, such as "Lang shi chunri feng" ("My Love Is Like the Spring Wind") and "Maomao yü" ("Drizzles"), a composition by the *shidai qu* pioneer Li Jinhui that is considered to be the first Shanghai modern pop song. "Drizzles" received a boost from its inclusion as one of the musical numbers in the song-and-dance extravaganza *Long xiangfeng wu* (*Calendar Girl*, 1959) and had a second life as a pop hit, along with several other Shanghai-era oldies recycled by the film.[93] Another one of these tunes was "Heri jun zai la?" ("When Will You Return?"), first recorded by Zhou Xuan in 1938.[94] Indeed, the fortunes of "When Will You Return?" in the postwar years serve as an apt illustration of the extent to which old songs were recirculated in new forms. The song was adapted as a number in *Hudie furen* (*Madame Butterfly*, 1956), a *gechang pian* based on the Puccini opera; rearranged as a tango number for *Calendar Girl*; adapted yet again in a blockbuster period drama from Shaw Brothers, *Lan yu hei* (*The Blue and the Black*, 1966); and also translated and performed in two Cantonese films from this period.[95] Similarly, the 1929 popular hit "Taohua jiang" ("Peach Blossom River," also composed by Li Jinhui) appeared in not one but four different versions in the late 1950s and early 1960s, each one associated with a movie soundtrack. The most notable of these is *Songs of the Peach Blossom River*, whose Chinese title is the same as that of the song: *Taohua jiang*. The song appears again as the climactic musical number of the songstress film *Tao li zheng chun* (*It's Always Spring*, 1962), where it is the melodic backbone for an extended medley that switches between the styles of calypso, hula, and military march.[96] Other postwar films also borrowed the titles of popular Shanghai-era songs, such as the Grace Chang vehicle *Jiao wo ruhe bu xiang ta* (*Because of Her*, 1963) and *Heri jun zai la* (*Till the End of Time*, 1966).

Listening to the Mandarin films of this period, one cannot but be struck by the familiar refrains, encore turns, and melodic fragments from other times and places that stream continuously throughout these productions. New compositions circulated alongside translation songs and cover versions, but original versions of classic oldies also maintained a constant presence on the airwaves and in the affections of listeners. The soundscape of postwar Hong Kong mass culture consisted of an echo chamber of already heard tunes and hybrid combinations, resonating across cultural and historical borders. This characteristic has been attributed to the peculiar conditions that confronted the postwar culture industry: on the one hand, there was great public demand for musical entertainment, and, on the other hand, there was a dearth of skilled songwriters and composers. Beyond a reflection of material constraints, we can also understand it as an effect of the tightly interwoven relationship of film and music. Far from merely giving rise to film songs as a subcategory of popular music, cinema functioned as a productive resource for the latter, providing a framework through which familiar melodies could acquire a fresh set of meanings for popular audiences. In a milieu where original compositions were not the sole driving force of musical cultural production, film emerged as a critical medium for the propagation of popular music, endowing old songs with a renewed life and relevance.

In turn, musical practices of covering and rearranging existing works served as a model for a film industry that relied heavily on strategies of copying, remaking, adapting, and recycling plot tropes and scenarios. Just as film soundtracks were filled with already heard tunes, so their narratives drew from a repertory of twice-told tales. In some instances, postwar filmmakers remade works of an earlier period of Chinese cinema—like *Tiyu huanghou* (*Queen of Sports*, 1961), which updated the Shanghai silent film of the same title, or *Yu ge* (*The Fisherman's Daughter*, 1956), a remake of a 1943 production by the same director, Bu Wancang, titled *Yu jia nü*. Hollywood movies also leave visible tracks across the terrain of postwar Chinese filmmaking. For instance, *Mambo Girl*, discussed in chapter 4, draws on the formula of American rock and roll films of the early 1950s while also appropriating elements of the 1937 classical maternal melodrama *Stella Dallas*. Adaptations of literary classics were common, as chapter 5 shows. The genres of historical costume epics and opera films drew on a familiar trove of ancient tales, legends, and folklore, including *The Water Margin*, *The Dream of the Red Chamber*, and the legends of Hua Mulan and the White Snake. The practice of remaking a film in one dialect into a version in another dialect was common as well, with the phenomenon of the translation song finding a parallel in the Amoy and Cantonese film industries' practice of copying well-known Mandarin releases.[97]

A Residual Cinema

In his overview of film music in postwar Hong Kong Mandarin films, Yu Mo-wan lays out a classificatory schema based on five major musical categories: Western, regional opera, Shanghai-era *shidai qu*, Chinese folk tunes, and original compositions.[98] Yu's taxonomy offers a way to grasp the plurality of musical styles in postwar film culture, based on a detailed statistical breakdown of two decades of filmmaking. Yet the sense of order that it imposes on this multiplicity is provisional at best. In the face of the high degree of cannibalization and cross-fertilization taking place within this soundscape, these categories quickly lose their distinctness. For instance, where in this schema would we place a tune like "Kamen" ("Carmen"), sung by Grace Chang in *Ye meigui zhi lian* (*The Wild, Wild Rose*, 1961), which pairs the tune of the "Habañera" from the opera *Carmen* with Mandarin lyrics, simultaneously injecting it with a mambo and rumba dance rhythm?[99] Rather than relying on clear-cut differences of musical type to navigate the complex field of postwar cinema, by way of wrestling its heterogeneity into a semblance of order, we might instead take the constitutive impurity of Mandarin popular music as a starting point—a means of focalizing the hybrid, translational, and residual qualities that make this cinema otherwise difficult to place.

The persistent resonance of familiar tunes from an earlier historical era might be heard as another symptom of Shanghai hangover, as a musical expression of émigrés' nostalgia for a lost homeland and cultural milieu. Indeed, such a reading is borne out by the trope of the songstress as a figure of displacement—an orphan, refugee, or exile—that embodies the collective losses of a generation of migrants at the same time that her songs preserve an aural memory of the past. But to focus exclusively on the point of origin of these already heard tunes as the key to the meaning they held for listeners is to overlook the "performative reinvention" and mutation of these meanings in the process of revision and circulation.[100] The repackaged melodies of postwar film culture, Lily Wong writes, necessarily "shift our focus away from fidelity to origins and redirect our attention to the (re)formulations of meaning in its very rhizomorphic movements that are decentered, dispersed and in a constant process of becoming."[101] As old songs are recoded in new contexts, and as echoes accumulate, historical referents become ever more obscure. The rituals of listening do not so much duplicate a past world or a shared national identity as they point to the increasing pliability and contingency of identity in the fractured cultural geography of the postwar diaspora.

Likewise, the cinema of this period must be situated in a zone of liminal temporality where old and new come together in unpredictable ways. As a point of contact between film and musical culture, the songstress allows us to grasp this liminal status in audiovisual terms. The following chapters take a twofold approach to the evolution of the songstress, paying careful attention to the residues that cling to this figure even as she is held up as a sign of modernity. For the songstress herself is nothing if not an ambivalent, composite historical sign. A throwback to earlier traditions who also embodies the new, she amalgamates traditional and modern ideals of femininity and blends native and foreign performance idioms. Gazing critically across the most iconic faces and voices of Mandarin cinema, and looking deeply into the textual dynamics of individual works, we discover that the tragic chanteuses of old do not simply fall by the wayside but linger on, reincarnated in a younger generation of performers who simultaneously point ahead to the future.

THE LITTLE WILDCAT

One of the faces standing out in the new generation of songstresses was that of Chung Ching (Zhong Qing). Born in 1932, she was a mainland émigré who began acting in Hong Kong at the age of twenty-one. Although Chung would eventually sign a contract with the Motion Picture and General Investment Co. Ltd. (MP&GI), her most memorable films were made at the beginning of her career, when she starred in a series of highly popular song-and-dance pictures produced by Xinhua (New China) Film Company. Xinhua was one of Hong Kong's more successful smaller film studios, originally founded in Shanghai in 1934 by the legendary producer and entertainment mogul Zhang Shankun and reestablished in Hong Kong in 1952.[1] Responsible for some of the biggest box-office hits of the 1930s—like *Yeban gesheng* (*Song of Midnight*, 1937), inspired by the *Phantom of the Opera*—Xinhua reprised its commercial success in its postwar phase with a string of musical extravaganzas and adaptations of romantic legends and literary works. Among these were Hollywood-style underwater musicals like *Bi shui honglian* (*Fleur-de-Lys*, 1960), Japanese-influenced musicals like *Ying du yan ji*

(*Beauty of Tokyo*, 1955), an adaption of Alexandre Dumas *fils*'s *The Lady of the Camellias* titled *Chahua nü* (*Camellia*, 1955), and a retelling of Puccini's *Madame Butterfly* with the same title as the opera, *Hudie furen* (1956)—which was one of the first Hong Kong productions to use color cinematography.[2]

In 1956 Xinhua released *Songs of the Peach Blossom River*—in Chinese *Taohua jiang*, or *Peach Blossom River*—which featured Chung Ching in her first starring role as a plucky country lass nicknamed Wildcat, known in her village for her lovely voice and fondness for singing. The film achieved resounding commercial success, inspiring a cycle of *xiangcun gechang pian* (rustic singing films) that featured song performance against a pastoral backdrop, with characters drawn from a stock of rustic village types. In addition to making a star of Chung, the film exerted a lasting influence on her public image. For the remainder of her career, she would be referred to as Little Wildcat (Xiao Yemao) and cast in the role of a songstress. From a historical standpoint, *Songs of the Peach Blossom River* also marked a pivotal turn in the development of the *gechang pian*, with its innovative melding of song and story. In it, Stephen Teo observes, "the characters now sing to each other instead of the solo episodes which were invariably the only scenes that would indicate that a picture was a musical. Now, the music and songs spring forth naturally as a function of both scene and plot."[3] Teo argues that the film breaks from the traditional *chaqu* format, in which music is typically experienced as a disruption of the story, by putting music to work in the service of narrative. With its twelve song scenes, the film at once affirms the centrality of musical spectacle in feature filmmaking and lays out a new direction for the singing picture. On the one hand, the song scenes still bear the traces of the freestanding format of the inserted film song, most evidently in the appearance during each song of subtitles that give the lyrics. The interruptive effect of this convention—conspicuously signaling a rupture in diegetic space and a shift into a different mode of address—is still evident in this film, although it would disappear from *gechang pian* within the next few years. On the other hand, the song scenes are increasingly anchored in the fictional world as the film moves through a spectrum of musical scenarios. These scenarios range from the substitution of song for dialogue as a communicative medium (for instance, substituting for dialogue during a musical duet between the film's two main characters) to various diegetic situations of performance (in the open air and in private spaces, as well as on the public stage). Therefore, following Teo's cue, many critics have singled out *Songs of the Peach Blossom River* as "Mandarin cinema's first integrated musical."[4]

Against this background, Chung Ching might be seen as a principal player in the postwar evolution of *gechang pian*, her debut as a songstress making her the dramatic agent of a turn toward a more naturalized, integrative approach to song performance in films. Yet many aspects of Chung's performance do not seem to follow such a mandate, as a closer look at the film quickly reveals. The character of Wildcat is distinctly modulated by an acting style in which the exaggerated gesture trumps subtle characterization. Playing her role with the exuberance of a comic, Chung injects the film with a playful, at times campy and cartoonish, quality that jars with the codes of realistic transparency. Throughout the film, she displays a certain self-consciousness in her performance. Rather than disappearing behind the veil of her character, the actress seems to peek and wink at the audience from behind that veil. There is a coquettish dimension to her acting approach, aiming to elicit not so much the audience's belief in the fictional construct of the wholesome country lass, but rather its delighted recognition of Chung the sex symbol vamping at the camera. In the tug of war between performer and character, Wildcat emerges as an ambiguous and layered sign, referring to Chung's defining star attribute as well as to an individuated narrative persona. The coyly kittenish posture she adopts in *Songs of the Peach Blossom River* subsequently becomes an indelible part of her dramatic signature, inscribed in her public moniker, in the titles of her productions like *Duoqing de yemao* (*Passionate Wildcat*, 1960), and even in her film songs ("You are too naughty, like a little kitty-cat," she croons in one lyrical self-portrait).[5] Another production puns on the actress's name, which can be translated by a phrase that means "to fall in love": Chung Ching's name is part of the title of *Yi jian zhong qing* (*Love at First Sight*, 1958).

In Chung's case, we are confronted with a manner of performance and presentation that constantly steps outside of the bounds of the fiction and reflexively gestures at the extradiegetic identity of the star. Indeed, if integration means a harnessing of representational elements to an overriding narrative logic, in *Songs of the Peach Blossom River* this process stumbles over the figure of the songstress, who cannot be fully absorbed by the framework of the character as a cohesive and unified entity. The instability of Chung's presence in the film is such that the film seems compelled to acknowledge it by incorporating it into the plot. In the course of the story, Wildcat relinquishes her rustic identity when she travels from the countryside to the city (explicitly named as Hong Kong), is discovered, and is made over into a singing star. The natural-born singer is reborn in an updated modern guise as an entertainment professional, in a plot twist that bears more than a passing resemblance to Chung's life story.[6] With this sudden turnaround, the film settles the contest between performer and character by giving up on Wildcat and offering up the image of Chung Ching, looking every bit the glamorous star that *Songs of the*

Peach Blossom River would make of her. The star text is superimposed on the filmic text, and this reflexive turn of events attests not to the successful diegetic containment of an extraneous star presence, but rather to the capacity of that presence to dictate the terms of filmic representation. The star-is-born narrative ends with a playful reference to the film itself, as the characters pile into a car and pull up in front of a movie theater where a prominently placed poster announces the screening of *Taohua jiang*.

Such gestures of discursive self-awareness can be seen as instanciations of a reflexive disposition that underpins the musical film. Jane Feuer argues that "the musical appears to be constantly breaking through its own glossy surface," with its frequent moments of direct address, detours across multiple levels of reality, and divided characters.[7] In contrast to classical realist cinema's concealment of its representational mechanisms, the film musical breaks the framework of illusionism and demystifies itself as a show. Feuer attributes these self-reflexive tendencies to the fundamental heterogeneity of the genre, whose form resides in "the contrast between narrative and number."[8] Such a contrast also lies at the heart of *gechang pian*, notwithstanding the other differences between these and American musicals. As I argue in this chapter, *Songs of the Peach Blossom River* displays a comparable drive to expose and thus demystify the mechanics of musical performance—especially insofar as these are materially grounded in technologies of recording and transmission. To laud the film as a feat of integration is to overlook the way that its song numbers push outward at the edges of the film and open onto a broader sphere of electromagnetic sound media. Many other songstress films offer their audience a unique vantage point onto the technological means by which the singing voice is reproduced and recirculated. But in transposing Feuer's critical observations to the realm of Chinese musical productions, one particular distinction merits further consideration. Unlike Hollywood musicals, where music making is heavily coded as a collective enterprise, laden with values of communality and folk culture, in *gechang pian* it devolves on the solo female singer. Given the uneven distribution of musical labor in this body of films, and their obsessive focus on the feminine lyrical voice, the effects of this structural heterogeneity concentrate around the figure of the songstress, who embodies the transitions between narrative and number. The self-conscious quality of Chung's acting and the oscillation between her star persona and the fictional character she portrays thus emerge as direct outcomes of the intrinsic formal disjunctions of *gechang pian*.

From another angle, we might say that Wildcat generates an effect of expressive incoherence, or what James Naremore describes as a breakdown in the unity of the acted persona. According to Naremore, expressive incoherence typically arises as a discord between reality and appearance, for instance in situations of deception, "where we see persons in the drama trying to conceal or repress their 'sincere' feelings."[9] In certain cases, expressive incoherence can extend beyond the bounds of the fiction to manifest itself in a physical manner that goes even further to stage a breakdown in the relationship between actor and role. Naremore makes note of the genre of comedy, which frequently relies on "alienated styles of performance" and "exaggerated forms of bodily incoherence."[10] As Songs of the Peach Blossom River suggests, musical films are another genre in which bodily incoherence tends to be exaggerated, insofar as these films mobilize the performer's body as a vehicle of lyrical expression as well as a medium of the character. In the scene of song, a sense of the physicality of the performing body intervenes in the fictional persona, rendering it unstable and transitive. Speaking a part is fundamentally different from singing a song, as the fixation on integration in the critical discourse about musicals makes clear. What Naremore terms as an incoherence stemming from the split between actor and role might also be described as an effect of doubling. As Scott McMillin argues in his study of musical theater, when the characters in a narrative sing, they undergo a transformation, stepping outside of their role without ever fully leaving it behind. In singing they become "new versions of themselves. . . . They are said to be the same characters, but clearly they are different, and the incongruity is theatrically arresting."[11]

These effects of incoherence and doubling are given yet another twist in Chung Ching's case, for a disjunction between body and voice marks her musical performances. The Little Wildcat was typecast as a songstress for the best part of her career in spite of her lack of vocal talent. Unlike her peer and counterpart Grace Chang, whose vocal powers factored heavily in her filmmaking career, Chung had no aptitude for singing. Consequently, her song scenes were always dubbed. Yet this limitation did not prevent her from building a successful and prolific career as a star of gechang pian, appearing in numerous productions that were each packed with musical interludes. In many of her screen appearances, including Songs of the Peach Blossom River, Chung's songs were dubbed by the pop singer Yao Lee, discussed in the previous chapter. The film's program brochure even features an image of Yao on its cover, attesting to the drawing power wielded by the singer despite her behind-the-scenes role. The film marked the beginning of an enduring partnership between Chung and Yao: the two would collaborate in many subsequent productions, with Yao providing the vocals for Chung's musical scenes. In these films, the act of singing provokes an even more literal sense of doubling, bringing together two performing bodies in an audiovisual palimpsest. Song activates the audience's prior experience of the singing voice, familiar from a reality outside of the fiction, and sets into motion a double articulation of stardom.

The paradox of a songstress who does not actually sing might be interpreted as grounds for Chung's dismissal as an aberration, an outlier in the lineage of the Mandarin songstress. This chapter takes an opposed view, making a claim for Chung as a paradigmatic exemplar of this lineage, precisely because of the insights she offers on the expressive capacities of the songstress. The vagaries of her case help us grasp the core conceptions of performance and dramatic authorship underpinning the *gechang pian*. By attending to the gaps between sound and image, between the aurally and the visually perceived body, between the character and the performer, we can begin to articulate the singing film's distinctive performance codes and modes of address. This chapter presents disjunction and incoherence as engrained aspects of the *gechang pian* and the musical pleasures of the songstress. Approached from this perspective, *Songs of the Peach Blossom River* becomes an illustration of how the performance idiom deployed by the songstress derives its impact from the musical interlude, whose suspension of diegetic time and identity is not readily dismissed. It entails a different relation to and identification with the performer, not only as a character within a fiction but also an embodied agent of musical expression. Moreover, this effect is not confined to the musical sequence per se; rather, it infects the entire narrative topography, giving rise to a proliferation of roles premised on the mutability and permeability of character—doublings, disguises, transferences, transformative makeovers, and the like. The discussion below tracks the interplay of mismatched voices, bodies, identities, and temporalities in the films of Chung Ching, who pushes the songstress's expressive incoherence to its extreme. In her work, we find a persuasive argument for the fundamentally incongruous pleasures of musical performance.

The Rustic Songstress

The idyllic vision of the country that characterizes the rustic singing film is set forth at the outset of *Songs of the Peach Blossom River*, with an opening song number set in a grove of flowering trees on a river bank. A fresh-faced young woman, dressed in a traditional peasant costume with her hair in two braids, wanders singing in the midst of the trees, her verse an ode to the natural beauty that she reflects in her appearance (figure 3.1). A chorus of voices harmonizes with her song and evokes a sense of communal solidarity, which

· · · FIGURE 3.1 · · ·
Chung Ching as the rustic songstress, *Songs of the Peach Blossom River*, 1956.

is also visually anchored in images of rural laborers happily at work and at one with the arcadian setting, rounding out this highly idealized portrait of country life. Song scenes of this kind become a standard introductory number for rustic singing films. They stand in an ambiguous relation to the film—on the one establishing the mise-en-scène and main personages, but on the other hand, taking place in an abstracted time with respect to the story. Such scenes compose a lyrical portrait of the songstress, concentrating on her musical and iconic presence. A more multidimensional sense of her character comes only later, with the switch from musical montage to narrative exposition.

In *Songs of the Peach Blossom River*, such a presentation befits Wildcat's entrance onto the larger stage of Hong Kong cinema. As Sam Ho argues, the film introduced a new songstress archetype to the *gechang pian*: the "farmer's daughter." In his inventory of postwar songstresses, Ho defines the farmer's daughter as a melodious child of nature. Nature itself, he notes, is thematically equated with "goodness, spontaneity and creativity," and the singer with a wholesome and earthy ideal of femininity—with occasional flashes of ferocity, in keeping with the primitivist notions subtending this ideal.[12] In the wake of the film's enthusiastic reception, the farmer's daughter archetype spread as other filmmakers rushed to imitate its formula. Moreover, because of Hong Kong's littoral geography, the pastoral is commonly evoked in a seaside setting, so the farmer's daughter is more often than not in fact a fisherman's daughter. These interrelated types can be subsumed within the more general category of the rustic songstress.

But contrary to what Ho argues, *Songs of the Peach Blossom River* did not wholly invent the rustic songstress. A musical clue to the origins of this figure is proffered in the film's opening musical number. Wildcat performs the song from which the film borrows its title, "Taohua Jiang" ("Peach Blossom River"), composed by Li Jinhui in 1929. The song carries a distinct historical cachet as one of the most popular hits of the prewar period, when *shidai qu* was emerging as an idiom of modern music. Its resonance with the listening public also made the song an object of parody by left-wing composers critical of the decadent and apolitical values that they perceived in *shidai qu*. "Taohua Jiang" appeared in the 1935 film *Xin nüxing* (*New Woman*), set to new lyrics by the film's songwriter Nie Er that transformed it from a paean to the temptations of urban life into a revolutionary anthem about the working-class vanguard— one of what Andrew Jones notes were numerous instances in which popular songs were "rewritten as narratives of national salvation."[13] Thus *Songs of the Peach Blossom River* flaunts its participation in a tradition of cinematic appropriations and recastings of popular songs dating back to the prewar period—a tradition that would reach a new apogee in postwar Hong Kong, where the practice of recycling familiar oldies became a mainstay of the film industry. In this new version, set to lyrics penned by the film's screenwriter Chen Dieyi, the song takes yet another detour in meaning, turning the phrase "Peach Blossom River" into a denotation of rural natural beauty.

Songs of the Peach Blossom River also invokes an earlier period of film history with the name it gives to Chung's character, Wildcat, which recalls another screen icon of a feline and feral bent: the 1930s actress Wang Renmei. Just as the film overwrites a familiar tune of the prewar era, so it reappropriates the image of one of that period's best-known actresses. Wang starred in notable productions of the Shanghai film industry such as *Ye meigui* (*The Wild Rose*, 1932) and *Yu guang qu* (*Song of the Fishermen*, 1934), one of the earliest films to include a theme song. In her heyday Wang was commonly known by the nickname of Wildcat, a reference to the character she portrays in *Song of the Fisherman*, a poor girl from a fishing village named Little Cat.

A closer look at these productions sheds light on the mold from which the rustic songstress is cast. Despite being a silent film, *The Wild Rose* lays a foundation for this archetype with its portrayal of Little Phoenix, played by Wang with panache as a rough-and-tumble, barefoot child of nature. Little Phoenix is motherless and spends her days in the company of her brutish father in the village she calls home, until a man from the city—Jiang Bo, a painter from a family of wealth and social standing—comes into her life and introduces her to his world. The primitive nature incarnated by Little Phoenix is set into relief by an opposition between the two locales. Alternating between the village and metropolitan Shanghai, the film contrasts her spontaneous ease in the one setting with her conspicuous awkwardness in the other. The wildness projected by Wang is nowhere more apparent than in the scene where Jiang Bo tries to make her over as a civilized young lady so that she can be presented to his father. His scheme ends in utter failure: in a virtuoso scene of physical comedy, Little Phoenix does a full split and tumbles down the stairs while attempting to walk in high-heeled shoes; upends a pastry cart; and unceremoniously adjusts her drooping silk stockings, to the consternation of the elegant company assembled at Jiang Bo's home. The wild child proves to be inassimilable to the civilized urban milieu and is promptly expelled by the patriarch who rules over it. In its inability to comply with the physical and behavioral demands of proper feminine decorum, Little Phoenix's unruly body performs a satirical dissection of modern bourgeois manners. In this satire, we can also discern a counterdiscourse of feminine beauty. Wang Renmei is often considered to be an incarnation of the early twentieth-century physical ideal of *jianmei* (robust beauty), and the rustic types she portrays in productions like *The Wild Rose* display the attributes of athleticism, healthy vigor, and unadorned simplicity prized by *jianmei*'s standard.[14]

In *Song of the Fishermen*, Wang returns to the role of the spirited country lass with her portrayal of Little Cat, the daughter of a poor fishing family. As I discuss in chapter 1, the soundtrack of this early partial-sound production included three performances by Wang of the theme song from which the film takes its name. The film took the important step of endowing the country lass with a singing voice, while presenting song as a key conduit of expression for the values of the countryside, with its plaintive folk ballad about the hard lot of fishermen. The name of Chung's character therefore deliberately conjures up one of the earliest incarnations of the rustic songstress.[15] Between Wang's Little Cat and Chung's Wildcat, we can identify an entire series of singing fishermen's daughters that take their inspiration from the prototype forged by *Song of the Fishermen*. Zhou Xuan portrays one of these in *Yü jia nü* (*The Fisherman's*

Daughter, 1943), made in Shanghai during the Japanese occupation and directed by Bu Wancang. *The Fisherman's Daughter* reprises plot motifs from *The Wild Rose*, with its story about the bond that develops between the wholesome country lass and a painter from the city, whose artistic sensibility leads him to appreciate her pure nature despite their different backgrounds. The film opens with a pastoral ballad performed by the rustic songstress on a boat as she returns from the day's fishing. Bu was part of the wave of migrants from Shanghai to Hong Kong, and in 1956 he remade his own film as the vogue for rustic singing films was taking off. The remake, *Yü ge* (*The Fisherman's Daughter*), featured Linda Lin Dai in the role originally played by Zhou Xuan.[16] Many other prominent singing actresses—such as Grace Chang and Julie Yeh Feng—played the part of the rustic songstress at some point in their career.[17]

A survey of these productions discloses the thematic elements, narrative structures, and musical motifs that define the rustic songstress cycle. Its stories center on female protagonists who live in humble circumstances with their fathers. Like Wildcat, other rustic songstresses are bereft of maternal love, and their fathers are consistently painted as rough types who are ill suited to understand them with any depth. The fate of the rustic songstress is to fall in love with a man who enters her sheltered world as an outsider, and whose romantic interest in her is piqued by the sound of her voice. Although the wave of rustic singing films crested in the late 1950s, their basic formula, iconography, and folk melody sounds were revived some years later in the Shaw Brothers' blockbuster *Shan ge lian* (*The Shepherd Girl*, 1964), starring Yeh as a singing shepherdess and featuring indigenous songs from the Xiangnan, Jiangsu, and Shandong regions.[18] Yeh's character falls in love with a fisherman passing through her village, and the developing feelings between the two are conveyed in the form of the duet, with a call-and-response structure that alternates between the male and female voice. With its frequent recourse to such duets, the rustic singing film creates a limited space for the male singer, in contrast to the prevailing exclusion of men from vocal participation in musical spectacles.[19] The first encounter between the two characters occurs across an expanse of space, when the fisherman hears Yeh's singing from a hilltop and calls out to her from his boat. Back and forth, they engage in a flirtatious repartee without ever laying eyes on one another, the harmonization of their voices predicting the eventual unification of the couple. As a preview article on *The Shepherd Girl* states, this is a story of "love at first sound."[20]

Similarly in *Songs of the Peach Blossom River*, music is the chosen medium of courtship for Wildcat. Early in the film, when her father urges her to respond to the advances of a young man from their village, she reminds him that her mother agreed to marry him only after he serenaded her for three nights, insisting that she will accept no less from any of her own would-be suitors. Shortly thereafter, Wildcat meets a man from the city who is attracted by her singing. He introduces himself as Li Ming, tells her that he has come to the country from Hong Kong in search of folk songs, and asks Wildcat to come to his home so that he can record her songs. When Wildcat demands that he prove his seriousness by singing to her for three nights, he gladly rises to the challenge and, after a moonlight duet between the two, she grants his wish. But although *Songs of the Peach Blossom River* raises the expectation of a vocal match between its rustic songstress and the man from the city, this ultimately proves to be a red herring. We soon learn that Li's primary function is to cultivate Wildcat's talents as her coach and impresario, rather than to assume the role of lover or companion.

The detouring of their relationship from romance into a different register corresponds to an abrupt shift in the story's geographic locus. Halfway through the film, Wildcat's secluded existence is ended by a montage of images of fleeing refugees on mountain paths, set to the sounds of falling bombs, artillery fire, and dramatic orchestral accompaniment. These scenes of war give way to a series of images of Hong Kong's cityscape: aerial views of the skyline, Western-style architecture, dense thickets of commercial signs, and electric trams. We return to Wildcat in this new environment, where she is wandering the streets alone after having lost her father in the exodus from the village. She miraculously reconnects with Li Ming in this unfamiliar metropolis, as a result of a chain of events triggered when she hears one of her own tunes playing on the radio. Li's interest in her songs, it turns out, was motivated by entrepreneurial impulses. Since his return to Hong Kong, he has been making a success in the music industry by producing Wildcat's folk songs and forming a song-and-dance troupe—one of whose singers, Miss Fang, he has married. He invites Wildcat to join the troupe. She accepts and subsequently makes a smashing debut on the stage. Her public appearance leads to a reunion with her old sweetheart from the village, by another stroke of coincidence. The drama concludes with a celebratory outing by the entire group to watch a movie titled "Taohua jiang"—an ending that affords another glimpse of city lights and modern nightlife, shot on location outside the Victoria Theater. By the end of the film, Wildcat is no longer recognizable as the village girl she once was. *Songs of the Peach Blossom River* revives the rustic songstress only to stage her disappearance in the modern world.

What motivates the film's sudden relocation from country to city is never fully elucidated for the viewer. But the portrayal of battle and flight in the transitional montage sequence, followed immediately by Wildcat's arrival in an urban environment identified as Hong Kong, would certainly have been understood as an allusion to the recent wars by audiences for whom the experience of displacement and migration was still a recent memory. In its highly allusive and roundabout method of referring to these events, *Songs of the Peach Blossom River* conforms to the conventions of a period when colonial censors forbade any explicit mention of recent political events such as the Nationalist-Communist conflict. Consequently filmmakers resorted to a code in which the countryside represented the lost homeland and the city stood for the colonial port of Hong Kong.[21] This code was not restricted to filmic representations, but also operated across a range of mass media. We see it at work, for instance, in an August 1954 issue of the pictorial journal *Young Companion Illustrated* (*Liangyou huabao*), which contains a two-page spread titled "Views of the Hometown."[22] The spread is dominated by a collage of photographic views of Fujian's picturesque rural landscape, and the accompanying text reads: "Rice, buffaloes, hills, valleys, streams and villages of Fukien stir up our feelings for the country we have left behind." Elaborating the point in more sentimental terms, the article goes on to describe these as images from an exile's beautiful dream, offerings for the many who have "left their beloved hometown for a strange alien land, to lead a wanderer's existence."[23]

In consideration of the tacit subtext that weighs the country-city antinomy, many critics have viewed the film's happy ending in allegorical terms. Teo describes it as an affirmation of Hong Kong itself, unlike earlier films that treated the port city as "a vague urban locality standing in for Shanghai." In his reading, Hong Kong now "comes into its own as a place of both the mind and the heart," no longer erased by a nostalgic gaze fixed on the lost homeland.[24] The reconstitution of community and the professional success achieved by Wildcat at the film's conclusion reflect an optimistic view of the rosy future that awaits the migrant in her newly adopted home. Such an interpretation is borne out by the peculiarity of the film's pastoral imaginary. The documentary views of the cityscape that set the stage for the second part of the story—containing real buildings, streets, and people—contrast sharply with the plastic artifice of the country setting. In its visualization of rural life, *Songs of the Peach Blossom River* dispenses with attempts at scenic naturalism. The few location shots of the countryside that appear in the opening musical interlude only serve to underscore the fakeness of the sets where most of its scenes take place, as if to flaunt the phantasmatic basis of its rural vision. In the very act of galvanizing the *xiangcun gechang pian* trend, the film simultaneously exorcises the fantasy to which it speaks, dissolving the timeless arcadia of Peach Blossom River in the streams of modern life. And in this paradox we begin to discern the film's critical import as a work disclosing the complex layers that constitute the rustic as a conjured image of the past, steeped in a preestablished filmic repertory and refracted through the concerns of the present. To the extent that the film displays its own negotiations between past and present with a notable degree of transparency—acknowledging the fragility of its nostalgic pastoral vision in the very act of leaving it behind—it also presents us with an especially rich case study through which to track the historical resonances carried by the figure of the rustic songstress.

In the Shanghai tradition of filmmaking, the countryside is painted in an idealized light, as a locus of virtue, honesty, and fraternity. This idyllic portrait is consistently set in stark opposition to the fallen and ethically bankrupt world of the city, in keeping with what Yingjin Zhang describes as an anti-urbanist strain of thought subscribing to "a fundamental suspicion of the moral implications of the modern city."[25] The city stands for a set of values that must be repudiated—even at the cost of the songstress herself, who must remain true to her roots as a child of nature. The insistence on the authenticity of her character seems to necessitate her demise when she leaves her natural rustic habitat, as the outcome and proof of her innocence and incorruptibility. The misfortunes of so many fishermen's daughters mirror the vulnerability of a social habitus imperiled by modernity, with their exposure to the city resulting in adversity, madness, or death—all outcomes that reinforce the radical incommensurability and spiritual divide that separates these realms. But in contrast with the negative image that we see in a film like *The Wild Rose* (where the story's transposition across the two locales is announced with the sardonic intertitle, "Our so-called prosperous city") or *The Song of the Fisherman* (where Shanghai is praised as a wonderful place by a blind character who cannot see its true ugliness), *Songs of the Peach Blossom River* offers an image of the metropolis purged of cruelty, rapacity, and ironic editorial commentary. Although Wildcat follows in the footsteps of the many rustic heroines who precede her, the end result is her good fortune, not the tragedy and suffering encountered by her predecessors. Just as the city no longer automatically stands in for Shanghai, so the image of the metropolis sheds its previous associations with corruption, decadence, and danger in the Shanghai filmmaking tradition and acquires a new set of inflections when it is overwritten in the image of Hong Kong.[26]

Wildcat's journey also retraces a path mapped out by predecessors like Yueying in *Two Stars in the Milky Way* (1931), another country girl whose songs are overheard. The premise of the natural-born singer inducted into a glamorous life of stardom is taken up in countless songstress films that frame this passage by a narrative of professionalization. In many iterations of this familiar tale, the making of the star is followed by her unmaking, and the gains of fame and fortune are eventually reversed in a downward spiral of loss, heartbreak, or tragedy. Recall that for Yueying, career success leads to personal heartbreak and her ultimate retreat from the silvery world of stardom. As cautionary tales on the dangers of quick riches and hedonistic gratification, such narratives are steeped in the anti-urbanist sensibility of the leftist filmmaking tradition. *Songs of the Peach Blossom River*, however, dispenses with such pedagogical aims. It weaves a dream of stardom not to finally deflate it, but rather to augment its potency by linking it to a fantasy of upward mobility. Along the way, the familiar leftist critique of urban modernity is supplanted by an unreservedly aspirational view of class mobility. The film draws on an entrenched country-city dichotomy only to break down its ideological underpinnings, presenting the city as a place of possibility and promise, where economic rewards await those who have the determination to face up to its conditions. The values distinguishing the two realms lose much of their distinction in the rustic songstress's felicitous transposition from the one to the other.

The Detachable Voice

Just as *Songs of the Peach Blossom River* composes an idealized mise-en-scène of pastoral life only to turn away from it, so it constructs the figure of the rustic songstress only to have her be transformed into something quite different by the film's end. Devices like the camera, tape recorder, microphone, and radio all play a role in this transformation, as the film spotlights the various devices and media that facilitate Wildcat's makeover from child of nature to urban denizen. The marvels of technology come to stand for the city itself, and the rustic songstress's introduction to these marvels marks a crucial step in her gradual assimilation, rather than absolute alterity, to urban modernity. This assimilation process begins early in the film, when she first meets the man from the city, Li Ming. When he tells her that he is from Hong Kong, her curiosity is aroused and she responds, "That's a big city, isn't it?" The meeting also marks her introduction to a mechanical recording device. After complimenting Wildcat on her singing, Li reaches for the camera hanging around his neck, tells her to hold still, and snaps a photograph. In complete bafflement, Wildcat points to his camera and asks, "What is that?" "A camera," he replies. "What does it do?" "It takes photos." As in *The Wild Rose*, the callow innocence of the country lass is registered in her lack of familiarity with the accouterments of modern life. The situation is reprised in a scene that soon follows, involving the recording of sound rather than image. Li invites Wildcat to the home of his country relatives so that he can make a recording of her song. Her naïve response to the effects of playback repeats the comedic effect of the country rube confronted with a modern unknown: she stares in amazement at the tape recorder, approaches it, hesitantly touches it, and even sniffs it. Li Ming proceeds to tell her about all of the other marvelous machines to be found in the city, like the phonograph and the radio, which he describes as a box that one can turn on to listen to "songs, opera, storytelling, and many other things; no matter where the song is sung, you can listen in your home."

Li's words prove to be prophetic, for Wildcat's journey from country to city is plotted by the film as a series of encounters with instruments of recording and reproduction. The series begins with photography (when she sees her picture for the first time, Wildcat exclaims, "This drawing looks just like me!"), proceeds to the tape recorder, and then crosses over to broadcast media. After landing in Hong Kong, she hears a radio playing in a café and is shocked to recognize the song as one of her own—"Hua er bi jie er," performed by her earlier in the film. To the amusement of the other characters inside the café, she demands, "Where is the singer?" The answer to this query comes in the scene that follows, which takes place outside a nightclub as loudspeakers transmit the performance taking place within. By a stroke of lucky coincidence, Wildcat hears her song again as she walks past the nightclub and thus learns the identity of the singer from the placard advertising the show. She approaches the singer, Miss Fang, who happens to be married to Li Ming and brings Wildcat to him. During their reunion, he convinces Wildcat to join his stage troupe and maps out his grand vision for her, which includes a career as a recording artist and television performer. The final scene of *Songs of the Peach Blossom River*, when they all go the movies, holds a mirror to the film itself as the endpoint of this technological series. As the story progresses, the mediated existence for which the songstress is destined becomes increasingly apparent.

Thus the film telescopes a span of entertainment media and reproductive technologies—recapitulating these as it establishes its own belonging to this larger, mass-mediated cultural industry, not just as a constituent element but as a point of culmination. The concluding image of the urban picture palace stands in stark contrast to the natural setting in which Wildcat is introduced, where her song is accessible only to a small, physically present community of listeners. But consonant with its departure from a tradition that sets an idealized vision of rural life against the vices of the city, the film likewise retreats from a nostalgic stance that would privilege the spontaneous and intimate mode of performance presented in the first scene. If technologies of recording and transmission interrupt the organic circuit of pastoral performance, turning the rustic songstress into a mediated voice and image, the endpoint of this process is not the disenchantment of her music. Far from favoring the immediate over the mediated, spontaneity over mechanical repetition, or the original song of nature over its recirculation in an urbanized commodity sphere, *Songs of the Peach Blossom River* redeems this technological progression as the basis for the restitution of historical trauma and the rectification of a broken social order. Only by relinquishing her song to the apparatus is Wildcat able to rediscover it, and thus to be refound herself, in a narrative recuperation of the uncanny effects of recording. Far from a force of alienation, technology operates as an instrument for the restitution of community, capable of overcoming the daunting conditions of urban life. It delivers the songstress to the rosy future held in store by the city.

The scenes of recording described above, in their staging of a primal encounter with the apparatus, also recall a trope of early cinema in which the mimetic powers of technological media are registered in their mystification of a viewer who is ignorant of the processes at work in the manufacturing of illusion. Consider, for instance, the 1902 short *Uncle Josh at the Moving Picture Show*, where the overexcited Uncle Josh tears down the screen in his attempt to interact with the lifelike figures projected onto it. In such scenes, the depiction of the apparatus becomes a self-reflexive display by which the film discloses its own mechanical operations. We encounter a similar moment of disclosure in *Songs of the Peach Blossom River*, one centering on the relation of sound and image, in the scene in which Li Ming records Wildcat's voice. It begins with a long shot of Wildcat singing into a microphone while Li looks on with delight and operates a magnetic tape recorder. The sound of her voice continues over a dissolve into a medium close-up of Li. The camera then pans back to Wildcat staring at the device in wonder as her song is played back to her (figures 3.2–3.5). The temporal interval between the actions of recording and replaying is elided in the sonic construction of the scene, for the song continues without interruption as the film shifts from one point in time to a later point. Put another way, the scene turns on an ellipsis in time that is visually registered but sonically denied—an inaudible cut, a trick designed to impress on the audience the virtual identity between the live and the technologically mediated voice.[27]

In Wildcat's uncanny confrontation with her recorded voice, we are offered a momentary glimpse into the workings of playback technology. Soundtracks in this period were constructed in the postproduction phase, with playback technology used in the making of song sequences. Actors would move their lips in synch with songs that had been recorded in a studio. The synthesis of sound and image at the end of this process amounts to a technological reintegration of these two separate registers. But if Wildcat's voice breaks free of the singer's body at the moment when she becomes her own listener, it is only to demonstrate that it never really belonged to this body in the first place. The lack of any audible difference between the "live" and replayed performance of the song retroactively reveals liveness itself to be an effect of mediation. On the basis of this opening of a fissure between body and voice, we can begin to draw out the particular terms of the audiovisual contract that *Songs of the Peach Blossom River* holds out to its audience.[28] In doing so, we gain a deeper insight into the logics of sound and image governing the songstress film as a broader category. These contractual terms do not conform to a standard of synchronization that aims at effectively "[binding] the voice to a body in a unity whose immediacy can only be perceived as given," in the words of Mary Ann Doane.[29] The calculated display of technological prowess in the foregoing scene is made at the expense of a necessary, immediate, and self-evident relation of sound and image. No longer the property of the visible body, the voice announces its machinic origins and lays bare the composite nature of song performance as a trick of the playback process, along with the status of the songstress's body as a chimeric sign, divided across the visual and audial registers.

The audiovisual unity that Doane describes above is a product of the illusionism of narrative cinema, whose norms of sound reproduction generally strive to deny the material heterogeneity of the filmed body. Yet in *Songs of the Peach Blossom River*, the disclosure of the mechanisms of playback is unaccompanied by laments for a loss of authenticity, originality, or other such notions of ontological purity—befitting the film's thematic emphasis on the essential reproducibility and detachability of the voice. The film's lack of anxiety about the proper place of the voice, in contrast to the Western cinema to which Doane primarily refers, reflects a different set of practical assumptions about its status and relation to the image. This discrepancy can perhaps be accounted for by the "no film without a song" mentality of postwar Hong Kong film culture, where musical performance was not confined to particular genres

春天的花兒朵朵

春天的花兒朵朵開

· · · FIGURES 3.2–3.5 · · ·
Recording Wildcat's singing, *Songs of the Peach Blossom River*, 1956.

but was pervasive throughout narrative films. As Rick Altman has pointed out, the film musical pushes cinema's constitutive material heterogeneity to a limit, insofar as "more than any other type of film the musical has resorted to dubbing, rerecording, hopping, postsynchronization, and other techniques which involve separate recording of the image and diegetic music."[30] The far-reaching scope of musical spectacle in Hong Kong cinema renders the asynchrony of film performance inescapable, a normal condition hardly meriting disavowal.

The detachability of Chung Ching's singing voice in the scene discussed above may ultimately have been rationalized by the audience's knowledge that this voice did not belong to her in the first place but rather was dubbed by the pop singer Yao Lee. Yao built her reputation as a recording artist in 1930s Shanghai, and her participation in the film's production constitutes another link to the prewar period. The substitution of voices not belonging to the actors, especially during on-screen performances of song, is far from uncommon— although in many contexts, such as Hollywood, the practice tends to be hidden from the public. But Yao's dubbing of Chung's song scenes, far from being hidden or denied, was publicized as a marketing strategy in *Songs of the Peach Blossom River* as well as the many subsequent productions in which the two performers collaborated. Besides Chung, many other well-known actresses of postwar Mandarin cinema relied on professional vocalists to dub their songs. And even in the case of singers who fell short of Yao's celebrity status as the queen of Mandarin pop, the practice of substitute singing was no secret to the public.[31] Playback singers were known as behind-the-screen singers, and their names were regularly included in film credits, inscribed on song sheets, and featured on the covers of record releases of film songs.

The Duplicity of Vocal Performance

The partnership between Chung Ching and Yao Lee calls to mind the conventions of another regional cinema distinguished for its emphasis on musical expression. As Neepa Majumdar discusses in her study of Hindi cinema, although song sequences were introduced to Indian filmmaking with the beginnings of sound, until the 1940s a certain unease surrounded the practice of dubbing film songs with the voices of people other than the actors. Concerns about the mismatch between voices and bodies abounded in the filmic discourse of this period, and the habit of referring to film singers as "ghost voices" reflected the marginalization and erasure of these uncredited artists.[32] By the 1950s, a shift had taken place: the nonidentity of voice and body had become the norm as the singers began to acquire a star identity of their own, independent of the movie actor. This shift was registered linguistically in the replacement of "ghost voices" by "playback singers" who had well-known and marketable names—the most famous being Lata Mangeshkar, who more than any other single vocalist dominated the soundscape of Hindi cinema in the second half of the twentieth century. As the singing voice emerged as an aural locus of fan identification and idealization, Majumdar writes, what mattered "was no longer whether the voice and body matched, but whether the singing voice was recognizable in and of itself."[33] From this point in time, "Hindi cinema's song sequences simultaneously draw upon two different star texts, those of the singer and of the actor. Putting together the ideal voice with the ideal body results in an ideal cinematic construct, a composite star."[34] In Majumdar's analysis, the composite star is rooted in a particular kind of audiovisual contract: "Song performances are here authenticated precisely through knowledge of the star persona of the singing voice. The morality of vocal substitution becomes irrelevant when the dual star reference makes it *equally a question of borrowing a body or of borrowing a voice*."[35]

In Hindi cinema we find a case for comparison that sheds light on the modes of musical expression driving the songstress film.[36] In Hong Kong just as in India, song performance was a universal feature of popular cinema, and the landscape of popular music was heavily populated by film songs. The conditions for the emergence of the composite star are discernible in both contexts, with film songs claiming a life beyond the film as independent cultural commodities. (In contrast, in American cinema in this period, Alan Williams notes, "the musical, to be successful, did not *need* good songs, merely serviceable songs" whose life did not extend far beyond the film.[37]) For a parallel example of the recognition commanded by Indian playback singers, we can look to the image of Yao Lee's visage printed on the cover of the playbill for *Songs of the Peach Blossom River* (figure 3.6). As this marketing maneuver suggests, Yao's star power equaled or exceeded that of the many actresses whose song performances she dubbed. Hers was one of the most recognizable voices of postwar popular Chinese music, and her celebrity was boosted further by the frequent publicity she received in movie journals like *International Screen*. Moreover, far from being unique in its approach to film music, *Songs of the Peach Blossom River* has a precedent in the early sound era of Chinese cinema, when songs were also sometimes dubbed by famous vocalists rather than the actors themselves. As Zhang Zhen has pointed out, in the earliest years of synchronized sound technology "the possibility of conflating the singing voice of an opera star (such as Mei Lanfang in the case of [*Songstress Red Peony*]) and the face of a film star like Hu Die was one of the attractions of the sound film."[38]

桃花江

The example of Hindi cinema further serves to delineate the ways in which different logics of audiovisual presentation can give rise to divergent forms of performance and audience identification. Pamela Wojcik argues that in the classical Hollywood movie, "integration of body and voice becomes key to perceptions of 'authentic' film acting; the recorded voice is effaced as recorded, assumed to emanate from the actor's body."[39] (This limited conception of acting is illustrated in the bylaws of the Academy for Motion Picture Arts and Sciences, Wojcik points out, which state explicitly that actors whose voices have been dubbed by others cannot be nominated for the Academy Award for acting.) In contrast, the composite singing star described by Majumdar activates the audience's knowledge and pleasure at different levels, beyond a straightforward belief in the illusionistic copresence of voice and body.[40] An enjoyment of the momentary fusion of these separate entities does not preclude, but rather coexists with, an awareness of the material heterogeneity of the performing body in the musical interlude. As *Songs of the Peach Blossom River* suggests, a similar mode of reception occurs with *gechang pian*, where the pleasures of absorption into a self-contained diegetic universe are intercepted by a metadiegetic interplay of borrowed voices and borrowed bodies. The spectacle of the film song centers on the performing body as an audiovisual composite and a pleasurable oscillation of different star identities—the one seen but unheard, the other invisible yet audible. This oscillation also inscribes a temporal dimension, given the generational difference between the two stars—one firmly planted in the postwar generation, the other possessing a voice laden with associations of the soundscape of the prewar period.

Another contemporary film featuring Yao Lee's songs reveals the other possible directions that such an interplay might take. Yao made very few screen appearances in her career, despite providing the vocals for numerous films. One exception is *Gemi xiaojie* (*Miss Songbird*, 1959), in which she makes a cameo appearance. The film stars another well-known postwar songstress, Julie Yeh Feng, as a staunch Yao Lee fan and aspiring chanteuse. Early in the film, Yeh's character attends an open recording session taking place at Pathé-EMI's studios in hopes of meeting her idol. The scene, shot on location in Causeway Bay, offers filmgoers an opportunity to witness the inner workings of the recording studio as well as Yao's performance.[41] The singer approaches the microphone to perform "Good Flowers Don't Always Blossom," and in the course of the song, the camera alternates between shots of Yao in medium close-up and views of the conductor and musicians playing alongside her, the engineer in the sound booth, and the window through which Yeh watches the session from an adjoining room. At the end of the session, the latter rushes into the studio hoping to meet Yao and is disappointed to discover that she has already departed. Her wish is realized at the end of the film, however, when the two finally meet and perform alongside one another in a concert.[42]

Miss Songbird features many musical interludes with Yeh playing the songstress role, her songs dubbed by Yao (although Yeh would later become a singer in her own right). The scene at Pathé's studio marks yet another instance of technological self-reference, revealing not only the mechanics of musical recording but also the site where the film's songs were produced. Yao's appearance here precipitates a further disclosure, for as in *Songs of the Peach Blossom River*, the scene of recording introduces a split between body and voice. The same voice attached to Yeh's body in the preceding song scenes is now visually "returned" to Yao; a few scenes later, it migrates back to its original anchor when Yeh's character launches into another song. The thematic bond of admiration and emulation tying the fictional character to the real-life chanteuse here motivates a transfer of the voice through space and from body to body. As if to acknowledge the duplicity of this interchangeable voice, the film delays the face-to-face meeting between the two songstresses and thus avoids the strange echo effect that such a meeting would entail. The culminating song number of *Miss Songbird* brings the two together in a joint performance that cleverly solves the one voice–two body problem in its orchestration. The number begins with Yao Li taking the stage, announced as the "queen of modern pop." After she performs a song, she introduces the younger singer. There is a cut to Yeh as she makes an unexpected entrance from the rear of the room and then, crooning the film's theme song, winds her way through the crowd before joining Yao on the stage. The uncanny repetition of the same voice across these consecutive song performances is mitigated by the cut and its cuing of a perceptible spatial distance between the two singers. The voice is tossed like a ball from one body to the other, and the two come together in the same shot only after the voice has had time to properly detach itself from the one image and settle into the other.

The playful interchange of voices and bodies in *Miss Songbird* corroborates the sense that the *gechang pian* entails a distinctive idiom of performance, one flexible enough to accommodate a shifting field of sound-image correspondences. To the extent that it functions as a conduit of musical expression, the voice becomes detachable and autonomous, floating in and out of character. The musical number invites an altered perception of the body as a material audiovisual entity. Moreover, this effect is not confined to instances of behind-the-screen singing, when the voice does not belong to the actress, or even to the musical interlude. Rather, it infects the entire performative range of the songstress as a figure in whom the character as a naturalistically integral entity yields to other forms of cinematic presence. In her position at the crossroads of different representational modes, the songstress raises a question—what happens to acting in its proximity to music spectacle? And returning to Naremore's phrase, what other forms of expressive incoherence are activated by her performance? The remaining sections of this chapter explore these questions in connection with Chung Ching's films. The analysis is guided by Richard Dyer's observation that the inclusion of the musical number necessarily spins the rules of performance. Musicals (and comedies) rely on an acting style that is "problematic in relation to novelistic character," he writes, leading to "shifts of performance gear between comic and/or musical sections of a film and the rest of it." This makes it "particularly interesting to study such shifts of gear for the mischief they may do to the assumptions of the non-comic or non-musical aspects of a film."[43] Such mischievous effects find an especially vivid animation in Chung's roles.

Xinhua rehashed the winning combination of Chung Ching's image and Yao Li's voice in a series of *gechang pian* made during the three years after the release of *Songs of the Peach Blossom River*. Among these is *Bai hua gongzhu* (*Flower Princess*, 1959), whose title refers to Chung's character, a teenager working in her family's florist shop. Viewing the film alongside *Songs of the Peach Blossom River*, one is immediately struck by its higher production values and technical polish, strikingly modern décor and mise-en-scène, and Eastmancolor palette. The stylistic contrast between the two films is far greater than the three years separating their production would otherwise suggest—a testimony not only to the rising fortunes of Xinhua but also to the rapid development of the Hong Kong film industry at this historical juncture. Yet many elements of *Flower Princess* also hark back to the earlier film. The opening musical number is set in a field of flowers that visually evokes the pastoral backdrop of *Songs of the Peach Blossom River* and the lyrical formula of the nature ballad. The number introduces the character of Yueying, singing the praises of spring blossoms as she harvests flowers from a country field and transports them on her bicycle to the florist shop. Along the way, she passes by a large Coca-Cola sign. Clearly this is not the world of a prewar village, so we find the farmer's daughter updated as the florist's daughter, sporting the modernized garb of a tomboyish teenager—capri pants, colorful jumper, and a knit cap pulled over a braided ponytail—while still retaining her predecessor's air of unaffected vivacity. To the extent that she appears equally at home in rural and urban settings, the flower princess embodies the integration of these realms in a smoothly functioning commercial enterprise. Her movement across these spaces is tied to her contribution to the family business, as both a diligent worker and a dutiful child.

Flower Princess derives much of its interest from the conceit of the double role, with Chung playing two separate characters (figures 3.7 and 3.8). Unlike the florist's daughter hard at work in the fields, the second character is introduced as a figure who is draped odalisque-style on a settee. Our first glimpse consists of a shot of immaculately pedicured feet; the camera pans right to reveal bare legs and then a torso garbed in a sumptuous emerald gown, and finally comes to rest on Chung's heavily made-up face. We find ourselves in the lavishly decorated apartment of Miss Ding, a former nightclub singer now living off the largesse of her many admirers. Her demeanor throughout the film remains true to the cartoonish portrait of the vamp presented here. Miss Ding

··· FIGURES 3.7–3.8 ···
Chung Ching's double role in *Flower Princess*, 1959.

walks with an exaggerated wiggle of the hips and seductive simper, eliciting a chorus of whistles in her wake. Occasionally she throws champagne parties for her suitors, who for their part shower her with expensive presents. Both characters have an aptitude for singing, with Yueying spontaneously bursting into song at regular intervals throughout the film, and Miss Ding unveiling her musical talents at one of her parties. But despite their similar looks, they represent polarized types: the one a wholesome teenager, the other a calculating gold digger. The narrative link between the two characters comes in the form of Fang, a young man who rents a room in the house where Yueying lives with her parents and tutors her in English. Yueying harbors an unrequited crush on Fang, who is in turn enamored of Miss Ding, despite the fact that she repeatedly rebuffs his overtures. Thus the plot of *Flower Princess* hangs on a love triangle between a man and two women who appear identical.

The casting of stars in double roles was a fairly common practice in postwar Hong Kong cinema, although in contemporary practice it is more commonly encountered in the realm of art cinema than commercial filmmaking. To offer some examples, in *Jin lianhua* (*Golden Lotus*, 1957), Lin Dai plays both the poor songstress with whom the male lead falls in love and the genteel woman his family forces him to marry. In *Xiangrufeifei* (*Sweet Sister-in-Law*, 1958), the bombshell actress Diana Chang Chung-wen plays a pair of identical twins. *Qian mian nülang* (*Girl of a Thousand Guises*, 1959) presents Grace Chang in a mother-daughter double role, embedding the mother's story as an extended flashback. Chang again portrays two different characters in *Ti xiao yinyuan* (*A Story of Three Loves*, 1964), an impoverished street singer and her wealthy rival in love. Lucilla You Min plays a mortal woman and her immortal look-alike in *Zhenzhu lei* (*Her Pearly Tears*, 1962). As these examples suggest, double roles in this period were dominated by actresses.[44] The double typically finds a narrative basis in a family resemblance, as in the mother-daughter and twin motifs, or in the fantastic realm of deceptive spirits. Sometimes it is attributed to pure coincidence—as in *Flower Princess*, where no explanation is offered for the physical resemblance between Yueying and Miss Ding, even though the other characters remark on it with astonishment. In many instances, the doubled presence of the actress functions rhetorically to draw a contrast: differences are set into sharper relief against the background of surface resemblance. Here they acquire a further narrative significance through a romantic counterpart who must choose one of the two characters. Thus *Flower Princess* lays out a series of binaries as it alternates between Yueying and Miss Ding, with the rather clueless Fang caught in the middle: naiveté and worldliness, naturalness and artifice, spontaneity and affectation, sincerity and cynicism, kindness and cruelty, and production and consumption. Yueying labors diligently and loans Fang money for flowers and presents to lavish on Miss Ding, out of concern and affection for him. Her look-alike spends her time lounging about and extracting offerings from her suitors, and she shows only contempt for Fang.

Commenting on double casting in postwar Mandarin cinema, Chiao Hsiung-ping points out that the practice has a direct precedent in the Shanghai tradition. She cites a well-known classic of leftist filmmaking, *Zimei hua* (*Twin Sisters*, 1933), in which Hu Die plays two sisters separated since early childhood. One is left to an impoverished existence in the countryside with her mother; the other is taken by her father to the city, where she leads a comfortable and privileged existence. The two unwittingly cross paths when the poor sister is hired as a nursemaid by her wealthy sibling, and their kinship finally comes to light after a melodramatic turn of events. In *Twin Sisters*, the double role serves as the basis for a parallel structure highlighting the disparities between the siblings' social identity. Despite their shared blood, one is a member of the ruling class, pampered and imperious, while the other is a member of the working class, humble and struggling for survival. The parallel drawn between the two characters ultimately serves a critique of class hierarchy, with the sisters' divergent fates framed as the outcome of social injustice. In Chiao's reading, the reappearance of the double role in postwar Hong Kong evidences the lingering influence of the Shanghai filmic tradition. The figure of the double, she argues, held a special appeal for émigré filmmakers, reflecting their own dislocated sense of self. Corroborating the connection drawn by Chiao, we can discern the traces of *Twin Sisters* in the class distinctions highlighted by the double in films like *Golden Lotus* and *A Story of Three Loves*, or even in the contrast drawn by *Flower Princess* between Yueying as a worker and Miss Ding as the stereotypical female consumer.

For Chiao, however, the significance of the double changes markedly from the prewar to the postwar period. The political meaning that *Twin Sisters* attaches to the double recedes into the background, and consequently the trope becomes the exclusive province of the historical romance, romantic comedy, and melodrama. In the context of a film culture catering mainly to a collective desire to escape from reality, she argues, the social-realist edge of the double is blunted, devolving into a gimmick whose only purpose is to elicit comedic and pathetic effects.[45] Chiao's analysis usefully calls attention to the broad ideological divide that separates these golden ages of Mandarin cinema, yet it fails to provide a more nuanced insight into the changing ideological valences of the double in time. The distinction she draws rehearses the terms of a key polemical battle of the leftist era, the "hard film" versus "soft film" debate, which pitted cinema's political efficacy against its entertainment value. But even in its time, this distinction was unstable, as evidenced by the critical responses garnered by *Twin Sisters*. Paul Clark has observed that the film was viewed with ambivalence by left-wing critics. For instance, Tang Na, writing in 1934, described the film as being expressive of "the reality of social inequality," but also steeped in a "petit-bourgeois backward fantasy of social harmony."[46] Whatever their political convictions, filmmakers still had to defer to popular tastes. As polyvalent texts, films readily lend themselves to multiple, even dissonant, messages.

The latter are readily detected in *Twin Sister*'s twofold presentation of its star, Hu Die, as it registers the emotional impact of injustice in the decidedly nonprogressive feminine stereotypes of the suffering woman of virtue and the decadent modern woman. Indeed, the gendering of the double complicates Chiao's reading, bringing into view a set of ideological meanings that do not neatly map onto a leftist class critique. These same gender stereotypes continue to inform the double vision of *Flower Princess*, with Chung Ching's alternating depiction of heroine and villain—the virtuous worker with the desexualized tomboy demeanor, on the one hand, and the smoldering siren with mercenary motives, on the other hand. The double meaning of the star's body becomes symptomatic of the ideological incoherence of the cinematically represented female body, which is at once exploited as an object of display and sexual objectification (Miss Ding) and idealized with reference to ethical and disciplinary discourses of family and capitalism (Yueying). In the double role, it is as if the centrifugal pressure of the dueling mandates with which the actress must comply results directly in the splitting of the star herself. The need to have the female body both ways is answered by the multiplication of that body. In this regard, a postwar film like *Flower Princess* does not so much neutralize the critical sensibility of an earlier filmmaking tradition as it highlights the conflicting discourses and agendas that have all along constituted this tradition. The double brings to the surface underlying tensions between didacticism and entertainment and between the female body as good and bad object that are common to both periods.[47]

Furthermore, the notion of amusement value cannot fully account for the persistence of the double role in postwar film culture, given that narrative cinema as a general rule shies away from the practice. Double casting inevitably comes at the expense of a significant degree of narrative plausibility, as it calls attention to the artifice of dramatic enactment. The work of performance is foregrounded, and a gap opens up between the role and the actor, who becomes visible to the audience as an actor rather than as a singular fictional persona.

To borrow a phrase from Jean Comolli, the double role constitutes a case of the "body too much," which can only interfere in the game of belief that the film plays with its audience.[48] The tight fit between the character and the actor is disrupted by the return of that body in another character. A seam in the fiction is thereby exposed. For these reasons, the use of double role tends to be restricted to films that consciously reflect on questions of performance, identity, history and time, alternate universes, and other forms of virtuality.[49] When deployed in a classical realist mode, it typically requires a narrative pretext (such as identical twins) or a generic dispensation (for example, science fiction, horror, and other fantastical genres that mine the uncanny terrain of the doppelgänger). The prevalence of the double in Hong Kong popular films with a realistic setting therefore warrants further attention.

As *Flower Princess* alternates between Yueying and Miss Ding, and as Chung Ching switches between these roles, this oscillation becomes a source of fascination in its own right. The differences between the two characters become an opportunity for the actress to showcase her range as a dramatic player. The naturalism sacrificed by the trick of the double is therefore recuperated in the spectacle of performance, with the audience's interest held less by the individual characters and more by the display of Chung's acting skills as she switches between different personas.[50] Thus the spectacle of role-playing itself supplants the character's believability and psychological realism as a dramatic objective. A further emphasis is placed on impersonation and the transfer of personas when Yueying schemes to disguise herself as Miss Ding in order to deceive Fang. With this plot development, we find Chung playing not just two characters, but also one of them in the act of imitating the other. The binary structure of the double gives way to an even more fungible interchange of identities, and impersonation acquires a momentum with which the narrative struggles to keep pace. Rather than the performance of a role, what we witness in *Flower Princess* is better described as a performance of performance—a metaperformance. Thus we find ourselves back in the domain of expressive incoherence, as a routine effect of "acting persons who are acting," to return to Naremore's formulation.[51]

The same combination of doubling and impersonation that injects *Flower Princess* with a playfully self-conscious, almost campy, quality arises with surprising frequency in postwar cinema. An example is *Sweet Sister-in-Law*, in which Diana Chang Chung-wen plays twin sisters: the older one a buttoned-up housewife who quarrels incessantly with her husband, and the younger a free-spirited sophisticate who flies in from Paris to pay her sister a visit. When the older sister's husband begins to flirt with her twin, the two sisters scheme to teach him a lesson, disguising themselves as one another as they encourage his romantic advances. A closer examination of the film brings to light the specific forms of expressive incoherence mobilized by the double, which both evoke and go beyond the definition offered by Naremore. The twin sisters' scheme in *Sweet Sister-in-Law* calls to mind his account of situations of deception in which we see characters assume a mask. In such situations, Naremore writes, expressive incoherence is narratively recuperated as a legible discrepancy between an interior truth and a false surface, rendered visible for the audience if not for the other characters in the fiction. The metaperformance of deception therefore remains confined to the level of plot, whereas "at the level of professional acting itself, the film requires an absolute coherence, so that everyone plays *in character*."[52] The convention of the unified character remains intact, its sense of interiority reinforced and rendered in greater depth, despite a momentary fluctuation of identity.

On the one hand, the ruse in *Sweet Sister-in-Law* works in a similar fashion, insofar as the audience is always in on the joke played on the wayward husband, given access to an omniscient position from which expressive incoherence can be deciphered. But on the other hand, the ultimate effect of the sisters' role-playing is to point to their substitutability, to impress on the audience the ease with which a mask can be assumed or discarded, thereby calling into question the distinction between depth and surface. So when the twins' deception is revealed to the husband at the end of the film, he laughs at his own foolishness and embraces his wife. Desire does not insist on the singularity of its object, but rather reinforces the sense of the two women's interchangeability. The truth behind this game of impersonation, the film seems to suggest, resides not inside these characters, but somewhere on the outside. As Chang moves through every possible permutation of her double role—the older twin, the younger twin, the older twin pretending to be the younger twin, and vice versa—she becomes increasingly difficult to identify with any one of these roles, appearing instead as a constant presence poised at a distance from the diegetic world. As an agent of metaperformance, she occupies a role like that of a showman who mediates between the fiction and the audience. The last shot of the film affirms this status: Zhang looks directly at the camera, gives a playful laugh, and nods her head as if taking a bow.

The connection between the double and the idea of expressive incoherence comes from Majumdar, writing on the prevalence of double casting in Indian cinema. "Doubling films offer many occasions for displaying expressive incoherence," she observes, with their built-in emphasis on the playing of roles and transfer of identities.[53] Here as well, the incoherence of the doubly signifying body is not fully explicable by narrative rationale or character motive. Rather, Majumdar argues, it is a *discursive* incoherence: the double predicates a definition of cinematic fiction as "a palimpsest on which are multiple traces of metanarratives other than the primary one of the immediate film itself."[54] Key among these metanarratives is the star text, which necessarily exceeds the parameters of any given fictional character. The double role in Indian cinema represents the logical outcome of a culture industry heavily invested in stardom, "creating multiple avenues of exposure for the star body within the films."[55] The connection drawn by Majumdar between double casting and the star system is relevant to Mandarin popular cinema, where doubling also functions as an index of star presence. In *Flower Princess*, the appeal of that presence alone seems to warrant Chung Ching's reinscription in the form of multiple characters, in the absence of a narrative motive for doubling. And in *Sweet Sister-in-Law*, a film entirely constructed around a voyeuristic fascination with Chang Chung-wen's body, doubling serves as a means for the intensified display of that body. It is the physicality of her presence that remains a constant behind all of the alternating façades, so that metaperformance creates the sense of a more direct access to the star, a heightened intimacy that stems from being in on the prank. The gesture of the film's final shot, when the star steps outside of her character to directly address the audience, acknowledges a rapport that was there all along in the film.

Becoming a Songstress

The double role is bound up with stardom, Majumdar argues, as the outgrowth of a discourse that strains against the film's textual boundaries. But stardom also inflects the narrative of *Flower Princess* by means of other reflexive strategies. Yueying's scheme does not achieve its goal of deceiving Fang but leads instead to an unanticipated result. She is invited to try out as a performer for a televised song-and-dance program, a job previously turned down by Miss Ding. She pulls off the audition with great success and is offered a contract by the television station. The impression made by Yueying during the audition presents a striking contrast to the clumsiness of her previous attempts to impersonate Miss Ding. Until this point in the story, she has failed to project the worldly self-assurance of the seductress—a failure that highlights the contrast between the natural beauty of the flower princess and the artifice of Miss Ding's brand of femininity. Yet before the camera Yueying undergoes a magical transfiguration, suddenly, and somewhat unbelievably, shedding her ordinary identity as a gawky adolescent to fully inhabit the persona of the glamorous songstress. At this moment, we might very well confuse her with Miss Ding, for the two are no longer distinguishable.

With this ending, the film discloses its ideological break from the leftist tradition. In *Twin Sisters* the parallel identities of worker and bourgeois consumer are rooted in a social universe that is ineluctably divided between the disempowered and their masters. Therefore the overcoming of class inequality and restoration of harmony can be imagined only through a return to a prior state of unity, allegorized in the reunion of the broken family at the story's conclusion. But in *Flower Princess* these categories become permeable against the backdrop of a world defined by social mobility and opportunity. The resolution of social differences thus occurs on a different plane. Yueying's fairy tale of transformation recasts the female consumer as a producer, for whom the trappings of fashion and glamour serve as a working uniform. Those feminized signifiers of consumption that previously stood for frivolity and luxury are recoded as tools for professional achievement and social advancement, crucial instruments in a process of disciplining the self and producing a modern subject. Just as the persona of Miss Ding has been fully internalized by Yueying by the end of the film, so production and consumption are effectively collapsed into one another, in a magical reconciliation made to the measure of a capitalist mythos. In addition, this reconciliation neutralizes the threat of female sexuality embodied by the coquette, while also setting forth a gendered vision of upward mobility.

Such a turn of events recalls the plotline of *Songs of the Peach Blossom River*, which also culminates with Wildcat's makeover from rustic singer to polished stage star. Here as well, the change of identity transpires with a remarkable ease and instantaneity. It is encapsulated in a single sequence, which separates the scene of Wildcat's reunion with Li Ming—when she listens incredulously to his promises of stardom and questions her own ability to realize his vision—and her first appearance onstage. The sequence begins with a shot of an unoccupied, sumptuously furnished bedroom, and as the camera pans to the right, we see a bed with two evening gowns laid on it. A dissolve brings us into the adjoining bathroom, where the camera reverses its pan to reveal first a vanity table covered with toiletries, then Wildcat in a bathtub filled with bubbles, her silhouette visible behind a semitransparent curtain. A cut brings us to the other side of the curtain and lingers there as she launches into a song, "On Cloud Nine," delivering up a fetishic display that focuses as much on the luxuries of modern plumbing as her unclothed body. In *Songs of the Peach Blossom River*, the metamorphosis of the farmer's daughter boils down to a matter of toilette. Within the confines of that bourgeois temple of grooming, the

Western bathroom, and in the hiatus of a bubble bath, a star is born. Unlike her predecessor Little Phoenix—who, despite the head-to-toe makeover she is given, cannot help but betray her rural origins—Wildcat adapts to the unfamiliar metropolis as easily as she steps into a new outfit, in the most literal sense.

In both of these films, expressive incoherence results from a particular version of the familiar star-is-born tale, one that emphasizes the malleability of identity. Dreams of success and achievement are filtered through a tableau of transformation, and professionalization is coded in terms of the feminine concerns of beauty and fashion. These concerns reappear throughout Chung Ching's films and become key components of her star image. In *Love at First Sight*, she again demonstrates that acquiring a new identity is like acquiring a new set of clothes—in this instance, a wardrobe of exquisite dresses that were custom-tailored for another woman but that happen to fit her perfectly. Her character Meili has been mistaken for the fiancée of Zhiming by his wealthy family, following a plane crash that has killed the real fiancée. She is fetched to their hilltop home where, awaiting the arrival of the young master, she bides her time by lounging, sunbathing, and beautifying herself in a manner appropriate to the ornamental role of the scion's wife. The entire narrative can be seen as an extension of the grooming scene in *Songs of the Peach Blossom River*, built on intermittent repetitions of primping, adorning, and changing clothes as well as song performances that often accompany these actions. One of *Love at First Sight*'s many musical numbers is "Shuzhuang ge" ("The Dressing Song"), which is crooned by Chung as she stares into her reflection in a vanity mirror. The lyrics describe the details of her toilette "because," as the song says, "everyone loves feminine beauty." Another of her songs emphasizes the magical instantaneity of this identity change: "Life is too strange, too strange, in a split second I've become a young mistress, young mistress." Eventually Zhiming returns and catches on to her ruse. However, he decides that he prefers her to his deceased fiancée, which leads to a happy romantic resolution.

Love at First Sight attests to the extreme degree to which Chung's roles spotlight themes of class mobility and feminine adornment, even in comparison with the many other films of its time that take fashion as a key source of visual and thematic interest. The amalgamation of the romantic comedy of mistaken identity with a metanarrative of class climbing appears repeatedly in postwar film culture, symptomatic of what has been described as a pervasive "Cinderella complex[,] . . . a belief that anyone might climb to the top from the bottom."[56] In this notion we can discern the ideological sway exerted by the spectacle of metamorphic femininity at this historical moment, when regimes of fashion and beautification emerge as visual building blocks of a postwar capitalist mythos that links economic striving, upward mobility, and self-improvement. Chung's embodiment of this mythic cluster calls to mind the persona of one of her Western contemporaries. As another Cinderella-like figure, Audrey Hepburn was also indelibly linked with the possibilities of self-fashioning against the background of postwar prosperity. Her stardom hinged on what Rachel Moseley describes as a "fairytale narrative of growing up and transformation in which discourses of beauty, dress and class are brought together as social mobility."[57] The parallels between the two performers bring to light another significant aspect of the animal coding of Chung's star image, in which the woman as kitten connotes not just a coy and playful expression of female sexuality, but also what Roland Barthes would describe as a "peculiar thematics" of metamorphosis. Hepburn, Barthes writes, embodies a quality of mutability, of "an infinite complexity of morphological functions," that reflects the values of the contemporary moment.[58] Her star appeal is rooted in a capacity for transformation and a theatrical conception of identity, having "nothing of the essence left in it."[59]

A similar ideal can be discerned in Chung Ching's Wildcat persona, which consists not just of a set of traits that map onto a fixed and determinate character type, but also of an indeterminate reservoir of potentiality and capacity for metamorphosis. The wildcat enacts a perpetual drama of self-reinvention, an unfolding of different versions of the self. The trope of transformative femininity crosses multiple axes of distinction, related to geography, modernity, profession, class, and sexuality. And as Chung demonstrates, these tableaux of transformation are inextricably interwoven with tableaux of musical performance, drawing on the sense of becoming other that is spurred by the act of singing. Across her films, metamorphosis is staged as a musical spectacle—whether in venues like the revue theater and recording studio where the songstress makes her public debut, or in the more private confines of the bathroom and vanity, where her display is addressed to a narcissistic gaze. The performance of song endows the process of self-reinvention with a visible reflection, telos, and platform for exhibition. Song carves out a virtual zone in which transformational femininity finds its most unhindered realization, where the old self can be fully shed for something more desirable. Hence the tendency in her films to signal the endpoint of her transformation with a musical number, as in the conclusion of *Songs of the Peach Blossom River*, which uses the stage as a grand metaphor for self-fashioning. Similarly Yueying's transformation in *Flower Princess* culminates with an image of her singing, broadcast on a television screen.

Although framed by the small screen, the songstress simultaneously breaks free from an earthbound existence, highlighting performance as a projective space of virtuality.[60]

The expressive force of the musical interlude therefore resides primarily in its condensation of a process that eludes causal exposition. The fantasy of becoming embodied by a performer like Chung Ching relies on the representational capacities of what Amy Herzog calls the "musical moment," when time is suspended and space "completely reconfigured into a fantastical realm that abandons linear rationality."[61] By definition, the musical moment lies outside the stream of narrative time. Concomitantly, it activates a mode of performance that does not answer to the demand for a realistic and coherent identity. To return to McMillin's formulations, in the discrepant interval of lyrical performance, characters acquire a new dimensionality and become "new versions of themselves that lay against our normal sense of identity and story," versions that are "multiple" rather than unified.[62] In Chung's films, we see how the mode of performance authorized by musical numbers is sutured to an imagination of identity that privileges flux over stability, incoherence over consistency, and plurality over singularity. In bringing these qualities into play, the songstress emerges as a conduit for the ideologies that distinguish the postwar era from an earlier phase of modernity.

4

THE MAMBO GIRL

The rustic songstress has deep roots in Chinese cinema of the prewar period, as described in the previous chapter. Even a film like *Songs of the Peach Blossom River*, which heralded an obvious turn in Mandarin film culture, simultaneously draws deeply from an interconnected set of themes, tropes, and personages rooted in earlier screen narratives depicting farmers' daughters, urban migrants, and budding stars. But postwar Hong Kong also provided the conditions for the emergence of a new songstress type, one entirely without precedent in past filmmaking traditions. She makes a dramatic debut in *Manbo nülang* (*Mambo Girl*, 1957), one of the biggest hits from Motion Picture and General Investment Co. Ltd. (MP&GI) and considered by many critics to be the single most representative work of postwar Mandarin cinema. *Mambo Girl* featured in its title role the young star Grace Chang, who had recently signed an exclusive contract with MP&GI. The film would prove to be her breakthrough vehicle, its success securing her standing as one of the biggest stars of the Hong Kong film world.

Chang's character is introduced with flourish in the film's opening scene, which commences with a shot of a pair of feet in white ballet flats tautly poised in a dance step, accompanied by the vigorous pounding of bongo drums. As the shout, "Mambo—oomph!" is sounded by the chorus, the feet launch into action. The camera tilts up to reveal legs clad in capri pants imprinted with a bold harlequin print that echoes the checkered floor, then a torso, then a bouncing ponytail. A female voice bursts into song. Finally the dancing body with her back to the camera turns to reveal the radiantly beaming visage of Chang herself (figures 4.1–4.3). The careful orchestration of her moves, the music, and the movements of the camera produces a seamless gestalt of rhythm, energy, and dynamism through which the figure of the songstress springs to life and takes musical flight—as unforgettable an action image as there ever was.

Here we witness the birth of the songstress as "mambo girl," to invoke Sam Ho's christening.[1] *Mambo Girl* introduced to Mandarin cinema the persona of the vivacious, carefree, singing and dancing teenager. This archetype would quickly catch on and reappear in numerous other films in the mold of *Mambo Girl*—on the one hand, affiliated with the emerging global genre of the youth film, and on the other hand, bearing obvious debts to the American rock and roll musical. The film's reenvisaging of the songstress rides the wave of the invention of the teenager, a phenomenon rooted in the socioeconomic conditions of postwar prosperity; the institution of the nuclear family; and a budding consumer culture of fashion, music and dance, and automobiles. The teenager's connection to a set of modern cultural styles was cemented in the global popular imagination by films from *Rebel without a Cause* (1955) to *Crazed Fruit* (1956). The reification of the teenager as a pop icon is announced in no uncertain terms by *Mambo Girl*'s unusual opening credit sequence. A series of line drawings of dynamic dancing figures provide the backdrop for a doll that is realistically rendered as a young adult woman, reminiscent of Mattel's Barbie in its general appearance, and posed as if in interaction with the two-dimensional images. The doll is styled to resemble Chang as she appears in the opening scene, with dark hair pulled into a ponytail and attired in the mode of a stylish Western teenager. With the shift from the credit sequence to the narrative, the image of the inert doll is replaced by the animated figure of Chang herself—an uncanny juxtaposition that reinforces both the sense of a rhythmic transition from stillness to motion and the self-conscious drama of the springing to life of a static prototype. The transition also foreshadows the character's repeated association with dolls and toys in the course of the film, an association motivated by her parents' occupation as the proprietors of a toy shop above which the family lives.[2] The visual rhyming of Chang's character in the doll as commodity object discloses the basis of that character—modeled on and revivifying the preexisting iconography of the teenager, setting forth an object of identification and consumption aimed at a youth market.

Chang's sprightly persona in *Mambo Girl* has marked commonalities with the gamine types regularly portrayed by Chung Ching, her contemporary. The two built their careers on close parallel tracks: they were born one year apart, migrated from mainland China to Hong Kong as young adults in 1949, and led the pack of the first generation of stars to emerge in the postwar film industry.[3] The image projected by these actresses anticipates the tide of young female stars who would soon follow in their footsteps to fill the screens of Mandarin cinema. Another performer who stands out in this group is Jeanette Lin Tsui. Also a contemporary of Chang and Chung, Lin was nicknamed the student's sweetheart for her adolescent appeal. Lin's roles frequently emphasized her athletic vigor as much as her youthful qualities. For instance, in the MP&GI production *Qingchung ernü* (*Spring Song*, 1959) Lin and Chang costar as rival college coeds. Lin's character is a sports star who shows off her physical prowess in scenes of archery, swimming, water skiing, and horseback riding. Her role here harks back to the athletic *jianmei* type earlier embodied by Li Lili in *Tiyu huanghou* (*Queen of Sports*, 1934).[4] Just as Lin's queen of sports descends from a republican-era prototype, so the schoolgirls populating so many postwar films might also recall a familiar icon from the early twentieth century. The female student was one commonly circulated model of the new woman, embodying May Fourth political ideals of egalitarianism and gender parity as well as the concrete gains of feminist struggles for education reform.[5]

But with the fading of the leftist Shanghai tradition in postwar Hong Kong cinema, the historical meanings attached to the female student recede into the background. She comes to seem less a figure of radical politics than a representative of an ascendant modern middle class, and coeducation itself less a hard-won right than a signifier of class privilege and a channel of upward mobility. The schoolgirls portrayed by actresses like Chang, Chung, and Lin point to the emergence of the teenager as a demographic category, defined in terms of a distinct set of social rituals, mannerisms, and cultural styles. The youthful turn taken by film culture in this moment finds a basis in the colony's material circumstances during the phase of postwar stabilization. Hong Kong's economy was entering a phase of rapid growth and industrialization, which would lay the foundation for the economic boom of the 1970s—although it must be noted that the distribution of wealth in the growing economy was grossly uneven, with nearly half of all households subsisting below the poverty line. The institution of the family was undergoing a reconstruction of its

· · · FIGURES 4.1–4.3 · · ·
Grace Chang in the opening number of *Mambo Girl*, 1957.

own, as the traditional Chinese household consisting of a multigenerational extended family came to be supplanted by the modern-style nuclear family.[6] Most striking is the downward demographic shift experienced by Hong Kong in this period: in 1961, fully half of the colony's population was nineteen years old or younger.[7] Even if its young people could not necessarily lay claim to many of the indulgences and privileges of their counterparts in wealthier parts of the world, they still exerted a great impact on the cinematic imaginary.[8]

It might be argued that the teenager did not fully arrive on the scene in Hong Kong cinema until nearly a decade after *Mambo Girl*, when the colony's baby boomer generation came of age and made its presence felt across a broad spectrum of popular media—from film to television shows and radio programs, and from tea dances to guitar bands and their screaming fans. Poshek Fu dates the beginnings of the Hong Kong youth film (*qingchun pian*) to the latter half of the 1960s and the rise to stardom of teen idols like Josephine Fong-fong Siao (Xiao Fanfang) and Connie Po-chu Chan (Chen Baozhu). The *qingchun pian* discussed by Fu emphasize the rebellious streaks of their teenage characters, who came to be known as *ah fei* ("flown off"), or by the Anglicism "teddy boys."[9] The *ah fei* generation found a compelling idol in Siao, star of the enormously successful *Feinü zhengzhuan* (*Teddy Girls*, 1969), whose representations of antisocial impulses, delinquent behavior, and youthful rage against a hypocritical and morally corrupt adult society resonate with youth films from other parts of the world. The pulsing go-go dance club scene with which *Teddy Girls* begins forms a fascinating counterpoint to the mambo number that launches *Mambo Girl*, a point that I will elaborate on in the book's coda. For the purposes of the present discussion, a brief comparison of the two films will highlight the particular contours of Chang's teenage protagonist—no juvenile delinquent or teddy girl, but rather the paragon of a filial Chinese daughter.[10] As the camera pulls back from its tight focus on her dancing form, we find her positioned at the center of a circle of peers who clap and chant along with good-natured enthusiasm (figure 4.2). Chang's character, a high-school student named Li Kailing, sings:

> Clinking glasses, bumping chairs,
> Shaking bodies, racing pulses,
> Loud shouts and frenzied dances,
> Everything is wild as I am,
> As wild, as wild, as wild as I am.

> Everybody clap, everybody cheer.
> If you feel the rhythm, jump right in.

Loosen your ties, take off your coats,
Everybody come and join in and be
As wild, as wild, as wild as I am.[11]

Despite the impression of raucous all-night partying that the song's lyrics conjure up, the scene's visual framing negates this impression. What we see is in fact a rather anodyne picture of teenage revelry: a group of respectable middle-class young people whose abundant energies are channeled into a coordinated performance of song and dance under Kailing's musical leadership, as they clap in time with the melody she sings. As if to announce that this is a representation of youth intended to reassure adults as much as to appeal to young people, Kailing's mother enters the room with a tray of refreshments and is warmly greeted by the gang. The gathering, we discover, is taking place in her family's home with the full benefit of parental supervision, a fact reiterated by her song in due course: "No matter how wild the party is / Sing and dance till dawn, it's all right / Just revel to your heart's delight / Because this is my home, my heaven." The lyrics encapsulate the scene's constitutive incongruity as a (both literally and figuratively) domesticated portrait of modern teenage culture, whose newness and strangeness are brought into the safe fold of the family home.[12] The effect of the songstress's performance is not to transgress the protocols of polite sociality but rather to bring together friends and family, to consolidate a community. This incongruity is mirrored by the song: despite its verbal invocation of disinhibition and unruliness, its musical idiom is conventional and old-fashioned by the pop standards of the time, calling for a disciplined style of vocal delivery that conforms to traditional ideals of bel canto and expressly shows off Chang's classical training.[13]

A sense of discordance momentarily interrupts this happy scene in the person of a matronly neighbor who complains to Kailing's father about the noises of the party and the unseemly behavior of his daughter. Mr. Li's response is to express genuine bafflement at the woman's objections to the party and to defend his daughter's activities as the well-deserved fun of a hard-working student. He proudly describes his daughter's natural gift (*tiancai*) for all forms of musical expression and pedantically explains to the neighbor that when a child shows such genius, "her parents must encourage and nurture her talents." Although unorthodox in the eyes of the old-fashioned neighbor, Kailing's singing and dancing are redeemed from reactionary disapproval and recuperated as a sign of liberal parenting rather than teenage abandon.

In this opening scene, music functions as the medium of youth's physical expression, and the link between the two is cemented further in the course of

Mambo Girl. Musical performance is associated with the social spaces of youth culture and folded into a rhythmic alternation of school and play. In particular, the film mines the sensational interest of the social rituals of modern teenage life. Not only does it begin with a teenage dance party, but it also ends with a scene that mirrors the first: Kailing and her friends gather once again in her home and dance to a rock and roll medley reminiscent of contemporaneous Hollywood films like *Rock around the Clock* (1956).[14] The musical idiom of the last scene and its choreographic display of rocking, rolling, and swinging bodies points to *Mambo Girl*'s debts to the emerging genre of the American rock and roll musical. These musicals, as David James argues, played an important role in propagating not just the sounds of rock and roll but also "the visual components of the cultures that formed around it: dance styles and body language, fashions in dress and hairstyle, posters and album covers, and so on."[15] *Mambo Girl* coincides with the initial phase of a cycle that began in the mid-1950s and underwent intense development for the next decade. The film marks the global reach of the rock and roll wave and participates in a process by which new popular musics of the postwar era were disseminated, remediated, and socially recoded in their encounter with cinema. In purging the potentially transgressive components of youthful musical expression, the film colludes in what James identifies as a dominant tendency in American rock and roll musicals of the late 50s. The filmic remediation of rock music, he notes, worked to narratively sever the music's associations with juvenile delinquency, sexual release, and working-class and African-American culture.[16]

Mambo Girl established the key traits that would define Chang's star persona— her multifaceted musical genius and her charismatic embodiment of modern feminine identity. Like Zhou Xuan, Chang was a gifted singer who could lay equal claim to the title of movie star and pop recording artist, her presence in the mass cultural media sphere as dependent on the dissemination of her voice as on the projection of her image. She consistently sang her own songs in her films, nearly all of which contain musical sequences expressly designed to showcase her vocal talent. In the course of her career, she also released numerous recordings with the Great Wall Record Company and Pathé-EMI. The foundation of Chang's stardom in her singing voice is conveyed in the first moments of *Mambo Girl*, which can be described as a drama of embodiment, staging an expressively forceful convergence of body and voice. Just as the vertically moving camera shows us fragments of a female figure in sequence—feet, legs, hips, torso, head—so the voice that sings the first notes of the song is cut off from this figure, which is seen from behind. Chang whips around to face the camera, and with this gesture asserts her ownership of the voice, now synchronized with her facial movements. The camera tracks back gradually to frame her entire body, caught up in the physical exertion of song performance. The remainder of the scene alternates between frontally framed medium close-ups that capture the action of singing and long shots that display her dance moves, cutting with the rhythm of the song. Throughout the performance the camera does not stray from Chang; thus the performance is authenticated by the collocation of voice and body, grounded in the aura of the singing star.

Moreover, unlike most of her predecessors, Chang was as gifted a dancer as she was a vocalist. This fact was broadcasted by *Mambo Girl* and further capitalized on by subsequent productions. Her extensive training in a wide range of musical styles—from traditional Chinese opera to classical and contemporary Western music—was noted repeatedly in the publicity about her films. Such variety and flexibility may be one factor in the complexity of Chang's star image and the depth she brings to the familiar figure of the songstress. Surveying her body of work, we discover a portrait of the postwar songstress that is more multifaceted and nuanced than can be discerned in the films of any other single performer of her time. For example, in *The Wild, Wild Rose*, discussed in detail in the next chapter, she gives a memorable performance as a vampish lounge singer. In the widescreen color extravaganza *Jiao wo ruhe bu xiang ta* (*Because of Her*, 1963), she plays an unwed mother and stage star. In the historical drama blockbuster *Ti xiao yinyuan* (*A Story of Three Loves*, 1964), she plays a drum singer who performs in teahouses and on the street, in keeping with the types of traditional entertainers associated with the republican period.

Just as Chang's musical personas run a gamut of different stripes and periods, so her fictitious roles in the contemporary dramas in which MP&GI specialized add up to a comprehensive portrait of the modern woman. At various times she plays the role of the college student, ambivalent fiancée, young wife, and career woman. Her characters dress in the latest Western fashions, drive cars, play sports, smoke, drink, frequent cafés and nightclubs, travel by plane and boat, speak multiple languages, fall in love, engage in premarital sex, and prioritize their careers over marriage. This pattern of behaviors upholds the prevailing critical view of MP&GI as a studio with a progressive and forward-looking bent, clearly distinguishable from the more conservative, tradition-based cinematic worldview of Shaw Brothers. The latter studio was known for its historical epics, but MP&GI's productions for the most part were staged in contemporary urban settings, thereby capturing "the sensibility of an evolving time and city," in the words of Shu Kei.[17] Their films revolved around the everyday intrigues of the white-collar middle class and reflected an evolving capitalist culture of consumption, leisure, and fashion—envisioned through spatial loci like restaurants, hotels, cafés, nightclubs, automobiles, and the single-family home; activities like social dancing, tourism, seaside vacations, sports and fitness, fashion shows, and beauty contests; and technological media such as radio, television, and records. Mary Wong points out that this modern sensibility goes hand in hand with a specific gender orientation, as MP&GI also tended to favor stories that were centered on female protagonists and shaped around the talents of the actresses who dominated its stable of stars. Discussing Chang's roles in films such as *Liu yue xinniang* (*June Bride*, 1960), where she portrays a soon-to-be bride who begins to question the marriage her father has arranged for her, and *Kongzhong xiaojie* (*Air Hostess*, 1959), where she plays a recent college graduate who spurns a proposal to pursue a demanding career in the glamorous air travel industry, Wong comments on the prominent place in MP&GI films of women who "travel abroad, speak many languages, and who are educated in modern ways and open to foreign cultures." Their presence, which is all the more striking since such female characters are "rare for 1950s and 60s Hong Kong films," suggests an active reflection on modernity, mediated through a feminine point of view and channeled by the dilemmas and choices faced by these characters.[18] Viewed from this angle, Chang's films reveal much about the new ideals of femininity promulgated by the studio in the context of an industrializing, capitalist, and cosmopolitan society.

But as we have already seen, this depiction of the modern female subject also carefully filters out those elements that might strike a disconcerting chord. Even when engaged in activities that fly in the face of conventions of proper feminine behavior, Chang's characters rarely stray from the approval of the family members, peers, and coworkers who surround her. As the dispute between Mr. Li and the neighbor in *Mambo Girl* illustrates, the potential for conflict between modern and traditional mind-sets hovers at the edges of her films and must be actively defused—in this case by being displaced on the neighbor, who is cast in a decidedly negative light as old-fashioned and intransigently narrow-minded. *Mambo Girl* is illustrative of the ways in which Chang's films address the implicit threat of her unconventional behaviors by domesticating her characters, bringing them into line with dominant familial values and gender norms. The figure she cuts here and in many other films is sunny to the point of relentlessness, wholesome and upright to the point of unbelievability.

But if these films seem rather too insistent on positioning Chang within the bounds of propriety, we need only look at their extreme dependence on modes of corporeal display that push those very bounds for the reason why.

More than any other performer of her time, Chang was identified with new, unfamiliar musical fashions from the West as well as other parts of the world. Indeed *Mambo Girl*, as her breakout vehicle, cemented her affiliation not just with American rock and roll, but also with Latin Caribbean dance and music. Halfway through the first musical number, Kailing stops her singing and—as a rhythmic percussive beat surges to the fore of the soundtrack—shimmies, shakes her hips, and throws herself into an energetic solo mambo routine. Later in the film, she dances a cha-cha, set to one of Chang's most popular hit songs, "I Love Cha-Cha." At direct odds with Chang's projection of exemplary Chinese femininity is her active role in the cinematic remediation of foreign musical styles, channeling and absorbing their connotations of otherness, exoticism, and threatening sensuality. And if Chang's films often fail in the final instance to reconcile the contradictions in her persona, this failure is precisely where their fascination as historical texts begins. Rather than straightforward illustrations of liberal or progressive gender values, they demand to be viewed as instantiations of conflicting norms of gender identity in the postwar period. Indeed, Chang's star persona reflects less a fixed, unidimensional ideal of Chinese womanhood than the very incoherence of such a construct at a time when codes of feminine conduct were being radically rewritten. And in her films, the fault lines subtending the idealized image of modern femininity acquire a particular clarity in the performance of song and dance.

The Postwar Family Romance

Mambo Girl can be described as a family melodrama-cum-song-and-dance film. Its plot centers on Li Kailing, an ordinary high-school student with extraordinary musical talents. She eventually makes a traumatic discovery that shakes the foundations of her perfect life in the bosom of a doting family and admiring circle of classmates. At the end of the dance party scene at the film's beginning, Mr. Li announces to the group that Kailing's twentieth birthday is a just few days away and invites them to a celebration of the event. One of her friends, a young man named Danian, volunteers to host the party. Later in the evening, Mrs. Li tells her husband that he has misremembered the date of the birthday, and the couple consult a document hidden in a box under their bed. At that moment, Kailing's little sister Baoling bursts into the bedroom and catches sight of the document, which is thus revealed to be not a birth certificate, but an adoption certificate. The parents confess that this is their family secret and attempt to reassure the stunned Baoling. At school the next day, Baoling unwisely shares the secret with a classmate who, envious of Kailing's popularity, harbors a grudge against her. When the day of the birthday party arrives, everyone gathers at Danian's luxurious and lavishly decorated home. Kailing is presented with an enormous birthday cake inscribed with her name and lit with candles, and serenaded with a song by her classmates: "You are the sweetheart of your family, you are the queen of our school . . . today we sing to you, blessed mambo girl." During the festive dancing that follows, the jealous classmate maliciously leaks the secret to Kailing, and she flees the party in tears.

Thus the warm picture of the home as heaven constructed at the film's opening number is torn apart, in the midst of another round of festivities that otherwise construct a fantasy image of the Western-style, middle-class birthday party in which no expense is spared and no expression of affection withheld. Such a setting befits the nature of the rupture in Kailing's world caused by the revelation of this secret. Against the background of comforting familiarity, a discordant sense of unhomeliness rears its head. In the midst of the birthday celebration as a ritual affirmation of modern individuality, Kailing is confronted with the unsettling enigma of her identity and origins. She is plunged into a state of doubt and a process of questioning, during which she turns away from her family and friends. Eventually Kailing's self-searching drives her out of the home itself. In the middle of that same night, she wakes up and makes her way up to the roof of the house, where she has a vision of her mother as an aged and weary woman in humble dress, singing a plaintive tune about her lost daughter. The vision prompts her to run away and, with her adoption papers in hand, embark on a search for her birth mother. The course of this search draws Kailing into a series of spaces that are increasingly alien and removed from middle-class domesticity—the orphanage, a sanctuary for homeless children; the slum, a metonymy of the class reality held at bay from the idealized fictitious world of middle-class teenagers; and lastly the nightclub, the diametrical opposite of the home.

Across these locales, we can plot the turns of a narrative problematic of identity, knowledge, and belonging. Deprived of a sense of her place in the world, Kailing wanders from her domicile; with the eventual resolution of this conundrum, she returns to it, reclaims her place, and reaffirms the sense of home. Notably, the trajectory of Kailing's wandering also pulls the camera away from the controlled environment of the studio and into the real spaces of Hong Kong, offering the audience brief glimpses of its streets, neighborhoods, and places of leisure. At her first stop, the orphanage, Kailing obtains the name—Yu Suying—and address of the woman who left her there as a baby. The address leads her to a poor neighborhood, shot on location in Kowloon, whose residents she questions about Yu's whereabouts. Kailing is disappointed to find that the woman no longer lives there, but she obtains a new clue when one of the residents tells her that she works in a nightclub. Kailing's ensuing pursuit of this lead takes her through the pleasure palaces of Hong Kong nightlife. A series of images of Kailing questioning various uniformed servers is projected on a montage of successive neon signs, each flashing the names of establishments such as the Crystal Lounge Night Club, Silver City, Metro, Empire, Nice, and the Lichi.

At this last stop, she learns from a kindly waiter that a woman named Yu Suying works as an attendant in the ladies' washroom. She enters, asks the woman her name, and falteringly declares, "Twenty years ago, did you turn over your child to the orphanage? I'm . . ." The two then enter into an emotionally charged and circuitous exchange in which Yu denies that she ever had a child but unambiguously betrays the truth of their relationship in the manner of her acting and in the barely repressed interest she takes in Kailing, interrogating her in great detail about her life and adoptive family. The two circle each other carefully until Kailing makes a last urgent plea, "Isn't it you?" Yu responds with the question, "How can I possibly have a daughter like you?" Her performance convinces Kailing enough to leave the nightclub, although after she has gone, Yu confesses to the waiter that she is indeed the girl's mother. For her part, Kailing takes refuge at a friend's house as she ponders the conversation, and finally goes home, where her family anxiously awaits her. When she walks through the door and sees the concern on their faces, she cries out, "Father! Mother!" They tearfully embrace, and—rounding out the happy ending—her friends rush in and resume the interrupted birthday festivities. The film ends with a final party scene of singing, dancing, and youthful merriment.

Mambo Girl has been read by many critics as a parable of postwar diasporic identity, with Kailing's acceptance of her parents at the film's conclusion standing in for a younger generation's renunciation of an absent motherland in favor of Hong Kong as their adopted home. In his discussion of the film, Ho points out that "the surrogate family is an important motif in the post-war cinema. This is at once a result of the many real families being broken during their exile from the mainland and reflective of the refugee generation's adoption of a new homeland in Hong Kong."[19] The film critic Sek Kei takes a similar allegorical view of the motif of surrogate parenthood in the films of this period. "Characters are often forced to choose between birth mothers and adoptive mothers," he writes, a choice that symbolically resonates "for the Chinese population of Hong Kong, torn between living in the colony and wishing to return to the mainland."[20] Li Kailing is but one of many foundlings of the screen, for in the Mandarin films of this period, abandoned children and orphans who live with surrogate parents abound. Alongside *Mambo Girl*, we can consider other works like *Yunü siqing* (*Her Tender Heart*, 1959), in which a young woman must choose between the birth parents who left her behind as a baby and the foster father who raised her in their absence. In *Xue ran haitang hong* (*Blood-Stained Begonia*, 1949), a young woman becomes the object of a battle between the surrogate parents who lovingly brought her up and a manipulative biological mother who returns to claim her after having previously abandoned her. The latter film was remade in 1955 as *Haitang hong* (*Blood Will Tell*), with Li Lihua cast in the bad mother role that had been played with gusto by Bai Guang in the previous version. The remake remains true to the original plot: the daughter's biological father, the notorious but noble-minded jewel thief known as the Red Begonia, breaks out of jail to fend off the mother and ensure that Aizhu remains with the foster family to whose care he entrusted her many years ago. Another example is *Yun chang yan hou* (*Cinderella and Her Little Angels*, 1959), which takes place in an orphanage; Linda Lin Dai plays a young woman who lives there. Lin's role as an orphan is reprised in many of her best-known films—*Cui Cui* (*Singing under the Moon*, 1953), *Jin lianhua* (*Golden Lotus*, 1957), *Diao Chan* (*Diau Charn*, 1958), *Bu liao qing* (*Love without End*, 1961), and *Lan yu hei* (*The Blue and the Black*, 1966). Finally, we can recall the motherless Wildcat from *Songs of the Peach Blossom River*, who loses her only remaining parent but acquires a surrogate family in the course of the narrative.

These films constitute just a partial sampling of the "symbolic potency" of the orphan or foundling figure in postwar Chinese cinema, to borrow a phrase from Zhang Zhen. The orphan, Zhang writes, "crystallized the abject suffering and traumatic experiences under decolonization and modernization that impacted the lives of millions of people, including the Chinese and Sinophone communities, in the Asia-Pacific [region] during the 1940s to 1960s."[21] Although rarely thematized in an explicit fashion, the recent political conflicts that had overturned so many lives left their imprint on screen culture in the pervasive presence of broken families. Along with foundlings and surrogate families, postwar cinema is also rife with widows and widowers. Single-parent families are the norm, and intact two-parent families a rarity. The orphan is not just a reminder of historical pain, Zhang maintains, but also an avatar of hope and futurity, allied with a sense of "ontological openness and biological malleability."[22] In this light, we can begin to further unpack the progressive definition of family advanced by films like *Mambo Girl*, *Her Tender Heart*, and *Blood-Stained Begonia* or *Blood Will Tell*, all of which clearly prioritize the bonds of surrogacy over claims of blood. As well as setting forth an allegorical affirmation of Hong Kong as an adopted home, these works construct a melo-dramatic rescue fantasy around the foundling, who must be saved from her blood kin as she approaches a crucial moment at the threshold of adulthood. Focusing on the child in the family romance of postwar Chinese cinema, we can approach the foundling in Zhang's terms of openness and malleability, as a figure who embodies a desire for release from the past and a wish for a re-made identity purged of past traumas. The figuration of modernity in terms of youth—student and teenager as well as foundling—thus acquires an additional set of inflections during the Cold War period.

If such inflections help explain the identificatory power of the young woman between childhood and adulthood who is positioned as the object of these rescue fantasies, then a closer examination of the role of music sheds further light on what the songstress brings to the family romance narrative. In a personal meditation on *Blood-Stained Begonia*, Sek focuses on a song insert as the moment that the film comes to life for him as a historical text. The song, "Blessing," is sung by the foster mother as she plays the piano with Aizhu by her side, and it sums up Aizhu's development from child to young woman as a member of the household.

How peaceful is our family,
Serene and beautiful like heaven.
You are a flower of fortune,
Blooming joyously in the spring breeze.
Bless you child, may you grow up in happiness.

How many new shoes for you to fill,
How many pathways for you to forge,
There will be no obstacles on your road,
No barriers from South to North.
Bless you child, may your journey be unimpeded.

Like fishes in water,
Drifting about as they will.
Like birds in the sky,
Flying where they please.
Bless you child, may you grow up in freedom.

Sek describes the musical interlude as the vehicle by which a larger reality intervenes in the plot. "What moves me most," he writes, "is the concern for the younger generation expressed by director Yue Feng and songwriters Li Ping and Fang Zhi, who had gone through all the sufferings of WWII and the civil war that followed. . . . The film is adamant about not letting the past generation's conflicts damage the younger generation's future."[23] Paradoxically, it is through the device of the *chaqu* and the theatrical interval of song performance that this historical reality penetrates the veneer of fiction. A similar lyrical inscription of hope for the future can be found in *Mambo Girl*, where, as Ho observes, music is instrumental to the repair of the family.[24] Kailing is finally convinced to give up her search and return to her family after a friend plays her a recording of herself singing. The song's exhortation to count blessings and forget worries picks up on the message of "Blessing," and Kailing visibly undergoes a change of heart as she listens to the lyrics.

> Life is meaningful,
> Life has a reason.
> The sun shines and the moon smiles,
> There is radiance in the universe and mystery in the world.
> A brave person can face all hardships,
> A persevering person can solve any problem.
> Only cowards cannot bear any sorrow—
> Do re mi fa so la ti, hey!
> Hurry and leave your worries behind.

Here again, song performance draws out the subtext of the family melodrama as a coded reflection on the recent past, of the reconciliation of historical trauma in the fictitious register of private crises. As a paean to the virtues of forgetfulness and optimistic perseverance, the song also serves as a starting point from which to complicate the dismissive portrayal of postwar cinema as inward looking and escapist. Technology plays an important role in this reconciliation: somewhat paradoxically, Kailing's existential restlessness is alleviated by a confrontation with her voice as a disembodied and externalized entity. The scene calls to mind the imagination of technology in *Songs of the Peach Blossom River*, where the reproduced and recirculated voice also plays a key role in the reparation of historical wounds and the restitution of community.

In its bid to move onward and forward, *Mambo Girl* does not neglect to cast a final glance at what is left behind. Indeed much of its emotional force resides in its attention to the cost and sacrifice underpinning the good life secured for Kailing. Many critics have taken note of the film's withholding of moral judgment on Kailing's biological mother. Far from being vilified for her actions, Yu is depicted in a dignified and sympathetic light, her reasons for giving up her daughter neither disclosed nor called into question. The standoff between the two characters in the ladies' room at the nightclub is a tour de force of melodramatic pathos, with Yu obliquely expressing the depth of her love for her daughter in the tension of the willed repression of that love. Although this repression is clearly signaled for the audience, it escapes Kailing's notice. The theme of maternal sacrifice is reiterated and accentuated in the film's ending. In the midst of the final round of partying prompted by Kailing's return, Yu and the waiter from the nightclub peer through the front door of the house and catch a glimpse of these goings-on. The waiter offers to go inside to fetch Kailing, but Yu tells him, "I have no right to tell her. Those wonderful people, they deserve to be her parents. I have nothing to give her. I don't deserve her," and walks away sadly.

With this mother-daughter drama, *Mambo Girl* reprises several familiar motifs from the maternal melodrama. Gary Needham has observed that the film's ending appropriates the memorable concluding scene of the Hollywood maternal melodrama *Stella Dallas* (1937). Stella watches her daughter as a distanced spectator, from outside the home of the family to which she has relinquished her for her own good. Likewise in *Mambo Girl* we witness the gaze of an "estranged lower class mother," Needham writes, who "watches in exclusion her daughter and her adoptive family in a happy reunion."[25] Similar themes of maternal sacrifice also appear in several Chinese films of the silent era, such as *Lianai yu yiwu* (*Love and Duty*, 1931), *Xiao wanyi* (*Little Toys*, 1933), and *Shennü* (*Goddess*, 1934). In all of these films, the great silent film star Ruan Lingyu is cast as a loving mother who—like Kailing's biological mother—must be removed as an obstacle to her child's upward mobility. *Love and Duty* and *Little Toys* are particularly significant intertexts for *Mambo Girl*, insofar as these films stage an emotionally wrenching reunion between the mother and a child who no longer recognizes her. In both of the earlier films, the reunion also serves to display in stark relief the contrasting social positions of the separated mother and child.[26] These antecedents raise the point of the bad class conscience of the postwar family romance, in which the viability of the middle-class family and the promises of modernity necessitate the sacrifice and expulsion of the mother who hails from the slum. If Kailing can take her own destiny in hand and overcome history, this is only because the mother has already resigned herself to fate. After Yu's departure, the waiter continues to watch the revelry until Kailing catches sight of him at the door and recognizes him. He makes up an excuse about passing by and overhearing the music and tells her as he leaves, "If you like dancing, you should come to our nightclub some time." Kailing shrugs off the odd encounter and rejoins the party, and the afterimage of maternal suffering is expunged by the upbeat swing tune and lively choreography as she dances away her worries.

Through this series of events, the elementary diegetic mystery of Kailing's parentage is answered, the crisis of her identity resolved, and the threads of the story tied up. Such an account of *Mambo Girl*, however, is incomplete. At another narrative level, the questions of who the mambo girl is and where she comes from linger. The enigma of birth finds another articulation in the film, one that emerges only if we shift our analytic focus away from the causal sequence of story events and toward the framing and structuring of musical performance. In this double articulation, the question of Kailing's identity is reformulated by the film as a question of the roots of musical spectacle itself. If the natural talents of the mambo girl warrant repeated displays of song and dance, then where do these musical gifts come from? From the beginning of the film, Kailing's character is individualized and defined by her community in terms of her aptitude for singing and dancing, as the title makes clear. When the truth about her birth is disclosed, the very traits that have carved out her place in a social world become a source of self-doubt. How is it that I possess such talents, Kailing asks, "when my father can't sing, my mother can't dance, and even my sister can't sing or dance?" The mark of her identity as a song-stress becomes a sign of an alienating difference and otherness. The narrative poses an answer to this problem in the single clue offered to Kailing concerning the whereabouts of her birth mother—the fact that she works in a night-club, an establishment whose existence is premised on the entertainments of singing and dancing. The mambo girl's search for her roots brings her face to face with the nightclub as the place of the mother and locus of her true origins.

Kailing's flight from her home takes her into the nightclub, a space commonly portrayed in postwar cinema as "an illicit place . . . the Other (place) of the family," in the words of Roger Garcia.[27] The significance of the nightclub can be grasped in contradistinction to the home as a spatial microcosm of a social order founded on traditional Confucian values and the authority of the patriarch. Garcia observes that the diametrical opposition between the respectable family home and the disreputable nightclub simultaneously reinforces a familiar stereotypical binary of female sexuality, for "dutiful mothers, daughters, sisters, [and] wives" are never to be found in nightclubs, and "the only question surrounding the women found in them does not concern their virtue, but their price."[28] For Garcia, the confrontation between the mother and daughter in *Mambo Girl*, constructed in a series of shot–reverse shots against a background of mirrors, exposes the spatial logic that binds these spaces in an oppositional relationship. Here the nightclub emerges clearly as an "other" space, "the representation of the family's hidden desire, the expression of its unconscious."[29]

Yet Garcia's analysis overlooks the ways in which *Mambo Girl* does not just invoke but actively deconstructs the binary of the nightclub and home, of the virtuous and the fallen woman. Upon entering the spaces of nightlife, Kailing is confronted with a series of musical spectacles that uncannily echo her own performances. On the nightclub's stage and dance floor, we behold a mirroring of the song-and-dance scenes that earlier transpired in the home and the school. The first stop on Kailing's nightclub tour brings us into a venue where a singer belts out a jazzy dance tune from the stage as smartly dressed couples swing on a small dance floor, their moves and appearance indistinguishable from those of Kailing's teenage friends. Kailing's songbird role is reprised here by the lounge singer, identified by a neon sign behind her as Miss Mona Fong. The scene entices the viewer with a glimpse into urban nightlife that lasts for the entire duration of the song "Enjoy Yourself Tonight," an incitement to pleasure in the same spirit as the film's opening musical number. Our first glimpse of the nightclub comes in a long shot that encompasses a view of the stage, dance floor, and a door from which Kailing enters the venue. As she regards the performance with earnestly searching eyes, the camera cuts between Kailing and Mona Fong, both frontally framed in medium shots. Fong now occupies the visual and sonic spotlight, as Kailing did earlier in the film. The shot–reverse shot editing pattern emphasizes Kailing's position as the onlooker in this performance and her intense concentration on the singer.

The question left hanging here, posed in the visual syntax of the face-off between the mambo girl and the lounge singer, is whether the singer is Kailing's mother. Concomitantly, we are invited to consider the home of the lounge singer, the nightclub, as the font of Kailing's genetically unaccountable musical talent. The question is put into words by Kailing herself at the final stop of her nightlife tour when, entering the Lichi Nightclub, she asks a waiter if a person named Yu Suying works on the premises. The waiter asks, "What sort of work does she do here?" Kailing replies, "I'm not sure what kind of work. Perhaps she sings or performs or something like that?" "Never heard of her," the waiter says, "and it's show time now. Everyone is here to see Margo. Why don't you stay and watch for a while? This way, please." Kailing reluctantly allows herself to be directed to the side of the dance floor as the band strikes up an allegro arrangement of the jazz classic "Summertime," enlivened by the addition of a pounding timbale drumbeat throughout. To this accompaniment a lone performer, Margo, makes her way onto the floor and proceeds to mesmerize the audience with a display of explosive carnal energy. Barefoot and costumed in a beaded and tassled bikini, she shakes, spins, and thrusts her hips with suggestive abandon in a burlesque dance that draws from a mélange of Latin Caribbean elements. The performance culminates with a frenzied percussion solo during which Margo goes into high gear and drops to the floor in a none too subtle mimicry of sexual intercourse, to the applause and evident thrills of the nightclub clientele. As in the earlier nightclub scene, the camera cuts to Kailing at moments throughout the performance, so that we watch her watching. Her reaction sets her apart from the other patrons in the nightclub. She appears distracted by rather than immersed in the spectacle of the dance, ill at ease and, in the grand finale, quite scandalized by what she witnesses.

At this point in Kailing's search, the confrontation between the wholesome singing teenager and the semirespectable nightclub entertainer reaches an intense pitch as a primal encounter. Kailing's hidden identity returns to her in the form of a *danse sauvage*, and the shadow of the fallen woman falls on the youthful mambo girl. During such scenes of nightlife spectacle, the film's unwinding of the narrative problem of biological origins takes a reflexive turn, directing our attention to the nightclub performer as the mambo girl's mother in the figurative sense of a historical precursor and tropological ancestor. The enigma of Kailing's parentage condenses the obscured history of the postwar songstress: before the mambo girl, musical spectacle was supplied by the lounge singer and cabaret dancer, whose narrative abode was the nightclub stage. Kailing reacts by refusing this implied parentage, turning away from the performance she witnesses, and the narrative conspires in her gesture of disavowal by defusing the tension of this confrontation in the immediately ensuing meeting with the real mother. Yet the force of this distancing gesture, the conviction of Kailing's refusal to look, are also significantly undermined by the film's presentation of the nightclub entertainer, which flagrantly caters to the filmgoer's desire to look. Most striking here are the concessions granted to the sensuous appeal of these musical performances, which are presented in their entire duration and real time as well as staged in an exhibitionist mode that directly addresses the spectator- auditor.

The sense of exhibitionism is especially pronounced in Margo's dance, which is filmed so as to dramatize the self-consciousness of its corporeal display: at several points Margo acknowledges the presence of the camera by looking at it and moving directly toward it, thereby offering the audience close-up views of her dancing body that are quite jolting in their tactile impact and intimate physicality. Her dance is undeniably *Mambo Girl's* spectacular high point, and its extremely erotic tenor discloses the stakes of the film's attempt to distance Kailing from such a choreographic exercise. Just as the mambo girl needs to be rescued from her working-class past, so she must also be delivered from the sexually charged atmosphere surrounding the nightclub performer whose vocation is to arouse the desires of her audience. As the fulfillment of the dangling promise of "wild and crazy" dancing made in Kailing's song at the beginning of the film, the *danse sauvage* is the counterimage of the teenage party, flagrantly displaying all of those seamy and provocative elements that are carefully excised from the mambo girl's image. If Kailing's physical effusions have been drained of their libidinal overtones and channeled toward a more socially acceptable signification of youthful vitality, these overtones return with a renewed force in the nightclub setting, where social dancing's associations with courtship and sexual expression come to the fore. Thus the film calls attention to the mambo girl's buried kinship with performers like Mona Fong and Margo in the very process of exorcising that kinship. Musical spectacle offers a key to Kailing's secret history, and, viewed against the background of these nightclub shows, she emerges with a greater complexity and depth than the film's story would otherwise grant her.

The intimation that the mambo girl is mirrored in the nightclub performer is reinforced by an earlier scene in the film, which presents Kailing's mother as her double. In the teenager's vision of her real mother on the rooftop, a figure descends from the sky like a fairy, singing a woeful tune of maternal longing, and disappears as soon as she finishes her song. Chang, made up as an older version of herself, plays the object of this vision, her image juxtaposed with Kailing's by means of the technique of multiple exposure. The use of the double role as a signifier of family resemblance dates back to the silent period. For instance, in *Love and Duty*, Ruan Lingyu plays both an aged mother and her daughter, juxtaposed with one another through the use of split-screen cinematography. Chang would perform another mother-daughter double role in a film released in the wake of *Mambo Girl*. In *Qian mian nülang* (*Girl of a Thousand Guises*), she plays Linxiu, an aspiring stage performer whose ambitions meet with resistance from her father and grandmother. The reason for their objection comes to light in an extended flashback sequence taking place two decades earlier and representing the courtship of Linxiu's father and mother. A brief glimpse at *Girl of a Thousand Guises* reveals the significance of the double as not merely a visual coding of family resemblance, but a pointed articulation of kinship as a kind of cross-generational haunting, one experienced by the younger generation as a crisis of identity and a specter to be purged. The metaphor of haunting finds a thematic realization in the film when Linxiu, practicing Peking opera in the middle of the night, is mistaken by her father and grandmother for a ghost. This mistake prompts the confession of the grandmother:

Linxiu's mother was an opera singer, deemed by the grandmother to be an unfit companion for Linxiu's father for that very reason. In the process of describing the series of actions by which she forcibly drove the mother away, against the wishes of her son, the grandmother acknowledges the error of her ways to Linxiu.

The casting of Chang as both mother and daughter creates some awkwardness, given that the same actor, Zhang Yang, plays Linxiu's father in both strands of the narrative. Chang and Zhang are initially presented as father and daughter and then as a pair of lovers. The film's apparent lack of concern for the incestuous implications of these overlaid pairings only further stresses the particular distribution of its dramatic investments. The redemption of the grandmother's mistake lies not in the reunification of the broken couple—an event that is suggested but is not a part of the depicted plot—but rather in her relinquishing of her prejudice against entertainers and ultimate acceptance of Linxiu's choice of profession. That is, *Girl of a Thousand Guises* is not a romantic drama but a family drama, its axis of narrative tension plotted out by the bodily mirroring of mother and daughter. Unlike *Mambo Girl*, which disavows the bonds between the mambo girl and the nightclub performer, it affirms the resemblance of mother and daughter while vindicating the vocation of the songstress. Nonetheless the similarities between the two films are conspicuous—as tales of concealed origins, absent mothers, and repressed pasts that must be acknowledged so they can truly be laid to rest; and as narrative rites of exorcism intended to release a future generation from the burdens of its predecessors. The mother-daughter double role fulfills a unique function in the unremitting family romances and melodramas of postwar Chinese cinema, disclosing the historical stakes of these dramas in its symptomatic reiterations.

The Cinema Goes Nightclubbing

Nightclub scenes appear with striking frequency in the era of *Mambo Girl*, with countless films playing out against the backdrop of nightlife establishments for drinking, dining, and musical entertainment—leading one commentator to wryly observe that "night clubs seem to be places where most movie characters who live in Hong Kong spend an inordinate amount of their time."[30] In the universe of Mandarin cinema—like that in the cinema of many other parts of the world—in both the pre- and postwar periods, the nightclub signifies urban leisure, affluence, glamour, and cosmopolitanism. It is, in the words of Vivian Sobchack, "an idyllic capitalist chronotope . . . [a] lavish [place] of social leisure, romantic encounter, and public display."[31] Nightlife institutions were also associated with risqué sexual and social behaviors, as public places where men and women could freely mingle. Frequently portrayed on-screen as an arena of illicit behavior, delinquency, and forbidden desire, the nightclub functioned as a site for the projection of social fantasies of moral transgression and dissolution.

But just as *Mambo Girl* breaks down the opposition between the home and the nightclub, with its disclosure of the secret history of the songstress, so the film also introduces a more expansive understanding of the significance of the nightclub for postwar film culture. More than an ideological node in an imaginary landscape, nightclubs were a material and historical fixture of urban space, existing alongside cinema in a modern capitalist culture of consumption, leisure, and fashion. As many historians of Hong Kong have observed, the nightclub was a transplant from prewar Shanghai—like Mandarin film and pop music, a cultural import brought to the colony by cosmopolitan exiles. There it would take root and flourish throughout the 1950s and 1960s, giving rise to vibrant nightlife scene of cabarets, supper clubs, and dance halls whose traces abound in the screen representations of the period. In this respect, the nightclub in postwar Hong Kong cinema can be compared to the cocktail lounges, bars, and cabarets that litter the landscape of the Hollywood noir films of the 1940s. Sobchack describes these as "common places in wartime and postwar American culture that, transported to the screen, gain hyperbolized presence and overdetermined meaning."[32] In treating these spaces as the "material premises" of film noir, as the ground "from which narrative and character emerge," she proposes a compelling framework for understanding how a set of films can be "'about' its historical and cultural moment."[33] Sobchack describes the complex interplay of the historical and symbolic that are lodged in such material premises—"premises that, in existing concretely and visibly in both the films and the culture, materially ground both the internal logic of the films and the external logic of the culture and allow each to be intelligible in terms of the other."[34]

The idea of a mutually determining encounter between an external cultural logic and an internal filmic logic has particular relevance for the case at hand given that, in an even more literal sense, the mambo girl was born in a nightclub. As Chang recounts, the initial idea for *Mambo Girl* came about during an evening on the town in the company of Loke Wan Tho, the MP&GI studio head, who was so taken with her dancing that he suggested making a film of it.[35] The film is inspired by—even takes its name from—the dance styles then sweeping the club and cabaret circuit. Its musical idiom is indebted not only to Western popular music trends and the rock and swing styles of Hollywood youth musicals, but also to the latest trends in the Hong Kong nightlife scene. By her own account, Chang was an avid participant in this culture of social dancing, hitting the nightclubs on a regular basis with other MP&GI personnel like the actress Jeanette Lin Tsui and her *Mambo Girl* costar, Peter Chen Hou.[36] Thus the mambo girl's moves originate in the glamorous, worldly, and risqué environs of the nightclub and are imbued with its color, notwithstanding the film's attempt to recode her dances with reference to the spaces of the home and school. The rhythms and choreography that are the film's main attractions are a direct import from the nightclub, appropriated and set on display in the framework of cinematic spectacle.

Moreover, the film's debts to the nightclub extend beyond the story of its genesis. Although countless films made before and after *Mambo Girl* have used the nightclub as a fictional setting, the film stands out for its material connections to this milieu, as one of the first productions to solicit the extensive collaboration of entertainment professionals from the local cabaret scene. It contains footage of an actual cabaret act, filmed on location in one of Hong Kong's most famous nightclubs. The sumptuous Lichi, located in the North Point district, is sometimes referred to in English as the Ritz, although a better translation of its name—which means swimming pool, a metaphorical reference to the dance floor—would be the Lido, borrowing from the well-known Paris cabaret. The bikini-clad dancer who takes the stage inside is Lolinda Raquel, better known by her stage name of Margo the Z-Bomb, who at the time of *Mambo Girl*'s production was a sensation on the cabaret circuit in Hong Kong, Southeast Asia, and the United States (figure 4.4). The timbale player sharing the stage with Margo is Ollie Delfino, a specialist in Latin percussion who was renowned as one of top bongo players in his native Philippines. And the "Summertime" number in which the two perform is compiled from footage of the entire length of one of Margo's live shows, recorded in multiple takes by a handheld camera from the edge of the dance floor. The footage captures not only the act itself, but also the real-life audience it attracted, with the film's actors stationed among the nightclub patrons. In this picture of an evening at the Lichi Nightclub, we are therefore given a rare documentary glimpse into the postwar nightlife scene. A similar moment occurs in the preceding scene, which features a live performance by Mona Fong, one of Hong Kong's most popular cabaret singers.[37] Through the material premise of the nightclub, the historical reality of musical spectacle comes to the fore.

Fong, Delfino, and Raquel (referred to as "Margo") are named as guest performers in *Mambo Girl*'s opening credit sequence. Their presence in the film is also highlighted in the publicity discourse surrounding the film—for instance,

caption
· · · FIGURE 4.4 · · ·
Lolinda Raquel, or Margo the Z-Bomb, photograph by Harry Jay. Courtesy of the
Performing Arts Collection at Arts Centre Melbourne.

an article in the film journal *International Screen* devotes considerable space to a description of Margo's talents, accompanied by action shots of her dancing. The piece announces that Margo, who "drives audiences wild" with her dancing, has never before been captured on film, most "regrettably for those unaccustomed to the nightclub scene." But fortunately, it continues, she has selected one of her most popular programs to be recorded for *Mambo Girl*.[38] The article at once plays up voyeuristic interest in Margo's guest appearance and promises the reader a vicarious taste of nightlife indulgences, targeting a mass audience whose members include those "unaccustomed to," or lacking access to, the nightclub experience. In this regard, the film can be seen as yet another instance of cinema's insatiable cannibalization of adjacent entertainment forms, evincing a high degree of marketing savvy concerning its own operations as an audiovisual channel for urban nightlife culture. But in flaunting its unique appropriation of the cabaret show, *Mambo Girl* is the exception that proves the rule of the omnipresent imprint of the nightclub on postwar cinema. The film catalyzes a far-reaching shift in which the goings-on of the dance floor begin to influence screen culture to a greater degree than in the past, and choreography assumes a more emphatic presence in film's musical lexicon.

Until this period, singing films (*gechang pian*) far outnumbered song-and-dance films (*gewu pian*). Even in the latter category, the balance was decisively weighed toward song. Although displays of dance were featured occasionally in the sound films of the Shanghai period, musical expression centered for the most part on vocal performance. As Shaoyi Sun and Chuan Shi point out, "it is quite hard to identify an early Chinese film that fits the definition of the 'all-talking, all-singing, and all-dancing' Hollywood musical. Early Chinese 'musicals' are marked by interpolated songs, but with few dancing sequences."[39] Apart from the opera films drawing on a stylized gestural repertory associated specifically with traditional Chinese opera, dance was not a prominent feature of films with modern settings. Many films of this period contained scenes set in urban venues for social dancing like the nightclub and dance hall, reflecting the dance madness (*wu kuang*) of jazz age Shanghai. In the images of couples crowding the dance floor that are so familiar in films of this period, however, dance remained tethered to mise-en-scène, confined to the status of a represented activity that enhances the spatial realism of its setting. A handful of films from this period featured dance routines in the context of the musical revue stage show, using the format of the play within the play (*xi zhong xi*), like *Two Stars in the Milky Way*, *Feng yun ernü* (*Children of Troubled Times*), and *Yasuiqian* (*New Year's Coin*). But in contrast to the performance of song, dance was not elaborated further as an autonomous attraction, with a distinct set of formal and choreographic effects. This tendency persisted into the 1950s, as demonstrated by *Songs of the Peach Blossom River*. The only dancing seen in the film is performed by an anonymous couple in the background of one of its singing acts.

Starting in the late 1950s, however, dance gradually came to assume the status of a choreographed spectacle in its own right—promoted to an equal partner of song, incorporated into songstress routines on a regular basis, and even in some instances supplanting vocal performance as a main musical attraction. This shift was concomitant with a general revamping of the form of the Chinese musical picture. Siu Leung Li observes that from this moment on, "the genre gradually transformed from the less sophisticated format of a romance film with added song sequences—as exemplified by the 1956 [*Peach Blossom River*]—to the fully developed, glamorous wide-screen, color, Hollywood-style movie musical culminating in the productions of the Shaws."[40] By many accounts, this transformation was announced by MP&GI's 1959 release of *Calendar Girl*, Mandarin cinema's first Technicolor widescreen musical extravaganza. The film's story of two sisters, both employed as showgirls, afforded a pretext for the inclusion of numerous elaborately staged song-and-dance numbers. *Calendar Girl* heralded the age of the "Mandarin revue film," in Ho's reading, based on the Hollywood formula of the backstage musical, "with stories revolving around entertainment troupes trying to put shows together" and the galvanizing spirit of "the show that must go on."[41] Li similarly identifies a turning point in the advent of the "Chinese movie musical à la Hollywood," most fully realized in the *gewu pian* produced by Shaw Brothers in the 1960s— for example, *Qian jiao bai mei* (*Les Belles*, 1961), *Hua tuan jin cu* (*Love Parade*, 1963), and *Xiang jiang hua yueyu* (*Hong Kong Nocturne*, 1967).[42]

Mambo Girl has little in common with such musical revue films in terms of style and structure, and its song-and-dance numbers do not nearly approach the scale of the extravagant spectacles that characterize this cycle. But even if the film does not belong to the new wave of Hollywood-style musicals, it nonetheless marks a turning point in the evolution of what can be broadly termed the Mandarin musical picture. Of the nine musical numbers contained in *Mambo Girl*, four consist of song inserts in the traditional *chaqu* format and five break with this format to highlight hot dances like the mambo, cha-cha, and swing. Several of the film's songs also describe the experience of dancing in their lyrics, such as "I Love Cha-Cha" and Fong's "Enjoy Yourself Tonight." The opening mambo number is illustrative of the film's compositional approach: instead of relegating dance to a visual backdrop for vocal performance, it foregrounds dance as a key driving force in the spectacle. The number revolves around the coordinated interaction of voice and body, which it uses for a unified expressive effect: song and dance join in an integrated rhythmic flow. Rather than repeating the distracted gestures of a songstress whose primary concentration is on the act of singing, Chang emphatically and consciously uses her entire body as an expressive instrument. Halfway through the number, she stops singing and shifts her performance entirely into the register of dance, increasing the intricacy and pace of her choreographed moves. This nonvocal portion of the number is longer than the singing portion. Moreover, Chang's actions determine the positioning and movements of the camera, so that interspersed among the medium shots of her singing are long low-angle shots taken at floor level and high-angle shots from the ceiling that capture the full effect of her movements. The representation of dance thereby liberates the camera and motivates its vertical fluidity with respect to the performing body (although the shots themselves generally remain static). The sequence constitutes a choreographed spectacle in its totality, in the interrelations of its individual compositional elements as well as in the represented content.

Using such strategies, *Mambo Girl* shines a spotlight on dance as a form of musical expression. In doing so, the film stands out from mainstream Mandarin cinema of its time and points to the new direction that the film industry would take in the following years. Despite the prevailing view of *Calendar Girl* as the most conspicuous forerunner of the new-style song-and-dance film, that work is indebted to the choreographic innovations of *Mambo Girl*. Indeed the very first musical number in *Calendar Girl* recycles one of Chang's songs, "I Love Cha-Cha," and evokes the dance styles of the earlier film. In this regard *Mambo Girl* serves as a starting point for a different parsing of Hong Kong cinema's unfolding musical idiom, one that does not look solely to the Hollywood musical as a dominant influence and developmental telos. In looking more closely at the modes of musical expression in *Mambo Girl*, we arrive at a more expansive and nuanced mapping of cinema's embedded place in the larger terrain of postwar audiovisual culture, its dialogic interplay with both live and mass-mediated entertainment forms, and a panoply of cross-cultural transpositions beyond a Hong Kong–Hollywood axis. Such a mapping in turn yields a fuller picture of the culture of music that was so inextricably interwoven with the cinema of this period, looking beyond the intersections between film and the recording industry described in the last chapter and extending to other sites of public and embodied musical consumption, such as the nightclub.

Given that a lack of choreographic expertise is frequently invoked as one reason for the long-standing absence of dance from Chinese cinema, a question that immediately arises concerns the talent behind *Mambo Girl*. The demand for songs found a ready solution in a thriving popular music industry that could supply filmmakers with lyrical content, personnel (vocalists, composers, and musicians), and a technological and material apparatus for musical production, but the incorporation of dance posed greater difficulties. Mandarin cinema has long been hindered by a shortage of choreographers and dancers versed in modern dance styles—in contrast to the rich resources for traditional dance located in Chinese theater, productively mined by the genres of the opera film and martial arts action cinema. Against such a background, the constitution of *Mambo Girl*'s musical spectacles is of particular interest. According to Chang, Delfino's participation in the film was not limited to his on-screen appearance but extended behind the scenes, where he played a crucial role both as *Mambo Girl*'s principal choreographer and as Chang's dance coach.[43] At the time of the film's production, Delfino was an established figure in the Hong Kong music scene, known to the public as an accomplished musician and bandleader as well as the husband of the popular *shidai qu* singer Chang Loo. His involvement in the crafting of Chang's mambo girl persona illustrates the deep intermedia connections between the cinema and the nightclub, as linked nodes in an urban mass culture of entertainment.

With live musical performance as its main attraction, the nightclub came to have a significant impact on the popular music soundscape as one of the key sites for the dissemination of Mandarin pop. Some of the biggest names of postwar *shidai qu* (like Mona Fong and Rebecca Pan) hailed from the cabaret stage, eventually moving on to larger concert venues as their fame attracted larger and more far-flung audiences.[44] As their examples suggest, the songstress occupied a central position in the realm of nightclubs, cabarets, and supper clubs—hence their ubiquity as settings for many a songstress film. Most establishments employed a female singer with top billing and at least two bands to supply a continuous stream of jazz music, with the occasional special attraction of an overseas touring show.[45] Relegated to the underside of the nightclub's star culture were the unnamed instrumentalists playing in these bands. Most of them were, like Delfino, of Filipino descent, and many worked in Shanghai's cabaret scene before the war years, serving an indispensable function in the modern music culture of cosmopolitan Shanghai.[46] Although often lacking in the classical training of their White Russian and European counterparts, their accomplishments as jazz musicians created a great demand for their services, in Shanghai as well as other entertainment centers throughout Asia beginning in the early twentieth century.[47] The importance of Filipino musicians persisted into the postwar decades in Hong Kong, where they continued to provide the

instrumental foundations of modern Chinese music—supplying accompaniment for recording artists, working for the film industry, and performing in
nightclubs.

A *Southern Screen* article describes the musicians responsible for film
soundtracks as "invisible heroes behind the scenes," whose vital contribution
to filmmaking is all too often overlooked by audiences because they lack an
onscreen presence.[48] Against this background of invisibility, the involvement
of a well-known figure like Delfino in the design of *Mambo Girl's* musical spectacles only hints at the degree to which the Hong Kong culture industry de-
pended on the Filipino music scene. But even if these instrumentalists tended
to remain out of sight and unacknowledged, their impact on postwar Mandarin movie and music culture is explicitly registered in its styles and idioms.
This is especially evident when we consider one of the signal trends of the
postwar years, the craze for Latin Caribbean dance and music, which marks a
dividing line between the jazz-influenced Mandarin pop of the prewar years
and the guitar-driven rock styles that would dominate the latter half of the
1960s. Chang's musical performances, Andrew Jones writes, were plugged
into a "circuit routed by way of Havana, Mexico City, New York, Hollywood
to Hong Kong, that reproduces 'mambo' as a global vernacular."[49] At this time,
the vogue for mambo, Latin-style jazz, and Afro-Caribbean music was a global
phenomenon. It originated in Latin and North America, where it was popularized by musicians and bandleaders like Xavier Cugat (credited with introducing Latin music to the American big band scene) and Pérez Prado (known as
the king of mambo) and spread to centers of live music throughout the world,
including Manila, Singapore, and Tokyo.[50] Crucial to this dissemination were
recordings and radio, as technologies enabling the circulation of music across
space, as well as live performances by touring and traveling musicians.[51] In this
regard, Delfino's trajectory from the Philippines to Hong Kong illustrates the
channels by which this phenomenon made its way to the colony, as part of a
circulation of musical styles from the Americas and the Caribbean across the
Pacific to East and Southeast Asia. The influence of Filipino musicians on the
soundscape of postwar Hong Kong accounts for a significant measure of its hybrid and cosmopolitan flavor and points to the sway of cross-cultural currents
that cannot be mapped solely along an East-West axis.[52]

The Songstress as Dancer

In transposing the nightlife vogue for Latin dance music to the screen, *Mambo
Girl* accelerated postwar film culture's absorption of the imprint of these mu-

sicians. In the wake of its success, numerous other films attempted to reproduce its formula, so that the rhythms of mambo, calypso, rumba, and cha-cha
quickly became a common musical feature of Mandarin cinema. The popular
appeal of these dances is evidenced not just on-screen but also in the advertising and print materials surrounding the films. Promotional articles began to
place special emphasis on the dances in individual pictures, supplementing
the long-standing practice of advertising their song content. Moreover, the
increasing prominence of dance speaks not only to the changing contours of
musical expression in film, but also to the fluctuating social meanings of the
activity itself, which were irrevocably altered in its drift from the nightclub to
the screen. *Mambo Girl* registers this flux at multiple levels, in the shifting locations of dance—between the indecorous nightclub and the respectable home,
from the stage to the spaces of everyday life—as well as in its refiguring of the
songstress, now a skilled dancer as much as a vocalist. More than any of her
contemporaries, Chang embodied the rebirth of the songstress as dancer. The
prototype of the mambo girl set the parameters for Chang's stardom: dance
would become an integral element of her persona, featured in nearly all of her
films as well as emphasized in the publicity discourse about her. Moreover, the
ambivalent identity of the mambo girl would continue to haunt her star image
as a structuring tension. In Chang's performances, we discover a seismograph
of the process by which dance is recoded in its filmic remediation, emerging as
a critical part of the imaginary of postwar Chinese modernity.

The "I Love Cha-Cha" number in *Mambo Girl* offers a telling example of
the specific terms of this transposing process (figure 4.5). As in the opening
mambo performance, the sequence's main thematic interest resides in the display of a specific dance style, extending the temporal duration of the song with
a long instrumental section, in which Chang stops singing to immerse herself in the steps of the cha-cha. Similar transitions from vocal performance to
wordless dancing are found throughout Chang's subsequent films, as so many
restagings of the emergence of the dancer from the chrysalis of the singer.
The shift across these modes of musical performance also entails a shift in
the film's representational strategies. Although the first part of the number
alternates between medium close-ups and long shots of Chang as she sings, the
second part consists largely of longer shots, staged with respect to a static camera positioned to offer an ideal vantage point for observing the dance steps.[53]
At regular intervals, the camera moves to a position at the ceiling of the school
gymnasium, thus providing an extremely high-angle view of the actors' movements. The overall effect of the composition is highly theatrical, calculated to
capture the dance as an action taking place in real space and time.

··· FIGURE 4.5 ···
"I Love Cha-Cha," *Mambo Girl*, 1957.

"I Love Cha-Cha" also goes one step further than the earlier mambo number. Beyond prioritizing movement and choreography, it also frames its musical spectacle as a pedagogical display. The sequence is structured as a dance lesson, during which Kailing teaches Danian and their other classmates how to do the cha-cha. The lyrics reinforce the number's instructional purport, as she sings, "Listen to the beat carefully / Follow the steps closely / Don't be afraid, anybody can dance. . . . / If you can't dance, then I'll show you how." The extended dance interlude that follows consists of a duet between Kailing and Daning, displaying his success in mastering the steps of cha-cha.[54] Moreover, Kailing's words are an invitation to the film's viewer as much as to the characters in the fiction, an invitation visually reinforced in the careful framing of their duet, which offers the camera a clear and unimpeded view of their bodily movements, and in the oddly deliberate pacing of their steps. The scene's mode of address is therefore participatory as well as theatrical, aimed to corporeally engross the viewer with a display to be emulated. By interpellating its audience members as recipients of a cha-cha lesson, *Mambo Girl* evinces an awareness of its own capacity to channel the kinetic experience of dance—a capacity, as we have seen, yet to be fully used by the cinema of its time. The participatory and mimetic address of "I Love Cha-Cha" can be traced to the conventions of the *chaqu*, or song insert, in which lyrical subtitles and a bouncing ball cue the audience to follow along in the musical performance.

The compositional emphasis on dance in the film finds an echo in the publicity materials surrounding *Mambo Girl*. For instance, a promotional feature on the film in *International Screen* includes a visually striking two-page spread of Chang photographed in various dance postures, under the heading "Grace in Her Mambo Poses" (figure 4.6).[55] One of these same images appears again on a film poster for *Mambo Girl*, which features a full-body image of Chang with her costar, Peter Chen Ho, playing the bongo drums by her side. The program brochure distributed for the film is also dominated by production stills of Chang and Chen dancing together. From this time on, photographic representations of dance appear with increasing frequency in major film magazines, offering the reader a visual preview of cinematic dance scenes by transposing their choreography into a series of iconic poses. Typically the actors are photographed in costume (ball gowns, sarongs, leotards, and so on) to further give the general flavor of a choreographic style or scene. Such images tend to appear as a set of multiple action shots of dancing figures—for instance, a story on the "scintillating" tango performed by Peter Chen Ho and Diana Chang Chung-wen in *Calendar Girl* is illustrated with images of the two actors photographed in costume on the set as they perform the tango scene.[56] Apart from production stills of dance numbers, we also begin to see other methods of assimilating dance to star discourse. A two-page spread of the Cantonese film star Patricia Lam Fung dancing in *Yunü qun qing* (*Teen-Age Love*) appears in an issue of *Southern Screen* from 1958, consisting of a series of separately framed photographs of Lam posed against a plain white background (figure 4.7). The text accompanying the photos tells us nothing about the film's plot, instead describing the dances in the film—a cha-cha and calypso, reflecting Lam's status as the Grace Chang of Cantonese cinema.[57] Here dance is absorbed into the conventions of the star portrait, rendered as a distinguishing attribute of the performer herself, a sign of what makes this particular body a star body. The isolation of the pose in itself, abstracted from the scene of production, paves the way for compositional strategies like the dance collage, with different poses presented as juxtaposed individual images (as in the Lam feature) or brought together on a single picture plane (as in the *Mambo Girl* article). Collages of both kinds became a common means of branding certain stars as dancers, as in the case of Lam, Chang, and the young Shaw Brothers actress and soon-to-be martial arts superstar Cheng Pei-pei.

Such images speak to the growing visual fascination that dance comes to exert in and of itself, independent of its connotations in any particular film. By

舞姿

GRACE IN HER
MAMBO POSES.

Among the contemporary starlets,
Grace Chang is noted for her representation of youth and vitality. She is
recently casted to play the role of an
ultra modern flapper in the picture
titled "Mambo Girl". As the Mambo
girl, she is being featured in the various lively accompanying poses.

· · · FIGURE 4.6 · · ·
(above and opposite) "Grace in Her Mambo Poses," *International Screen*, December 1956.
Permission of Cathay-Keris Films Pte. Ltd. Courtesy of the Hong Kong Film Archive.

葛蘭

加

力騷是先有「歌」後有「舞」，發源地爲西印度群島的千里達。加力騷歌是黑奴勞動時的呼吟加上現代樂器，舞是拉丁舞韻的支流與變形。步法簡單而感情熱烈。它的特點是不論歌唱和舞韻，它所需要的只是節奏之旋律。加力騷盛行於「查查」以後，會得跳「恰恰」只需一小時的時間便可學會加力騷，重要在腰部之外，上身也要擺動。英國皇家舞院曾對此舞多方研究，撮著取材，近來所見「加力騷」中，尤以「恰恰」最爲近花步，多數原出於此。林鳳對流行舞蹈凮有心得，一跳最近在邵氏新片「玉女春情」中大展所長，本版所刊的花步，均將在該片出現。騷與恰恰舞姿搖擺動人，神態飄逸，

「格力騷」與「恰恰」

DANCING STEPS IN "TEEN-AGE LOVE" *by Ling Feng*

Calypso

and *Cha Cha*

The definition of the word "Calypso" in an English dictionary is: lively, rhythmic and tropical ballad improvised and sung by natives of Trinidad. It is characterized by wrenched syllabic stress and loose rhyme. Its history dates back to the 18th Century when slavery was still in practice in Trinidad of the British West Indies. The Negro slaves, after a day's hard work amused themselves by song and dances. This kind of dance and music is called "Calypso". It is easy to learn. Anyone who knows Latin American dance will be able to master it within an hour. On the spread of two pages are pictures of Ling Feng who will appear with her dancing steps like these in her new film the 'Teen-age Love'.

· · · FIGURE 4.7 · · ·

(above and opposite) "Dancing Steps in 'Teen-Age Love,'" *Southern Screen*, February 1958. Permission of Shaw Movie City Hong Kong Limited. Courtesy of the Hong Kong Film Archive.

林鳳在「玉女春情」中的舞姿

means of the collage format in mass-circulated print media, dance is distilled into a set of poses evoking its distinctive spirit or style. With their ability to dissect choreographic movement, photo collages share in the pedagogical purport of the "I Love Cha-Cha" number, offering a sequence of frozen postures that can be studied at leisure and emulated if desired, in the manner of a step-by-step instruction manual. Across these print representations, dance comes to the fore as an object of mass consumption, available to be visually possessed, imitated, and absorbed by the reader—not unlike the clothing, hairstyles, and lifestyle practices also showcased in the pages of these movie magazines. The link between dance and current fashions can already be glimpsed in the marketing of *Mambo Girl* as a window onto contemporary nightclub trends. It is further underscored in the lyrics of "I Love Cha-Cha":

The foxtrot is a bore—
Ya cha chaaaaaaa cha cha cha.
The waltz is ancient—
Ya cha chaaaaaaa cha cha cha.
Your rumba's out of date,
Your samba's unromantic.
If you give it a try you'll know how cool cha-cha is,
How nimble cha-cha is.

The film's poster entices viewers with the bold print promise of "Eight new songs" and "Wild tunes, hot dances!," while a promotional article bills it as a film containing "the newest mambo, cha-cha, and rock and swing [*ah fei*] dances."[58] Such descriptions come to permeate the mass media of the period, which repeatedly refer to choreographic styles as the "hottest," "latest," and "newest." Dance assumes the connotations of fashion and modishness, linked with the perpetual overturns of consumer desire. A 1966 article in *International Screen* explicitly spells out the association between changing dance styles and the cyclical life of the commodity. Introducing the newest dance fad from the Philippines, the author writes: "In the last few decades, dance styles have incessantly changed, with each new dance in vogue for only one or two years before it is replaced by an even newer one, as you can see from this string of names: Rock and Roll, Cha-Cha-Cha, Off-beat Cha-Cha, Twist, Mashed Potatoes, Tahitian Twist, Monkey Dance, A-Go-Go Dance . . . [and] the newest dance to come into vogue, the Hala Hala."[59]

The invocation of dance as a signifier of newness and fashion was not unique to this moment of Chinese modernity. It found a precedent in what Andrew Field has termed the "dancing world" of cosmopolitan Shanghai, in his description of the urban cult of leisure and dance incubated in the budding cabaret scene of the late 1920s and 1930s.[60] In this milieu, dancing as a social practice stood out as a Western import, with no close equivalent in Chinese culture. In the words of Eileen Chang, an author and keen observer of modern life, "China is a land without dance. Perhaps it existed in the past. I have seen it in costume dramas and plays on historical themes. . . . Even in the days when there was dance, people merely watched the performance, rather than actually participating in it. . . . Yet social dancing has become quite common among the Chinese in recent years. Some feel that it is improper, while others defend it as a form of art and decry the salacious minds of those who find it sexually suggestive."[61] Dancing was seen on the one hand as socially and morally suspect, facilitating inappropriate interactions between the sexes, and on the other hand as a thrilling expression of modernity.[62] In films of the Shanghai era, we encounter representations of dance that emphasize its exoticism and glamour—for instance, *Two Stars in the Milky Way*, which contains a stage performance of an Egyptian dance by Violet Wong as well as an elegant tango that she performs with her costar, Jin Yan. In contrast, leftist productions of the 1930s often subscribe to a cultural logic that equates dance with hedonistic excess (in *New Woman*, dancing revelers are contrasted with laboring factory workers); sexual exploitation (the abuse suffered by a taxi dancer in *New Year's Coin*); and perverse decadence (the sadomasochistic tango performed by two women, one dressed as a man, in *Children of Troubled Times*).[63]

The dancing world of the postwar era can be seen as a transplanted version of prewar nightlife culture and a continuation of a longer historical process of popularizing dance, as suggested by press descriptions of Grace Chang's mambo girl as an "ultra modern flapper."[64] From Shanghai to Hong Kong, dance persisted as a fashionable pastime, absorbed into a modern style of living built on practices of consumption and leisure and the structured division of work and play. In the postwar decades, however, the assimilation of social dancing reached a new threshold, and the values attached to this practice irreversibly shifted as it was firmly instituted as an object of mass consumption. Dance became mainstream and consequently was no longer outré. To be sure, the long-standing sexual connotations of some forms of dance did not entirely subside, as Margo's performance in *Mambo Girl* makes clear. But they lost their power to overdetermine social perceptions of dance. The pleasures and physicality of dancing were no longer defined solely with reference to eroticism and hedonistic indulgence but were rather overwritten by a wider set of concepts: playfulness, artistry and creative expression, technique, physical fitness, and recreation.

Filmic remediations of dance played a critical role in this process of its recoding and rehabilitation. For instance, alongside *Mambo Girl*'s spatial dislocation of the dance floor to the family domicile, the film draws parallels between dancing and more innocuous forms of exercise and physical fitness. As Emilie Yeh observes, the film "redirected a prejudice against modern dance from atavistic hedonism to a healthy, athletic and kinetic art form."[65] "I Love Cha-Cha" takes place in a high-school gymnasium, and the song's lyrics include the phrases: "We merrily go to school together, / We happily exercise together . . . / You have a clear and sharp mind, / You have a fit and agile body, / So listen closely to the beat . . . / It's okay to shake your body!" A similar equation can be seen at work in print representations of Chang, where we frequently find her in the dance studio, another setting identified with physical training. Indeed the marked resonance between on- and offscreen constructions of Chang as the mambo girl points to the ways in which film and print media converged around the agenda of reshaping popular perceptions of dance. Mr. Li's defense of the artistic merit of his daughter's musical proclivities resurfaces in numerous promotional articles accentuating the artistry and technical rigor in Chang's dancing. Time and again, she is billed as an "accomplished danseuse," her films as displays of the "art" and "beauty" of choreographic expression, and her performances as the products of arduous training and perfecting of technique.[66] In journalistic accounts of the particular demands made by the *gewu pian* on its performers, dance crosses the line between work and play. For instance, a production report on *Because of Her*, illustrated by images of Chang rehearsing in the studio with her dance coach and fellow actors, emphasizes the "intense behind-the-scenes work of choreographic training" involved in the making of this musical revue. The article tells us that the performance of dance requires artistic and technical expertise, which can be acquired only by diligent practice. To prepare for her role, the article notes, Chang has absorbed herself in a grueling rehearsal schedule for the past three months.[67] The emphasis on such rigorous preparations runs throughout her publicity. Across these accounts, dance (and musical training in general) emerges as the centerpiece of a disciplinary regime of labor and physical conditioning, a sign of Chang's professionalism and work ethic. These values intercept the dubious moral values traditionally assigned to dance and thus pave the way for its cultural legitimization as a form of work. What makes this flapper ultramodern is determined by the demands of modern industry as much as up-to-the-minute trends.

By tracking the intersections between filmic inscriptions and print discourses of song and dance, we begin to grasp the ways in which a star like Chang became not just an agent of musical expression but also a medium through which music was infused with a larger constellation of cultural meanings. In Chang's case, this constellation circles back to the prominent position of foreign musical styles in her public image. Even before the release of *Mambo Girl*, she was a key force in the trans-Pacific vogue of Latin dance, reportedly triggering a mambo craze in Taiwan with one of her live concerts there.[68] On the occasion of *Mambo Girl's* premiere, Chang went on a forty-five-day tour of Singapore and Malaysia, appearing at live concerts and mambo dance contests to promote the film.[69] Her next picture, *Air Hostess*, added calypso to her repertoire, with a number reprising the earlier film's display of choreography by means of extended instrumental interludes. In "I Love Calypso," Chang's singing serves as an introduction for a lengthy dance duet with Guo Shengsheng, a celebrity on the Hong Kong nightclub circuit for his fancy footwork whose contribution to *Air Hostess* as a choreographer and guest performer lends this sequence a certain charm and flair. Chang was one of the few actresses of her time who could keep pace with a figure like Guo, but the progression of her career saw the extension of her exotic appeal beyond the ambit of Latin Caribbean dance tunes, encompassing an even wider range of musical styles. Throughout the discursive construction of Chang's stardom, her singular talents were consistently equated with her ability to cross cultural boundaries in the act of performance. Chang's career illustrates how in this era of Hong Kong modernity, ideals of stardom were modulated by an aspiration to cosmopolitan worldliness and embodied in the songstress as a kind of cultural chameleon able to absorb, adapt to, and enact cultural differences with virtuosic grace.

This aspiration constitutes one of the key traits that distinguished Hong Kong popular cinema from that of the mainland and Taiwan in this period. It reflects the imperatives of a film industry with transregional ambitions, and perhaps also the territory's ambivalent identity in the context of the Cold War and British colonialism.[70] Brian Hu traces an emerging transnational strand in the Hong Kong film industry, evident in practices such as cross-regional coproduction (especially with Japanese companies) and shooting in overseas locations; the rising importance of regional festivals like the Asian Pacific Film Festival; and expanding distribution networks throughout Southeast Asia. The increasingly international orientation of the Hong Kong postwar film culture was nowhere more visually apparent than in the representation of female stars as a point of access to a world beyond local borders. Hu writes that the cosmopolitan imaginary of postwar cinema centered on "the body of the Chinese actress standing on the world stage, a metaphor that provided much visual splendour and exotic appeal."[71] A close look at the screen performances of major stars like Linda Lin Dai reveals how cosmopolitanism had a feminine accent. Hu analyzes the fantasy of mobility and fluidity enacted in the around-the-world musical spectacles that became a staple of *gewu pian* in the 1960s, best exemplified by a series of Hollywood-style extravaganzas produced by Shaw Brothers. For instance, in *Les Belles*, Lin sings and dances in a musical medley that shifts from a French can-can to a Thai folk dance, Spanish *paso doble*, Japanese *odori*, and Chinese drum storytelling, with corresponding changes of costume. In several other films, Lin's body serves as a platform for sartorial displays of worldliness, posing in a series of different ethnic costumes in the format of an around-the-world fashion show.[72] Screen performances like these found a counterpart in magazine reports on the overseas travels of these same actresses—for instance, Lin Dai touring the United States and Grace Chang on her honeymoon in Europe. As Hu notes, "this emphasis on actresses' foreign travel and worldly skills re-enforced their multicultural song-and-dance performances on-screen by giving them off-screen validity."[73]

Another example of the around-the-world song-and-dance number can be found in the backstage musical *Because of Her*, in which Chang plays a revue star. Halfway through the film, she performs onstage a medley that moves through a number of geographically distinct settings, with appropriate changes of costume and musical idiom. It begins with Hong Kong, signaled by the *qi pao* worn by the backup performers and the painted backdrop of a pagoda, then shifts to a hula dance against a set of palm trees; Japan, evoked by kimonos and screen doors; America, with skyscrapers and neon signs visible as Chang sings of freedom, fast cars, and President John Kennedy; Venice, with its gondolas and romance; and Spain, with its toreadors and guitarists. The number begins and ends with a song that joins the musical celebration of international diversity with a liberal rhetoric of universal harmony and understanding, set to a Latin tune:

> Hong Kong, Kowloon, muchacha,
> Taipei, Jinmen, muchacha,
> Singapore and Malaysia, muchacha,
> You and me, muchacha,
> Everybody, muchacha,
> Muchacha, muchacha, . . .

All the young brothers and sisters,
All the old fathers and mothers
Belong to one world, one family, regardless of color.

As the scene illustrates, around-the-world numbers functioned in the manner of a musical grand tour, moving through a series of condensed audiovisual clichés, with Chang, whose vocals remain a constant throughout the alternation of locales, playing the role of a singing tour guide.

Such musical medleys, however, constituted only one of numerous channels by which international diversity would come to define Chang's identity as a songstress. A discourse of cosmopolitan musicianship runs throughout her filmmaking career, indexed by the unusual breadth of performance styles that she mastered in her films and recordings. Her songs ran a gamut from modern Mandarin pop to traditional Chinese idioms like *kunqu* opera, performed by Chang in *Qingchung ernü (Spring Song)*; Peking opera in *Girl of a Thousand Guises*; and drum song (*dagu shu*) in *A Story of Three Loves*. Press accounts of these films emphasized the extensive practice demanded by these performances and extolled the rarity of a modern pop singer who was also versed in traditional musical forms. In *The Wild, Wild Rose*, Chang's musical range is pushed even further, to encompass Western opera, American blues, and a choreographic display of Spanish flamenco. In one of the film's numbers, Chang dons a kimono to sing an aria from Puccini's *Madame Butterfly* (figure 4.8), in what can only be described as an instance of layered cross-cultural drag, split between a visual enactment of traditional Japanese femininity and a vocal display of Western operatic virtuosity. If Chang's films evince an imperative to showcase her musical versatility as much as possible, her publicity materials corroborate the authenticity and "purity" of these performances by pointing to her educational background (she learned classical piano at an early age) and tutelage under well-known figures from the music world (such as the Peking opera actor Zhu Qinxin and the modern pop vocalist Huang Feiran).[74] Across these representations, song and dance emerge as markers of international fluency, with Chang embodying the ethos of an era distinguished for its insatiable assimilation of foreign musics.

One of the most striking features of Chang's stardom has to do with the emphasis placed on her voice as a locus of authenticity. What made her voice extraordinary was its flexibility in bending not only to the demands of disparate cultural traditions of singing—from open-throated bel canto to the nasal melismatic vocalizations of Chinese opera—but also to the phonetic exercise of multiple languages. Her publicity repeatedly drew a parallel between her abilities to assimilate foreign musical styles and to learn different languages.

··· FIGURE 4.8 ···

Grace Chang in costume, publicity still for *The Wild, Wild Rose*,
printed in *International Screen*, July 1960. Permission of Cathay-Keris Films
Pte. Ltd. Courtesy of the Hong Kong Film Archive.

Just as she can move fluidly from one performance idiom to the next, so she can also switch effortlessly and fluently between languages like Mandarin, Cantonese, and English. These two strands of expertise converge in her rendition of bilingual songs, like the pop hit "I Want You to Be My Baby," a Mandarin cover of the 1953 American jump blues tune. Chang's recording of the tune preserves most of the original English lyrics, sung at a rollicking allegro pace. According to one article, when the song was recorded at Pathé's music studio, the band members spontaneously broke into applause at the end of Chang's performance. The singer's linguistic skills, the article goes on, place her in the ranks of vocalists like Mona Fong and Chang Loo, renowned for their mastery of translation songs; but Chang surpasses them in the precision of her American-accented English and her ability to thus capture the song's original flavor.[75] Notwithstanding the hyperbolic tone of promotional articles like this, the portrait it paints received a confirmation with Chang's guest appearance on the *Dinah Shore Show* in the fall of 1959, where instead of bringing American pop to Mandarin listeners, she played the opposite role of Chinese cultural ambassador. During her appearance—viewed by "sixty million American viewers," as the Hong Kong press proudly announced—Chang sang "The Autumn Song" in Mandarin and "Getting to Know You" in English (in a trio with Shore and the Japanese singer Yukiji Asaoka). When complimented by the host on her English skills at the end of the show, Chang suavely replied, "I learned in Shanghai . . . at a French convent."[76]

The linguistic dexterity that defined Chang as a performer would become incorporated into the character she played in *Air Hostess*, a film in which the mambo girl grows up to become a working woman. Having completed her studies, Keping spurns a proposal of marriage to pursue a career in the glamorous air travel industry. She undergoes a demanding series of interviews and auditions at the airline company, one of which requires her to repeat the phrase "Would you like some coffee?" in Cantonese, Shanghainese, and English. Keping pulls off the test with aplomb, even throwing in the French and Thai versions of the phrase as a bonus. Her performance of "I Love Calypso" comes later in the film, after she has successfully passed the test and goes on her first trip to Singapore. The other travel scenes in the film—to Taiwan and Bangkok—are also highlighted with flights of a musical nature. Indeed *Air Hostess* symbolically equates shifting between languages, alternating musical idioms, and the crossing of geographical borders in its portrayal of the jet-setting stewardess. The film offers a thematic commentary on the songstress's role as a mediator of cultural difference, making such difference translatable, consumable, and pleasurable for mass audiences.

CARMEN, CAMILLE, AND THE
UNDOING OF WOMEN

Grace Chang's identity as the star of a thousand guises—capable of fluidly switching between different languages, adopting heterogeneous musical styles, and inhabiting diverse cultural personas—weaves throughout her films as a performative discourse. The roles she played were designed with her unique musical talents in mind, showcasing these in spectacles of song and dance, in films from independent productions like *Qian mian nülang* (*Girl of a Thousand Guises*, 1959) to big-budget extravaganzas from the Motion Picture and General Investment Co. Ltd. (MP&GI) like *Jiao wo ruhe bu xiang ta* (*Because of Her*, 1963). Another film clearly driven by this imperative is *Ye meigui zhi lian* (*The Wild, Wild Rose*, 1960), directed by Wong Tin-lam (Wang Tianlin), one of the most prolific filmmakers of postwar Hong Kong cinema. If *Mambo Girl* hints at the genealogical ties that bind the youthful songbirds of postwar cinema together with an earlier generation of tragic singers, then *The Wild, Wild Rose* situates Chang even more squarely in this lineage by casting her as a lounge singer, a figure who harks back to the Shanghai era. The film even refers to one of *Mambo Girl's* key locations in its very first shot, a neon sign of the New Ritz (Lichi) Nightclub, although it soon becomes apparent that the setting here is far from the grand and upscale pleasure palace glimpsed in the earlier film. Rather, it consists of a rather more modest, run-down establishment with a boisterous clientele, shot with low-key lighting that evokes the nocturnal and seedy ambiance of film noir. As if to further emphasize the status of Chang's songstress as a denizen of the lower depths—or perhaps an angel of the street reminiscent of Zhou Xuan's Xiaohong—the lounge singer is reduced to performing for a smaller crowd in the nightclub's smoky back room, while a different singer occupies the main stage as the star act. The nightclub setting motivates the insertion of seven scenes of song and dance that encompass an unusual range of musical idioms: Western opera, bluesy torch songs, Spanish flamenco, and Latin mambo beats.

The Wild, Wild Rose follows the conventional format of the song-and-dance film by anchoring these displays in diegetic situations of performance, using a technique that harks back to the early sound era's convention of the *xi zhong xi* (play within the play). The nightclub stage on which all of these scenes take place therefore serves as a playground for Chang to show off her multifaceted musicianship, while simultaneously playing her part as a character in the drama. The visible division between onstage and offstage space creates a boundary between the real and ordinary world of the lounge singer Deng Sijia, on the one hand, and a virtual world populated by a host of roles associated with Sijia's songs, on the other hand. Sijia does not just sing and dance during these musical interludes. In many instances, she also momentarily assumes a different guise—by donning costumes, making herself over in an image that evokes the music's original sources, and adopting a persona described by the lyrics. For example, in one number she dons a kimono and Japanese hairstyle to sing the aria "Un bel dì vedremo" from the Puccini opera *Madame Butterfly*. At another point, she appears attired in a man's cape and hat for a rendition of "La donna è mobile" from Verdi's *Rigoletto*. This act of cross-dressing complements her assumption of the masculine vocal role of the tenor, for which the song was originally written as a comic lament on the fickleness of women. In another operatic number, Sijia switches back to a soprano voice to sing the waltz from Lehár's *The Merry Widow*. When she performs a flamenco in the film's final musical number, she appears again in a form of drag that crosses both ethnic and gender lines, dressed in the garb of a male flamenco dancer. These visual transformations find a parallel in the shifting vocal styles that Chang deploys throughout the film, from the throaty contralto croon of the torch singer to the coloratura of the operatic soprano. As another character remarks of Sijia, "when she sings, she can sound like anyone she wants." A distinctive sense of theatricality infuses *The Wild, Wild Rose* as it repeatedly detours into scenarios of metaperformance, where we see acting at work and the character becomes other than who she is.[1]

Yet the film also stands apart from the standard song-and-dance films of its time for the way it ultimately breaks down these divisions between onstage and offstage, performance and reality. The dizzying multiplication of roles around Chang's character overruns the space of the stage and crosses over into the narrative. Even when she is not performing, Sijia cuts a remarkably unstable figure, appearing at some moments as a coquette and unconscionable home wrecker and at others as a paragon of virtue and loyalty, ready to sacrifice herself for the sake of others. Chang's character is introduced in the film's opening scene, when a young piano player reports for his first night of work at the New Ritz Nightclub. While he is waiting inside the lounge area, the lights go down and a spotlight reveals a woman in silhouette strumming a guitar in the rear of the room (figure 5.1). The lights come up again as she begins to dance and sing:

Love is just an ordinary thing,
Nothing special at all.
What are men but just a way to pass the time,
Nothing so wonderful either.
L'amour, l'amour, l'amour, l'amour—

What is love, what is affection?
Isn't it all a delusion?
What is infatuation, what is temptation?
It's only people playacting.
I like all kinds of men, no matter rich or poor;
I'll leave any man, no matter how charming. . . .

If you fall in love with me
You're in for trouble;
If I fall in love with you
You'll die in my hand.

The tune here is instantly recognizable as the "Habañera" from Georges Bizet's opera *Carmen*, set to Mandarin lyrics that preserve its spirit as a paean to the wild, fickle, and treacherous nature of desire.[2] As this opening scene announces in no uncertain terms, *The Wild, Wild Rose* is a retelling of a familiar tale and its songstress a temptress in the mold of Carmen, updated from a gypsy factory girl to a denizen of the nightlife underworld—just as the "Habañera" itself is jazzed up with a fashionable "Latin-American" beat.[3] Sijia meets her Don

· · · FIGURE 5.1 · · ·
Grace Chang channels Carmen, *The Wild, Wild Rose*, 1960.

José in Liang Hanhua, a musician and teacher down on his luck, with no recourse but to take a job as a piano player with the nightclub band so he can support his mother and fiancée. Despite his initial disdain for the singer and the
demimonde milieu into which he has been reluctantly thrust, Hanhua is eventually seduced, then abandoned by Sijia. The film appropriates many elements
of *Carmen's* cautionary story of dangerous passion. Similar to the iconic diva,
Sijia makes numerous declarations of her capricious nature, laughs callously
at the distress of Hanhua's fiancée (who, like Micaëla in the opera, represents
the good woman as the polar opposite of the temptress), and openly plots to
seduce Hanhua. The latter's consuming, obsessive love for Sijia becomes his
undoing, leading him to throw away his career and social standing, break the
law, and land himself in jail, much like Don José. And as in the opera, the film
concludes with a violent crime of passion. Fragments of *Carmen's* music are
woven throughout the underscore of *The Wild, Wild Rose*, often to highlight
those moments when the parallels between the two stories are most apparent.

Notwithstanding its many obvious debts to *Carmen*, however, *The Wild, Wild
Rose* cannot be described as a straightforward adaptation. As the story pro-

gresses, we discover that Sijia is not the vamp she initially appears to be. The narrative's most decisive detour comes when Sijia falls in love with Hanhua and declares her undying devotion to him. Unlike Carmen, who by and by becomes bored with Don José and leaves him for a new lover, Sijia leaves Hanhua for his own good, to save him from the life she has brought him into. As Leo Lee suggests, her character "is in fact more inspired by Camille than Carmen."[4] Although Lee does not elaborate on this brief comment, it points to the fictional inspiration for the plot twist that occurs in the film: the 1848 novel *La dame aux camélias* (*The Lady of the Camellias*), by Alexandre Dumas *fils*. Sijia's determination to give up Hanhua for his own sake parallels the sacrifice made by the book's eponymous protagonist, a high-class courtesan who offers up the ultimate proof of her devotion by giving up the man she loves. Sijia is an uneasy amalgam of two very different iconic prototypes—Carmen, the woman with the rose, and Marguerite Gautier, the lady of the camellias—and *The Wild, Wild Rose* a pastiche that combines two of the most frequently adapted narratives of Western romantic literature.

The same incoherence that haunts Sijia's character also plagues the narrative, which barely holds together given its numerous plot detours and bizarre (although not unusual for its time) episodic digressions. Even as Sijia puts on a cynical face in placing a bet with her fellow musicians on how long it will take her to seduce the new piano player, she shows a different side to another coworker who lacks the money to pay for a medical operation to save his ailing wife. In a tangential subplot that taps into the cliché of the prostitute with the heart of gold, Sijia spends the night with a wealthy man she finds repugnant to obtain the funds for the operation. Amid the various intrigues of the nightclub employees, Sijia's dark past returns in the form of her husband, a brutal one-eyed gangster known as the Cyclops. When the Cyclops attempts to assert his control over the singer, Hanhua intervenes and lands in jail for nearly killing him. After Hanhua is released, he and Sijia move in together and struggle to survive. The gangster returns and threatens to kill Hanhua if he and Sijia stay together. Meanwhile, Sijia's friend convinces her that Hanhua will never find respectable employment as long as he is associated with her. Sijia finally concludes that her love will do him no good and that she must give him up for his sake, however painful the consequences are to her. The film ends as it begins, with a conspicuous reference to *Carmen*: Hanhua, under the mistaken belief that Sijia has left him for another man, strangles her to death in a jealous rage.

As even this highly condensed plot synopsis makes clear, *The Wild, Wild Rose* falls somewhat short in terms of narrative consistency, legibility, and believability. Yet it is precisely its patchwork quality that makes the film a paradigmatic case of postwar Hong Kong cinema. On the one hand, the citational mélange that makes up the film can be seen as the inevitable end product of a film industry that freely adapted, appropriated, and recycled preexisting plot material, as I outlined in chapter 2. For the chameleon-like star Grace Chang, Deng Sijia must have appeared to be an ideal role, as an amalgam of feminine stereotypes and familiar fictional prototypes. Sijia evokes not only Carmen and Camille, but also the feisty Scarlett O'Hara, taking her name from the translation of the heroine's name when *Gone with the Wind* (1939) was shown to Chinese audiences. Her character spins out even further with her multiple stage performances. The personas and voices she adopts in these scenes echo throughout the film, resonate with its plot twists, and further dissolve her identity within a network of references.

On the other hand, the film's two primary intertexts also carry a particular significance, as signposts on the pathways by which the songstress became entrenched as a dominant feature of the film culture of this period. As *The Wild, Wild Rose* suggests, these pathways cut across the boundaries of disparate media and cultural traditions. Female singers and film songs emerged from a rich intertextual field, as products of translations between East and West and cross-pollinations among cinema, literature, theater, and opera. The encounter with classical compositions from Bizet, Verdi, Lehár, and Puccini in a Mandarin movie from 1960 becomes less surprising when considered in the context of the widespread practice of transposing elements of the musical stage to the screen throughout postwar Hong Kong film culture. These practices left an imprint on a wide range of genres—martial arts pictures, dramas, *gechang pian*, and the opera films more obviously indebted to the tradition of *xiqu* (Chinese opera). *The Wild, Wild Rose*'s references to well-known Western operas constituted but one facet of a cinematic landscape rife with inventive combinations of song, music, and narration that amalgamated traditional and modern forms from both Chinese culture and foreign sources.

Moreover, *The Lady of the Camellias* was a highly influential text in the cultural milieu of late Qing and republican-era China, exerting a significant impact on the literary and cinematic productions of this period. In appropriating the central character and plot motifs from the French novel, *The Wild, Wild Rose* participates in a longer history of translational practices and hybridizing exchanges that extend back to the prewar Shanghai-based film industry. The film's debts to the novel clearly display the continuities that anchor postwar film culture in a tradition of popular sentimental fiction dating to the early twentieth century, a tradition constituted in the contact zones of adaptation across media as well as translation across languages. Such continuities account for the entrenchment of the singing woman as a stock character of the first four decades of Chinese sound cinema. In the ill-fated songstresses of the early sound era—who were plagued by social injustice and bad luck—we find a reflection of this longer tradition of female-centered romance narratives, whose stock in trade consisted in the spectacle of suffering women. And in postwar Hong Kong, the cinematic imagination of the songstress as a tragic heroine carried on a longer history of literary representations of melodramatic heroines. The unruly referentiality of The Wild, Wild Rose offers a means of mapping the pathways by which this tradition passed from page to screen, thus generating a distinctive strand of Chinese filmic melodrama. It also suggests the ways in which this tradition was in turn transformed and revivified in its contact with the expressive capacities of cinema. Although the relationship between cinema and sentimental literature has been explored by scholars through the lens of wenyi pian (literary arts film), the insertion of the songstress into this discourse opens up another perspective by calling attention to the important role of song and music in an expanded field of melodrama.

Seductive Songs

The Wild, Wild Rose belongs to a storied lineage of Carmen adaptations, a lineage inaugurated by a novella about strange lands and exotic women written by Prosper Mérimée in 1845–46. The novella served as the source text for Bizet's opera, which debuted at the Opéra-Comique in 1875. Then seen as scandalous, it is now one of the most popular operas of all time and regarded as the composer's sole masterpiece.[5] The story of Carmen has been adapted for the screen in countless versions—including a 1915 American silent version starring the opera singer Geraldine Ferrar; Ernst Lubitsch's Gypsy Blood (1918), starring Pola Negri and Charlie Chaplin; Jean-Luc Godard's Prénom Carmen (1983), which dispenses entirely with Bizet's music and recasts the gypsy tribe as a radical political terrorist gang; and, in the following year, a version directed by Francesco Rosi that adheres faithfully to the libretto while critiquing the politics of class, gender, and race in the original.[6] Of particular salience to The Wild, Wild Rose is Carmen Jones (1954), directed by Otto Preminger and starring Dorothy Dandridge and Harry Belafonte in the lead roles of Carmen and Joe. Many elements of the Hong Kong film appear to be drawn from Carmen Jones, which was itself based on a 1943 Broadway stage production of the same title, featuring Bizet's compositions rearranged by Oscar Hammerstein II, translated into English, and performed by an all–African American cast against the backdrop of 1940s America.[7] As Marshall Leicester writes, "to a degree unparalleled by any other opera, *Carmen* has become a *discourse*, a multiply-authored, historically developing tangle of bits and pieces from Bizet, Mérimée, high-art criticism, the folk imagination and the movie; of stock images of Spain, opera, melodrama, *femmes fatales* and doomed lovers, and heaven knows what else."[8]

In casting Chang as Carmen—her first role as an outright vamp—*The Wild, Wild Rose* banks on her established reputation as a conduit for foreign culture and musical styles at the same time that it perpetuates the link between female sexuality and racial otherness that is central to what might be called the global Carmen discourse. Since her beginnings as a literary character in Mérimée's novella, a gypsy woman described from the point of view of a Frenchman, Carmen has been equated with racial and ethnic alterity, whether by way of the Orient, Caribbean, Mediterranean, Africa, or American South. The film's beginning credit sequence is designed to trigger the memory of Chang's earlier performances of Latin Caribbean dances (in films like *Mambo Girl* and *Air Hostess*) and to relate this memory to Carmen as an embodiment of nebulous yet alluring exoticism. Chang appears on a starkly expressionist set, a stage with a giant rose in the background, from which a cascade of steps descends (figure 5.2). Dressed in a strapless evening gown decorated with Spanish lace, clutching a single rose between her teeth, she performs a Latin-style dance as an orchestra strikes up an accompaniment meshing the melody of the opera's third entr'acte with generic Spanish *paso doble* music (double-step music typically played at bullfights) and blending classical instrumentation with Latin jazz percussion. The images of the rose in this credit sequence, along with the title of the film, allude to the single flower that Bizet's Carmen throws at Don José when they first meet, picking up on this floral motif of intoxicating feminine beauty and further infusing it with the exotic symbolic associations of the rose in the modern Chinese literary imagination.[9] These graphic motifs and musical clichés come together in a coordinated display of sensuality and fiery passion, thus making explicit the undercurrents of transgressive female sexuality that course below the surface of Chang's star persona.

The "Habañera" number that follows soon after builds on this constellation of motifs. In her important work on the gender politics of Bizet's opera, Susan McClary describes the song as an "instrumental vamp," a celebration of "sexual pleasure and promiscuity" that serves as an introduction to the character of Carmen.[10] In the film it also marks our first encounter with Sijia, and Chang's performance strives to attain a similar register of untamed sexual bravado. The spotlight switches on to reveal her strumming a guitar and striking a pose that flaunts her legs and accentuates the revealing cut of her dress. As she launches

··· FIGURE 5.2 ···
Credit sequence, *The Wild, Wild Rose*, 1960.

into song, she begins each verse with a low, guttural growl that slowly builds into an open-throated note, a vocal stylization that powerfully evokes the sense of primal animal passions. Dispensing with the guitar, she struts around the room, boldly comes on to the men in the audience, and twists her hips in a dance that recalls her mambo girl persona. The rearrangement of the song in a Latin-style rhythm with the accompaniment of bongo drums represents a clear deviation from its operatic form. But quite ironically, in the very creative liberties undertaken by the film's composers to update Bizet's music for a modern audience, they return this music to its original roots. For the "Habañera" was itself based on an Afro-Cuban song, "El Arreglito," part of a corpus of Creole music that came into vogue in the *café-concerts* and cabarets of nineteenth-century Paris at the time of the opera's composition.[11] In appropriating the song as a signifier of Carmen's otherness, McClary observes, the composer fused an "African-Latin rhythmic impulse" with a primal gypsy dance, the setting of Seville, and the suggestion of the cabaret demimonde.[12] The resulting ethnic mishmash in the opera is not dissimilar to the exotic mélange that we encounter in *The Wild, Wild Rose*.

In the film, the "Habañera" marks the first encounter between two characters destined for love and tragedy, as prefigured by the intertwining of desire and trauma in Sijia's song. The staging of the number emphasizes the spectacular impact of Sijia's performance. In accordance with the conventions of the song insert, all other narratively significant actions cease in the interval of the number. The arresting power of the song is visually signaled by the change in lighting that precedes the performance: the lights go down, suddenly submerging the scene in darkness and interrupting the conversations of the nightclub's clients. Then a spotlight bathes Sijia in dazzling illumination. From this point on, space contracts around and perceptions converge on the singer, who commands the attention of all the other characters, holds the gaze of the camera for the full duration of her song, and dominates the soundtrack with her voice. We find ourselves, along with the fictional onlookers, drawn into an intense rapport with the performer who plays directly to her audience.

The sense of direct address activated by the performance of song and dance is encoded with a particular narrative significance in this instance. At moments the camera breaks its intense concentration on Sijia to show the musicians playing beside her and, more importantly, to single out Hanhua's reaction at several moments during the show. We see him in a close-up shot as the lights dim to announce the start of the number. The film cuts from his face plunged into shadow to a long shot of the cocktail lounge, cloaked in darkness except for a spot of light that casts the silhouette of the singer against the rear wall. The lights come back on to reveal Sijia, as if for his eyes alone; then the camera returns to Hanhua in his seat, clearly intrigued by the spectacle that unfolds in front of him. Only after this emphasis on his point of view are we made aware of the others in the nightclub audience. Later in the number, his visual perspective is again singled out from the crowd with a shot–reverse shot pattern. The camera frames Sijia's upper body in one of many medium close-ups then cuts into a very tight close-up on her face. The effect is one of startling proximity, made more disorienting by a subtle change in framing as the camera moves along a vertical axis from eye level to a higher angle. A reverse shot of Hanhua in medium close-up, completely transfixed by Sijia, codes the preceding shot in terms of his perspective, although not as a literal duplication of his visual point of view; instead, it is an approximation of the heady effect of Sijia's bigger-than-life presence. The editing pattern conveys the power of song to create a zone of intimacy, to break down physical distance and social barriers, and thus to enable the emergence of illicit desires and sexual tension—in this case, between two characters who have otherwise exchanged no words. The "Habañera" number draws an analogy between the performance of song and the act of seduction, so that the relationship between the songstress and her spectator-auditor becomes the kernel of a drama of temptation, entanglement, and eventual undoing. In this regard, *The Wild, Wild Rose* not only draws on the trope of the femme fatale but also gives this trope a musical inflection by relating it to the myth of the siren, which intertwines female sexuality and musicality. The siren myth of the dangerous sensory powers of song—capable of overcoming reason, ruining men, and disrupting order—has deep roots in both the Western imagination, codified in works like *Carmen*, and Chinese historical discourses in which "beautiful females and their licentious music are like an ax that cut[s] short the lives of men and nations." In the words of Joseph Lam, "female music is the femme fatale."[13]

The conflation of performance and seduction, which makes the sensory pleasure afforded by the song and dance indistinguishable from feelings of desire for the performer herself, is a leitmotif in Hong Kong's songstress films. *The Wild, Wild Rose* may present a somewhat exaggerated example of music as an advertisement for the charms of the singer, but many other films use the scenario of a man who falls under the spell of the songstress's song as an essential narrative building block. Several examples can be found in Grace Chang's films. In *Girl of a Thousand Guises*, she again appears with Chang Yang, the actor who plays Hanhua in *The Wild, Wild Rose*. Chang Yang's character, a university student, falls in love with the Peking opera singer played by Grace Chang after watching her perform. In *Ti xiao yinyuan* (*A Story of Three Loves*, 1964), a film set in republican-era Beijing, Grace Chang's character, Fengxi, is a drum singer who performs on the streets. Her singing catches the attention of Jiashu, a young man from a wealthy family, as he wanders through the entertainment district. When he hears Fengxi's voice, he turns around, notices her performing, and wanders in her direction. His fascination with the singer is signaled by the movements of the camera as it cuts back and forth between the two characters, in rhythm with the music. Jiashu walks toward Fengxi, and in the next shot the camera tracks in towards the singer from the side, her face not fully visible. A reverse shot shows him enraptured by her performance, and in the next shot of Fengxi, the camera tracks in closer at an angle, so that it faces her directly at the moment she sings a verse about the shock of encountering the famous beauty Cui Yingying. The verse identifies her song as an account of love at first sight from the classical drama *The Story of the Western Chamber*, between the scholar Zhang Sheng and the beauty Cui Yingying. With this reference, it serves also as a reflexive commentary on the scene unfolding in the moment, situating it in a longer history of scholar-beauty romances. Fengxi notices the young man watching her intently and their eyes meet. A corresponding track-in toward Jiashu conveys its impact on his composure. As they continue to gaze directly at one another, their faces are captured in two successive close-ups, followed by a third long shot in which both characters can clearly be seen standing face-to-face. The repeated movements of the camera toward the two characters, tracking along a perpendicular axis, and the progressively tighter framing of their faces suggest the magnetic attraction that builds between them, virtually inscribing a sense of affinity and intimacy. The characters seem to come together and interact in an interior drama of love at first sight and sound, even when they do not physically move from their positions on the street, with Jiashu standing back at a distance from the small group that has gathered around Fengxi. The bond between them is conveyed not by means of realistic depiction, but rather through a cinematically mediated situation of performance—of looking, listening, and singing—that amplifies the impact they have on each other's perceptions (figures 5.3–5.8).

In both of these examples, the songstress entrances a male listener with her performance, reprising a familiar schema in which the female body is marked as an object of eroticized display for a male subject whose perspective is allied with that of the film's audience. The seduction scenario sets forth a consonance between the alluring quality of the singer's voice and her visual appearance, both oriented toward the pleasure of a male listening and viewing subject. In doing so, it colludes in what Kaja Silverman has described as "the close identification of the female voice with spectacle and the body" and perpetuates a gendered opposition between the active, mastering masculine gaze and the passive, objectified female body.[14] Yet to conflate the voice with the visual presence of the body from which it issues is to perpetuate a fallacious conception of sound as a mere property of the image, and thus to neglect the ways in which the audiovisual dynamics of these scenes of musical performance complicate the power relations inscribed in the mastering gaze. On closer analysis it becomes clear that the voice here cannot be reduced to a single, localized point in space as an object of visual perception within the diegesis. Rather, musical performance marks an interval in which the singing voice collapses the distance between subject and object as it surrounds, saturates space, and envelops both singer and listener in an affectively charged bubble of intimacy. In the two numbers described above, the tactile address of the voice is conveyed by its literally arresting effect—on both Hanhua, immobilized by the performance taking place before him, and Jiashu, drawn as if by magnetic force into the orbit of the song. Song ushers in a contraction of space, not only in the composition of the image but also in its discursive construction, as the camera work in both sequences deliberately undermines the perception of distance in

··· FIGURES 5.3–5.4 ···
Space contracts around the songstress, *A Story of Three Loves*, 1964.

··· FIGURES 5.5–5.8 ···
Space contracts around the songstress, *A Story of Three Loves*, 1964.

profilmic space. The sense of a shift away from ordinary phenomenal reality is also signaled on the soundtrack, as the song ushers in a break from an objective sonic perspective. Alan Williams notes that the conventions of recording film music run counter to the codes of realism. The clear and tightly controlled sound that results from close recording "depends on the abolition of spatial impressions," he writes. "Not only does the sound seem very close, but it also conveys a sense of relative *spacelessness*."[15] What becomes apparent in the musical numbers above is the difference between visually and acoustically perceived space, a difference that is coded diegetically as a space for unsanctioned intimacies. The musical seduction scenario allegorizes the power of song to create its own reality while it harnesses this power to a dramatic formula of love that transgresses the boundaries of class and social position.

Transplanted Camellias

Discussing the opera *Carmen*, McClary calls attention to those moments when its gender and racial politics tip over into ironic self-exposure, when the main character escapes the stereotypes that would frame her and in turn "controls the frame" of the audience's experience by means of her dominant musical voice.[16] The highly exhibitionistic tone of Carmen's performances, she writes, introduces an ambiguity: "When she sings, does she express herself, or is she just performing a number? Do we ever have access to 'Carmen herself,' or only to a stage persona?"[17] The sense of uncertainty entailed by Carmen's self-conscious displays calls to mind the "epistemological trouble" that Mary Ann Doane identifies in the femme fatale.[18] The mystique of this figure stems from her intimation of the unknown (or the unknowable), even as she makes herself available to a desiring gaze. In a seductive stance that uses her sexuality as bait, the femme fatale provokes an awareness of what remains hidden behind the façade of performance. Hence the films surrounding this figure frequently take shape around what Doane terms a "dialectic of concealing and revealing." Doane turns to Rita Hayworth's song-and-dance number "Put the Blame on Mame" in *Gilda* (1946), where Gilda starts to peel off her clothing while singing, as a demonstration of this formula: "There is a sense in which the narrative itself takes the form of a striptease, peeling away the layers of Gilda's disguises in order to reveal the 'good' woman underneath, the one who will 'go home' with Johnny."[19] Hayworth's femme fatale—a good woman who is in fact only pretending to be bad, using the cabaret stage as a platform for her disguise—resurfaces in Grace Chang's temptress in *The Wild, Wild Rose*. This film also takes the form of a narrative striptease, peeling away the layers of Sijia's character to reveal the good woman hidden beneath the façade of the bad temptress. The musically drawn parallels between Sijia and Carmen turn out to be only an act, while the alternation between on- and offstage space is tied to a "dialectic of concealing and revealing," turning on the central question of whether Sijia is who she appears to be, to us in the audience as well as to the other characters in the fiction. But what *The Wild, Wild Rose*'s striptease lays bare is less an authentic reality behind the veneer of performance than a *mise-en-abyme* of interlinked mimetic personas. The role of Carmen dissolves into yet another unknown woman, the lady of the camellias, the protagonist of yet another drama of veiling and disclosure.

Like *Carmen*, *The Lady of the Camellias* represents a discourse unto itself more than a self-contained work, constituting a set of interrelated romantic motifs that have reappeared in countless multiple versions on the printed page, stage, and screen. The 1848 novel by Dumas tells the story of a doomed love affair against the backdrop of the nineteenth-century Parisian demimonde. Its two protagonists are the young bourgeois Armand Duval and Marguerite Gautier, an upscale courtesan famed for her beauty and extravagant lifestyle. Armand's devotion holds out a promise of both spiritual and physical rehabilitation for Marguerite, who suffers from tuberculosis, and she leaves behind decadent high society for a simpler, happier, and more wholesome life in the countryside with him. But things take a turn when Armand's father pays her a visit to tell her that Armand's association with her, a fallen woman, is harming his future prospects, as well as those of his younger sister. Capitulating to the man's plea for his family's reputation, Marguerite determines to sacrifice herself and sever her ties with Armand by whatever means necessary. Pretending that she no longer loves him and misses the luxury of her previous life as a kept woman, she leaves him for another man. Armand vilifies her, and Marguerite's health deteriorates. Too late, he comes to realize what her real motives were and regret his inability to see the truth, and the story ends with her death as a martyr. With this tale of a fallen woman redeemed by true love, *The Lady of the Camellias* brought forth "a new, enduring myth of femininity," Toril Moi writes. "Uniting libertine sexuality with enduring love proved by self-sacrifice, Marguerite Gautier becomes the incarnation of a particularly powerful male fantasy. Sexually free and experienced, desirable and desiring, Marguerite is also truly loving, utterly selfless, ready to sacrifice every interest of her own on the altar of bourgeois respectability."[20]

The Wild, Wild Rose engages this myth by modeling its protagonist Deng Sijia on Marguerite—desirable, desiring, and transformed by love. On one level, the scene in which Sijia ends her relationship with Hanhua plays out like the episode in *Carmen* when the temptress abandons Don José for Escamillo, the toreador to whom she has transferred her affections. Sijia callously informs Hanhua that she has found a new lover and flaunts the presents she says that he has given her (which actually come from the job she has just taken at a new nightclub). But what is apparent to the audience, if not to Hanhua, is that this is a performance calculated to mask her true feelings and convince him to forget her. With this performance, the narrative of Carmen is intercepted by that of *The Lady of the Camellias*, and Sijia's actions are recoded as a sacrifice that attests to her selfless nature. Like Marguerite Gautier, she ultimately accepts society's judgment of her as unworthy and makes Hanhua believe that she no longer loves him to save him from her love. Her reconciliation with family values is shown in the visit that she pays to Hanhua's widowed mother to inform her that she has given up Hanhua. Just as Marguerite receives the blessing of the father, so Sijia's sacrifice is recognized by the mother, who tells her that she understands her "good intentions." The film's ending draws from both *Carmen* and *The Lady of the Camellias*: Hanhua tracks down Sijia at the nightclub where she works and strangles her to death, reprising Carmen's death at the hands of Don José, who would rather kill her than lose her. The shock of the murder is followed immediately by the pathos of Hanhua's realization that he has misunderstood Sijia, as the other characters rush in and tell him the real reason for her actions. Like Armand Duval, he realizes the truth and recognizes her sacrifice only after it is too late.

The Lady of the Camellias was performed as a stage play in 1852. Like *Carmen*, it was adapted as the libretto for an opera, *La Traviata*, composed by Giuseppe Verdi in the following year, with its title character renamed Violetta. The story has also found a rich afterlife on the big screen, as Moi notes, with more than forty film versions of *The Lady of the Camellias*. In many of these, Marguerite is renamed Camille, after the type of flower worn by the courtesan as a symbol of her sexual availability.[21] The best known of these adaptations is the 1936 Hollywood production *Camille*, which cast Greta Garbo in one of her most memorable roles. The enduring appeal of this story of "champagne and tears," as Henry James once called it, points to the potency of its romantic myth of true love, ennobled by adversity and authenticated by its contrast to external markers of social distinction and class hierarchy. In the view of many contemporary critics, however, this mythology of love itself functions as an ideological sleight of hand that ultimately reaffirms the supremacy of the patriarchal bourgeois family. Moi points out that the novel idealizes a free woman's willing subjugation of herself in the name of love, in a fantasy of "absolute emotional submission."[22] Writing in 1957 about *The Lady of the Camellias*, Roland Barthes invokes the text as an instantiation of the prevalent "mythologies" of postwar French society. For Barthes, however, the central myth that it perpetuates ultimately has less to do with romantic love than with a disempowered subject's blind quest for recognition on the basis of the reigning values of the dominant class, thereby embracing the conditions of her own subjugation. "The alienation of Marguerite Gautier in relation to the class of her masters," he suggests, "is not fundamentally different from that of today's petit-bourgeois women in a world which is just as stratified."[23]

Furthermore, the story's resonance in Hong Kong film culture must be considered in light of the remarkable history of its reception in China. When *La dame aux camélias* was translated into Chinese in 1899, the book created a sensation—captivating readers, spawning numerous imitations, and igniting a vogue for translated foreign literature. Camille, as Hu Ying argues, "was without question the most popular figure in the late Qing imaginary of the West," with the runaway success of the translated novel giving rise to a host of "transplanted camellias" in Chinese literature for the next two decades.[24] The story of *Chahua nü*, as the book was titled in Chinese, would become one of the founding texts of early twentieth-century popular Chinese fiction, consolidating a set of motifs that figured centrally in the Mandarin Duck and Butterfly school of sentimental literature. In addition, the character Marguerite Gautier was highly legible for Chinese readers versed in a tradition of literary representations of high-minded courtesans willing to die for their ideals. Haiyan Lee situates the translated novel at the beginning of a "moral and epistemological transformation in early twentieth-century China."[25] In codifying the romanticist ideal of *le grand amour*, Lee argues, the book catalyzed the emergence of a modern cult of feeling and a new concept of personhood, in which love functioned as a measure of the individual.

The significance of the book for Chinese readers, Lee writes, stems from its successful fusion of a late Qing discourse of valorized sentiment with a modern ideal of free love as "a politicized symbol of the absolute hypergoods of the May Fourth modern: freedom, equality, rights."[26] In this new context, the political implications of *La dame aux camélias* reside less in an affirmation of traditional values and paternal authority than in the book's staging of a generational conflict between desiring youth and controlling parents around the question of marriage. The story of young love run aground by parental interdiction becomes the template for what Lee describes as a May Fourth morality play, turning on the struggle between "free will and moral integrity of the individual on the one hand, and the hypocrisy and tyranny of family, society, and Confucian morality on the other."[27] At the same time, the gendered narrative structure of the French novel—in which the woman dies to prove her love and the man lives to tell their story—finds a correlate in what Rey Chow describes as an intrinsic structural asymmetry in Butterfly fiction. For the female protagonists in these stories, "'love' is not a cherished state of being endowed with the meaning of a 'completed' life; it is rather a disaster that befalls them."[28] Or, in the words of Lee, romantic heroines "must be loyal, faithful, devoted, and self-sacrificing, so much so that only death—almost always self-induced—is [an] adequate authentication of her identity as a woman of feeling."[29]

The story of *chahua nü* was not only referenced and reworked in literary productions of the period, but it was also adapted for the stage by one of China's first modern theater troupes in 1907.[30] Zhang Zhen points out that the earliest Chinese screen version of Camille's story, titled *Xin chahua* (*New Camellias*), appeared in 1913 and was one of a string of film adaptations from well-known Western literary works during the silent period.[31] The acclaimed director Sun Yu credits the novel as the inspiration for *Yecao xianhua* (*Wild Flowers*, 1930), one of the earliest films to incorporate synchronized sound effects into its design and to use a theme song. *Wild Flowers'* story of a young man from a wealthy family who falls in love with a poor flower seller (played by the screen luminaries Jin Yan and Ruan Lingyu) transposed the story of Camille to a contemporary setting, concomitantly reimagining the courtesan as a street singer. As Sun wrote in an article about the film, "The story is from Dumas, not much is new . . . women often sacrifice themselves. Dancers, singers, actresses, and ill-fated women, from ancient times, even outside of China, have supplied the materials of tragedy."[32] Besides such direct adaptations, many of the Chinese novels inspired by Dumas were also made into movies, such as *Yu li hun* (*Jade Pear Spirit*) which, Zhang notes, was a big box-office hit on its release in 1924.[33] In this filmmaking environment, scriptwriters relied heavily on preexisting literary materials, and many filmmakers themselves came from the world of literature. In particular, Emilie Yeh writes, the authors of popular Duck and Butterfly fiction "were among the most sought after to adapt their own stories for movies or to write new screenplays."[34] Beyond adaptation narrowly defined as a direct treatment of an original source text, then, Camille's impact on early Chinese cinema ripples across a dense intertextual field constituted in practices of allusion, creative appropriation, and transmigration between languages and mediums. Its significance can be framed in the context of what Lydia Liu terms the "translated modernity" of early twentieth-century Chinese culture.[35]

The impact of this story is not confined to the period of early Chinese cinema, moreover, for the transplanted camellias of the romantic imagination would also find fertile ground on which to blossom in postwar Hong Kong. Filmmakers in the 1950s and 1960s continued to draw on the story of *La dame aux camélias* in various ways. These include direct adaptations that explicitly refer to the French novel as a source text, such as *Chahua nü* (*Camellia*, 1955), produced by Xinhua Film Company. The film was one of the early projects on which Wong Tin-lam honed his skills as an assistant director, and thus it was a likely inspiration for *The Wild, Wild Rose*'s envisioning of the songstress as a transplanted camellia. The opening credit sequence of *Camellia* announces that the film is based on the book by Alexander Dumas *fils*—although, as the first scene reveals, it owes more to the 1936 Hollywood film version than to the original novel. Like Cukor's *Camille*, the film begins with a scene at the florist shop that provides the main character with a regular fresh supply of her namesake flower. The remainder of its story adheres closely to the plot outline of Cukor's film, while replacing its historical mise-en-scène with a modern setting. Like *Wild Flowers*, *Camellia* turns to the figure of the songstress as a modern-day counterpart to the nineteenth-century courtesan. The film featured the actress Li Lihua as a worldly courtesan (euphemistically referred to as a "social butterfly") and singer suffering from tuberculosis. Li began her career in the Shanghai film industry during the years of the Japanese occupation, a fact that exposed her to accusations of collaboration at the end of the war. After relocating to Hong Kong, she recommenced her filmmaking career and went on to become one of the biggest stars of her time. Although she never established a separate career as a recording artist in the way of songstresses like Zhou Xuan and Grace Chang, Li sang in many of her productions, and in keeping with this tendency, *Camellia* contains two song inserts performed by the star.[36] *Camellia* had such success that it was imitated in the following year by Shaw Brothers in a production titled *Hua luo you feng jun* (*Till We Meet Again*, 1956). The publicity materials for the film include a program synopsis with a preface written by its director, Doe Ching: "In the mid-nineteenth century, there emerged a woman in Paris. Her beautiful, tragic story was written by Alexander Dumas *fils* as a novel and play. One hundred years later, there has emerged among us another woman like Marguerite Gautier. Her story astonishes us, because she shares the fate of that famous Parisian lady."[37]

Apart from adaptations like these that lay direct claim to the literary prestige of the original work, the Camille ur-narrative also weaves throughout postwar Hong Kong cinema through more indirect channels of circulation, its components broken down and incorporated in various recombinations. For instance, one of Grace Chang's earlier films, *Girl of a Thousand Guises*, contains the theme of love between a young man from a respectable family and a woman deemed to be socially unfit because of her occupation as an opera singer. The mother convinces the singer to leave her son for his own good, and like Marguerite, she does so by pretending to take up with another man. The son realizes what has happened too late, after she has run away from their home. *A Story of Three Loves* takes its Chinese title from the 1930 novel from which it is adapted—*Ti xiao yinyuan* (*Fate in Tears and Laughter*), one of the most popular works of fiction from the Duck and Butterfly period[38]—but fuses this well-known story with elements from *The Lady of the Camellias*. In *Fate in Tears and Laughter*, a high-born man falls in love with Fengxi, the lowly street singer played by Chang. But although the novel portrays Fengxi as materialistically driven in her romantic pursuits, the film overlays the image of Camille on this character, presenting her as unwaveringly loyal to her lover, Jiasu. By way of emphasizing her self-sacrificing virtue, the film reprises the episode in which Armand caustically confronts Marguerite after she has left him and insults her by hurling a fistful of dollars at her, along with the ending of teary deathbed regrets. Traces of the Camille ur-narrative are also found in cycle of songstress films produced by Shaw Brothers. One of these, *Chiqing lie* (*Pink Tears*, 1965), conjures up the suffering Camille in the figure of a high-class call girl and songstress, featuring in its lead role one of Chang's contemporaries, the singer and actress Julie Yeh Feng. *Pink Tears* combines the story of ill-fated romance with motifs from American maternal melodramas like *Imitation of Life* (1959). When the young widow Lilan meets her true love, a piano player, the couple encounter opposition on two fronts, from both his mother and her daughter. What follows plays out like a remake of Camille, with tubercular coughing fits, flung money, and deathbed regrets. Another Shaw Brothers film in this cycle is *Bu liao qing* (*Love without End*, 1961). Starring Linda Lin Dai as a nightclub singer, the film rehashes the theme of love blighted by a man's misrecognition of a woman's surreptitious sacrifice, on the one hand, and doomed by terminal disease, on the other. And finally *Heri jun zai lai* (*Till the End of Time*, 1966) bisects the tragic romance with a cross-generational family drama with its story about a wealthy young man who marries a nightclub singer over the objections of his family. Notably, the film served as a launching pad for the young star Jenny Hu, the last of postwar Hong Kong cinema's singing actresses.

As these examples indicate, the figure of the *chahua nü* was constantly revisited and reimagined by the postwar Mandarin film industry. As in the prewar years, her story supplied filmmakers with a set of tropes and scenarios that could be appropriated, reworked, amplified, and transformed in what seem to be endless variations. The enduring appeal of *The Lady of the Camellias* across the two periods brings into view an important strand of continuity between the film cultures of prewar Shanghai and postwar Hong Kong. Not only are the interconnections between these cultures embodied in the film workers who migrated from one context to the other, but they also extend to their fictional landscapes, both deeply ingrained by the tradition of sentimental literature. The literary disposition of filmmaking in the republican era continues to be evident in the reliance of postwar filmmakers on adaptation as a "generative grammar," to borrow a phrase from Robert Stam.[39] Popular literary works from the early twentieth century proved to be a resource for adaptation well into the 1960s. For instance, *A Story of Three Loves* was produced by MP&GI in an endeavor to capitalize on a literary classic, and Shaw Brothers responded in the same year with its own adaptation, *Xin ti xiao yinyuan* (*Between Tears and Smiles*), released in the same year to compete with their rival's version. The echoes of the romantic literary theme of free love versus tradition reverberated throughout the postwar years. Analogously, fiction writers continued to play an active role in the film industry. In particular, MP&GI was known for its close ties to the cosmopolitan literati class.[40]

Music, Melodrama, and the Undoing of Women

In each of the films noted above, the cultural memory of the lady of the camellias is linked to the figure of the songstress, reanimated time and again by the most celebrated singing actresses of Chinese film history—Grace Chang, Li Lihua, Linda Lin Dai, Julie Yeh Feng, and Jenny Hu. The association between the songstress and this literary prototype is revealing on many counts. To begin with, it attests to the ways in which the imagination of the modern-day singer is tinged by the afterimage of the courtesan, her fascination framed by references to the female entertainers of an earlier era. Although this association upholds the mythology of the songstress as an embodiment of feminine ideals of beauty and talent, it also cements a social perception of the female singer as little more than a prostitute, as a figure who cannot be assimilated to gender norms that contain female sexuality within the sphere of domesticity and who is therefore viewed as a threat to the identity of daughter, wife, or mother. The cultural paradox of the songstress—desirable and idealized, yet also contemptible and stigmatized—becomes dramatic fodder in many Camille-like narratives, where these attitudes are personified in different characters and set in conflict with one another. Almost invariably this conflict plays out between young men of feeling, in the mold of Armand, and their parents, depicted as little more than stock figures of social prejudice and knee-jerk traditionalism. *The Lady of the Camellias* supplies the songstress film with a set of motifs that are repeated, reworked, and reified as a dramatic template for romantic melo-drama. Moreover, through the lens of Camille, we can also begin to account for the bizarre fusion that produces a character like Deng Sijia, who is less an internally consistent entity than a pastiche of familiar feminine stereotypes. Viewed as a transplanted camellia, Sijia assumes a position in a long line of incoherent and contradictory feminine types. As Hu Ying argues, the cultural imagination of women entered a markedly dynamic phase in the early twen-tieth century—drawing on imported models of femininity, such as Marguerite Gautier, along with traditional icons of virtuous women, and amalgamating these into composite signs that were neither "original" nor "coherent."[41] These earlier figurations of the new woman were central to the imagination of mo-dernity, circulating as emblems of historical ambivalence and of the interplay between the global and the local. In subsequent decades, cinema would in-tercept this discourse of femininity, emerging as a crucial platform on which gendered ideals of modernity were projected, translated, and domesticated.

As an embodiment of conventions shared by cinema and literature, the song-stress can be positioned within the history of *wenyi pian* (literary arts film), a genre designation that came into usage in the 1920s to refer to film adaptations of Western fiction. In her important critical genealogy of *wenyi pian*, Emilie Yeh traces its origins to the sphere of literary criticism, where the Japanese loan word *wenyi* was invoked as a name for works of translated fiction from the West. As these works became a resource for filmmakers, the term was ad-opted by film critics to denominate both local productions based on *wenyi* fic-tion and Western productions drawing on literary sources.[42] The meaning of *wenyi pian* incorporated a broader set of associations during its evolution as a genre category in film criticism, acquiring connotations of artistic distinc-tion as well as progressive political values. It is the latter progressive strand of *wenyi pian*, rooted in 1930s leftist filmmaking and extending into the era of the People's Republic of China, that has attracted the bulk of scholarly attention. The earliest writings in English on this topic approach it through the rubric of melodrama, and in their wake, melodrama continues to be invoked as a criti-cal equivalent for *wenyi pian*.[43] But, Yeh argues, *wenyi pian* is not reducible to melodrama, and to conflate these terms too readily is to overlook the specific cultural and historical inflections that each carries in its respective regional context. While *wenyi* emerges from and emphasizes "literary value and artistic space," she writes, melodrama originates in musical theater, defined by values of sensationalism, "theatrical display . . . and emotional excess." Yeh builds a case for recovering *wenyi pian*'s distinctiveness as a mode of filmmaking that points to translation and adaptation as driving forces in the "mass production of modern sentiment" by Chinese cinema.[44] As a product of the intertextual, cross-referential field of postwar filmmaking, *The Wild, Wild Rose* stands out as an exemplary case study of how these intertwined forces affected film culture throughout the twentieth century and stimulated the development of genres like *gechang pian*.[45]

But at the same time, *The Wild, Wild Rose* also points to the impossibility of fully separating the literary and artistic ambitions of *wenyi pian* from the more sensationalist aspects of melodrama. The film fully conforms with melodrama defined most broadly, as a cinematic mode rooted in an appeal to emotion. In the words of Linda Williams, "if emotional and moral registers are sounded, if a work invites us to feel sympathy for the virtues of beset victims, if the narrative trajectory is ultimately more concerned with a retrieval and staging of innocence than with the psychological causes of motives and action, then the operative mode is melodrama."[46] Within the larger constellation of sentimental songstress narratives to which the film belongs, we can also readily discern numerous other defining attributes of melodrama: a black-and-white moral universe, with characters who fall clearly on one side of the boundary or the other; a reliance on coincidence as a plot device; a fascination with suffering and, in particular, female victimhood; and, increasingly in the 1960s, a displacement of meaning onto aesthetic components of lighting, décor, color, gesture, and music.[47] The difficulty of distinguishing between *wenyi pian* and melodrama in the context of specific films ultimately stems from the fact that the two were historically constituted in dialogue with one another.[48] To the extent that *wenyi* denotes a set of translingual practices, it paved the way for an encounter with, and the absorption of, the conventions of Western melodrama. Thus in his book-length study of *wenyi pian*, Cai Guorong refers both to the literary dimension of this category and to its elicitation of "emotion and sympathy" from the audience. In this definition, *wenyi pian* rests on spectatorial affects as much as narrative attributes.[49]

The role of the songstress is important here because it shows how performed songs were absorbed into the conventions of film melodrama. As much as female-centered sentimental dramas continued to command the interest of filmgoers, the endowment of the tragic heroines of the screen with singing voices brought a new dimension to these stories, by adding musical vocalization to cinema's arsenal of melodramatic effects. Songs served to punctuate the plights of the characters and the pathos of their position, to give voice to their experiences of suffering and longing, and thus to materialize emotional truths and an inner realm of feeling. They emerged as crucial audiovisual conduits through which the themes of sacrifice, virtue, and romantic idealism were amplified for movie audiences. These connotations are already evident in one of the earliest instances of a film containing song performance, *Liangxin fuhuo* (*Resurrection of Conscience*, 1926), a *wenyi pian* adapted from Tolstoy's novel *Resurrection*, discussed in chapter 1. This silent film forged a link between sentimental drama and musical drama by punctuating a climactic scene in which a single mother discovers that her child has died with a live song performance by the actress. The subsequent development of singing pictures solidifies and deepens this link. If songs found their way into Chinese cinema as part of the legacy of sentimental literature, here they would constitute the seeds for a strand of film melodrama that emerged from the conjunction of music and narrative—a strand that harks back to the term's original definition as *melos* plus drama. Breaking into the film at regular intervals, songs operate in the manner of a theatrical monologue, as manifestations of the feelings and thoughts of the singer and hence expressions of an inner truth. Yet even as they seem to offer a privileged insight into the character, they also come into direct conflict with the way she is perceived in her fictional universe, given that the songstress as *wenyi* heroine is consistently not seen for who she really is, and her actions and motives are misapprehended by others. Song performance thus materializes the gap between truth and perception, sounding a plea on behalf of the singer and in the name of a "retrieval and staging of innocence." Its function derives from the drama of misrecognition that *gechang pian* has in common with melodrama, as a narrative mode directed at the vindication of truth and virtue.[50] Thus the problem of identity that drives *The Wild, Wild Rose*—whether Sijia is a Carmen or a Camille—is representative of the strategies by which melodrama generates effects of pathos. By positioning the songstress as the source and center of an emotional reality to which only music can do justice, these films reinforce the focus on female characters as a locus of melodrama.

The potent truth effect of song—its evocation of emotional authenticity—is capable of overcoming even the most theatrically contrived situations of performance, as demonstrated by Sijia's final song number in *The Wild, Wild Rose*. Costumed as the character Cio-Cio San in *Madame Butterfly*, in a kimono and traditional Japanese chignon, Sijia sings a Mandarin version of "Un bel dì vedremo." (*Madame Butterfly* was popularized in an Italian film version of 1955, starring the Japanese soprano Kaoru Yachigusa, and the kimono worn by Chang in this scene was reportedly given to her by Yachigusa.[51]) In the opera, Cio-Cio San sings the aria as she awaits the return of her American husband Pinkerton, expressing her unwavering faithfulness to him although—as we soon learn—he has already betrayed her. The lyrics of Sijia's rendition describe her feelings for Hanhua. She sings of her regret for having treated their love as a "game," referring to and revoking the sentiments expressed in the opening "Habañera" number, and of the hopeless bind in which she now finds herself, unable to love him or to leave him. "Love only hurts people," she sings, "and now I have no escape." The performance adds yet another layer to the collage of voices and personas that make up Chang's character. In conjuring up the figure of Cio-Cio San as a familiar icon of virtuous love, the song ultimately affirms Sijia's rehabilitation by true feeling, her transformation from a Carmen into a Camille.

Somewhat curiously, the music that would most directly convey this transformation, that of the opera La Traviata, is absent from the repertoire of The Wild, Wild Rose. This exclusion may be owing to the extreme technical difficulty of La Traviata's prima donna role and the fact that its music, unlike that of other operas, would not have been recognized as readily by Chinese audiences at the time. But the interjection of "Un bel dì vedremo" at this point in the film calls attention to the parallels between the stories of Camille and Madame Butterfly, both featuring romantic heroines who sacrifice their lives in the name of love and for the sake of men incapable of rising to their level of intensity. When we consider Madame Butterfly alongside Carmen, another parallel emerges: their common reliance on the death of the woman as a mechanism of narrative closure. Indeed The Wild, Wild Rose cites a total of three well-known operas that culminate in the death of the soprano.[52] With this intertextual gesture, the film discloses a consonance between the sacrificial structure of the literary tradition on which it draws and the "undoing of women" in the classical musical tradition, to quote from Catherine Clément's famous critique of the regressive gender politics of Western opera. Clément writes: "On the opera stage women perpetually sing their eternal undoing. The emotion is never more poignant than at the moment when the voice is lifted to die."[53] Across the operatic canon, "there is always this constant: death by a man," so that the beautiful death amounts to a patriarchal ritual, an "infinitely repetitive spectacle of a woman who dies."[54]

The debates launched in the wake of Clément's critique help shed light on the ambivalent positioning of the voice in songstress films. Operas like Carmen, La Traviata, and Madame Butterfly stage in hyperbolic terms the paradox of the female singing voice. Responding to Clément's critique, various commentators have argued that the libretto does not fully account for the experience of the work.[55] To reduce the meaning of the opera to the actions of the plot or the fate of the fictional character is to miss something vital about the music's effects on the listener. The analysis of gender in opera must also take into account the power of the voice raised in song—particularly, the voice of the prima donna—and its conquest of the audience, or even the text itself. Along these lines, Adriana Cavarero describes opera as not a ritual restaging of the unambiguous death of women, but as a struggle between the vocal and the semantic, music and story, and the feminine and masculine. "The mixing of words and song of which opera consists works precisely as an anomalous site of challenge and confusion, or seduction and trickery," she writes. "The problem remains that opera can be received by different subjects precisely because the power of song triumphs over the words."[56]

The double edge of opera, endowing the singer with an outlet for expression only to eventually silence her, can also be seen at work in *gechang pian*. These films dramatize the intrinsic tension between the protagonist's capacity to move the audience and—beyond any other character in the fiction—command their identification with her voice and her lack of agency within the story, which more often than not traces a trajectory of victimization and eventual death. The central paradox of the songstress film rests on the decided contrast between the affective power concentrated in the singing voice and the extreme disempowerment of the owner of that voice in the diegetic universe. In tapping into the feminine death drive that animates opera, *The Wild, Wild Rose* brings to light the perverse narrative impulses of sentimental songstress films, with their fixation on female suffering, elaborately contrived acts of sacrifice, and masochistic heroines who actively elicit the contempt of the people they love. Viewed in this context, the manner in which Sijia dies—strangled, and hence both literally and figuratively silenced—is especially symbolically loaded. But even while characters like Sijia are allowed "no escape" from their vulnerability as women from the lower depths, their songs constitute a residue that cannot be entirely integrated into or dispatched by these narrative systems of control. When there is nothing left to do, no recourse for action, what remains is the act of singing. Song carves out a space for dissonant musical voices in the film, and these voices lay claim to the attention and the memory of the audience with an insistence that surpasses that of the story itself.

CODA

Like *Manbo nülang* (*Mambo Girl*), the 1969 youth film *Feinü zhengzhuan* (*Teddy Girls*) begins with an energetic scene of musical revelry. Boys and girls crowd together on a dance floor beneath a glittering disco ball, moving in time with a driving rock beat. Joyful hoots and yelps mingle with the howl of an electric guitar and punctuate the beat at irregular intervals. The camera plunges into the scene in medias res and weaves erratically among the bobbing and shaking bodies, as if infected by the kinetic propulsion of the music. It singles out two young women clad in minidresses who are dancing together with evident glee. They throw their arms around, careen their hips this way and that, swimming and twisting. A tight close-up on one of them reveals the face of the teen idol Josephine Siao (Sia Fong-fong), masked partially by her long locks as she wildly tosses her head. Immersed in the music, the two friends are oblivious to the aggressive lecherous stares of a trio of men sitting at a table nearby. Thus the scene reprises a scenario of sexual objectification familiar from so many songstress films. The three men rise from their seats with a menacing manner and make their way toward the dance floor. We see a medium close-up of Siao's friend from behind at hip level, and a hand enters into the frame to paw at her derriere. She screams and Siao comes to her defense, slapping the offender full in the face. When he responds by grabbing Siao and forcing a kiss on her, she fights back, and the altercation ends when she breaks a glass bottle over his head and he drops to the floor in pain. This is abruptly followed by a cut to a courtroom scene, where Siao is sentenced to incarceration in a juvenile detention center.

Comparing this opening scene to that of *Mambo Girl*, we can track the twelve years separating the two films by means of musical styles. The jazzy big band tunes of the 1950s have been drowned out by the amplifier-enhanced sounds of rock and roll, and Grace Chang's carefully choreographed mambo moves replaced by Siao's writhing go-go dance. The orderly, precise orchestration of Chang's mambo number gives way to a freewheeling presentation more in keeping with musical codes of spontaneity, abandon, and youthful kicks. Indeed *Teddy Girls* evokes *Mambo Girl* only to stage the return of the libidinal and antisocial impulses that were repressed in the earlier film's portrayal of the teenage songstress. Even the violence that breaks out in the dance club becomes an expression of the music, which does not pause until the cut to the courtroom. By exploding the values previously assigned to music and dance, *Teddy Girls* also displays the conditions for the disappearance of the songstress from postwar Chinese cinema in the latter half of the 1960s. The film's enormous box-office success points to the gulf in taste and sensibility that separated the wartime generation of migrants from a new generation of moviegoers. The latter were born in Hong Kong; had no direct memories of war and displacement; and came of age in a period marked by social unrest, mass demonstrations, and political violence.[1] In *Teddy Girls*, the performance of the Cantonese-speaking Josephine Siao channels rebellion and rage, rather than submission to suffering. For the younger postwar demographic, the plaintive ballads of the songstress held no emotional sway, and the melodramatic conventions in which they were embedded could only appear atrophied and outdated.[2]

The reign of singing actresses over the Hong Kong movie world was eventually challenged by a different screen icon, one who heralded a novel chapter in the colony's film history: the male action hero. The death knell of the songstress was sounded by the revival of the martial arts film, first in the genre of the historical swordplay film (*wuxia pian*) and then in the kung fu craze ignited by Bruce Lee. Singing women were edged out by fighting men (and sometimes fighting women, too), and the lyrical display of the voice gave way to a choreography of bodies clashing in violent battle. Along with this swing of the pendulum of popular taste, the extinction of the songstress was also hastened by the demise of the system that had sustained her. The golden era of Mandarin filmmaking in Hong Kong was a short-lived phenomenon. The death of Loke Wan Tho in an airplane crash in 1964 was a blow from which the studio that he headed, the Motion Picture and General Investment Co. Ltd. (MP&GI), never completely recovered: following a period of declining production, the studio closed in 1971. Around this time the fortunes of Shaw Brothers also went into a decline. Demand for Mandarin films shrank in response to competition from broadcast television, which became established on a mass scale in the late 1960s, and import quotas imposed in Southeast Asia, where a large part of the films' overseas markets was located. In Hong Kong, the monolithic Shaw Brothers saw its dominance challenged by smaller, nimbler competitors.

By the middle of the 1970s, Cantonese had become the dominant language of Hong Kong's film, music, and media industries. Hong Kong cinema as we know it today has roots in this moment of reorientation.

Thus the songstress disappeared from the screen, yet she did not remain completely forgotten, lingering in the attics of film history to be occasionally revived for an encore turn. In recent years, she has haunted the soundtracks of films from all three Chinese territories that reflect on historical events of the twentieth century. For instance, *Huang tudi* (*Yellow Earth*), one of the defining productions of the Fifth Generation of mainland Chinese cinema, revives the figure of the farmer's daughter in the character Cuiqiao, a peasant girl whose singing punctuates the soundtrack. The 1998 Hong Kong film *Yanzhi kou* (*Rouge*) casts the Cantonese pop singer and actress Anita Mui in its leading role, a courtesan and entertainer from the 1930s who returns from the dead seeking her old lover. The first scene of the film introduces her character as a young woman working in a brothel, as she performs a Cantonese opera song for a group of customers. The song number taps into Mui's identity as one of Hong Kong's most famed recording artists in the 1980s and 1990s, an enormously popular performer of the Cantonese soft rock music commonly known as Cantopop.[3] The Taiwan-made film *Zui hao de shiguang* (*Three Times*) also features a courtesan in one of its three vignettes, set in China in the 1910s. In one of its scenes, we see her playing a *pipa* as she sings *nanyin*, a style of vocal music from the southern region of Fujian. Notably, her voice receives a special emphasis as the only one that is audible on the soundtrack, given that the entirety of the vignette is shot as a silent film. These films speak to the diffusion of the songstress figure in Chinese films of different languages and regions, beyond the Mandarin films this book has focused on.

To return to the examples set forth at the beginning of this book, the espionage drama *Se jie* (*Lust, Caution*) follows its principal players from Hong Kong to Shanghai, tracing routes of passage carved out by the upheavals of the wartime era. When Wang Jiazhi performs "The Wandering Songstress"—a song originally made famous by Zhou Xuan in *Malu tianshi* (*Street Angel*)—the lyrics acquire a pointed resonance in this historical context, with their avowal of steadfast love in the face of displacement and suffering. "Gazing north from my mountain nest, my tears fall and wet my blouse," she sings. "Only love that lasts through adversity is deep. In life who does not cherish the springtime of youth?" *Hua yang nianhua* (*In the Mood for Love*) presents Hong Kong as another stopping point on a similar route of passage, with its depiction of the insular Shanghainese émigré community living there in the postwar years. In the words of Giorgio Biancorosso, this community inhabits "an almost fictitious realm defined by visual and auditory images of Shanghai"—cheongsams, songs, dialect, food, mahjong, and daily rituals—as signs of "a mythologisation of a time and a place in the mind of these homesick characters."[4] Here again, Zhou Xuan's music serves to evoke a sense of dislocation. The selection of her song "The Blooming Years" is doubly significant in this regard, with its lyrical lament for a lost homeland and its historical status as one of the tunes recorded by the singer after she fled Shanghai for Hong Kong. Lastly, the Taiwan-made film *Dong* (*The Hole*) has been described by its Malaysian-born director as a tribute to one of his favorite singers, Grace Chang. The circulation of Chang's songs from Hong Kong to listeners in Malaysia and Taiwan further extends the network of migration and diaspora delineated in the previous examples. In all of these instances, familiar tunes and distinctive voices function as both a means of mapping movements across a territorial expanse and an index of the temporal rifts also engendered by these passages. In direct proportion to her anachronistic status, the songstress conjures up a sense of pastness and provokes an awareness of distance and loss.

In the Mood for Love derives its Chinese title from the Zhou Xuan song that is played in its entirety in the film, "Hua yang de nianhua." The phrase, commonly translated as "The Blooming Years," metaphorically describes a bygone golden age in the beauty and brevity of a flowering blossom. The same song lends its title to, and serves as a soundtrack for, a short film made by Wong Kar-wai with his longtime collaborator and editor William Chang Suk Ping in the same year as the feature. The short consists of a montage of found footage fragments, compiled from a cache of nitrate prints of old Hong Kong movies discovered in a warehouse in southern California, where they once were screened in Chinatown theaters. It begins with a dedication from the filmmaker: "To the blooming years we will always remember." The first image is of a young ballerina spinning in pirouettes, her movements rendered even more flickeringly weightless by the use of fast motion compression.[5] The melody begins, and a series of opening credits from different productions flashes by too quickly to read, followed by a shot of a round clock face (an object that appears in nearly all of Wong's films) and then by an image of the same ballerina blowing out the candles on a birthday cake—now in extreme slow motion. As Zhou's voice commences to sing, we are offered a glimpse of the scene in which she originally performed the song, from the 1947 film *Chang xiang si* (*All-Consuming Love*).[6] Thus sound and image align in synchronization for a brief moment in the body of the singer, only to diverge once again as the film resumes its rapid-fire montage. A parade of the glamorous leading ladies of bygone years floats across the screen—styled in the fashions of the times, beaming in close-up for the camera, twirling with their partners on the dance floor, running to greet their lovers, swooning in their arms, and bidding them farewell. Clips of Zhou taken from various other films appear throughout the montage, which lasts for the duration of her song. At the point when she croons, "Suddenly this orphan island is overshadowed by miseries and sorrows, miseries and sorrows," the events to which the lyrics refer are illustrated with shots of falling bombs and explosions, waves that suggest travel by sea, and then a Hong Kong street scene.

The short film can be seen as an epilogue to the feature, constituting an archive of material traces of the era that *In the Mood for Love* strives to recreate, a catalog of the feminine details so central to its visualization of history: *qipao*, elaborate hairdos, stockings, and high-heeled shoes. The romantic mood of these golden years is boiled down to a repertory of repeated gestures and facial expressions, tropes of arrival and departure, and boudoir scenarios. These present themselves with the instant legibility of the melodramatic cliché, but at the same time they undergo a process of defamiliarization in their detachment from narrative and deprivation of sound. In succession they appear and disappear in the blink of an eye, ephemeral and fragile like images in a dream. A blue tint intermittently washes over the black-and-white images and contributes to the film's nocturnal atmosphere; this manipulation of color calls to mind *Rose Hobart*, directed by Joseph Cornell in 1936, another found footage work that pays homage to actresses of the past. Similar to Cornell's film, *The Blooming Years* eliminates all of the sound from the original footage and replaces it with music selected by the filmmaker. Zhou Xuan's song frames the montage from beginning to end and rhythmically structures the flow of its images. The meanings previously inscribed in the film fragments are submerged in the emotional matrix of the music, recoded as signs of the wistful longing expressed by the singer. Conversely, the song undergoes a transformation of its own in this encounter. The metaphor of blossoms shifts into a figure of feminine beauty with the film's last images, consisting of a pageant-like procession of lovely starlets—unattainable fantasy objects in their own time and further mythologized as emblems of an idealized past for subsequent generations. The sentiments stirred up by the song expand in an infinite regress of desire and nostalgia, and the phrase *the blooming years* comes to stand for a longing that manifests itself in a mode of belatedness.

By distilling an entire era of history into the space of a song, the short film suggests why the songs of the songstress remain compelling across the reaches of time—even when the films in which they originally featured have either faded from sight or contracted into brief moments standing apart from a filmic stream. To the extent that film songs like this one were never fully integrated into the narratives in which they featured, they exist on a different timeline and make special claims on the memory of the audience. Yet the difference constituted by the musical moment was once an entrenched feature of film culture, built into its genre system and industrial networks. The ubiquitous presence of film songs complicates questions of address and identification, and how films construct what we remember of them. The voice of songstress sounds an exhortation to listen again by activating an awareness of something more to be heard, residual meanings yet to be fully deciphered.

NOTES

Introduction

1 *Hua yang nianhua* (*In the Mood for Love*).

2 *Chang xiang si* (*All-Consuming Love*).

3 This translation is from Deppman, *Adapted for the Screen*, 206, note 19. As Deppman points out, Zhou Xuan herself fled from Shanghai to Hong Kong in 1946, returning to the mainland in 1950 and remaining there until her death in 1957 at the age of thirty-nine. Ironically, the song was banned from Hong Kong's airwaves in the 1960s, possibly for the political subtext of its lyrics, with their references to the mainland (the "lovely country") and pro-Kuomindang patriotism. See K. Wong, *The Age of Shanghainese Pops*, 29.

4 The film's casting of the well-known émigré singing star Rebecca Pan in the role of the landlady Mrs. Suen further emphasizes the Shanghainese presence in postwar Hong Kong.

5 The term *punctum* comes from Barthes, *Camera Lucida*.

6 *Se jie* (*Lust, Caution*).

7 *Malu tianshi* (*Street Angel*).

8 *Dong* (*The Hole*).

9 For a detailed discussion of this film's songstress references, see J. Ma, "Delayed Voices."

10 Indeed, this symbiosis even predates sound cinema: the great silent film star Ruan Lingyu, Jones points out, was a recording artist in Hong Kong's popular music industry prior to her acting career (*Yellow Music*, 67).

11 Jones, *Yellow Music*; Touhy, "Metropolitan Sounds"; Yeh Y., *Gesheng meiying*; Zhang Z., *An Amorous History of the Silver Screen*, chapter 8; J. Ma and Johnson, "Sound and Music."

12 For an overview of Chinese opera films (focusing on productions from the People's Republic of China), see Iovene and Zeitlin, "Chinese Opera Film." Chapter 2 contains a more detailed account of opera films and the conventions of song performance, including specific examples.

13 Y. Yeh, "Historiography and Sinification," 79.

14 The parallels between the two films are discussed in Harris, "*Two Stars on the Silver Screen*."

15 For more on these works, see Jones, *Yellow Music*, 131–32; Zhang Z., *An Amorous History of the Silver Screen*, chapter 8; and Y. Wang, "The 'Transnational' as Methodology," 13–14.

16 Zhou, "*Genü Hong mudan* duiyu Zhongguo dianyingjie de gongxian jiqi yingxiang," 14.

17 Needham, "Fashioning Modernity," 45.

18 This gloss on the film musical and its "harmonious unity" of marriage comes from Altman, *The American Film Musical*, 24. Altman's definition of the musical forms the backbone for Needham's comparative reading. Needham also comments on the general absence of dance and choreographic spectacle in the group of films he describes as Mandarin musicals ("Fashioning Modernity," 50).

19 Needham, "Fashioning Modernity," 42. It is telling that several of the entries in Creekmur and Mokdad, *The International Film Musical*—a recent volume that surveys international film musicals by country—reflect on the difficulty of reconciling the film musical as understood in an American context with their particular region of focus, at both the semantic and syntactic levels.

20 Dyer, *In the Space of a Song*, 57–58.

21 McMillin, *The Musical as Drama*, 1.

22 McMillin, *The Musical as Drama*, 3.

23 Teo, "Oh, Karaoke!," 35.

24 Teo, *Hong Kong Cinema*, 31. Chapter 2 of *Hong Kong Cinema* revisits and expands on the arguments of Teo's earlier essay on this topic, "Oh, Karaoke!" My discussion here synthesizes and responds to both of these works.

25 Teo, "Oh, Karaoke!," 32.

26 Teo, *Hong Kong Cinema*, 34.

27 Altman, *The American Film Musical*, 13.

28 Dyer, *In the Space of a Song*, 5. This last point echoes observations by other theorists of the musical. For example, Altman writes about how musical numbers unfold at a different level of reality, in "a 'place' or transcendence where time stands still, where contingent concerns are stripped away to reveal the essence of things," "a utopian space in which all singers and dancers achieve a unity unimaginable in the now superseded world of temporal, psychological causality" (*The American Film Musical*, 66, 69). McMillin emphasizes the repetitive (rather than static) temporality of song: "there is another order of time in the theatre, not just the cause-and-effect sequencing of plot but the lyrical repetitions of song and dance" (*The Musical as Drama*, 9). And Herzog writes: "Unfettered by the demands of causality, the sensorial spectacles in the musical often subsume the narrative framework, creating configurations of time and space completely unlike those found in other filmic works" (*Dreams of Difference*, 2).

29 The crux of McMillin's book lies in his assertion that "the musical depends more on the differences that make the close fit interesting than on the suppression of difference in a seamless whole" (*The Musical as Drama*, 2). Herzog's analysis focuses on those "breaks and stutters on the level of the image and the sound track" that open onto the "noise" of social differences (*Dreams of Difference*, 4). And Dyer's most recent book relates the affective dimension of song performance to questions about such is-

sues as racial difference and the tension between the musical's explicit heteronorma-
tivity and its queer reception (*In the Space of a Song*). See also Mast, *Can't Help Singin'*.

30 Herzog, *Dreams of Difference*, 2, 8.

31 Zhang takes the idea of the dominant from Roman Jakobson, referring to "the focusing component of a work of art: it rules, determines, and transforms the remaining components" (*An Amorous History of the Silver Screen*, 302).

32 Zhang Z., *An Amorous History of the Silver Screen*, 307. Hu Die's song scenes in the
film were dubbed by the famed Mei Lanfang, a male opera performer who specialized in female roles; this fact was not widely advertised at the time of the film's
release. One of the very few exceptions to this pattern in the early sound period, discussed by Zhang, was *Song at Midnight*, a second-generation (by means of Universal's
1925 film) adaptation of Gaston Leroux's *The Phantom of the Opera*, which features a
deformed male singer.

33 Wong K., "A Song in Every Film." A more accurate translation of his phrase (*wu ge bu
cheng pian*) would be "no film without a song."

34 One of the most iconic *enka* singers of postwar Japanese film, Misora Hibari appeared in over 150 films and recorded 1,500 songs between 1949 and 1981. Her
early career was based on her performances of American jazz music. See Tansman,
"Misora Hibari"; Yano, *Tears of Longing*. My thanks to Alan Tansman for introducing
me to Misora's work.

35 Conway, *Chanteuse in the City*, 3. Such lyrical performances are a long way from the
Hollywood musical, with its overtones of utopia, euphoria, and wish fulfillment.

36 Another comparative example worth considering here is song in American noir and
crime thrillers. These songs are typically performed by women and often give explicit voice to undercurrents of pain, perversity, and violence. Examples include Rita
Hayworth's performance of "Put the Blame on Mame" in *Gilda* and Lauren Bacall
crooning "And Her Tears Flowed Like Wine" in *The Big Sleep*, both released in 1946.
Indeed, rather than Hollywood musicals, a more salient reference point for Chinese
songstress films might be the American noir film—which, as Adrienne McLean
observes, tends to "feature women as singers or showgirls" and to frame song performance within the story as "straight (often in a nightclub or other underworld
setting)" ("'It's Only That I Do What I Love and Love What I Do,'" 3).

37 Yeh, "China," 173.

38 Yue, *Shanghai and the Edges of Empire*, 98.

39 *Genü zhi ge* (*Song of a Songstress*).

40 The popular music historian Szu-Wei Chen writes: "In traditional Chinese operas or
folk songs, both genders participate in singing, but most of the historical recordings
of Shanghai popular songs were sung by female performers. Male performers often
served as characters who were secondary in importance to the main female role
in duets and choruses, or as vocalists for backing harmonies. Though some male
singers also made their own recordings, such as Yao Min, Yan Hua and classically
trained Sheng Jialun and Huang Feiran, overall, they left behind considerably fewer
works than their female counterparts" ("The Rise and Generic Features of Shanghai
Popular Songs in the 1930s and 1940s," 116).

41 Zeitlin, "'Notes of Flesh,'" 92.

42 Fong, "Engendering the Lyric," 110, 111.

43 Zeitlin situates these exchanges within the gift economy: the courtesan is understood as the recipient of "gifts" rather than "payments" from her clients because this implies that she "bestows her favors voluntarily as a return gift, rather than fulfilling a set payment for service" ("'Notes of Flesh,'" 77).

44 Hershatter, *Dangerous Pleasures*, 42. This aspect of the courtesan's identity is linguistically inscribed in the English term *singsong girl*, a transliteration of the Chinese honorific sometimes used to refer to courtesans, *xiansheng*.

45 Zeitlin, "'Notes of Flesh,'" 79–80.

46 Hershatter, *Dangerous Pleasures*, 43.

47 Jones, *Yellow Music*, 29, 113. Music, he demonstrates, was "central to the efforts of leftist intellectuals to transform media culture in China and, in doing do, mobilize the citizenry to resist the twin specters of Western imperialism and Japanese territorial encroachment" (112).

48 Leo Lee observes that the "display of the female body . . . marked the beginnings of a new discourse which was made problematic precisely because it was derived from the courtesan journals, in which female bodies indeed carried a market value" (*Shanghai Modern*, 73).

49 Zhang Z., *An Amorous History of the Silver Screen*, 70.

50 Russell, Introduction, 3.

51 As Laikwan Pang maintains, from an early stage in the iconography of the New Woman, "political messages were highly intertwined with trends and consumerism, and commercialism was as powerful as revolution in the shaping of China's modernity" (*The Distorting Mirror*, 109). In view of Pang's insights, I do not make a distinction between the New Woman and the Modern Girl for the purposes of this discussion, although to be sure, these figures are not identical.

52 Kracauer, "The Mass Ornament," 67.

53 Bao, "From Pearl White to White Rose Woo," 203.

54 Shih, "Shanghai Women of 1939," 205. See also Dong, "Who Is Afraid of the Chinese Modern Girl?"; Shen, "From *Xin nüxing* to *Liren xing*."

55 In an analysis of *Goddess*, Rey Chow writes: "the spotlight it gives to a prostitute amplifies in a unique manner the epistemic contradiction that accompanies the status of 'woman' in film . . . perhaps more peculiar to the media involving visuality" ("'Woman,' Fetish, Particularism," 211). William Rothman relates *Goddess* to a claim about film melodrama: "the camera is always also an instrument of villainy and cannot 'nominate' innocence without at the same time violating it" ("*The Goddess*," 68).

56 Hansen, "Fallen Women, Rising Stars, New Horizons," 15.

57 Hansen, "The Gender of Vernacular Modernism," 34.

58 The progressive political ideal of the New Woman, who predates mass cultural imaginations of the modern girl, was equally caught up in this nexus of fantasy and social policing. As Louise Edwards writes, "the Chinese new woman had less potency for the women's movement than she did with the nationalist project of state building. . . . The Chinese new woman was an intellectual class (and, therefore,

overwhelmingly male) invention, and discussions about her relate more to the concerns of this demographic than they do to any lived reality for the women of Republican China or the women's movement of the time" ("Policing the Modern Woman in Republican China," 117).

59 Hansen, "Fallen Women, Rising Stars, New Horizons," 15, 16.

60 Jones, *Yellow Music*, 114.

61 Jones, *Yellow Music*, 125, 126.

62 Jones, *Yellow Music*, 135–36.

63 Editors of *Cahiers du cinéma*, "John Ford's *Young Mr. Lincoln*," 446.

64 Hansen, *Babel and Babylon*, introduction.

65 Hansen, "Pleasure, Ambivalence, Identification," 7.

66 Hansen, *Babel and Babylon*, 123.

67 Hansen, "Pleasure, Ambivalence, Identification," 9.

68 Hansen, "Fallen Women, Rising Stars, New Horizons," 12.

69 Hansen, "The Gender of Vernacular Modernism," 30.

70 Fu, *Between Shanghai and Hong Kong*. Fu positions his study as a deliberate move away from a mainland-centric view of Chinese film history, toward the border-crossing and panregional movements that shaped its trajectory. In contrast, Zhang Zhen proposes a view of Shanghai cinema as the "preconscious" of Hong Kong cinema ("The 'Shanghai Factor' in Hong Kong Cinema," 147).

71 Fu, introduction, 6.

72 Taylor, *Rethinking Transnational Chinese Cinemas*, chapter 2.

73 The Cantonese dialect community includes Guangdong Province, Hong Kong, and Southeast Asia. Amoy, also called Hokkien and Minnan, is spoken in southeastern China, Taiwan, and Chinese communities in Southeast Asia.

74 Exceptions include two important surveys of the history of Hong Kong cinema: Teo, *Hong Kong Cinema*; Law and Bren, *Hong Kong Cinema*. See also Chu, *Hong Kong Cinema*; Fu, *China Forever*. The Hong Kong Film Archive has made important contributions to the foundational historiography of Hong Kong cinema through an ongoing publication series. In particular, see *The Cathay Story* and *The Shaw Screen*, both edited by Wong Ain-ling.

75 An example of writing in this vein is Bordwell, *Planet Hong Kong*. See also Stokes and Hoover, *City on Fire*; E. Yau, *At Full Speed*.

76 The project of theorizing about Hong Kong identity acquired a particular urgency in the years surrounding the handing over of the colony to the People's Republic of China, and the pressure to reckon with such concepts is impressed on filmmakers and critics alike. This much is suggested by the numerous catchphrases advanced as descriptors of Hong Kong cinema—*ethnic cinema, quasi-national cinema, urban cinema, transnational cinema*, and *crisis cinema*—as well as by the volume of writings that approach films singly or collectively as expressions of some strain of postcolonial identity crisis. These are enumerated and discussed in detail in Cheung and Chu, introduction.

77 Teo, *Hong Kong Cinema*, 15.

78 *Manbo nülang* (*Mambo Girl*).

79 *Ye meigui zhi lian* (*The Wild, Wild Rose*).

Chapter 1. A SONGSTRESS IS BORN

1 Sue Touhy notes that the film was accompanied by a record released by Pathé ("Metropolitan Sounds," 205).

2 Jones, *Yellow Music*, 6.

3 Zhang Z., *An Amorous History of the Silver Screen*, 317, 308.

4 Li and Hu, *Zhongguo wusheng dianying shi*, 6.

5 An advertisement for *Pleasures of the Opera* declares: "All talking and singing picture topples fake dubbed wax disc sound films . . . leading the way to real sound-on-film pictures (*Shenbao*, October 28, 1931, page 9). The claim to realness echoes the marketing rhetoric used for *Peace after Storm*, which described the film as "a first real talkie of China" (quoted in Zhang Z., *An Amorous History of the Silver Screen*, 306).

6 Li and Hu, *Zhongguo wusheng dianying shi*, 7.

7 Local supplement, *Shenbao*, May 25, 1931.

8 To offer another example, a full-page ad for *Pleasures of the Opera* includes a summary of its story, about an affair between a married man and a singing girl, and a listing of six of the songs, each accompanied by the name of the star who performs it in the film and a few stanzas of the lyrics (local supplement, *Shenbao*, October 28, 1931).

9 For a richly detailed discussion of *Two Stars in the Milky Way* as a "metafilm" dramatizing the relationships between "fiction and film, art and life, stage and screen, silent and sound film, opera and film, players and play, motion pictures and still photographs," see Harris, "*Two Stars on the Silver Screen*," 193.

10 Even if live transmission accounts but for a small fraction of broadcasting practices, the idea of "liveness" has been embedded ideologically in the very definition of television, as Jane Feuer argues in "The Concept of Live Television." Her argument can be extended to radio as well.

11 Quoted in Xu, "Dianyingyuan yu yinyue" (translated by Hsinyi Tiffany Lee).

12 Zhang Yiwei, "Shengyin yu xiandaixing: mopian zhi youshengpian guodu shiqi de Zhongguo yingyuan shengyin shi wenti," 89.

13 Xu, "Dianyingyuan yu yinyue" (translated by Hsinyi Tiffany Lee).

14 Bu Wancang would go on to direct some of the most acclaimed silent films of the 1930s, including *Lianai yu yiwu* (*Love and Duty*), *Taohua qi xue ji* (*Peach Blossom Weeps Tears of Blood*), and *Yijian mei* (*A Spray of Plum Blossoms*,).

15 Yang Naimei was a member of an early generation of film stars who, even before entering the movie business, garnered public notoriety as a flamboyant modern girl with a penchant for outrageous fashions and scandalizing antics. Often cast as a vamp, she eventually founded her own production company. For a discussion of Yang's career, see Zhang Z., *An Amorous History of the Silver Screen*, 39.

16 Qiu, "Ping *Liangxin fuhuo*."

17 Gui, "Wanren zheng ting 'Ru niang qu.'"

18 Jones, *Yellow Music*, 73.

19 Lu, "Ji *Kelian de Qiuxiang*." The gramophone record produced by Great China included "Putao xianzi" ("The Grape Fairy"), a runaway hit among Li Jinhui's

children's songs. Li Minghui's stage performances of this song ignited a trend of fairy dances in this period.

20 With its origins in a song, *The Miserable Life of Qiuxiang* resembles the Japanese category of *kouta eiga*, or ballad films from the silent era based on popular songs. On *kouta eiga*, see Lewis, "Media Fantasies." Songs played an important role throughout the extended transition to sound in the Japanese film industry, thus giving rise to many other parallels to Chinese cinema in this period—such as referring to film songs as *sonyu-uta*, or "insert songs," which is also the literal translation of the Chinese term for film song, *chaqu*. On *sonyu-uta*, see Baskett, *The Attractive Empire*, 53.

21 Local supplement, *Shenbao*, June 3, 1927.

22 Jones discusses the historical parallels between Li's musical dramas, including his children's "performance songs" like "Kelian de Qiuxiang," and avant-garde spoken drama of the same period. Both had an antifeudalist, emancipatory agenda that placed women on the stage and celebrated the natural beauty of their bodies, and both consequently drew the ire of traditionalists (*Yellow Music*, 86–90).

23 Geng, "*Lian xiang* xiaoji."

24 For a discussion of the two films—*Xiao Xiang lei* (*Tears of Xiao Xiang*) and *Gudu chun meng* (*Spring Dream in the Old Capitol*)—see Wang W., *Zhongguo dianying yinyue xunzong*, 8–9; Zhang Z., *An Amorous History of the Silver Screen*, 313.

25 The film and its theme song are discussed at length in Wang W., *Zhongguo dianying yinyue xunzong*, 9–10; Zhang Z., *An Amorous History of the Silver Screen*, 312–16.

26 Wang W., *Zhongguo dianying yinyue xunzong*, 10.

27 Philip Auslander's assertion that live and mediated performance in the twentieth century belong to "the same mediatic system" applies to this context (*Liveness*, 6).

28 Lastra, *Sound Technology and the American Cinema*, 133. Lastra develops this point in reference to the conventions of live symphonic performance, arguing that "the careful diminution or enhancement of various features of the sonic event (the very point of performing in specially designed spaces) constitutes a veritable technology of sound manipulation, as important as any microphone or loudspeaker" (ibid., 134). But the point applies equally to the cultural contexts and social practices of musical performance outside of Western classical music.

29 A similar tactic of reusing old theme songs in new films was discovered by Tianyi when it recruited Xu Qinfang, the songstress and star of *The Singing Beauty*, to perform that film's theme song "Fang cao meiren" ("Fragrant Beauty") in *Pleasures of the Opera*.

30 Wang W., *Zhongguo dianying yinyue xunzong*, 9.

31 Li Jinhui's contributions were "Work Hard" ("Nuli") and the *Two Stars* theme, "Shuang xing qu." Xiao Youmei, the president of the Shanghai Conservatory, was responsible for the nondiegetic score. The other two credited musical advisers were Jin Qingyu and A. Richter, the director of the Capitol Carlton Theatre's house orchestra (which performed the film's score).

32 Harris, "*Two Stars on the Silver Screen*," 196.

33 "Zi Luolan yu yousheng dianying," 36. Soon afterward, Wong moved from Shanghai to Hong Kong, where she caught a second wind as a star of Cantonese opera and films.

34　Harris notes that "Love's Sorrow in the Eastern Chamber" was frequently performed on the opera stage around this time, rendered in various regional styles ("*Two Stars on the Silver Screen*," 214).

35　Zhang Z., *An Amorous History of the Silver Screen*, 308.

36　Zhang Z., *An Amorous History of the Silver Screen*, 307.

37　For a discussion of these backstage plots—which anticipate the wave of backstage musicals that would breathe new life into the genre in the Depression era—see Altman, *The American Film Musical*, 204–11. Harris notes that the plot of *Two Stars* was derived from the 1928 Metro-Goldwyn-Mayer (MGM) musical *Show People*, about a Southern belle who arrives in Hollywood and becomes a movie star. United Photoplay Service even marketed its film as "China's *Show People*" ("*Two Stars on the Silver Screen*," 211).

38　The song's lyrics, which paint the labor of fishing against a backdrop of elements—sea, sky, clouds, and wind—sit rather uneasily with the class politics of the film. The hard lot of the fisher folk is naturalized as part of an unchanging elemental order, even as the narrative depicts the deterioration of their livelihood as caused by the socioeconomic forces of modernization and industrialization.

39　Si, "Chuangzao zhong de shengpian biaoxian yangshi," 183–84.

40　Tang, "Tan yijiusansi nian de dianying gequ" (translated by Jessica Ka Yee Chan). Thanks to Jason McGrath and Jessica Chan for sharing this article with me.

41　Nie, *Nie Er quanji*, 2:83. The strategic use of repetition was picked up on by Nie Er and other leftist composers. For instance, in *New Woman* he pairs the melody of the popular hit "Peach Blossom River" with rewritten lyrics, activating the memory contained in the familiar tune in order to redirect it to new political ends.

42　For a compilation of Zhou's recordings and films, see Hong F., *Tianya genü*.

43　The film's story of society's lower depths takes its inspiration from Frank Borzage's *7th Heaven*, even though its title is borrowed from another of the same director's films. Some of the scenes echo those from *7th Heaven*—for instance, when Zhou Xuan and her male costar Zhao Dan walk precariously along the rooftops and eaves of their apartment buildings. Zhao Dan offered another perspective on the story's origins in an interview: "Yuan Muzhi, the actor and director, Nie Er, the composer, Zheng Junli, the director, Tang Na, the critic, and myself used to meet in a certain tavern and have a snack and a drink. We called the place Cyrano's Café after *Cyrano de Bergerac*. . . . It was here we met the night-life people, the prostitutes, the garbage collectors, the news vendors. That's how we got the inspiration for the film. . . . We took the material from real life" (quoted in Wilson, "'I Sought the Jewel of Art,'" 83).

44　Des Forges, "Shanghai Alleys, Theatrical Practice, and Cinematic Spectatorship," 39. Des Forges situates the performances in *Street Angel* within a broader visual imaginary, where theater emerged as a metaphor for urban space and the new forms of sociality, interactivity, and seeing that were engendered by the architecture of the city.

45　Wang W., *Zhongguo dianying yinyue xunzong*, 40.

46 Ma N., "The Textual and Critical Difference of Being Radical," 27.

47 Zhang Z., *An Amorous History of the Silver Screen*, 309. For instance, in *Songstress Red Peony*, the female protagonist endures a betrayal by her husband, loses her voice, and sees her child sold to a brothel.

48 Hansen, "Fallen Women, Rising Stars, New Horizons," 15.

49 Jones, *Yellow Music*, 135. Ma Ning similarly notes the allegorical implication of the song scene: Xiaohong "is not only the virgin over whom the feudal forces and the lower classes contest, but also Mother China, who is now being violated by the Japanese invaders" ("The Textual and Critical Difference of Being Radical," 27).

50 The songstress as subaltern was immortalized in verse by Nie in "Songstress under the Iron Heel" ("Tieti xia de genü"), composed for the film *Feng yun ernü* (*Children of the Storm*).

51 *Flower Street* reprises some of the points in *Street Angel*'s plot, including the villainous figure of the gangster who tries to buy the teahouse singer and the contrasting character of the upright young man whose anger is aroused when she accepts the gangster's gifts. The film is also notable for its message of nationalism, portraying the devastating effects of the Japanese invasion of Manchuria and citing the political doctrines of Sun Yat-sen.

52 *Golden Lotus* might be described as a remake of *Flower Street* by the same director, Yue Feng, but one that tamps down the nationalist ideology of the earlier film while playing up the romantic melodrama between the singer and a man—in the later film, a high-born young man who falls for her while watching her perform. With this romantic plot, *Golden Lotus* incorporates plot motifs from a well-known work of the Mandarin Duck and Butterfly school of sentimental literature, *Ti xiao yinyuan* (*A Story of Three Loves*). I discuss this novel and its various filmic adaptations in chapter 5.

53 Sobchack, "Lounge Time," 153–54.

54 Some other examples are *New Woman*, which contains a striking montage of richly dressed revelers dancing and drinking champagne juxtaposed with factory workers laboring on the night shift, and *Yasuiqian* (*New Year's Coin*), where the nightclub serves as a setting for song-and-dance performances by the film's stars Gong Qiuxia, Li Minghui, and Hu Rongrong.

55 Goldstein, "From Teahouse to Playhouse," 770.

56 Goldstein, "From Teahouse to Playhouse," 772.

57 Vogel, *The Scene of Harlem Cabaret*, 62.

58 See Mulvey, "Visual Pleasure and Narrative Cinema."

59 Silverman, *The Acoustic Mirror*, 39, 56.

60 Silverman, *The Acoustic Mirror*, ix.

61 A similar scene can be found in *The Big Road*, when Li Lili's character sings the ballad "Fengyang Flower Drum" ("Fengyang huagu"). Accompanying her lyrics, which describe a woman driven away from her homeland, are documentary-like images of war and natural disaster. Laikwan Pang has argued that the song "creates a nondiegetic narrative space to introduce political messages, which are otherwise difficult to convey because of the censorship" (*Building a New China in Cinema*, 216).

62 Majumdar, *Wanted Cultured Ladies Only!*, 180.

63 As Altman notes, the very definition of the film musical "depends on a merging of the two tracks. . . . Music appears on the diegetic track, diegetic noises are transformed into [nondiegetic] music" (*The American Film Musical*, 63).

64 Stilwell, "The Fantastical Gap between Diegetic and Nondiegetic," 197. This description brings out the parallels between film music and character voice-overs, another prevalent form of metadiegetic sound.

65 Booth, *The Experience of Songs*, 15.

66 This paradox recalls the tension between "expression and repression" (Laing, *The Gendered Score*, 14) that underlies film melodrama, in which music is imbued with connotations of femininity and emotion.

67 Dyer, *In the Space of a Song*, 11.

68 For a nuanced consideration of the cultural and political milieu of occupation cinema, see Fu, *Between Shanghai and Hong Kong*, chapter 3. Fu discusses at length the Zhonglian production *Wanshi liufang* (*Eternity*), a historical epic about the Opium War that starred Li Xianglan as a singing candy seller. Both Bai Guang and Li Xianglan went on to work in the Hong Kong film industry after the war.

Chapter 2. FROM SHANGHAI TO HONG KONG

1 Wong Kee-chee, "A Song in Every Film."

2 Teo, *Hong Kong Cinema*, 29.

3 Law, introduction, 9.

4 Ho, "The Songstress, the Farmer's Daughter, the Mambo Girl and the Songstress Again," 63, 64.

5 Fu, *Between Shanghai and Hong Kong*, 68. The Central Plains syndrome, and its implicit mandate to sinicize local film culture, is evident in the attitude of mainland filmmakers toward Hong Kong's dialect film industry. As the Shanghai filmmaker Cai Chusheng said of the latter, "the *backwardness* of Hong Kong culture as a whole inevitably has a proportional effect on its cinema. . . . All the movies 'made' here are frivolous, vulgar commodities catering to the low taste of the uneducated" (quoted in ibid., 69–70).

6 Teo, *Hong Kong Cinema*, 15.

7 Teo, *Hong Kong Cinema*, 26.

8 Turner and Ngan, *Hong Kong Sixties*.

9 Turner, "60s/90s," 23–24.

10 Lau, "Intersection," 92.

11 E. Yau, introduction.

12 Sek, "Shaw Movie Town's 'China Dream' and 'Hong Kong Sentiments,'" 37.

13 Chiao H., "Guguo bei wang, zhongchanjieji de chuaijiji."

14 Teo, *Hong Kong Cinema*, 23.

15 Abbas, *Hong Kong*, 4.

16 In 1965, following Loke's death, MP&GI was reorganized and renamed the Cathay Organisation. Today the company's official name is Cathay-Keris Films.

17 For a condensed history of Cathay's film-related enterprises, see Chung, "A Southeast Asian Tycoon and His Movie Dream." For a more detailed portrait of the organization, see Lim, *Cathay*.

18 On the history of the Shaw movie empire, see Chung, "The Industrial Evolution of a Fraternal Enterprise"; Curtin, *Playing to the World's Biggest Audience*, chapter 1; and Shaw's official company website, http://www.shaw.sg/sw_about.aspx.

19 Most accounts—including that on the Shaw Brothers company website—give 1957 as the year that the land in Clearwater Bay was acquired by Run Run Shaw. According to I. C. Jarvie, the land was in fact acquired in 1954, although construction there did not begin until much later (*Window on Hong Kong*, 44).

20 "Shaw Studio, 1960," Shaw Online, stored at http://www.shaw.sg/sw_about.aspx (click on Shaw Studio, Hong Kong).

21 Cited in Chung, "The Industrial Evolution of a Fraternal Enterprise," 5.

22 Teo, *Hong Kong Cinema*, 74.

23 Figures from Kwok, *Hong Kong Filmography*, vols. 4 and 5.

24 Many accounts portray Run Run Shaw as an indefatigable micromanager, enamored of show business, whose imprimatur was stamped on every film put out by Shaw Brothers. For instance, see Jarvie's description based on firsthand observation in *Window on Hong Kong*, 46–47. See also Curtin, *Playing to the World's Biggest Audience*, chapter 2; Fu, introduction, 5–6.

25 The first issue of *International Screen* was published in Singapore in 1952, but its run as a regularly monthly magazine began only with its inaugural Hong Kong issue, which appeared in October 1955.

26 Zhang Z., *An Amorous History of the Silver Screen*, 73–74. According to Zhang, the first film magazine appeared in 1921, and by the middle of the decade there were nearly thirty in print (ibid., 73).

27 By the middle of the 1930s, Michael Chang writes, the stars of the Shanghai-based film industry "were constituted within the discourse of a well-established urban mass media and a highly efficient promotional system. Their film careers were entirely the products of this system and the speed of their ascendancy attests to the effectiveness of the new promotional machinery" ("The Good, the Bad, and the Beautiful," 147).

28 In these years producers took over a function previously associated with impresario figures like Li Jinhui, whose Bright Moon Song and Dance Troupe trained an early generation of actresses, and Bu Wancang, the émigré Chinese director who discovered and trained some of the key actresses of postwar Hong Kong cinema at his Taishan Training Institute.

29 Chung, "A Southeast Asian Tycoon and His Movie Dream," 14.

30 Cheng, "Reminiscences of the Life of an Actress in Shaw Brothers' Movietown," 247.

31 On the revivals of *wuxia pian*, see J. Ma, "Circuitous Action: Revenge Cinema."

32 Fu, introduction, 12.

33 One example is the Shaw-produced backstage musical *Qian jiao bai mei* (*Les Belles*), directed by Doe Ching, which received five awards at the eighth Asian Film Festival, including those for best art direction, best music, and best actress (for its lead

actress, Linda Lin Dai), as well as the awards for best director and best music at the Golden Horse Awards in Taiwan.

34 For instance, the two-part republican period drama *Xingxing, yueliang, taiyang* (*Sun, Moon, and Star*) won awards for best drama film, best screenplay, and best actress at the Golden Horse Awards in 1961 and was voted one of the ten most popular films of the year in a Hong Kong media poll.

35 Chung notes that both companies announced plans for an adaptation of *Dream of the Red Chamber* in 1961, bringing about the first of many "competing version" contests between Shaw and MP&GI ("A Southeast Asia Tycoon and His Movie Dream," 15).

36 The impact of the outsize public personas cultivated by Loke and Shaw is apparent in the tendency of critics and historians to discuss their studios in personalized terms. Darrell Davis writes: "This conforms to the Great Man theory of history, personifying the actions of organizations via executives' decision-making" ("Questioning Diaspora," 43). Davis notes that the tendency also finds a parallel in mogul-centered accounts of Hollywood history.

37 Fu, introduction, 6.

38 K. Ng, "Romantic Comedies of Cathay-MP&GI in the 1950s and 60s."

39 Hong Kong was ill equipped to absorb the massive influx of postwar migrants; hundreds of thousands of people lived in squatter settlements, and it was not uncommon for multiple families to share tiny apartments.

40 Sek, "Shaw Movie Town's 'China Dream' and 'Hong Kong Sentiments,'" 37.

41 Eberhard, *The Chinese Silver Screen*, 33.

42 Jarvie, *Window on Hong Kong*, 86.

43 Teo, *Hong Kong Cinema*, 49.

44 To be sure, "as much as Hong Kong during the 1950s and 60s remained a city of free trade, it was also a contact zone of covert espionage activities and intelligence gathering operated by the People's Republic of China, KMT, and US agencies," as Kenny Ng argues ("Inhibition vs. Exhibition," 24). As well as the political battles, the cultural wars of the previous years also persisted in Hong Kong during the Cold War era. See Leung, "Writing across Borders." Also see Wong A. and Lee, *Lengzhang yu Xianggang dianying*.

45 Wong A., Foreword, xi.

46 Taylor, *Rethinking Transnational Chinese Cinemas*, 54.

47 See Fu, "Cold War Politics and Hong Kong Mandarin Cinema," 125–26.

48 Accessing this large and lucrative market required conforming to the ideological strictures of the Republic of China's government, and both Loke and Shaw were active members of the Hong Kong and Kowloon Free Filmmakers General Association, whose clearance was required for all films exhibited in Taiwan. Emilie Yeh details the financial arrangements and history of coproductions binding the two studios with Taiwan in "Taiwan," 72–76. See also Davis, "Questioning Diaspora," 48–49.

49 The poor survival rate of dialect films, as well as the organizational incoherence and fly-by-night nature of their production outfits, have contributed to the marginalization of dialect cinemas in Chinese film scholarship.

50 See Law, "Shaw's Cantonese Productions and Their Interactions with Contemporary Local and Hollywood Cinema"; Li C., "A Look at MP&GI Cantonese Films through the Work of Tso Kea."

51 Taylor, *Rethinking Transnational Chinese Cinemas*, 11.

52 In this regard, the postwar Hong Kong film industry's investment in Mandarin can be distinguished from the promotion of *guohua pian*, or national-language films, in the 1930s. In this earlier period of filmmaking, the privileging of Mandarin as China's official standard language was bound up with the project of modern nation building. Until 1937 the Nanjing government even imposed a ban on dialect films. See Xiao, "Constructing a New National Culture." Although the complex cultural and ideological valences of Mandarin filmmaking are beyond the scope of the present discussion, my understanding of this issue has been considerably deepened by the research of Janet Y. Chen and Robert J. Culp.

53 Gan, "Tropical Hong Kong," 19.

54 Gan, "Tropical Hong Kong," 20.

55 In "Under Western Eyes," S. N. Ko argues that this cycle of American films began with *Hong Kong* (1952), a wartime thriller starring Ronald Reagan, and ended with *The Road to Hong Kong* (1962), the last of Bob Hope and Bing Crosby's international road movies.

56 For instance, *The World of Suzie Wong* begins with a ride on the iconic Star Ferry and contains many images of real street scenes and public markets filled with working-class residents of the colony as part of its setting in the Wanchai neighborhood (though many of these were shot in other parts of the island). The film also shows the typhoon shelter in Causeway Bay and even a hillside squatter community.

57 The bulk of these musical extravaganzas were Mandarin productions, made by Shaw Brothers and (to a lesser extent) MP&GI. See S. L. Li, "Embracing Glocalization and Hong Kong–Made Musical Films."

58 Taylor, *Rethinking Transnational Chinese Cinemas*, 88.

59 Taylor, *Rethinking Transnational Chinese Cinemas*, 89–90.

60 G. Hong, *Taiwan Cinema*, chapter 2.

61 Yung S., *Yueyun liusheng*, 23, and chapter 4.

62 Yung S., *Xunmi Yueju sheng ying*, xxvii.

63 A comprehensive listing can be found in D. Chen et al., "Filmography of Cantonese Cinema (1946–1959)." Film production of Cantonese opera tapered off in the following decade, with about a hundred films made during the 1960s.

64 A special issue of *Opera Quarterly* explores the intersection of operatic aesthetics and film practices, focusing on PRC-produced opera films from the 1950s to the Cultural Revolution (see Iovene and Zeitlin, "Chinese Opera Film"). Chris Berry and Mary Farquhar posit opera as a national cultural form that constitutes the early substrate of Chinese cinema, yet their elaboration of this thesis fails to account for the specificity of opera's forms, instead conflating *xiqu* with Tom Gunning's idea of a "cinema of attractions" (*China on Screen*, chapter 3; see also Gunning, "The Cinema of Attraction.").

65 B. Yung, *Cantonese Opera*, 6.

66 Judith Zeitlin notes that at least 115 opera films were made in the PRC between 1953 and 1966, a period when the government actively promoted popular folkloric traditions ("Operatic Ghosts on Screen," 220).

67 On the reception of *The Love Eterne* in Taiwan, see P. Chiao, "The Female Consciousness, the World of Signification and Safe Extramarital Affairs," 75–77. For a detailed discussion of *The Love Eterne* and *Huangmei diao pian*, see Tan, "Huangmei Opera Films, Shaw Brothers and Ling Bo."

68 E. Yeh, "China," 172. On operatic aesthetics, see Bao, "The Politics of Remediation."

69 Han, "The Design and Style of Opera Films," 447.

70 Chang also starred in *Bao lian deng* (*The Magic Lamp*), one of the few Huangmei opera films produced by MP&GI.

71 Quoted in X. Chen, "Woman, Generic Aesthetics, and the Vernacular," 184.

72 Wong Kee Chee, *The Age of Shanghainese Pops*, 198. This modernizing tendency is also found in the Cantonese opera films of this period, where opera songs are sometimes combined with contemporary settings, Western costumes, and versions of Hollywood plots. A well-known example is *Xuangong yanshi* (*My Kingdom for a Husband*), a remake of a 1934 Western-costume opera film that in turn was adapted from the 1929 Hollywood musical *The Love Parade*. For a discussion of this film, see Yung S., *Xunmi Yueju sheng ying*, 92; Y. Wang, "The 'Transnational' as Methodology," 12–15.

73 X. Chen, "Woman, Generic Aesthetics, and the Vernacular," 180.

74 Jones writes:"The modern songs of the urban petit bourgeoisie were thought to be tainted by both their commercial vulgarity and their cultural hybridity . . . the decadent sounds that filled the record stores, the airwaves, and the dance halls were seen as incitements to political indiscipline" (*Yellow Music*, 27).

75 See Jones, *Yellow Music*, chapter 4.

76 It must be noted that although Mandarin pop thrived in its new production base, the indigenous music that had dominated Hong Kong's soundscape before 1949, consisting primarily of Cantonese opera tunes and *yueyu liuxing ge* (Cantonese popular songs), maintained a continuous and significant presence in the postwar decades. This indigenous musical tradition informs the Cantopop style, which would come to displace Mandarin *shidai qu* and dominate Hong Kong popular music from the 1970s onward. The relation of Cantonese and Mandarin music can be likened to that of the two film industries: coexisting as separate culture industries divided by a linguistic gulf, yet joined by points of intersection and resonances.

77 Wong Kee Chee, *The Age of Shanghainese Pops*, 140, 212.

78 "Peiyin yu muhou gechang," 48.

79 Wong Kee Chee, *The Age of Shanghainese Pops*, 140.

80 "Baidai changpian gongshi wangluo Dianmau qunxing," 50.

81 An *International Screen* feature article in the following year on Grace Chang's vacation in Tokyo reports that the star was chaperoned on her travels by Wang, suggesting the extent of the latter's involvement with the artists whose careers she managed ("Ge Lan xiaoyou Riben," 54).

82 Jones, *Yellow Music*, 64.

83 Wong Kee Chee, *The Age of Shanghainese Pops*, 82.

84 Zhang Z., *An Amorous History of the Silver Screen*, 315–17.

85 See Jones, *Yellow Music*, chapter 3; M. Chang, "The Good, the Bad, and the Beautiful."

86 Chang cut her first record with Great Wall Records in 1954, but her vocal career took off only after she signed with Pathé-EMI.

87 Jones, *Yellow Music*, 18. See also S. Chen, "The Rise and Generic Features of Shanghai Popular Songs in the 1930s and 1940s"; I. Wong, "The Incantation of Shanghai."

88 Wong Kee-chee, "Two or Three Things about Mandarin Pop," 20.

89 The song is included as one of the musical numbers in Tsai Ming-liang's *The Hole*. For a detailed discussion of this film, see J. Ma, "Delayed Voices."

90 On English code-switching in Mandarin pop, see Chik, "Creative Multilingualism in Hong Kong Popular Music," 511. Diamond Records, an independent record company, even released "a series of albums made up of Mandarin and English originals, Mandarin versions of English originals, English versions of Mandarin originals, and 'bilingual' songs mixing English and Mandarin verses," Chik notes. Yet another variation on the bilingual cover song can be found in "Nianqing de ailü" ("Young Lovers"), a bilingual duet by *shidai qu* singer Chang Loo and her husband Ollie Delfino. In the duet Chang sings in Mandarin and Delfino in English.

91 Wong Kee Chee notes that there are precedents for this from the Shanghai era, offering examples of tunes by Japanese composers that were adapted as *shidai qu* (*The Age of Shanghainese Pops*, 173). Incidentally, these gestures of appreciation and appropriation were to a partial extent reciprocated in Western music culture, as demonstrated in instances of the reverse phenomenon of English-language covers of *shidai qu*. An American cover of the 1941 pop hit "Meigui meigui wo ai ni" ("Rose, Rose, I Love You") by Frankie Laine reached number three on the American pop charts in 1951. The 1959 London stage production of *The World of Suzie Wong* included an English version of a Mandarin pop tune, titled "The Ding Dong Song," which became a hit in Hong Kong as well.

92 "Shi nian lai zui liuxing de dianying gequ changpian," 62.

93 For a discussion of *Calendar Girl* and its songs, see L. Wong, "Moving Serenades."

94 "When Will You Return?" was the theme song for the film *Sanxing banyue* (*Orion Moon*).

95 The song also appeared in a more recent film with the same title, *Heri jun zai la* (*Au Revoir Mon Amour*), sung by the Cantopop star Anita Mui.

96 The other two films in which the song appears are from 1958: a song-and-dance picture, *Yinghai shengge* (*Stand Up and Cheer*), and a Cantonese production, *Xi linmen* (*Happiness at the Door*).

97 Taylor discusses the example of copycat films, or twin cases (*shuangbao an*): Amoy versions of successful Mandarin releases, like the 1958 *Manbo guniang*, a copy of *Mambo Girl* (*Rethinking Transnational Cinemas*, 63). For a discussion of Cantonese remakes of Mandarin films, see Y. Wang, *Remaking Chinese Cinema*, chapter 2.

98 Yu M., "Types and Sources of Hong Kong Mandarin Film Songs, 1940s to 60s."

99 The precedent for rearranging classical music with modern rhythms, we are told
by an article in *International Screen*, comes from the West, where Franz Schubert's
"Serenade" had been turned into a popular jazz style song by the Platters, titled "My
Serenade" ("Shi nian lai zui liuxing de dianying gequ changpian," 63.) Even a seem-
ingly self-contained category like regional opera poses problems here: as Wong Kee-
chee points out, Huangmei opera films, by far the most popular operatic style of the
postwar Mandarin cinema, display the influence of popular music in their singing
styles, and some films even include operatic versions of pop tunes in their repertory
("Two or Three Things about Mandarin Pop," 20). For a period in the late 1960s,
Shaw Brothers even made multiple versions of their own productions in different
languages, shooting repeat takes with different actors who spoke Mandarin, Korean,
Japanese, Malay, Thai, or Tagalog. See Chi, "Hong Kong Cinema before 1980," 89.
100 L. Wong, "Moving Serenades," 238.
101 L. Wong, "Moving Serenades," 238.

Chapter 3. THE LITTLE WILDCAT

1 Zhang Shankun played an active role in Shanghai cinema throughout the Japanese
occupation and war years, earning the moniker "king of Chinese cinema." In 1945
he was arrested by Japanese authorities on suspicion of collaborating with the Nationalist resistance. After his release he was arrested again, this time by Chinese authorities on charges of treason. Zhang fled to Hong Kong in 1946, where he played
an instrumental role in founding the Yonghua (China Forever) and Changcheng
(Great Wall) film companies before going on to resurrect Xinhua. For a detailed
account of Zhang's role in the film industry in the pre- and postwar periods, see Fu,
Between Shanghai and Hong Kong.

2 For a discussion of these works, see K. Yau, "Hong Kong and Japan," 104–5; Cai,
Zhongguo jindai wenyi dianying yanjiu, 51–55.

3 Teo, "Oh, Karaoke!," 34.

4 The phrase comes from Sam Ho, who argues that "although Hollywood had made
integrated musicals for years, the Mandarin cinema failed to follow suit. . . . With
Songs of the Peach Blossom River, the integrated format finally caught on" ("Lots of
Songs . . . and a Dance or Two," 63). Emilie Yeh similarly describes the film's songs
as "integrated closely into the stories" in "China," 176.

5 Chung sings this in a later Xinhua production, *Ru shi jiaren* (*A Challenge of Love*).

6 Like the character Wildcat, Chung was a mainland refugee who landed in Hong
Kong after losing her father to the war, eventually finding fame and fortune in her
new home.

7 Feuer, *The Hollywood Musical*, 47.

8 Feuer, *The Hollywood Musical*, 68.

9 Naremore, *Acting in the Cinema*, 76. Among his examples is Greta Garbo pretending
that she no longer loves Robert Taylor in *Camille* (1938), "alternating between the
imperious, coolly amused disdain we normally associate with a figure like Dietrich
and a wilting, passionate ardor typical of Victorian melodrama" (ibid., 75).

10 Naremore, *Acting in the Cinema*, 76.

11 McMillin, *The Musical as Drama*, 21.

12 Ho, "Lots of Songs . . . and a Dance or Two," 61.

13 Jones, *Yellow Music*, 113.

14 For an account of *jianmei* historically situated in the context of the New Life Movement, see Gao, "Nationalist and Feminist Discourses on *Jianmei* (Robust Beauty) during China's 'National Crisis' in the 1930s." Another star associated with *jianmei* in this time was Li Lili; by juxtaposing her character in *Tianming* (*Daybreak*)—a peasant girl who leaves a carefree and wholesome life in the country to become an urban factory worker—with Little Phoenix, we gain a clearer view of the country sprite's place in the iconography of *jianmei*.

15 Law Kar and Frank Bren also describe Chung as "the 1950s' answer to Wang Renmei and Li Lili" (*Hong Kong Cinema*, 270). Given the common practice of nicknaming performers as "little" versions of predecessors with a similar style—for instance, Julie Yeh Feng was known as "Little Bai Guang" because of her low singing voice—we might also interpret the "Little Wildcat" moniker as a deliberate marketing ploy that banked on the familiarity of Wang Renmei's star image.

16 Lin, one of the biggest female stars of postwar Hong Kong cinema, also played the role of a rustic songstress in the film in which she made her screen debut, *Cui Cui* (*Singing under the Moon*, 1953).

17 Grace Chang did so in *Shanhu* (*Torrents of Desire*).

18 With its spotlight on regional folk songs, *The Shepherd Girl* takes its inspiration from ethnic minority musicals from the PRC that similarly mined the visual and lyrical fascination of exotic folk cultures. One of the most commercially successful of these ethnic minority musicals was *Liu Sanjie* (*Third Sister Liu*), set among the Zhuang people of Guangxi Province and featuring the legendary figure of Third Sister Liu, a heroine of Guangxi folk legends who was renowned for her nimble verse and defiant spirit. *Third Sister Liu* suggestively points to the generic pathways through which the songstress circulated across mainland Chinese and Nanyang film culture. For a discussion of the film, see Clark, *Chinese Cinema*; Davis, "A Marriage of Convenience."

19 Although I have encountered a few isolated duets in other types of songstress films, the use of the device as a regular feature appears for the most part to be limited to the farmer's daughter films.

20 "*Shan ge lian*," 34. The *jianmei* ideal is especially present in Yeh's character, who asserts her physical strength by manhandling a village ruffian, thereby prompting him to exclaim, "She doesn't act like an unmarried maiden, she's more like a female bandit!"

21 Thus many characters in postwar cinema mention "going to the country" as an allusion to returning to the mainland. In an interview, the film's director Wang Tianlin described it as a story about migration from the mainland to Hong Kong (Youngs and Liu, "Interview," 85–86).

22 "*Fengjing ruhua de jiaxiang*." The English translation printed in the article is "Album from Homeside," an inaccurate translation of the Chinese title. The article appeared in

the first issue of the journal published in Hong Kong, after a two-decade run in Shanghai. *Liangyou huabao* was one of the most popular arts and entertainment magazines of the republican period, frequently noted in accounts of China's modern mass culture. It moved its home base to Hong Kong after the war, and its run there lasted until the late 1960s. Although the journal's cultural relevance and significance waned considerably toward the end of its life, its postwar phase of existence nonetheless attests to the depth of the connections between Shanghai and Hong Kong popular media.

23 "Fengjing ruhua de jiaxiang," 6–7.

24 Teo, "Oh, Karaoke!," 34. *Peach Blossom River*'s celebration of the move to the metropolis of Hong Kong can also be viewed in contrast to leftist films like *Jianghu ernu* (*The Show Must Go On*, the last production undertaken by the director Fei Mu before his death), which drive home a message of going back to the country as a coded exhortation to return to the mainland.

25 Yingjin Zhang, *The City in Modern Chinese Literature and Film*, 5. The rhetorical force of this contrast is evident in a film like *Daybreak*: shortly after she has been raped by the owner of the factory where she works, Li Lili's character recalls her halcyon days in the country, triggering a flashback that sets into sharp relief the depths to which she has now fallen.

26 Such a portrayal is consistent with what Ping-kwan Leung describes as a shift in the urban imaginary of postwar Hong Kong cinema. He argues that although the Shanghai tradition can still be detected in films that offer "a negative depiction of Hong Kong's urban space with a particular emphasis on its poor living conditions and the avarice and selfishness of the residents in a capitalist society," a more nuanced and ambivalent image of the city also begins to take shape in the 1950s ("Urban Cinema and the Cultural Identity of Hong Kong," 371).

27 My description of this as an "inaudible cut" is inspired by the technique of the invisible cut, associated with the trick films of George Méliès.

28 The idea of the audiovisual contact comes from Michel Chion, who defines it as "a sort of symbolic pact to which the audio-spectator agrees when she or he considers the elements of sound and image to be participating in one and the same entity or world" (*Audio-Vision*, 222).

29 Doane, "The Voice in the Cinema," 47.

30 Altman, *The American Film Musical*, 64.

31 There is an enormous degree of inconsistency in the recording of film songs. Although Chung's singing voice was dubbed on a regular basis (as was Lin Dai's), some actresses (like Julie Yeh Feng) did their own singing in some films and not in others, while others (like Grace Chang and Li Lihua) always sang in their own films. Chung's songs were dubbed by different singers in some of her productions.

32 Majumdar, *Wanted Cultured Ladies Only!*, 185–87.

33 Majumdar, *Wanted Cultured Ladies Only!*, 186.

34 Majumdar, *Wanted Cultured Ladies Only!*, 177.

35 Majumdar, *Wanted Cultured Ladies Only!*, 186 (my emphasis).

36 Davis also points to the similarities between song performance in Hindi and Chinese films ("A Marriage of Convenience," 440).

37 A. Williams, "The Musical Film and Recorded Popular Music," 156.

38 Zhang Z., *An Amorous History of the Silver Screen*, 308.

39 Wojcik, "The Sound of Film Acting," 74.

40 Majumdar formulates this in the framework of disavowal: "Knowledge of the use of technology enables the recognition of the singing voice as that of the playback star and not the actress, while the willful disavowal of technology allows the pleasure of watching this well-known voice embodied in the physical presence of another star" (*Wanted Cultured Ladies Only!*, 186).

41 *Miss Songbird* was produced by Yao Min, Yao Lee's brother and a prolific composer and producer. The film's access to Pathé's studio reflects the siblings' close relationship with the record company. Yao Min headed Pathé's film music division until his death, after which Yao Lee took over his job.

42 The song's title is a phrase from one of Zhou Xuan's hit songs, "When Will You Return." Yao was reportedly discovered by Zhou while singing an advertising jingle in a radio station, a fact to which *Miss Songbird* seems to slyly allude. My thanks to Andrew Jones for pointing out these historical resonances.

43 Dyer, *Stars*, 137.

44 My research into the films of the postwar period has yielded very few instances of male double roles, despite the large number of female ones. One rare example is *Singing under the Moon*, in which Yan Jun plays a double role of grandfather and grandson.

45 Chiao H., "Guguo bei wang, zhongchanjieji de chuaijiji," 13. In the case of *Her Pearly Tears*, Chiao argues that the double carries a politically regressive meaning: the mortal woman cannot attain the status of her immortal counterpart.

46 Quoted in Clark, *Chinese Cinema*, 9.

47 Dissecting the opposition between hard films and soft films, Zhang Zhen argues that "the seeming polarity in fact masks complex exchanges and interaction between the two camps" (*An Amorous History of the Silver Screen*, 297). Moreover, the most intense of these exchanges are centered on the representation of modern femininity.

48 Comolli, "A Body Too Much," 44. Discussing acting in the historical epic, Comolli argues that precisely because filmic characters require a material body to exist, a conundrum arises in the case of narratives about characters who happen also to be actual historical personages, once or still possessed of a real body with distinct features. In such films, "there are at least two bodies in competition, one body too much," he writes. The special challenge of the actor who must play the historical character is to contend with this extra body. Comolli's idea can be extrapolated to the double role, where the actor's body constitutes a body too much.

49 Some of the notable directors working in this vein are Krzysztof Kieslowski, Luis Buñuel, David Lynch, Hou Hsiao-hsien, Wong Kar-wai, and Apichatpong Weerasethakul. For a survey of the double role, see Ghillebaert, "The Double in Movies."

50 A promotional article on another of Chung Ching's double films, *Gei wo yi ge wen* (*Give Me a Kiss*), explicitly links the double role with a display of acting skill: "No matter what role she plays, whether a traditional Peking opera performer or overseas lady, Chung Ching pulls off the part" ("Duo cai duo yi de Zhong Qing," 10).

51 Naremore, *Acting in the Cinema*, 71.

52 Naremore, *Acting in the Cinema*, 71.

53 Majumdar, *Wanted Cultured Ladies Only!*, 138. Double roles in Indian cinema typically have a narrative basis in stories about identical siblings, multiple generations, and reincarnation.

54 Majumdar, *Wanted Cultured Ladies Only!*, 144.

55 Majumdar, *Wanted Cultured Ladies Only!*, 127.

56 Turner and Ngan, *Hong Kong Sixties*, 86. A similar plotline appears in the 1960 film *Xi xiang feng* (*Dreams Come True*), in which Kitty Ting Hao plays a poor flower seller who is taken in by a wealthy family that mistakes her for an acquaintance and who wins the affections of the son.

57 Moseley, "Trousers and Tiaras," 39. On Hepburn's relationship with postwar fashion, see Studlar, "'Chi-Chi Cinderella.'"

58 Barthes, *Mythologies*, 57.

59 Barthes, *Mythologies*, 57. The analysis of Hepburn serves as a foil to Barthes's ruminations on the face of Greta Garbo, which he associates with the absolute, the eternal, and the singular.

60 The presentation of Yueying as a television star is somewhat prophetic, given that television was far from a significant mass medium at the time of the film's release. Broadcast television had been introduced to Hong Kong only three years earlier, programming was still extremely limited, and television sets were seen as novel luxury items. See Hampton, "Early Hong Kong Television."

61 Herzog, *Dreams of Difference*, 7.

62 McMillin, *The Musical as Drama*, 21.

Chapter 4. THE MAMBO GIRL

1 Ho, "The Songstress, the Farmer's Daughter, the Mambo Girl and the Songstress Again."

2 The association of Chang's characters with toy dolls calls to mind a silent-era Shanghai film, *Xiao wanyi* (*Little Toys*), which draws a similar parallel between toys and children. For an analysis of this film, see Jones, *Developmental Fairy Tales*, chapter 4.

3 Chang and Chung both honed their talents at the Taishan Training Institute, under the supervision of the director Bu Wancang. The two made their screen debut in two films directed by Bu and released in 1953, *Lian chun qu* (*The Song of Spring*) and *Qi jiemei* (*Seven Maidens*). Chung vaulted to stardom in 1956 with the release of *Songs of the Peach Blossom River*, and Chang did the same in the following year with *Mambo Girl*.

4 *Queen of Sports* was remade in 1961 by MP&GI, using the same title.

5 See Chin, "Translating the New Woman."

6 See F. Wong, "Industrialization and Family Structure in Hong Kong."

7 Faure, *Colonialism and the Hong Kong Mentality*, 75.

8 A survey conducted in Hong Kong in 1968 revealed that in 30 percent of households, one or more children age fourteen or younger had a job, either on a part- or full-time

basis, to help support their households (Salaff, *Working Daughters of Hong Kong*, 23).
It bears reiterating that the relationship between the images of teenagers constructed by popular culture and the actual teenagers who made up the youth market was a mediated and indirect one.

9   Fu, "The 1960s." The mid-1960s also saw the publication of popular magazines aimed at a teen readership, such as *Young Hong Kong*; *Shao nan shao nü* (*Teenagers*); and *Shidai qingnian*, whose English tag line was "Mod—Strictly For Mods!" For examples of these magazines, see 140–42.

10 A comparison of the two films also complicates Fu's dating of the *qingchun pian* as a 1960s phenomenon. The "modern trappings" of dance parties, nightclubs, campus life, dating, picnics, cars, and Western fashion that figure so centrally in this cycle were present in earlier films like *Mambo Girl*, *Qingchung ernü* (*Spring Song*), and *Chang tui jiejie* (*Sister Long Legs*), to name just a few examples (Fu, "The 1960s," 82).

11 The translation of the lyrics here and throughout the chapter has been modified from the subtitles appearing in the Celestial Pictures DVD release of *Mambo Girl*.

12 It is worth noting that pop music itself was undergoing a process of domestication at this time, as the increasing availability of records and radio brought music into the home. The trend toward portable reproduced sound continued with the mass marketing of transistor radios, televisions, and tape recorders in the early 1960s, as Andrew Jones points out in "Circuit Listening."

13 Bel canto (which means beautiful singing) refers to the vocal style of the virtuosic opera or concert. Associated with Italian music from the seventeenth and eighteenth centuries, the style has been pedagogically instituted as a standard for classical voice training.

14 Gary Needham suggests *Rock 'n' Roll Revue* (1955) as a possible inspiration for *Mambo Girl* ("Fashioning Modernity," 46). Although the musical soundtrack bears out this link, the earlier revue film contains very few dance performances, with the exception of a few tap-dancing numbers. *Mambo Girl's* marked emphasis on choreographic spectacle suggests the influence of more mainstream rock musical productions like *Rock around the Clock*, which tended to feature elaborate dance displays.

15 James, "Rock 'n' Film," 10.

16 James writes: "In the 1950s, when films about rock 'n' roll were made from within the culture industries, their task was to disclaim the music's aesthetic and social menace and its associations with delinquent teenage working-class subcultures by legitimating the music as commodity entertainment assimilable to the existing cultural order within the hegemony of capitalist culture" ("Rock 'n' Film," 26).

17 Shu, "Notes on MP&GI," 49. See also K. Ng, "Romantic Comedies of Cathay-MP&GI in the 1950s and 60s."

18 M. Wong, "Women Who Cross Borders," 85–86.

19 Ho, "The Songstress, the Farmer's Daughter, the Mambo Girl and the Songstress Again," 66.

20 Sek, "Blessing, Bad Woman and Little Person," 40.

21 Zhang Z., "Ling Bo," 121, 129. Zhang's analysis is based on the example of Ivy Ling Bo, another actress and songstress who was known for her orphan roles and who

was an orphan herself. Notably, at the height of her stardom Bo became the object of what might be described as the most intense fan cult in Chinese film history.

22 Zhang Z., "Ling Bo," 129.

23 Sek, "Blessing, Bad Woman and Little Person," 40.

24 Ho, "The Songstress, the Farmer's Daughter, the Mambo Girl and the Songstress Again," 66.

25 Needham, "Fashioning Modernity," 46. The ending of *Blood Will Tell*, also directed by Yi Wen, borrows just as blatantly from *Stella Dallas*, although with a gender twist. Here the Red Begonia is allowed to witness his daughter's wedding before he is returned to prison. He attends the ceremony as a guest and expresses his good wishes to the daughter who does not know his identity; as she turns away, his outstretched hand is immediately handcuffed.

26 In *Love and Duty*, Ruan's character is kept from her children by her husband after she leaves him for another man; many years later, she meets them again when they call on her services as a seamstress. In *Little Toys*, mother and son are separated when he is kidnapped and sold to a wealthy woman; near the end of the film, when the mother has lost everything and supports herself as a street hawker, the little boy approaches her to buy one of the toys she is selling.

27 Garcia, "The Illicit Place," 147.

28 Garcia, "The Illicit Place," 147.

29 Garcia, "The Illicit Place," 148.

30 Jarvie, *Window on Hong Kong*, 92.

31 Sobchack, "Lounge Time," 153–54.

32 Sobchack, "Lounge Time," 130. She similarly positions the lounge as the antipode of the home and the negation of traditional domestic ideals.

33 Sobchack, "Lounge Time," 151, 130.

34 Sobchack, "Lounge Time," 130.

35 Cited in Shu, "Notes on MP&GI," 43. Another possible inspiration for *Mambo Girl* is the 1954 Italian film *Mambo*, starring Silvana Mangano as a professional dancer. The film features several performances of Afro-Caribbean dance by the Katherine Dunham Dance Company. Chang has recalled seeing *Mambo* before the filming of *Mambo Girl*, and the two films' credit sequences and opening dance scenes display some similarities. See G. Chang, "One Big Happy Family," 192.

36 Chang recalls: "We would eat dinner at home to save money and then go out and dance all night. We knew all the musicians at the clubs, having worked with them in the films and in the EMI studio. . . . I would dance with [fellow MP&GI actor Peter] Chen Hou and invent dance moves together, like the cha cha. After a while, we became quite good. We used some of those moves in the films we [made] together" (quoted in Ho, "Excerpts from an Interview with Ge Lan," 88).

37 The scene in which Fong appears to be shot on a studio sound stage, not in a real nightclub.

38 "Yi Wen xin zuo yi bu chongman qingqun qixi de gechang wudao pian," 14.

39 S. Sun and Shi, "Singing in Electric Shadows," 25.

40 S. L. Li, "Embracing Glocalization and Hong Kong–Made Musical Films," 76.

41 Ho, "The Songstress, the Farmer's Daughter, the Mambo Girl and the Songstress Again," 66.

42 Li, "Embracing Glocalization and Hong Kong–Made Musical Films," 74.

43 Ho, "Excerpts from an Interview with Ge Lan," 88; G. Chang, "One Big Happy Family," 192.

44 Fong often worked as a behind-the-scenes singer. She would eventually assume a highly visible role in the film industry as a senior executive of Shaw Brothers; to this day she is chiefly responsible for Shaw's enterprises in Hong Kong. Rebecca Pan makes occasional appearances in contemporary Hong Kong films—like Wong Kar-wai's *Hua yang nianhua* (*In the Mood for Love*), in which she is cast as the Shanghainese landlady Mrs. Suen.

45 Wu, "Yezonghui," 11.

46 Included among them were some of the most well-known and established musicians and bandleaders from that era: Lobing Samson, who led the house band at Ciro's, one of Shanghai's most extravagant nightclubs, and in Hong Kong led a band at the Luna Park Sky Room; the pianist and composer Vic Cristobal; and the violinist and jazz guitarist Fred Carpio. See Chik and Benson, "HK Pop History." Carpio's family would go on to establish itself as a key force in Hong Kong popular music: his son Fernando was an accomplished drummer, and the latter's daughter Teresa was a well-known Cantopop singer of the 1970s and 1980s.

47 Miller, *Garland Encyclopedia of World Music Volume* 4:885. Andrew Field points out that the leader of the Shanghai Musician's Association from the period of the occupation through the end of the 1940s was Jose Contreras, a Filipino bandleader (*Shanghai's Dancing World*, 207). For an overview of overseas Filipino entertainment professionals throughout the twentieth century, see S. Ng, "Performing the 'Filipino' at the Crossroads."

48 "Peiyin yu muhou gechang," 47.

49 Jones, "Circuit Listening."

50 By the late 1940s Latin jazz was sweeping the jazz venues of Manila. Cugat toured the city in 1953, and in the following decade, Tito Puente played a series of concerts "to near capacity audiences" at Hong Kong's City Hall before continuing to Singapore, Malaysia, and Japan. See Myatt, "Tito Puente Dates Boost Latin Music," 33. Delfino honed his drumming skills in the Philippines under the tutelage of Chino Santos, a Puerto Rican GI credited with an instrumental role in introducing Latin dance to the country. See Quirino, *Mabuhay Jazz*, 16–17.

51 Jones also discusses the intertwined "circuits of media and migration" by which Afro-Caribbean music made its way to Hong Kong and Taiwan as a "global musical vernacular" in this period ("Circuit Listening").

52 The role of Filipino musicians in Hong Kong's live music culture can be gleaned from Quirino, *Mabuhay Jazz*, a study based largely on interviews and oral history.

53 The program brochure for *Mambo Girl* notes that special care was taken by the filmmakers to capture the details of the choreography.

54 Kailing's lead here is significant when we consider Hollywood musicals of this era. As Richard Dyer points out, in scenes of couple dancing in the late 1940s and 1950s

we see "a dance style developed that gave more prominence to men. . . . Within couple-dances, it also meant a renewed sense of gender polarity [and] female dependency," with men leading and women following (*In the Space of a Song*, 99).

55 "Ge Lan wuzi."

56 *"Long xiangfeng wu zhong de 'Heri jun zai lai?'"*

57 "Lin Feng zai *Yunü chunqing* zhong de wuzi." Like Chang, Lam was typecast as a sunny modern girl and performed in numerous song-and-dance films throughout her prolific career. On the similarities between the two stars, see Law, "Shaw's Cantonese Productions and Their Interactions with Contemporary Local and Hollywood Cinema," 70–71.

58 *"Manbo nülang,"* 30.

59 "Maggie and Hala-hala," 38.

60 Field, *Shanghai's Dancing World*.

61 E. Chang, "Tan tiaowu," 151.

62 Even in the West, of course, social dancing had scandalous connotations—in particular, new jazz styles that broke from the formality of ballroom dancing. See Erenberg, "From New York to Middletown."

63 The cross-dressed woman in this dance scene is Zhou Xuan, making her first on-screen appearance.

64 "Ge Lan wuzi,"11.

65 E. Yeh, "China," 178.

66 See, for instance, "Zhihui zhi xing—Ge Lan."

67 "Ge Lan mai yi chang dagu," 43.

68 "Ge Lan shuo 'Wo lai gei nimen pai zhangxiang pian,'" 24. The article states that Chang was nicknamed Miss Mambo by her Taiwan audience.

69 "Ge Lan de yi feng gongkai xin."

70 In this same period the cliché of Hong Kong as a gateway between East and West—a crucial portal for the flows of international capital—took root.

71 B. Hu, "Star Discourse and the Cosmopolitan Chinese," 184.

72 Such fashion shows are a feature of films like *Cinderella and Her Little Angels* and *Love Parade*. Incidentally, both films are about the fashion and garment industry.

73 Hu, "Star Discourse and the Cosmopolitan Chinese," 186.

74 "Ge Lan de geren da yuedui," 22.

75 "Caihua jingren de Ge Lan," 32.

76 *The Dinah Shore Show* (NBC), October 25, 1959.

Chapter 5. CARMEN, CAMILLE, AND THE UNDOING OF WOMEN

1 Naremore, *Acting in the Cinema*, chapter 4.

2 The lyrics represent an approximation rather than direct translation of the original; for instance, the last stanza above appears to take its cue from the verses: "Si tu ne m'aimes pas, si tu ne m'aimes pas, je t'aime, mais si je t'aime, si je t'aime, prends garde à toi!"

3 It is so described by the film's musical director Yao Min, quoted in "Zhongguo ying-tan guibao—Ge Lan," 29.

4   L. Lee, "The Popular and the Classical," 99.

5   See McClary, *Georges Bizet*.

6   On these adaptations, see Tambling, *Opera, Ideology and Film*; McClary, *Georges Bizet*; Leicester, "Discourse and the Film Text"; Herzog, *Dreams of Difference, Songs of the Same*, chapter 2. It is estimated that more than two hundred film versions of *Carmen* have been produced.

7   The film was notorious for dubbing over the singing voices of the two stars with those of white, classically trained vocalists. See Smith, "Black Faces, White Voices."

8   Leicester, "Discourse and the Film Text," 246.

9   Bao, "From Pearl White to White Rose Woo," 213–14.

10 McClary, *Georges Bizet*, 75.

11 McClary, *Georges Bizet*, 51–52.

12 McClary, *Georges Bizet*, 75.

13 Lam, "The Presence and Absence of Female Musicians and Music in China," 100.

14 Silverman, *The Acoustic Mirror*, 39. Silverman's analysis deals primarily with classical Hollywood cinema, but her argument that "sexual difference is the effect of dominant cinema's *sound* regime as well as its visual regime, and that the female *voice* is as relentlessly held to normative representations and functions as is the female body" holds much relevance for the films discussed here (ibid., viii).

15 A. Williams, "The Musical Film and Recorded Popular Music," 151.

16 McClary, *Georges Bizet*, 89.

17 McClary, *Georges Bizet*, 75.

18 Doane, *Femmes Fatales*, 10.

19 Doane, *Femmes Fatales*, 15.

20 Moi, introduction, vi.

21 Moi, introduction, vii. In Dumas's novel, Marguerite always carries a bouquet of white camellias except for five days of every month, when they are replaced by red camellias.

22 Moi, introduction, vi.

23 Barthes, *Mythologies*, 103.

24 Y. Hu, *Tales of Translation*, 68–69.

25 H. Lee, *Revolution of the Heart*, 99.

26 H. Lee, *Revolution of the Heart*, 105. The two translators of Dumas's book, Lin Shu and Wang Shouchang, reportedly wept so profusely while working on the text that they could be heard from the street outside. Leo Lee writes: "When Lin was heard weeping for a foreign 'lady of the camellias,' he was well on his way beyond Confucian bounds toward the notion that personal sentiments, if genuinely expressed, can be the central *Weltanschauung* of a man" (*The Romantic Generation of Modern Chinese Writers*, 260).

27 H. Lee, *Revolution of the Heart*, 106–7.

28 Chow, *Woman and Chinese Modernity*, 51.

29 H. Lee, *Revolution of the Heart*, 102.

30 Y. Hu, *Tales of Translation*, 70. In this stage version by the theater troupe Chunliu she (Spring Willow Troupe), the role of Camille was played by a male actor and writer, Li Shutong.

31 Zhang Z., "Cosmopolitan Projections," 151.

32 Sun Y., *"Yecao xianhua,"* 55.

33 Zhang Z., "Cosmopolitan Projections," 151. *Yu li hun*, published in 1912, was one of the central texts of Duck and Butterfly literature. The book's narrator describes himself as "the Dumas *fils* of the east," and other features of the novel suggest that the author, Xu Zhenya, "was consciously using the work [by Dumas] as a model when composing his last two chapters" (Hsia, "Hsü Chen-ya's *Yü-li hun*," 219).

34 E. Yeh, *"Wenyi* and the Branding of Early Chinese Film," 69. Yeh offers a detailed survey of productions between 1926 and 1931 that were made with collaboration of Duck and Butterfly authors. On the topic of adaptation, see also Zhang Z., "Cosmopolitan Projections."

35 Liu, *Translingual Practice.*

36 The first number, "You and Me" ("Ni yu wo"), is a lyrical expression of the happiness that the two lovers find in the countryside together. The second number, "Frenzy of Song and Dance" ("Gewu fengkuang"), is performed when they meet again by chance at a casino after she has left him.

37 Doe [Tao], "Introduction," 5 (translated with the assistance of Hsinyi Tiffany Lee).

38 *Fate in Tears and Laughter* is another text with a rich history of adaptations in various media. Perry Link notes that "the story was performed as a play, a dialect play, an opera, a folk recitation (in Peking's *ch'u-yi*) and as a drum-song" (*Mandarin Ducks and Butterflies*, 257). It was adapted for the screen in 1932 (in a partial-sound production), 1945, 1956, and—in two competing versions from different studios—1963.

39 Stam, "Beyond Fidelity," 69.

40 For example, the modernist writer Eileen Chang wrote eight screenplays for the studio; some of these resulted in enormous success at the box office. For a discussion of this collaboration, see K. Ng, "The Screenwriter as Cultural Broker." The screenplay for both *A Story of Three Loves* and *The Wild, Wild Rose* was written by Nellie Chin Yu, another prolific contributor to MP&GI's screenwriting department. Chang and Yu stand out as prominent female authors in a cultural and literary milieu dominated by men, and their role in Chinese film history remains to be fully documented.

41 Y. Hu, *Tales of Translation*, 5.

42 E. Yeh, "Pitfalls of Cross-Cultural Analysis." See also E. Yeh, *"Wenyi* and the Branding of Early Chinese Film," 72–76. Theater constitutes another node in the cross-media dynamics of melodrama, as Li Jin argues in "Theater of Pathos."

43 Ma N., "Spatiality and Subjectivity in Xie Jin's Film Melodrama of the New Period"; Browne, "Society and Subjectivity."

44 E. Yeh, "Pitfalls of Cross-Cultural Analysis," 445, 450.

45 Emilie Yeh writes, "The new corpus of *wenyi* cinema may emerge as a distinct historiography in film scholarship," and maps out a trajectory that stretches from prewar Shanghai to the Mandarin and Cantonese film industries of postwar Hong Kong to Taiwan cinema in the Kuomintang era ("Pitfalls of Cross-Cultural Analysis," 438). See also Teo, "Chinese Melodrama."

46 L. Williams, "Melodrama Revised," 42.

47 This last set of attributes figures prominently in theorizations of American domestic melodrama. The expressive codes of this cycle of melodramas—summed up by Thomas Elsaesser as "an intensified symbolisation of everyday action" ("Tales of Sound and Fury," 56)—made their way into Hong Kong cinema through the influence of Douglas Sirk. Sirk's films were well received by Hong Kong audiences, inspired at least two credited remakes, and left a clear stylistic imprint on directors like Qin Jian. Thanks to Sam Ho for sharing his knowledge of Sirk's reception in the Hong Kong film world.

48 E. Yeh, "Pitfalls of Cross-Cultural Analysis," 446–49. Zhang Zhen discusses the "transcultural proliferation of melodrama," giving special consideration to the impact of the early film melodramas of D. W. Griffith on 1920s Shanghai cinema. She writes: "If Griffith drew on the ambivalent legacy of the French Revolution and European Enlightenment to address postbellum American society's sociocultural upheavals in nation building and industrialization, the Shanghai filmmakers further translated and adapted these Euro-American sources along with Chinese literary and theatrical traditions in the contradiction-ridden context of the Chinese new culture movement and Shanghai's semicolonial modernity" ("Transplanting Melodrama," 37).

49 Cai, *Zhongguo jindai wenyi dianying yanjiu*, 2.

50 Christine Gledhill writes: "Characteristically the melodramatic plot turns on an initial, often deliberately engineered, misrecognition of the innocence of a central protagonist. . . . Narrative is thus progressed through a struggle for clear moral identification of all protagonists and is finally resolved by public recognition of where guilt and innocence really lie" ("The Melodramatic Field," 30).

51 "Ge Lan de Riben zhuang." The story of *Madame Butterfly* was also adapted in *Hudie furen*, a Xinhua production of 1956 that starred Li Lihua as a Japanese singer who marries a Hong Kong businessman.

52 *Rigoletto* also ends with a woman's suicidal sacrifice for her beloved.

53 Clément, *Opera*, 5.

54 Clément, *Opera*, 47. Clément discusses the dagger "that will fix Butterfly . . . to the board of the white Occident" (ibid., 45), and that which kills Carmen, "a woman who refuses masculine yokes and who must pay for it with her life" (ibid., 48).

55 As Paul Robinson writes, "while the operatic text tells a story of woman's undoing, the music tells just the opposite story: of her empowerment" ("It's Not Over till the Soprano Dies"). Building on this assertion, Carolyn Abbate sets the role of the singer against that of the composer or librettist. It is the performer who endows music with a tangible, phenomenal existence; therefore "there are potentially multiple musical voices that inhabit a work" (*Unsung Voices*, x).

56 Cavarero, *For More Than One Voice*, 126.

Coda

1 For a discussion of *Teddy Girls* that places the film in dialogue with its historical context, see Fu, "The 1960s."

2 Siao sang in some of her films, not including *Teddy Girls*, but she never established a career as a recording artist.

3　For an overview of Mui's pop career, see Witzleben, "Cantopop and Mandopop in Pre-Postcolonial Hong Kong." Mui plays the songstress role again in *Heri jun zai lai* (*Au Revoir Mon Amour*), a historical drama set in Japanese-occupied Shanghai that takes its name from a hit song by Zhou Xuan.

4　Biancorosso, "Romance, Insularity and Representation," 91.

5　The sequence, with its distorted speed and dropped frames, bears the marks of William Chang's signature manipulations of footage.

6　For a discussion of the relationship between *In the Mood for Love*, *All-Consuming Love*, and the found footage short, see Biancorosso, "Popular Music and the Aesthetics of the Self in Wong Kar-wai's Cinema."

Bai hua gongzhu (百花公主 *Flower Princess*). Directed by Wong Tin-lam. Hong Kong: Xinhua Film Company, 1959.

Bai jin long (白金龍 *White Golden Dragon*). Directed by Tang Xiaodan. Hong Kong: Tianyi Film Company, 1933.

Bao lian deng (寶蓮燈 *The Magic Lamp*). Directed by Wong Tin-lam. Hong Kong: Motion Picture and General Investment Co. Ltd., 1964.

Bi shui honglian (碧水紅蓮 *Fleur-de-Lys*). Directed by Chiang Nan. Hong Kong: Xinhua Film Company, 1960.

Bu liao qing (不了情 *Love without End*). Directed by Doe Ching [Tao Qin]. Hong Kong: Shaw Brothers Ltd., 1961.

Chahua nü (茶花女 *Camilla*). Directed by Doe Ching [Tao Qin]. Hong Kong: Xinhua Film Company, 1955.

Chang tui jiejie (長腿姐姐 *Sister Long Legs*). Directed by Tang Huang. Hong Kong: Motion Picture and General Investment Co. Ltd., 1960.

Chang xiang si (長相思 *All-Consuming Love*). Directed by He Zhaozhang. Hong Kong: Huaxing Film Company, 1947.

Chiqing lie (痴情淚 *Pink Tears*). Directed by Chun Kim. Hong Kong: Shaw Brothers Ltd., 1965.

Cui Cui (翠翠 *Singing under the Moon*). Directed by Yan Jun. Hong Kong: Yonghua Film Company, 1953.

Da lu (大路 *The Big Road*). Directed by Sun Yu. China: Lianhua Film Company, 1934.

Diao Chan (貂蟬 *Diau Charn*). Directed by Li Han-hsiang. Hong Kong: Shaw Brothers Ltd., 1958.

Dong (洞 *The Hole*). Directed by Tsai Ming-liang. France, Taiwan: La Sept Arte, Haut et Court, Arc Light Films, China Television, and Central Motion Picture Corporation, 1998.

Duoqing de yemao (多情的野貓 *Nothing but Love*). Directed by Wong Tin-lam. Hong Kong: Xinhua Film Company, 1960.

Feinü zhengzhuan (飛女正傳 *Teddy Girls*). Directed by Patrick Lung Kong. Hong Kong: Eng Way & Company, 1969.

Feng yun ernü (風雲兒女 *Children of Troubled Times*). Directed by Xu Xingzhi. China: Diantong Film Company, 1935.

Gechang chunse (歌場春色 *Pleasures of the Opera*). Directed by Li Pingqian. China: Tianyi Film Company, 1931.

Gei wo yi ge wen (給我一個吻 *Give Me a Kiss*). Directed by Li Han-hsiang. Hong Kong: Shaw Brothers Ltd., 1958.

Gemi xiaojie (歌迷小姐 *Miss Songbird*). Directed by Chiang Nan. Hong Kong: Wanxiang Film Company, 1959.

Genü Hong mudan (歌女紅牡丹 *Songstress Red Peony*). Directed by Zhang Shichuan. China: Mingxing Film Company, 1931.

Genü zhi ge (歌女之歌 *Song of a Songstress*). Directed by Fang Peilin. Hong Kong: Qidong Film Company, 1948.

Gudu chun meng (故都春夢 *Spring Dream in the Old Capitol*). Directed by Sun Yu. China: Lianhua Film Company, 1929.

Haitang hong (海棠紅 *Blood Will Tell*). Directed by Evan Yang [Yi Wen]. Hong Kong: Xinhua Film Company, 1955.

Heri jun zai la (何日君再來 *Au Revoir Mon Amour*). Directed by Tony Au. Hong Kong: Golden Harvest Film Productions Ltd., 1991.

Heri jun zai la (何日君再來 *Till the End of Time*). Directed by Chun Kim. Hong Kong: Shaw Brothers Ltd., 1966.

Hua jie (花街 *Flower Street*). Directed by Griffin Yueh Feng [Yue Feng]. Hong Kong: Changcheng Pictures Corporation, 1950.

Hua luo you feng jun (花落又逢君 *Till We Meet Again*). Directed by Doe Ching [Tao Qin]. Hong Kong: Shaw Brothers Ltd., 1956.

Hua tuan jin cu (花團錦簇 *Love Parade*). Directed by Doe Ching [Tao Qin]. Hong Kong: Shaw Brothers Ltd., 1963.

Hua yang de nianhua (花樣的年華 *The Blooming Years*). Directed by Wong Kar-wai. Hong Kong, France: Block 2 Pictures, Jet Tone Production, and Paradis Films, 2000.

Hua yang nianhua (花樣年華 *In the Mood for Love*). Directed by Wong Kar-wai. Hong Kong: Jet Tone Productions Ltd., 2000.

Huang tudi (黃土地 *Yellow Earth*). Directed by Chen Kaige. China: Guangxi Film Studio, 1984.

Hudie furen (蝴蝶夫人 *Madame Butterfly*). Directed by Evan Yang [Yi Wen]. Hong Kong: Xinhua Film Company, 1956.

Jianghu ernu (江湖兒女 *The Show Must Go On*). Directed by Zhu Shilin and Qi Wenshao. Hong Kong: Longma Film Company, 1952.

Jiao wo ruhe bu xiang ta (教我如何不想她 *Because of Her*). Directed by Evan Yang [Yi Wen]. Hong Kong: Motion Picture and General Investment Co. Ltd., 1963.

Jin lianhua (金蓮花 *Golden Lotus*). Directed by Griffin Yueh Feng [Yue Feng]. Hong Kong: Yonghua Film Company, 1957.

Kelian de Qiuxiang (可憐的秋香 *The Miserable Life of Qiuxiang*). Directed by Wang Yuanlong. China: Dazhonghua Baihe Film Company, 1927.

Kongzhong xiaojie (空中小姐 *Air Hostess*). Directed by Evan Yang [Yi Wen]. Hong Kong: Motion Picture and General Investment Co. Ltd., 1959.

Lan yu hei (藍與黑 *The Blue and the Black*). Directed by Doe Ching [Tao Qin]. Hong Kong: Shaw Brothers Ltd., 1966.

Lian chun qu (戀春曲 *The Song of Spring*). Directed by Bu Wancang. Hong Kong: Taishan Film Company, 1953.

Lianai yu yiwu (戀愛與義務 *Love and Duty*). Directed by Bu Wancang. China: Lianhua Film Company, 1931.

Liang Shanbo yu Zhu Yingtai (梁山伯與祝英台 *The Love Eterne*). Directed by Li Han-hsiang. Hong Kong: Shaw Brothers Ltd., 1963.

Liangxin fuhuo (良心復活 *Resurrection of Conscience*). Directed by Bu Wancang. China: Mingxing Film Company, 1926.

Liu Sanjie (劉三姐 *Third Sister Liu*). Directed by Su Li. China: Changchun Film Studio, 1960.

Liu yue xinniang (六月新娘 *June Bride*). Directed by Tang Huang. Hong Kong: Motion Picture and General Investment Co. Ltd., 1960.

Long xiangfeng wu (龍翔鳳舞 *Calendar Girl*). Directed by Doe Ching [Tao Qin]. Hong Kong: Motion Picture and General Investment Co. Ltd., 1959.

Malu tianshi (馬路天使 *Street Angel*). Directed by Yuan Muzhi. China: Mingxing Film Company, 1937.

Manbo guniang (曼波姑娘 *Mambo Lady*). Director unknown. Hong Kong: Yicheng Film Company, 1958.

Manbo nülang (曼波女郎 *Mambo Girl*). Directed by Evan Yang [Yi Wen]. Hong Kong: Motion Picture and General Investment Co. Ltd., 1957.

Qi jiemei (七姊妹 *Seven Maidens*). Directed by Bu Wancang. Hong Kong: Taishan Film Company, 1953.

Qian jiao bai mei (千嬌百媚, *Les Belles*). Directed by Doe Ching [Tao Qin]. Hong Kong: Shaw Brothers Ltd., 1961.

Qian mian nülang (千面女郎 *Girl of a Thousand Guises*). Directed by Chiang Nan. Hong Kong: Tao Yuen Motion Picture Development Company, 1959.

Qingchun ernü (青春兒女 *Spring Song*). Directed by Evan Yang [Yi Wen]. Hong Kong: Motion Picture and General Investment Co. Ltd., 1959.

Ru shi jiaren (入室佳人 *A Challenge of Love*). Directed by Wong Tin-lam. Hong Kong: Xinhua Film Company, 1960.

Sanxing banyue (三星伴月 *Orion Moon*). Directed by Fang Peilin. China: Yihua Film Company, 1938.

Se jie (色戒 *Lust, Caution*). Directed by Ang Lee. United States, China: Focus Features, River Road Entertainment, and Haishang Films, 2007.

Shan ge lian (山歌戀 *The Shepherd Girl*). Directed by Lo Chen. Hong Kong: Shaw Brothers Ltd., 1964.

Shanhu (珊瑚 *Torrents of Desire*). Directed by Chiang Nan. Hong Kong: China Film Enterprise and Ziyou Dongnan Film Company, 1958.

Shennü (神女 *Goddess*). Directed by Wu Yonggang. China: Lianhua Film Company, 1934.

Tao li zheng chun (桃李爭春 *It's Always Spring*). Directed by Evan Yang [Yi Wen]. Hong Kong: Motion Picture and General Investment Co. Ltd., 1962.

Taohua jiang (桃花江 *Songs of the Peach Blossom River*). Directed by Zhang Shankun and Wong Tin-lam. Hong Kong: Xinhua Film Company, 1956.

Taohua qi xue ji (桃花泣血記 *Peach Blossom Weeps Tears of Blood*). Directed by Bu Wancang. China: Lianhua Film Company, 1931.

Ti xiao yinyuan (啼笑姻緣 *A Story of Three Loves*). Directed by Wong Tin-lam. Hong Kong: Motion Picture and General Investment Co. Ltd., 1964.

Tianming (天明 *Daybreak*). Directed by Sun Yu. China: Lianhua Film Company, 1933.

Tiyu huanghou (體育皇后 *Queen of Sports*). Directed by Sun Yu. China: Lianhua Film Company, 1934.

Tiyu huanghou (體育皇后 *Queen of Sports*). Directed by Tang Huang. Hong Kong: Motion Picture and General Investment Co. Ltd., 1961.

Wanshi liufang (萬世流芳 *Eternity*). Directed by Bu Wancang, Ma Xu Weibang, and Zhu Shilin. China: Zhonglian Film Company, 1943.

Xi linmen (喜臨門 *Happiness at the Door*). Directed by Fung Chi-kong. Hong Kong: Lap Tat Film Company, 1958.

Xi xiang feng (喜相逢 *Dreams Come True*). Directed by Bu Wancang. Hong Kong: Motion Picture and General Investment Co. Ltd., 1960.

Xiang jiang hua yueyu (香江花月夜 *Hong Kong Nocturne*). Directed by Inoue Umetsugu. Hong Kong: Shaw Brothers Ltd., 1967.

Xiangrufeifei (想入非非 *Sweet Sister-in-Law*). Directed by Yan Youxiang. Hong Kong: Yihua Film Company, 1958.

Xiao wanyi (小玩意 *Little Toys*). Directed by Sun Yu. China: Lianhua Film Company, 1933.

Xiao Xiang lei (瀟湘泪 *Tears of Xiao Xiang*). Directed by Sun Yu. China: Changcheng Film Company, 1928.

Xiao yunque (小雲雀 *The Lark*). Directed by Xue Qun. Hong Kong: Shaw Brothers Ltd., 1965.

Xin chahua (新茶花女 *New Camellias*). Director unknown. China: Asia Company, 1913.

Xin nüxing (新女性 *New Woman*). Directed by Cai Chusheng. China: Lianhua Film Company, 1935.

Xin ti xiao yinyuan (啼笑姻緣 *Between Tears and Smiles*). Directed by Griffin Yueh Feng [Yue Feng], Doe Ching [Tao Qin], Ho Meng-hua, Yan Jun, Lo Chen, Hsih Chun, Wang Xinglei, and Wen Shiling. Hong Kong: Shaw Brothers Ltd., 1964.

Xingxing, yueliang, taiyang (星星.月亮.太陽 *Sun, Moon, and Star*). Directed by Evan Yang [Yi Wen]. Hong Kong: Motion Picture and General Investment Co. Ltd., 1961.

Xuangong yanshi (璇宮豔史 *My Kingdom for a Husband*). Directed by Tso Kea. Hong Kong: Motion Picture and General Investment Co. Ltd., 1957.

Xue ran haitang hong (血染海棠紅 *Blood-Stained Begonia*). Directed by Griffin Yueh Feng [Yue Feng]. Hong Kong: Great Wall Film Company, 1949.

Yanzhi kou (胭脂扣 *Rouge*). Directed by Stanley Kwan. Hong Kong: Golden Harvest Film Productions Ltd., 1988.

Yasuiqian (壓歲錢 *New Year's Coin*). Directed by Zhang Shichuan. China: Mingxing Film Company, 1937.

Ye meigui (野玫瑰 *The Wild Rose*). Directed by Sun Yu. China: Lianhua Film Company, 1932.

Ye meigui zhi lian (野玫瑰之戀 *The Wild, Wild Rose*). Directed by Wong Tin-lam. Hong Kong: Motion Picture and General Investment Co. Ltd., 1960.

Yeban gesheng (夜半歌聲 *Song at Midnight*). Directed by Ma Xu Weibang. China: Xinhua Film Company, 1937.

Yecao xianhua (野草閑花 *Wild Flowers*). Directed by Sun Yu. China: Minxin/Lianhua Film Company, 1930.

Yi jian zhong qing (一見鍾情 *Love at First Sight*). Directed by Chiang Nan. Hong Kong: Xinhua Film Company, 1958.

Yijian mei (一剪梅 *A Spray of Plum Blossoms*). Directed by Bu Wancang. China: Lianhua Film Company, 1931.

Ying du yan ji (櫻都艷跡 *Beauty of Tokyo*). Directed by Evan Yang [Yi Wen]. Hong Kong: Xinhua Film Company, 1955.

Yinghai shengge (銀海笙歌 *Stand Up and Cheer*). Directed by Wong Tin-lam and Chiang Nan. Hong Kong: Xinhua Film Company, 1958.

Yinhan shuang xing (銀漢雙星 *Two Stars in the Milky Way*). Directed by Shi Dongshan. China: Lianhua Film Company, 1931.

Yu ge (漁歌 *The Fisherman's Daughter*). Directed by Bu Wancang. Hong Kong: Xinhua Film Company, 1956.

Yu guang qu (漁光曲 *Song of the Fishermen*). Directed by Cai Chusheng. China: Lianhua Film Company, 1934.

Yu guo tian qing (雨過天青 *Peace after Storm*). Directed by Xia Chifeng. China: Da Zhonghua Film Company and Jinan Film Company, 1931.

Yu jia nü (漁家女 *The Fisherman's Daughter*). Directed by Bu Wancang. Hong Kong: Zhonghua Film United Ltd., 1943.

Yu meiren (虞美人 *The Singing Beauty*). Directed by Chen Kengran. China: Youlian Film Company, 1931.

Yun chang yan hou (雲裳艷后 *Cinderella and Her Little Angels*). Directed by Tang Huang. Hong Kong: Motion Picture and General Investment Co. Ltd., 1959.

Yunü qunqing (玉女春情 *Teen-Age Love*). Directed by Chow Sze-luk. Hong Kong: Shaw Brothers Ltd., 1958.

Yunü siqing (玉女私情 *Her Tender Heart*). Directed by Tang Huang. Hong Kong: Motion Picture and General Investment Co. Ltd., 1959.

Zhenzhu lei (珍珠淚 *Her Pearly Tears*). Directed by Wong Tin-lam. Hong Kong: Motion Picture and General Investment Co. Ltd., 1962.

Zimei hua (姊妹花 *Twin Sisters*). Directed by Zhang Zhenqiu. China: Mingxing Film Company, 1933.

Zui hao de shiguang (最好的時光 *Three Times*). Directed by Hou Hsiao-hsien. Taiwan, France: 3H Films and Orly Films, 2005.

Abbas, Ackbar. *Hong Kong: Culture and the Politics of Disappearance*. Minneapolis: University of Minnesota Press, 1997.

Abbate, Carolyn. *Unsung Voices: Opera and Musical Narrative in the Nineteenth Century*. Princeton, NJ: Princeton University Press, 1996.

Altman, Rick. *The American Film Musical*. Bloomington: Indiana University Press, 1978.

Auslander, Philip. *Liveness: Performance in a Mediated Culture*. New York: Routledge, 1999.

"Baidai changpian gongshi wangluo Dianmau qunxing" [Pathé records Nets MP&GI's flock of stars]. *International Screen* 33 (July 1958), 50–51.

Bao, Weihong. "From Pearl White to White Rose Woo: The Vernacular Translation of the Serial Queen in Chinese Silent Films, 1927–1931." *Camera Obsura* 20, no. 3 (2005): 193–231.

———. "The Politics of Remediation: Mise-en-Scène and the Subjunctive Body of Chinese Opera Films." *Opera Quarterly* 26, nos. 2–3 (2010): 256–90.

Barthes, Roland. *Camera Lucida: Reflections on Photography*. Translated by Richard Howard. New York: Hill and Wang, 1982.

———. *Mythologies*. Translated by Annette Lavers. New York: Hill and Wang, 1972.

Baskett, Michael. *The Attractive Empire: Transnational Film Culture in Imperial Japan*. Honolulu: University of Hawaii Press, 2008.

Berry, Chris, and Mary Farquhar. *China on Screen: Cinema and Nation*. New York: Columbia University Press, 2006.

Biancorosso, Giorgio. "Popular Music and the Aesthetics of the Self in Wong Kar-wai's Cinema." In *Popular Music and the Post-MTV Auteur*, edited by Arved Ashby, 109–28. New York: Oxford University Press, 2013.

———. "Romance, Insularity and Representation: Wong Kar-wai's *In the Mood for Love* and Hong Kong Cinema." *Shima* 1, no. 1 (2007): 88–94.

Booth, Mark W. *The Experience of Songs*. New Haven, CT: Yale University Press, 1981.

Bordwell, David. *Planet Hong Kong: Popular Cinema and the Art of Entertainment*. Cambridge, MA: Harvard University Press, 2000.

Browne, Nick. "Society and Subjectivity: On the Political Economy of Chinese Melodrama." In *New Chinese Cinemas: Forms, Identities, Politics*, edited by Nick Browne,

Paul G. Pickowicz, Vivian Sobchack, and Esther Yau, 40–56. New York: Cambridge University Press, 1994.

Cai Guorong. *Zhongguo jindai wenyi dianying yanjiu* [Studies on modern Chinese *wenyi* cinema]. Taipei: Film Library, 1985.

"Caihua jingren di Ge Lan" [Grace Chang, the versatile genius]. *International Screen* 56 (June 1960): 32–33.

Cavarero, Adriana. *For More Than One Voice: Toward a Philosophy of Vocal Expression.* Translated by Paul A. Kottman. Stanford, CA: Stanford University Press, 2005.

Chang, Eileen. "Tan tiaowu" [On dancing]. In *Zhang Ailing wenji* [Collected works of Zhang Ailing], 4:151–62. Hefei, China: Anhui wenyi chubanshe, 1994.

Chang, Grace. "One Big Happy Family: Grace Chang's Cathay Story." In *The Cathay Story*, edited by Wong Ain-ling, 191–95. Hong Kong: Hong Kong Film Archive, 2002.

Chang, Michael G. "The Good, the Bad, and the Beautiful: Movie Actresses and Public Discourse in Shanghai, 1920s–1930s." In *Cinema and Urban Culture in Shanghai, 1922–1943*, edited by Yingjin Zhang, 128–59. Stanford, CA: Stanford University Press, 1999.

Chen, Dawn, et al. "Filmography of Cantonese Cinema (1946–1959)." In *Cantonese Opera Film Retrospective*, 134–99. Hong Kong: Urban Council, 1996.

Chen, Szu-wei. "The Rise and Generic Features of Shanghai Popular Songs in the 1930s and 1940s." *Popular Music* 24, no. 1 (2005): 107–25.

Chen, Xiangyang. "Woman, Generic Aesthetics, and the Vernacular: Huangmei Opera Films from China to Hong Kong." In *Gender Meets Genre in Postwar Cinemas*, edited by Christine Gledhill, 177–90. Urbana: University of Illinois Press, 2012.

Cheng Pei-pei, "Reminiscences of the Life of an Actress in Shaw Brothers' Movietown." In *China Forever: The Shaw Brothers and Diasporic Cinema*, edited by Poshek Fu, 246–54. Urbana: University of Illinois Press, 2008.

Cheung, Esther M. K., and Chu Yiu-wai. Introduction to *Between Home and World: A Reader in Hong Kong Cinema*, edited by Esther M. K. Cheung and Chu Yiu-wai, xii–xxxv. Hong Kong: Hong Kong University Press, 2004.

Chi, Robert. "Hong Kong Cinema before 1980." In *A Companion to Chinese Cinema*, edited by Yingjin Zhang, 75–94. Malden, MA: Wiley-Blackwell, 2012.

Chiao Hsiung-ping. "Guguo bei wang, zhongchanjieji de chuaijiji: tan Dianmao pianchang jiating tongsuju ji gewu xiju" [Homeland nostalgia and the middle class exodus: a discussion of MP&GI's family melodramas and musicals]. *Film Appreciation* 30 (spring 1987): 10–17.

Chiao, Peggy Hsiung-ping. "The Female Consciousness, the World of Signification and Safe Extramarital Affairs: A 40th Year Tribute to *The Love Eterne*." In *The Shaw Screen: A Preliminary Study*, edited by Wong Ain-ling, 75–85. Hong Kong: Hong Kong Film Archive, 2003.

Chik, Alice. "Creative Multilingualism in Hong Kong Popular Music." *World Englishes* 29, no. 4 (2010): 508–22.

Chik, Alice, and Phil Benson. "HK Pop History: 1930–59." Accessed July 6, 2012. http://home .ied.edu.hk/~hkpop/music/hkpophistory.html.

Chin, Carol. C. "Translating the New Woman: Chinese Feminists View the West, 1905–1915." *Gender and History* 18, no. 3 (2006): 490–518.

Chion, Michel. *Audio-Vision: Sound on Screen*. Edited and translated by Claudia Gorbman. New York: Columbia University Press, 1994.

Chow, Rey. *Woman and Chinese Modernity: The Politics of Reading between East and West*. Minneapolis: University of Minnesota Press, 1991.

———. "'Woman,' Fetish, Particularism: Articulating Chinese Cinema with a Cross-Cultural Problematic." *Journal of Chinese Cinemas* 1, no. 3 (2007): 209–22.

Chu, Yingchi. *Hong Kong Cinema: Coloniser, Motherland and Self*. New York: Routledge, 2003.

Chung, Stephanie Po-yin. "The Industrial Evolution of a Fraternal Enterprise: The Shaw Brothers and the Shaw Organisation." In *The Shaw Screen: A Preliminary Study*, edited by Wong Ain-ling, 1–17. Hong Kong: Hong Kong Film Archive, 2003.

———. "A Southeast Asian Tycoon and His Movie Dream: Loke Wan Tho and MP&GI." In *The Cathay Story*, edited by Wong Ain-ling, 10–17. Hong Kong: Hong Kong Film Archive, 2002.

Clark, Paul. *Chinese Cinema: Culture and Politics since 1949*. New York: Cambridge University Press, 1987.

Clément, Catherine. *Opera, or the Undoing of Women*. Translated by Betsy Wing. Minneapolis: University of Minnesota Press, 1988.

Comolli, Jean. "A Body Too Much." *Screen* 19, no. 2 (1978): 41–54.

Conway, Kelley. *Chanteuse in the City: The Realist Singer in French Film*. Berkeley: University of California Press, 2004.

Creekmur, Corey K., and Linda Y. Mokdad, eds. *The International Film Musical*. Edinburgh: Edinburgh University Press, 2012.

Curtin, Michael. *Playing to the World's Biggest Audience: The Globalization of Chinese Film and TV*. Berkeley: University of California Press, 2007.

Davis, Darrell W. "A Marriage of Convenience: Musical Moments in Chinese Movies." In *The Oxford Handbook of Chinese Cinemas*, edited by Carlos Rojas and Eileen Cheng-yin Chow, 438–51. New York: Oxford University Press, 2013.

———. "Questioning Diaspora: Mobility, Mutation, and Historiography of the Shaw Brothers Film Studio." *Chinese Journal of Communication* 4, no. 1 (2011): 40–59.

Deppman, Hsiu-Chuang. *Adapted for the Screen: The Cultural Politics of Modern Chinese Fiction and Film*. Honolulu: University of Hawaii Press, 2010.

Des Forges, Alexander. "Shanghai Alleys, Theatrical Practice, and Cinematic Spectatorship: From *Street Angel* (1937) to Fifth Generation Film." *Journal of Current Chinese Affairs* 39, no. 4 (2010): 29–51.

Doane, Mary Ann. *Femmes Fatales: Feminism, Film Theory, Psychoanalysis*. New York: Routledge, 1991.

———. "The Voice in the Cinema: The Articulation of Body and Space." *Yale French Studies* 60 (1980): 33–50.

Doe Ching [Tao Qin]. "Introduction." Hua luo you feng jun: *dianying gushi* [*Till We Meet Again*: the film's story]. Program brochure, 5. Hong Kong: Xinhua Film Company, 1955.

Dong, Madeleine Y. "Who Is Afraid of the Chinese Modern Girl?" In *The Modern Girl around the World: Consumption, Modernity, and Globalization*, edited by Alys Eve

Weinbaum, Lynn M. Thomas, Madeleine Yue Dong, and Tani E. Barlow, 194–219. Durham, NC: Duke University Press, 2008.

Dumas, Alexandre, *fils*. *The Lady of the Camellias*. Translated by Sir Edmond Gosse. New York: New American Library, 2004.

"Duo cai duo yi de Zhong Qing" [Chung Ching's great artistry and talent]. *Southern Screen* 2 (January 1958): 10–13.

Dyer, Richard. *In the Space of a Song: The Uses of Song in Film*. New York: Routledge, 2011.

———. *Stars*. London: BFI Publishing, 2007.

Eberhard, Wolfram. *The Chinese Silver Screen: Hong Kong and Taiwanese Motion Pictures in the 1960's*. Taipei: Orient Cultural Service, 1972.

Editors of *Cahiers du cinéma*. "John Ford's *Young Mr. Lincoln*." In *Narrative, Apparatus, Ideology*, edited by Philip Rosen, 444–82. New York: Columbia University Press, 1986.

Edwards, Louise. "Policing the Modern Woman in Republican China." *Modern China* 26, no. 2 (2000): 115–47.

Elsaesser, Thomas. "Tales of Sound and Fury: Observations on the Family Melodrama." In *Home Is Where the Heart Is: Studies in Melodrama and the Woman's Film*, edited by Christine Gledhill, 43–69. London: BFI, 1987.

Erenberg, Lewis A. "From New York to Middletown: Repeal and the Legitimization of Nightlife in the Great Depression." *American Quarterly* 38, no. 5 (1986): 761–78.

Faure, David. *Colonialism and the Hong Kong Mentality*. Hong Kong: Hong Kong University Press, 2003.

"Fengjing ruhua de jiaxiang" [Album from homeside]. *Liangyou huabao* 1 (August 1954): 6–7.

Feuer, Jane. "The Concept of Live Television: Ontology as Ideology." In *Regarding Television: Critical Approaches—An Anthology*, edited by E. Ann Kaplan, 12–21. Frederick, MD: University Publications of America, 1983.

———. *The Hollywood Musical*. London: Macmillan, 1993.

Field, Andrew David. *Shanghai's Dancing World: Cabaret Culture and Urban Politics, 1919–1954*. Hong Kong: Chinese University Press, 2010.

Fong, Grace S. "Engendering the Lyric: Her Image and Voice in Song." In *Voices of the Song Lyric in China*, edited by Pauline Yu, 107–44. Berkeley: University of California Press, 1994.

Fu, Poshek. "The 1960s: Modernity, Youth Culture, and Hong Kong Cantonese Cinema." In *The Cinema of Hong Kong: History, Arts, Identity*, edited by Poshek Fu and David Desser, 71–89. New York: Cambridge University Press, 2000.

———. *Between Shanghai and Hong Kong: The Politics of Chinese Cinemas*. Stanford, CA: Stanford University Press, 2003.

———, ed. *China Forever: The Shaw Brothers and Diasporic Cinema*. Urbana: University of Illinois Press, 2008.

———. "Cold War Politics and Hong Kong Mandarin Cinema." In *The Oxford Handbook of Chinese Cinemas*, edited by Carlos Rojas and Eileen Cheng-yin Chow, 116–33. New York: Oxford University Press, 2013.

———. Introduction to *China Forever: The Shaw Brothers and Diasporic Cinema*, edited by Poshek Fu, 1–25. Urbana: University of Illinois Press, 2008.

Fu, Poshek, and David Desser, eds. *The Cinema of Hong Kong: History, Arts, Identity*. New York: Cambridge University Press, 2000.

Gan, Wendy. "Tropical Hong Kong: Narratives of Absence and Presence in Hollywood and Hong Kong Films of the 1950s and 1960s." *Singapore Journal of Tropical Geography* 29, no. 1 (2008): 8–23.

Gao, Yunxiang. "Nationalist and Feminist Discourses on *Jianmei* (Robust Beauty) during China's 'National Crisis' in the 1930s." *Gender & History* 18, no. 3 (2006): 546–73.

Garcia, Roger. "The Illicit Place." In *The Seventh Hong Kong International Film Festival*, 147–49. Hong Kong: Urban Council, 1983.

"Ge Lan de geren da yuedui" [Grace Chang's one-woman band]. *International Screen* 23 (October 1957), 22–23.

"Ge Lan de Riben zhuang" [Grace Chang's Japanese costume]. *International Screen* 57 (July 1960): 18.

"Ge Lan de yi feng gongkai xin" [An open letter from Grace Chang]. *International Screen* 20 (July 1957), n.p.

"Ge Lan mai yi chang dagu" [Grace Chang in *Story of Three Loves*]. *International Screen* 90 (April 1963): 42–43.

"Ge Lan shuo 'Wo lai gei nimen pai zhangxiang pian'" [Grace takes a picture]. *International Screen* 13 (November 1956): 24–25.

"Ge Lan wuzi" [Grace in her mambo poses]. *International Screen* 14 (December 1956): 10–11.

"Ge Lan xiaoyou Riben" [Grace Chang tours Japan]. *International Screen* 44 (June 1959): 54.

Geng Kui. "*Lian xiang* xiaoji" [Brief notes on *Lian xiang*]. *Shenbao*, May 24, 1927.

Ghillebaert, Françoise, ed. "The Double in Movies." Special issue, *Post Script* 22, no. 3 (1999).

Gledhill, Christine. "The Melodramatic Field: An Investigation." In *Home Is Where the Heart Is: Studies in Melodrama and the Woman's Film*, edited by Christine Gledhill, 5–39. London: BFI Books, 1987.

Goldstein, Joshua. "From Teahouse to Playhouse: Theaters as Social Texts in Early Twentieth-Century China." *Journal of Asian Studies* 62, no. 3 (2003): 753–79.

Gui Yan. "Wanren zheng ting 'Ru niang qu'" [Crowds fight to hear "The Ballad of the Wet Nurse"]. *Shenbao*, December 24, 1926.

Gunning, Tom. "The Cinema of Attraction: Early Cinema, Its Spectator and the Avant-Garde." *Wide Angle* 8.3–4 (1986): 63–70.

Hampton, Mark. "Early Hong Kong Television, 1950s–1970s." *Media History* 17, no. 3 (2011): 305–22.

Han Shangyi. "The Design and Style of Opera Films." Translated by Jessica Ka Yee Chan and Judith T. Zeitlin. *Opera Quarterly* 26, nos. 2–3 (2010): 446–54.

Hansen, Miriam. *Babel and Babylon: Spectatorship in American Silent Cinema*. Cambridge, MA: Harvard University Press, 1991.

———. "Fallen Women, Rising Stars, New Horizons: Shanghai Silent Film as Vernacular Modernism." *Film Quarterly* 54, no. 1 (2000): 10–22.

———. "The Gender of Vernacular Modernism: Chinese and Japanese Films of the 1930s." *La Valle de l'Eden* 9, no. 19 (2007): 23–41.

———. "Pleasure, Ambivalence, Identification: Valentino and Female Spectatorship." *Cinema Journal* 25, no. 4 (1986): 6–32.

Harris, Kristine. "*Two Stars on the Silver Screen*: The Metafilm as Chinese Modern." In *History in Images: Pictures and Public Space in Modern China*, edited by Christian Henriot and Wen-hsin Yeh, 191–244. Berkeley, CA: Institute of East Asian Studies, 2012.

Hershatter, Gail. *Dangerous Pleasures: Prostitution and Modernity in Twentieth-Century Shanghai*. Berkeley: University of California Press, 1997.

Herzog, Amy. *Dreams of Difference, Songs of the Same: The Musical Moment in Film*. Minneapolis: University of Minnesota Press, 2010.

Ho, Sam. "Excerpts from an Interview with Ge Lan." In *Mandarin Films and Popular Songs: 40s–60s*, edited by Law Kar, 88–90. Hong Kong: Urban Council, 1993.

———. "Lots of Songs . . . and a Dance or Two: The Hong Kong Musical." In *Asia Sings! A Survey of Asian Musical Films*, edited by Roger Garcia with Chanel Kong, 53–79. Udine, Italy: Centro Espressione Cinematografiche, 2006.

———. "The Songstress, the Farmer's Daughter, the Mambo Girl and the Songstress Again." In *Mandarin Films and Popular Songs: 40s–60s*, edited by Law Kar, 59–68. Hong Kong: Urban Council, 1993.

Hong Fangyi. *Tianya genü : Zhou Xuan yu ta de ge* [The wandering songstress: Zhou Xuan and her songs]. Taipei: Xiu wei zixunkeji gufenyouxiangongsi, 2008.

Hong, Guo-Juin. *Taiwan Cinema: A Contested Nation on Screen*. New York: Palgrave Macmillan, 2011.

Hsia, C. T. "Hsü Chen-ya's *Yü -li hun*: An Essay in Literary History and Criticism." In *Chinese Middlebrow Fiction: From the Ch'ing and Early Republican Eras*, edited by Liu Ts'un-yan with the assistance of John Minford, 199–240. Hong Kong: Chinese University Press, 1984.

Hu, Brian. "Star Discourse and the Cosmopolitan Chinese: Linda Lin Dai Takes on the World." *Journal of Chinese Cinemas* 4, no. 3 (2010): 183–209.

Hu Ying. *Tales of Translation: Composing the New Woman in China, 1899–1918*. Stanford, CA: Stanford University Press, 2000.

Iovene, Paula, and Judith T. Zeitlin, eds. "Chinese Opera Film." Special issue, *Opera Quarterly* 26, nos. 2–3 (2010).

James, David. "Rock 'n' Film: Generic Permutations in Three Feature Films from 1964." *Grey Room* 49 (fall 2012): 6–31.

Jarvie, I. C. *Window on Hong Kong: A Sociological Study of the Hong Kong Film Industry and Its Audience*. Hong Kong: Centre of Asian Studies, University of Hong Kong, 1977.

Jones, Andrew F. "Circuit Listening: Musicals, Mambo, and the Chinese 1960s." Unpublished manuscript.

———. *Developmental Fairy Tales: Evolutionary Thinking and Modern Chinese Culture*. Cambridge, MA: Harvard University Press, 2011.

———. *Yellow Music: Media Culture and Colonial Modernity in the Chinese Jazz Age*. Durham, NC: Duke University Press, 2001.

Ko, S. N. "Under Western Eyes." In *Changes in Hong Kong Society through Cinema*, 64–67. Hong Kong: Urban Council, 1988.

Kracauer, Siegfried. "The Mass Ornament." Translated by Barbara Correll and Jack Zipes. *New German Critique* 5 (spring 1975): 67–76.

Kwok Ching-ling, ed. *Hong Kong Filmography*. Vol. 4, *1953–1959*. Hong Kong: Hong Kong Film Archive, 2003.

———, ed. *Xianggang yingpian daquan* [Hong Kong Filmography]. Vol. 5, *1960–1964*. Hong Kong: Hong Kong Film Archive, 2005.

Laing, Heather. *The Gendered Score: Music in 1940s Melodrama and the Woman's Film*. Burlington, VT: Ashgate, 2007.

Lam, Joseph S. C. "The Presence and Absence of Female Musicians and Music in China." In *Women and Confucian Cultures in Premodern China, Korea, and Japan*, edited by Dorothy Ko, JaHyun Kim Haboush, and Joan R. Piggott, 97–120. Berkeley: University of California Press, 2003.

Lastra, James. *Sound Technology and the American Cinema: Perception, Representation, Modernity*. New York: Columbia University Press, 2000.

Lau Yee Cheung [Liu Yichang]. "Intersection." Translated by Nancy Li. *Renditions* nos. 29–30 (spring and autumn 1988): 84–101.

Law Kar. Introduction to *Mandarin Films and Popular Songs: 40s–60s*, edited by Law Kar, 9. Hong Kong: Urban Council, 1993.

———. "Shaw's Cantonese Productions and Their Interactions with Contemporary Local and Hollywood Cinema." In *China Forever: The Shaw Brothers and Diasporic Cinema*, edited by Poshek Fu, 57–73. Urbana: University of Illinois Press, 2008.

Law Kar, and Frank Bren, with the collaboration of Sam Ho. *Hong Kong Cinema: A Cross-Cultural View*. Lanham, MD: Scarecrow, 2004.

Lee, Haiyan. *Revolution of the Heart: A Genealogy of Love in China, 1900–1950*. Stanford, CA: Stanford University Press, 2007.

Lee, Leo Ou-fan. "The Popular and the Classical: Reminiscences on *The Wild, Wild Rose*." In *The Cathay Story*, edited by Wong Ain-ling, 94–102. Hong Kong: Hong Kong Film Archive, 2002.

———. *The Romantic Generation of Modern Chinese Writers*. Cambridge, MA: Harvard University Press, 1973.

———. *Shanghai Modern: The Flowering of a New Urban Culture in China, 1930–1945*. Cambridge, MA: Harvard University Press, 1999.

Leicester, H. Marshall, Jr. "Discourse and the Film Text: Four Readings of *Carmen*." *Cambridge Opera Journal* 6, no. 3 (1994): 245–82.

Leung, Ping-kwan. "Urban Cinema and the Cultural Identity of Hong Kong." In *Between Home and World: A Reader in Hong Kong Cinema*, edited by Esther M. K. Cheung and Chu Yiu-wai, 369–98. Hong Kong: Hong Kong University Press, 2004.

———. "Writing across Borders: Hong Kong's 1950s and the Present." In *Diasporic Histories: Cultural Archives of Chinese Transnationalisms*, edited by Andrea Riemenschnitter and Deborah L. Madsen, 23–42. Hong Kong: Hong Kong University Press, 2009.

Lewis, Diane Wei. "Media Fantasies: Women, Mobility, and Silent-Era Japanese Ballad Films." *Cinema Journal* 52, no. 3 (2013): 99–119.

Li Cheuk-to. "A Look at MP&GI Cantonese Films through the Work of Tso Kea." In *The Cathay Story*, edited by Wong Ain-ling, 141–45. Hong Kong: Hong Kong Film Archive, 2002.

Li Jin. "Theater of Pathos: Sentimental Melodramas in the New Drama Legacy." *Modern Chinese Literature and Culture* 24, no. 2 (2012): 94–128.

Li, Siu Leung. "Embracing Glocalization and Hong Kong–Made Musical Films." In *China Forever: The Shaw Brothers and Diasporic Cinema*, edited by Poshek Fu, 74–94. Urbana: University of Illinois Press, 2008.

Li Suyuan and Hu Jubin. *Zhongguo wusheng dianying shi* [The history of Chinese silent film]. Beijing: Zhongguo dianing chuban she, 1996.

Lim Kay Tong. *Cathay: 55 Years of Cinema*. Singapore: Landmark, 1991.

"Lin Feng zai *Yunü chunqing* zhong de wuzi" [Dancing steps in 'Teen-Age Love']. *Southern Screen* 3 (February 1958): 38–39.

Link, Perry. *Mandarin Ducks and Butterflies: Popular Fiction in Early Twentieth-Century Chinese Cities*. Berkeley: University of California Press, 1981.

Liu, Lydia H. *Translingual Practice: Literature, National Culture, and Translated Modernity—China 1900–1937*. Stanford, CA: Stanford University Press, 1995.

"*Long xiangfeng wu zhong* de 'Heri jun zai lai?'" [Chang Chun Wan and Chen Hou doing scintillating tango steps]. *International Screen* 27 (January 1958): 6–7.

Lu Jie. "*Ji Kelian de Qiuxiang*" [Notes on *The Miserable Life of Qiuxiang*]. *Shenbao*, May 24, 1927.

Ma, Jean. "Circuitous Action: Revenge Cinema." *Criticism* 57, no. 1 (2015), forthcoming.

———. "Delayed Voices: Intertextuality, Music, and Gender in *The Hole*." *Journal of Chinese Cinemas* 5, no. 2 (2011): 123–39.

Ma, Jean, and Matthew Johnson, eds. "Sound and Music." Special issue, *Journal of Chinese Cinemas* 7, no. 3 (2013).

Ma Ning. "Spatiality and Subjectivity in Xie Jin's Film Melodrama of the New Period." In *New Chinese Cinemas: Forms, Identities, Politics*, edited by Nick Browne, Paul G. Pickowicz, Vivian Sobchack, and Esther Yau, 15–39. New York: Cambridge University Press, 1994.

———. "The Textual and Critical Difference of Being Radical: Reconstructing Chinese Leftist Films of the 1930s." *Wide Angle* 11, no. 2 (1989): 22–31.

"Maggie and Hala-hala." *International Screen* 131 (November 1966): 36–38.

Majumdar, Neepa. *Wanted Cultured Ladies Only! Female Stardom and Cinema in India, 1930s–1950s*. Durham, NC: Duke University Press, 2009.

"*Manbo nülang*" [Mambo Girl]. *International Screen* 15 (January 1957): 30–31.

Mast, Gerald. *Can't Help Singin': The American Musical on Stage and Screen*. Woodstock, NY: Overlook Press, 1987.

McClary, Susan. *Georges Bizet:* Carmen. New York: Cambridge University Press, 1992.

McLean, Adrienne. "'It's Only That I Do What I Love and Love What I Do': 'Film Noir' and the Musical Woman." *Cinema Journal* 33, no. 1 (1993): 3–16.

McMillin, Scott. *The Musical as Drama*. Princeton, NJ: Princton University Press, 2006.

Miller, Terry E. *Garland Encyclopedia of World Music Volume 4: Southeast Asia*. New York: Routledge, 1998.

Moi, Toril. Introduction to Alexandre Dumas *fils, Camille (The Lady of the Camellias)*, v–xiv. Translated by Sir Edmond Gosse. New York: New American Library, 2004.

Moseley, Rachel. "Trousers and Tiaras: Audrey Hepburn, a Woman's Star." *Feminist Review* 71 (2002): 37–51.

Mulvey, Laura. "Visual Pleasure and Narrative Cinema." *Screen* 16, no. 3 (1975): 6–18.

Myatt, Carl. "Tito Puente Dates Boost Latin Music." *Billboard Music Week*, November 17, 1962, 33.

Naremore, James. *Acting in the Cinema*. Berkeley: University of California Press, 1988.

Needham, Gary. "Fashioning Modernity: Hollywood and the Hong Kong Musical 1957–64." In *East Asian Cinemas: Exploring Transnational Connections on Film*, edited by Leon Hunt and Wing-Fai Leung, 41–56. New York: I. B. Tauris, 2008.

Ng, Kenny K. K. "Inhibition vs. Exhibition: Political Censorship of Chinese and Foreign Cinemas in Postwar Hong Kong." *Journal of Chinese Cinemas* 2, no. 1 (2008): 23–35.

———. "Romantic Comedies of Cathay-MP&GI in the 1950s and 60s: Language, Locality, and Urban Character." *Jump Cut*, no. 49 (spring 2007). Accessed July 2, 2012. http://ejumpcut.org/archive/jc49.2007/Ng-Cathay/index.html.

———. "The Screenwriter as Cultural Broker: Travels of Zhang Ailing's Comedy of Love." *Modern Chinese Literature and Culture* 20, no. 2 (2008): 131–84.

Ng, Stephanie. "Performing the 'Filipino' at the Crossroads: Filipino Bands in Five-Star Hotels throughout Asia." *Modern Drama* 48, no. 2 (2005): 272–96.

Nie Er. *Nie Er quanji* [Complete works of Nie Er]. Vol. 2. Edited by Zhou Weizhi. Beijing: Wenhua yishu chuban she; Renmin yinyue chuban she, 1985.

Pang, Laikwan. *Building a New China in Cinema: The Chinese Left-Wing Cinema Movement, 1932–1937*. Lanham, MD: Rowman and Littlefield, 2002.

———. *The Distorting Mirror: Visual Modernity in China*. Honolulu: University of Hawaii Press, 2007.

"Peiyin yu muhou gechang" [Dubbing and behind-the-scenes singing]. *Southern Screen* 11 (January 1959): 46–49.

Qiu Liu. "Ping *Liangxin fuhuo*: Mingxing yingpian gongsi chupin" [Review of *Resurrection*: a release from Mingxing Film Studio]. *Guowen zhoubao* 4, no. 3 (1927).

Quirino, Richie. *Mabuhay Jazz: Jazz in Postwar Philippines*. Pasig City, Philippines: Anvil, 2008.

Robinson, Paul. "It's Not Over till the Soprano Dies." *New York Times*, January 1, 1993.

Rothman, William. "*The Goddess*: Reflections on Melodrama East and West." In *Melodrama and Asian Cinema*, edited by Wimal Dissanayake, 59–72. Cambridge: Cambridge University Press, 1993.

Russell, Catherine. Introduction to "New Women of the Silent Screen." Special issue, *Camera Obscura* 20, no. 3 (2005): 1–13.

Salaff, Janet W. *Working Daughters of Hong Kong*. New York: Cambridge University Press, 1981.

Sek Kei. "Blessing, Bad Woman and Little Person," In *Mandarin Films and Popular Songs: 40s–60s*, edited by Law Kar, 39–40. Hong Kong: Urban Council, 1993.

———. "Shaw Movie Town's 'China Dream' and 'Hong Kong Sentiments.'" In *The Shaw Screen: A Preliminary Study*, edited by Wong Ain-ling, 37–47. Hong Kong: Hong Kong Film Archive, 2003.

"*Shan ge lian*" [The Shepherd Girl]. *Southern Screen* 76 (June 1964): 34–35.

Shen, Vivian. "From Xin nüxing to Liren xing: Changing Conceptions of the 'New Woman' in Republican Era Chinese Films." *Asian Cinema* 11, no. 1 (2000): 114–30.

"Shi nian lai zui liuxing de dianying gequ changpian" [The most popular film songs of the last decade]. *International Screen* 58 (August 1960), 62–63.

Shih, Shu-mei. "Shanghai Women of 1939: Visuality and the Limits of Feminine Modernity." In *Visual Culture in Shanghai, 1850s–1930s*, edited by Jason C. Kuo, 205–40. Washington: New Academia, 2007.

Shu Kei. "Notes on MP&GI." In *The Cathay Story*, edited by Wong Ain-ling, 40–50. Hong Kong: Hong Kong Film Archive, 2002.

Si Bai. "Chuangzao zhong de shengpian biaoxian yangshi" [Form of expression of sound film in the making]. 1934. In *Zhongguo dianying lilun wenxuan (1920–1989)* [Chinese film theory: an anthology], edited by Luo Yijun, Xu Hong, and Li Pusheng, 182–87. Beijing: Wenhua yishu chubanshe, 1992.

Silverman, Kaja. *The Acoustic Mirror: The Female Voice in Psychoanalysis and Film.* Bloomington: Indiana University Press, 1988.

Smith, Jeff. "Black Faces, White Voices: The Politics of Dubbing in *Carmen Jones*." *Velvet Light Trap* 51 (spring 2003): 29–42.

Sobchack, Vivian. "Lounge Time: Postwar Crises and the Chronotope of Film Noir." In *Refiguring American Film Genres*, edited by Nick Browne, 129–70. Berkeley: University of California Press, 1998.

Stam, Robert. "Beyond Fidelity: The Dialogics of Adaptation." In *Film Adaptation*, edited by James Naremore, 54–76. New Brunswick, NJ: Rutgers University Press, 2000.

Stilwell, Robynn J. "The Fantastical Gap between Diegetic and Nondiegetic." In *Beyond the Soundtrack: Representing Music in Cinema*, edited by Daniel Goldmark, Lawrence Kramer, and Richard Leppert, 184–202. Berkeley: University of California Press, 2007.

Stokes, Lisa Odham, and Michael Hoover. *City on Fire: Hong Kong Cinema.* New York: Verso, 1999.

Studlar, Gaylyn. "'Chi-Chi Cinderella': Audrey Hepburn as Couture Countermodel." In *Hollywood Goes Shopping*, edited by David Desser and Garth S. Jowett, 159–78. Minneapolis: University of Minnesota Press, 2000.

Sun, Shaoyi, and Chuan Shi. "Singing in Electric Shadows: A Survey of Chinese Musicals." In *Asia Sings! A Survey of Asian Musical Films*, edited by Roger Garcia with Chanel Kong, 22–41. Udine, Italy: Centro Espressione Cinematografiche, 2006.

Sun Yu, "Yecao *xianhua*—Daoyan de ganxiang" [*Wild Flowers*—the director's thoughts]. *Yingxi zazhi* 9, no. 1 (1930): 54–55.

Tambling, Jeremy. *Opera, Ideology and Film.* Manchester, UK: Manchester University Press, 1987.

Tan See-Kam. "Huangmei Opera Films, Shaw Brothers and Ling Bo—Chaste Love Stories, Genderless Cross-Dressers and Sexless Gender-Plays?" *Jump Cut*, no. 49 (spring 2007). Accessed July 4, 2004. http://www.ejumpcut.org/archive/jc49.2007/TanSee-Kam/text.html.

Tang Tangyin. "Tan yijiusansi nian de dianying gequ" [Film songs in 1934]. Translated by Jessica Kayee Chan. *Qingchun dianying* 1, no. 12 (1934), page unavailable.

Tansman, Alan. "Misora Hibari: The Postwar Myth of Mournful Tears and Sake." In *The Human Tradition in Modern Japan*, edited by Anne Walthall, 213–29. Wilmington, DE: Scholarly Resources, 2002.

Taylor, Jeremy E. *Rethinking Transnational Chinese Cinemas: The Amoy-Dialect Film Industry in Cold War Asia.* New York: Routledge, 2011.

Teo, Stephen. "Chinese Melodrama: The *Wenyi* Genre." In *Traditions in World Cinema*, edited by Linda Badley, R. Barton Palmer, and Steven Jay Schneider, 203–13. Edinburgh: Edinburgh University Press, 2006.

———. *Hong Kong Cinema: The Extra Dimensions.* London: BFI Publishing, 1997.

———. "Oh, Karaoke! Mandarin Pop and Musicals." In *Mandarin Films and Popular Songs: 40s–60s*, edited by Law Kar, 32–36. Hong Kong: Urban Council, 1993.

Touhy, Sue. "Metropolitan Sounds: Music in Chinese Films of the 1930s." In *Cinema and Urban Culture in Shanghai, 1922–1943*, edited by Yingjin Zhang, 200–221. Stanford, CA: Stanford University Press, 1999.

Turner, Matthew. "60s/90s: Dissolving the People." In *Hong Kong Sixties: Designing Identity*, edited by Matthew Turner and Irene Ngan, 13–34. Hong Kong: Hong Kong Arts Centre, 1995.

Turner, Matthew, and Irene Ngan, eds. *Hong Kong Sixties: Designing Identity.* Hong Kong: Hong Kong Arts Centre, 1995.

Vogel, Shane. *The Scene of Harlem Cabaret: Race Sexuality, Performance.* Chicago: University of Chicago Press, 2009.

Wang Wenhe. *Zhongguo dianying yinyue xunzong* [Tracing Chinese film music]. Beijing: Zhongguo guangbo dianshi chubanshe, 1995.

Wang, Yiman. *Remaking Chinese Cinema: Through the Prism of Shanghai, Hong Kong, and Hollywood.* Honolulu: University of Hawaii Press, 2013.

———. "The 'Transnational' as Methodology: Transnationalizing Chinese Film Studies through the Example of *The Love Parade* and Its Chinese Remakes." *Journal of Chinese Cinemas* 2, no. 1 (2008): 9–21.

Williams, Alan. "The Musical Film and Recorded Popular Music." In *Genre: The Musical*, edited by Rick Altman, 147–58. London: Routledge & Kegan Paul Ltd. and British Film Institute, 1981.

Williams, Linda. "Melodrama Revised." In *Refiguring American Film Genres: Theory and History*, edited by Nick Browne, 42–88. Berkeley: University of California Press, 1998.

Wilson, Patricia. "'I Sought the Jewel of Art: Introducing Zhao Dan.'" *Chinese Literature* 4 (April 1980): 73–92.

Witzleben, J. Lawrence. "Cantopop and Mandopop in Pre-Postcolonial Hong Kong: Identity Negotiation in the Performances of Anita Mui Yi-fong." *Popular Music* 18, no. 2 (1999): 241–58.

Wojcik, Pamela Robertson. "The Sound of Film Acting." *Journal of Film and Video* 58, nos. 1–2 (2006): 71–83.

Wong Ain-ling, ed. *The Cathay Story.* Hong Kong: Hong Kong Film Archive, 2002.

———. Foreword to *Hong Kong Filmography*, Vol. 4, *1953–1959*, x–xvii. Edited by Kwok Ching-ling. Hong Kong: Hong Kong Film Archive, 2003.

———, ed. *The Shaw Screen: A Preliminary Study.* Hong Kong: Hong Kong Film Archive, 2003.

Wong Ain-ling, and Lee Pui-tak, eds. *Lengzhang yu Xianggang dianying* [The Cold War and Hong Kong cinema]. Hong Kong: Hong Kong Film Archive, 2009.

Wong, Fai-Ming. "Industrialization and Family Structure in Hong Kong." *Journal of Marriage and Family* 37, no. 4 (1975): 985–1000.

Wong, Isabel. "The Incantation of Shanghai: Singing a City into Existence." In *Global Goes Local: Popular Culture in Asia*, edited by Timothy J. Craig and Richard King, 246–64. Vancouver: University of British Columbia Press, 2002.

Wong Kee Chee. *The Age of Shanghainese Pops: 1930–1970*. Hong Kong: Joint, 2001.

Wong Kee-chee. "A Song in Every Film." In *Hong Kong Cinema Survey 1946–1968*, 29–32. Hong Kong: Urban Council, 1979.

———. "Two or Three Things about Mandarin Pop." In *Mandarin Films and Popular Songs: 40s–60s*, edited by Law Kar, 18–20. Hong Kong: Urban Council, 1993.

Wong, Lily. "Moving Serenades: Hearing the Sinophonic in MP & GI's *Longxiang Fengwu*." *Journal of Chinese Cinemas* 7, no. 3 (2013): 225–40.

Wong, Mary. "Women Who Cross Borders: MP&GI's Modernity Programme." In *The Cathay Story*, edited by Wong Ain-ling, 85–93. Hong Kong: Hong Kong Film Archive, 2002.

Wu Hao. "Yezonghui" [Nightclubs]. In *Yishizhuxing: wushi liushiniandai de shenghuofangshi* [Living in Hong Kong: the 1950s and 1960s], 11. Hong Kong: Hong Kong Film Archive, 2001.

Xiao, Zhiwei. "Constructing a New National Culture: Film Censorship and the Issues of Cantonese Dialect, Superstition, and Sex in the Nanjing Decade." In *Cinema and Urban Culture in Shanghai, 1922–1943*, edited by Yingjin Zhang, 183–99. Stanford, CA: Stanford University Press, 1999.

Xu Mingshi. "Dianyingyuan yu yinyue" [Movie theaters and music]. *Shenbao*, February 25, 1929.

Yano, Christine R. *Tears of Longing: Nostalgia and the Nation in Japanese Popular Song*. Cambridge, MA.: Harvard University Asia Center, 2002.

Yau, Esther, ed. *At Full Speed: Hong Kong Cinema in a Borderless World*. Minneapolis: University of Minnesota Press, 2001.

———. "Introduction: Hong Kong Cinema in a Borderless World." In *At Full Speed: Hong Kong Cinema in a Borderless World*, edited by Esther Yau, 1–29. Minneapolis: University of Minnesota Press, 2001.

Yau, Kinnia Shuk-ting. "Hong Kong and Japan: Not One Less." In *Hong Kong Cinema Retrospective: Border Crossings in Hong Kong Cinema*, edited by Law Kar, 104–10. Hong Kong: Urban Council, 2000.

Yeh, Emilie Yueh-yu. "China." In *The International Film Musical*, edited by Corey K. Creekmur and Linda Y. Mokdad, 171–88. Edinburgh: Edinburgh University Press, 2012.

———. "Pitfalls of Cross-Cultural Analysis: Chinese *Wenyi* Film and Melodrama." *Asian Journal of Communication* 19, no. 4 (2009): 438–52.

———. "Taiwan: The Transnational Battlefield of Cathay and Shaws." In *The Cathay Story*, edited by Wong Ain-ling, 72–76. Hong Kong: Hong Kong Film Archive, 2002.

———. "*Wenyi* and the Branding of Early Chinese Film." *Journal of Chinese Cinemas* 6, no. 1 (2012): 65–94.

Yeh Yueh-yu. *Gesheng meiying: gequ xushi yu Zhongwen dianying* [Phantom of the music: song narration and Chinese-language cinema]. Taipei: Yuanliu chuban shiye gufen youxian gongsi, 2000.

———."Historiography and Sinification: Music in Chinese Cinema of the 1930s." *Cinema Journal* 41, no. 3 (2002): 78–97.

"Yi Wen xin zuo yi bu chongman qingqun qixi de gechang wudao pian" [Yi Wen makes a new song-and-dance film brimming over with youthful energy]. *International Screen* 14 (December 1956), 13–14.

Youngs, Tim, and Carol Liu. "Interview: Wang Tianlin." In *Asia Sings! A Survey of Asian Musical Films*, edited by Roger Garcia with Chanel Kong, 81–91. Udine, Italy: Centro Espressione Cinematografiche, 2006.

Yu Mo-wan. "Types and Sources of Hong Kong Mandarin Film Songs, 1940s to 60s." In *Mandarin Films and Popular Songs: 40s–60s*, edited by Law Kar, 69–75. Hong Kong: Urban Council, 1993.

Yue, Meng. *Shanghai and the Edges of Empire*. Minneapolis: University of Minnesota Press, 2006.

Yung, Bell. *Cantonese Opera: Performance as Creative Process*. New York: Cambridge University Press, 1989.

Yung Sai-shing. *Xunmi Yueju sheng ying: cong* Hong chuan *dao* Shuiyindeng [Sounds and images of Cantonese opera: from *Hong chuan* to *Shuiyindeng*]. Hong Kong: Oxford University Press, 2012.

———. *Yueyun liusheng: Changpian gongye yu Guangdong xuyi* [Cantonese recordings: the record industry and Cantonese opera, 1903–1953]. Hong Kong: Tiandi tushu youxian gongsi, 2006.

Zeitlin, Judith T. "'Notes of Flesh' and the Courtesan's Song in Seventeenth-Century China." In *The Courtesan's Arts: Cross-Cultural Perspectives*, edited by Martha Feldman and Bonnie Gordon, 75–98. New York: Oxford University Press, 2006.

———. "Operatic Ghosts on Screen: The Case of *A Test of Love*." *Opera Quarterly* 26, nos. 2–3 (2010): 220–55.

Zhang, Yingjin. *The City in Modern Chinese Literature and Film: Configurations of Space, Time, and Gender*. Stanford, CA: Stanford University Press, 1996.

Zhang Yiwei. "Shengyin yu xiandaixing: mopian zhi youshengpian guodu shiqi de Zhongguo yingyuan shengyin shi wenti" [Sound and modernity: issues in the history of sound in China's film theaters during the transition from silent to sound film]. *Wenyi yanjiu* 5 (2010): 85–96.

Zhang Zhen. *An Amorous History of the Silver Screen: Shanghai Cinema, 1896–1937*. Chicago: University of Chicago Press, 2005.

———. "Cosmopolitan Projections: World Literature on Chinese Screens." In *A Companion to Literature and Film*, edited by Robert Stam and Alessandra Raengo, 144–63. Malden, MA: Blackwell, 2008.

———. "Ling Bo: Orphanhood and Post-War Sinophone Film History." In *Chinese Film Stars*, edited by Mary Farquhar and Yingjin Zhang, 121–38. New York: Routledge, 2010.

———. "The 'Shanghai Factor' in Hong Kong Cinema: A Tale of Two Cities in Historical Perspectives." *Asian Cinema* 10, no. 1 (1998): 146–59.

———. "Transplanting Melodrama: Observations on the Emergence of Early Chinese Film Narrative." In *A Companion to Chinese Cinema*, edited by Yingjin Zhang, 25–41. Malden, MA: Wiley-Blackwell, 2012.

"Zhihui zhi xing—Ge Lan" [Grace Chang is accomplished danseuse]. *International Screen* 40 (February 1959): 12–13.

"Zhongguo yingtan guibao—Ge Lan" [The gem of the Chinese movie world—Grace Chang]. *International Screen* 64 (February 1961): 27–29.

Zhou Jianyun. "*Genü Hong mudan* duiyu Zhongguo dianyingjie de gongxian jiqi yingxiang" [The contribution and impact of *Songstress Red Peony* on the Chinese film world]. In *"Genü Hong mudan" tekan: Zhongguo diyibu yousheng yingpian* [Special edition on *Songstress Red Peony*: the first sound film in China], edited by Zhou Jianyun, 10–15. Shanghai: Hua wei maoyi gongsi, 1931.

"Zi Luolan yu yousheng dianying" [Violet Wong and Sound Films]. *Yingxi zazhi* 2, no. 1 (1931): 36.

INDEX

NOTE: Page numbers followed by *f* indicate a figure.

rustic songstresses of, 108–13, 235n14; Shanghai oldies of, 24–25; shifting sound-image correspondences in, 122–26

Gei wo yi ge wen (Give Me a Kiss), 237n50

Gemi xiaojie (Miss Songbird), 125–26, 237nn41–42

gendered spectatorship, 21–22

gendered vocal performance, 11–21, 66–67, 200–201; archetype of feminine victim-hood and, 61–70, 191, 227n47, 227n49; Chinese lyrical tradition of, 14; division of labor in, 11–13, 221nn31–32, 221nn34–36, 217n40; double roles and, 131; feminine virtue and, 12–13; masculine idioms of, 15, 222n47; modern femininity and, 16–21, 147–49, 222n51, 222n55, 222n58; revolutionary subalterns and, 20, 62, 227n50; sensual imaginings and, 14–16, 18–19, 66–67, 192–200, 222nn43–44, 222n48; in Western opera, 210–12, 245nn54–55

Genü Hong mudan (Songstress Red Peony). See *Songstress Red Peony*

"Getting to Know You," 183

gewu pian (song-and-dance films), 8, 28–29, 46; Chinese opera and, 91–93, 231n64; cosmopolitan worldliness of, 29, 179–83; emergence of dance numbers in, 164–68; inserted film songs in, 89–90, 231n57; Latin Caribbean music and dance in, 98, 149, 157–59, 168–69; nightclub scenes in, 160–68, 185–86; restaging of live performances in, 48–49; role of dance in, 168–79; songstresses as dancers in, 147, 161, 166, 168–78. See also *Mambo Girl; The Wild, Wild Rose*

ghost voices, 122–26. See also dubbing

Gilda, 200–201, 221n36

Girl of a Thousand Guises (Qian mian nülang), 185, 205–6; double role in, 129, 159–60; Peking opera numbers in, 93, 94f, 181; songstress seduction in, 195

Give Me a Kiss (Gei wo yi ge wen), 237n50

Gledhill, Christine, 245n50

Godard, Jean-Luc, 191

Goddess (Shennü), 17, 18–19, 155, 222n55

Golden Lotus (Jin lianhua), 63, 129, 130, 152–53, 227n52

Goldstein, Joshua, 65

Gone with the Wind, 190

Gong Quixia, 13

gramophone recordings, 43–44, 67, 90–91, 224n1, 224n19. See also music recording industry

Grand Beijing Theater, 39

Great Wall Records, 95, 146

Griffith, D. W., 245n48

Gu Mei, Carrie, 96

Gunning, Tom, 231n64

guohua pian (national-language films), 231n52

Guo Shengsheng, 179

Gypsy Blood, 191

"Habañera" (Bizet), 101, 187, 191–92, 242n2

Haitang hong (Blood Will Tell), 152–53, 240n23

Hansen, Miriam, 19–23, 62

Hanyu Pinyin system, 29

Happiness at the Door (Xi linmen), 233n96

Harris, Kristine, 47, 226n34, 226n37

Hayworth, Rita, 200, 221n36

Hepburn, Audrey, 137, 238n59

Heri jun zai la (Au Revoir Mon Amour), 206, 233n95, 246n3

Heri jun zai la (Till the End of Time), 99

"Heri jun zai la?" ("When Will You Return?"), 99, 233nn95–96

Her Pearly Tears (Zhenzhu lei), 129, 237n45

Hershatter, Gail, 14–15

Her Tender Heart (Yunü siqing), 152–53

Herzog, Amy, 11, 138, 220nn28–29

Hindi cinema: double casting in, 133–34, 238n53; on ghost voices, 237n40; playback singers in, 122–26

Ho, Sam, 109, 151, 165, 234n4, 245n47

Holden, William, 80

The Hole (Dong), 3, 216, 233n89

Hollywood productions: of American musicals, 7–10, 12, 48, 106, 165, 220nn18–19, 226n37; couple dancing in, 241n54; of maternal melodramas, 206; of noir films, 161; portrayals of Hong Kong in, 88–89, 231nn55–56; of rock-and-roll musicals, 140, 146, 161–62, 239n14, 239n16; Western values of, 84–86

Hong Kong, 28, 71–76, 230n48; American movies shown in, 85; colonial status of, 88, 116, 235n21; cosmopolitan diasporic culture of, 25–29, 76, 179–83, 223n76; economic boom and consumption in, 141, 147–48; Filipino musicians in, 167–68, 241n50, 241nn46–47; as geopolitical zone of contact, 76, 84, 230n44, 280n70; handover to PRC of, 223n76; location shots in, 89, 231nn55–56; migration from the mainland to, 24–25, 71–76, 95, 112, 215–16, 230n39, 235n21; modern femininity in, 18, 73, 115–16; nightlife in, 160–68; popular music industry of, 95–100, 232n76; scenic imaginary of, 88–89, 109; in *Songs of the Peach Blossom River*, 114–16; television broadcasting in, 238n60; youth culture of, 144, 238–39nn8–10

Hong Kong, 231n55

Hong Kong and Kowloon Free Filmmakers General Association, 230n48

Hong Kong Film Archive, 223n74

Hong Kong film industry, 18, 24–26, 223n70, 223n74, 228n68; Asian Film Festival and, 92, 179, 229n33; Cantonese films in, 86, 88, 91–93, 94f, 171, 215, 232n76, 242n57; decline of big studios in, 214–15; dialect films in, 87–88, 230n49; identity development of, 74–76, 114–16, 236n26; investment in Mandarin by, 231n52; leftwing studios of, 87; small studios of, 78, 87, 103–4, 214–15, 234n1; transnational cosmopolitanism of, 179–83. *See also* postwar Mandarin cinema; Shanghai-Hong Kong nexus

Hong Kong Nocturne (*Xiang jiang hua yueyu*), 165

"Hong shuilian" ("Red Lotus"), 98

Hope, Bob, 231n55

Hou Hsiao-hsien, 237n49

Hu, Brian, 179–80

Hu, Jenny, 4, 71, 81f, 207

Hua jie (*Flower Street*), 63, 227n51

Hua luo you feng jun (*Till We Meet Again*), 205

Huang Feiran, 181, 221n40

Huangmei opera films. *See* opera films (*xiqu*)

Huang tudi (*Yellow Earth*), 215

Hua tuan jin cu (*Love Parade*), 165

Hua yang de nianhua (*The Blooming Years*) (film), 216–17, 246n5

"Hua yang de nianhua" ("The Blooming Years") (song), 216

Hua yang nianhua (*In the Mood for Love*), 1–2, 216–17, 241n44

Hu Die, 12, 32, 131, 221n32

Hudie furen (*Madame Butterfly*), 99, 104, 181, 245n51

Hu Ying, 203, 208

"I Love Calypso," 179, 183

"I Love Cha-Cha," 149, 165, 166, 169–76, 178

Imitation of Life, 206

Indian cinema, 12

inserted film songs (*chaqu*), 9, 53, 89–94, 104, 171, 225n20

The International Film Musical (Creekmur and Mokdaad), 220n19

International Screen (*Guoji dianying*), 79–83, 229n24

In the Mood for Love (*Hua yang nianhua*), 1–2, 216–17, 241n44

It's Always Spring (*Tao li zheng chun*), 99

"I Want Your Love," 98

"I Want You to Be My Baby," 183

Jade Pear Spirit (*Yu li hun*), 204, 244n33

Jakobson, Roman, 221n31

James, David, 146, 239n16

Japan: cinema of, 12, 221n34, 225n20; invasion and occupation by, 24, 56, 62, 227nn51–52, 228n68

Jarvie, I. C., 86, 229n19

Jianghu ernu (*The Show Must Go On*), 236n24

jianmei (robust beauty), 111, 141, 235n14, 235n20

Jiao wo ruhe bu xiang ta (*Because of Her*), 99, 147, 178, 180–81, 185

Jiashu (character), 195–96, 197–99f, 206

Jinan Film Company, 35

Jin lianhua (*Golden Lotus*), 63, 129, 130, 152–53, 227n52

Jin Yan, 44, 177

Jones, Andrew, 5–6, 15; on connections of song with film, 33; on Li Jinhui, 42,